Unquiet Things

UNQUIET THINGS

Secularism in the Romantic Age

COLIN JAGER

PENN

UNIVERSITY OF PENNSYLVANIA PRESS

PHILADELPHIA

A volume in the Haney Foundation Series, established in
1961 with the generous support of Dr. John Louis Haney.

Published by
University of Pennsylvania Press
Philadelphia, Pennsylvania 19104-4112
www.upenn.edu/pennpress

Printed in the United States of America on acid-free paper
1 3 5 7 9 10 8 6 4 2

Library of Congress Cataloging-in-Publication Data
ISBN 978-0-8122-4664-3

For my parents, Ronald Jager and Grace Otten Jager,
with love and gratitude

CONTENTS

Introduction. Unquiet Things

the thin blue flame
Lies on my low-burnt fire, and quivers not;
Only that film, which fluttered on the grate,
Still flutters there, the sole unquiet thing.
—Samuel Taylor Coleridge, "Frost at Midnight" (1798)

I spent my childhood in a picturesque New England village whose architecture, as it happens, bears witness to the argument of this book. On one side of the village green was the town hall, built in 1787, where the community's business happened: here the selectmen had their offices, from here children graduated to bigger things, and here, every March, the townspeople gathered to complain about taxes, praise the road agent, and pass a budget. Less than a hundred yards away, on the other side of the common, stood the Congregational Church, where God's business happened: Sunday morning worship, mostly, and the occasional wedding or funeral. Except for Sunday, the church was usually closed. Except for Sunday, the town hall was usually open. As I was growing up, that seemed the right and proper order of things.

But, like many such distinctions, this one has a history.

In the case of my hometown, that history covers the early decades of the nineteenth century. The town's colonial-era founders, with their roots in England's Nonconformist and Dissenting communities, had been reluctant to build something that looked like a church. Like the communities nearby, they built a meetinghouse instead—a simple, white rectangular building that could house both God's business and the world's business. It is unlikely that those early New England pioneers even made the analytic distinction between what we today call the "religious" and the "secular."

By the 1820s, however, the increasing size and religious diversity of the village made it desirable to begin drawing some boundaries. It was not clear, for example, whether the town itself owned the meetinghouse, or whether the various denominations worshipping in the building did, nor how to allocate its various needs and functions—a question that mattered when it came time to collect taxes. So in the late 1830s the largest denomination (Congregationalist) built a church on the other end of the common. Their new church *looked* like a church: unlike the meetinghouse, it had a steeple and a belfry and two doors in the gable end.[1] And once the Congregationalists had moved out, others followed suit; Baptists, Methodists, and Seventh-Day Adventists, no longer tied to a single building, built their own churches. A diversified and clarified religious landscape followed in short order. And the meetinghouse, now emptied of religion, could become a town hall.

☙

Though my subject here is Great Britain, not the United States, the naturalized separations that defined my New England childhood are much like the ones I consider in this book.[2] Indeed, those separations were the cause of extensive commentary (and no small amount of self-congratulation) in and around eighteenth-century England. Voltaire, observing the English with admiration in 1733, remarked that "If there were only one religion in England, there would be danger of despotism, if there were only two they would cut each other's throats; but there are thirty, and they live in peace."[3] Religious pluralism, Voltaire thought, kept violence at bay (which is all he meant by *peace*). Joseph Addison's near-contemporary observation that there was "less appearance of religion in England than in any neighboring state, Catholic or Protestant" is only superficially opposed to Voltaire's.[4] It was the *appearance* of religion that Addison remarked on: the residue of a religious culture reduced now to a mere formality. Meanwhile, as Voltaire suggests, there was plenty of religion in England, but its very diversity meant that it was increasingly privatized; civil society was now organized by trade, not religious conformity. As they went about their daily business in the market, the field, or the coffee shop, the English kept their religion, or lack of it, to themselves.

☙

The metaphorical and literal space between the church and the town hall, the conceptual separation of religion and commerce—these distinctions characterize a modernity on whose modalities social scientists largely agree: rationalization and capitalism, industrialization and alienation, social and cultural differentiation, the autonomous subject, the power of science, the growth of cities, the advent of the liberal democratic state. The privatization of religion is perhaps the most salient factor of all, for it made possible the nation-state and the development of a market economy. Yet religion's role has typically been understood as transitional: however various in detail, most accounts of modernity agreed that by the twentieth century religion was a relic of the past, that it held on in some places only because the project of modernity was still incomplete, and that the inverse relationship of religion to modernity in Western Europe offered a template for the rest of the globe. Whether tinged with nostalgia or colored by triumph, this is a progressive narrative. It may contrast duplicity, superstition, and dogmatism with truth, science, and liberalism, or it may mourn alienation, the loss of connection, and the decline of magic; but in either case it left little room for the old enchantments, except perhaps as entertainment.

Paradoxically, however, the transformations that contained and privatized religion also made it more visible and more unruly. As Jose Casanova remarked some years ago, "What was new and unexpected in the 1980s" was the increasingly public role adopted by religious traditions whose demise had been widely predicted. "[R]eligious traditions throughout the world," he continued, "are refusing to accept the marginal and privatized role which theories of modernity as well as theories of secularization had reserved for them."[5] Casanova's target was the notion that all nations and cultures would eventually modernize, and secularize, according to a European model. As he and others began pointing out, many of the world's most rapidly modernizing societies—that is, those across the "global south"—were, at least for now, among its most religious.[6] Reviewing the current data in 2008, Philip Gorski and Ates Altinordu concluded that far from retreating into private life, "traditional, transcendent religion has become a key cleavage in domestic and international politics"—an observation that ought to surprise no one who regularly scans the news.[7]

What we typically mean by "modernity"—liberal, capitalist, secular, democratic—is not, it turns out, a universal aspiration, not even in the West, its supposed home. Moreover, as scholars working on "alternative" or "multiple" modernities have helped us to see, convergence theories of modernization give scant analytic attention to the force of local culture and its ability to take up and transform such aspects of modernity as the market society.[8] And even more, convergence theories make it too easy to forget that aspects of what we call "modernity" have existed in other times (premodern, "traditional") and places. Given the multivalent and finally provincial character of

European-style modernity, it seems likely that religion could be "repositioned" and differentiated within a secular world and yet find or create for itself new forms of social significance.[9] And given the very real constraints imposed by modernization, that significance may appear in noisy or, as I term it here, *unquiet*, forms.

Thus the present book, whose title comes from Samuel Taylor Coleridge's magnificent poem "Frost at Midnight" (1798). Coleridge writes there of one who, awake while everyone else sleeps, watches the film in his grate flutter and flap, the "sole unquiet thing" in his otherwise silent house. This restless film—not even a proper flame but a residue or ghost, pushed around by invisible air currents—inspires a mental journey through the speaker's own earlier life, and leads thereby to a series of hopes for his infant son, slumbering nearby in his cradle. The poem ends where it began, with the opening silence transformed into the "secret ministry" of the frost, hanging up its "silent icicles." However basically humanist the poem's ultimate sympathies, one cannot but be struck by the flickering disturbances it registers, from the flapping ghost of flame to a silence that is so silent that it "disturbs" and "vexes" meditation; even the secret, icy ministry of the frost is faintly sinister. Like so many romantic-era literary productions, Coleridge's poem permits us to enjoy its quiet finish, but invites us also to be caught by the "unquiet" that conditions it. In doing so, the poem allows me to pose the two questions that direct this study: By what means has the noise been banished? And are there frequencies at which those of us living in a secular age can nonetheless perceive its disquiet?[10]

The short answers to these questions are "Reform" and "Yes: romantic literature." The longer answers unfold over the course of this book.

ფ

Unquiet Things is a study of secularism during the romantic era. It treats some of the major writers of the British romantic period: Jane Austen, Samuel Taylor Coleridge, Walter Scott, James Hogg, Lord Byron, Percy Shelley. By subtitling the book *Secularism in the Romantic Age*, however, I indicate that the relationship between secularism and romanticism is not confined to a particular set of chronological dates. The last quarter of the twentieth century was marked by a remarkable and (to some) surprising resurgence in the public role of religion worldwide, a wave that has only increased during the early decades of the twenty-first century. What this means has been a matter of ongoing controversy. But it is clear that we have learned how to think about such phenomena from the writers and thinkers of the late eighteenth and early nineteenth centuries, when secularism had achieved the kind of cultural and intellectual importance that began to allow for some critical reflection. In part this is the story of romanticism's complex relationship to nationalism, whose conditions were set by the Westphalian model of the nation state as a container for religion. In part this is the story of romanticism's penchant both for history and for its losers—the anachronistic, the out-of-step, the people or cultural formations who in some fashion or other will be forced to adjust to the new reality. And in part this is the story of the invention of literature as we know it today: the great romantic-era thinkers, from Herder to Schleiermacher to Coleridge, inaugurated, systematized, and institutionalized a decisive shift toward appreciating the Bible's figurative, symbolic, and metaphorical resources, developing along the way a method for reading what was increasingly coming to be called "literature." In all these important senses we are still living in the "romantic age."

The association of romanticism with religion goes back almost a century, to T. E. Hulme's famous pronouncement that romanticism was "spilt religion" and Irving Babbitt's denunciation of it as a "sham spirituality."[11] In the 1960s Earl Wasserman and M. H. Abrams redrew that picture by arguing that romanticism was an example of secularization. Wasserman found in romanticism a "new poetic syntax" suitable to a postmetaphysical age, while Abrams saw it as a "secularization of inherited theological ideas and ways of thinking." Abrams meant not that religion was disappearing during the early nineteenth century but that it was being transformed: not "the deletion and replacement of religious ideas but rather the assimilation and reinterpretation of religious ideas, as constitutive elements in a world view founded on secular premises," he explained.[12]

The deconstructive and historicist scholarship of the 1970s and 1980s tended to leave the association between religious decline and modernity intact while positioning romanticism as obscuring rather than facilitating that connection.[13] Then in the 1990s a new wave of historicizing studies by Iain McCalman, Robert J. Ryan, and Martin Priestman restored to romanticism a richer and more diversified religious landscape.[14] Though various in their attitudes toward secularization, these books brought religion back into the conversation—but at the cost of treating it largely as a set of cognitive beliefs or mental dispositions. Only with a second wave of scholarship in the 2000s did literary criticism begin to absorb the lessons of scholars from other disciplines—history, anthropology, and religious studies—who were turning their attention to the historical and discursive constructions of both religion and secularism.[15] Those scholars reminded us that religion was not some "thing" in the world but rather a mobile discourse that answered particular needs at particular historical moments; that for Europe the crucial moment was an early modern crisis of authority within Christianity, and that around this time a newer, more cognitive definition of religion made it possible to invent "religions," in the plural, in order to name those activities and postures that characterized Europe's Others.[16] And they reminded us, too, that secularization could not be understood as a simple subtraction story, as though the modern secular self was always there, waiting to be liberated from false beliefs; that secularism was not a neutral governance structure but had its own interests, authorizing certain kinds of subjects and marginalizing others; that secularism was complexly intertwined with a particular religion (Christianity); that as part of that relationship it *produced*, at a certain historical moment, the apparently natural distinction between the religious and the secular; and that as a product of these contingent historical events secularism did not travel especially well.[17]

Contemporary scholarship directed at the confluence of what used to be called "religion and literature" therefore finds itself in a state of productive disequilibrium, since neither term seems to exist in the stable way that makes investigation easy. We continue to require genealogies that place both terms within the broader interpretive framework of what Charles Taylor calls the "secular age."[18] To be sure, the history and politics of secularism extend beyond romanticism, and beyond literary studies. Yet the following pages seek to demonstrate that literary culture of the long romantic period gave to the secular a particular and influential spin. It is romanticism that invented "difference," including religious and cultural difference, as we know it today; it is romanticism whose historical sensibility began to shape the way that we moderns look back at what used to be called the "age of faith"; it is romanticism that is largely responsible for transforming Christian hermeneutics into secular appreciation for the poetic resources of a tradition; it is romanticism that first took account, conceptually, ethically, and politically, of the changes wrought by Enlightenment culture. And because of all of these developments, it is romanticism that is best positioned to speak to our present moment, for the issues and problems it first identified and posed in recognizably modern form remain our issues and problems, even though much has changed since Percy Shelley declared that the language of the poets "marks the before un-apprehended relations of things."[19] In the romantic period, poetry (in the expansive definition Shelley gave to it, namely as the human faculty of *poiesis*) constitutes itself as *the* privileged, nondoctrinal place from which to speak about unexpected and surprising relations. It is with that capacity in mind that one can speak, not of "romanticism in a secular age," as though the latter term can capture and explain the former, but of "secularism in the romantic age."

ℝ

But this is to begin in medias res. In order to begin at the beginning, I have found it necessary to start with the changes imposed on the English nation by King Henry VIII. Chapter 1, "The Power of the Prince," shows that those changes involve, first of all, a literal secularization: between 1538 and 1540 Henry's government suppressed over 400 monasteries and abbeys, claiming their wealth and land for the Crown, refounding some as secular cathedrals, giving others away as gifts, and letting some decay into picturesque ruins. This deliberate "worlding" of the formerly sacred, while dramatic enough in its own right, was part of something bigger: a large-scale movement of Reform across early modern Europe.[20] That movement includes both the Reformation and Counter-Reformation, but encompasses also slower and subtler processes involving the adjustment of manners, bodily comportment, mental states, and notions of citizenship—all of which bolstered a rapidly centralizing state, including both absolutist and constitutional monarchies and issuing, eventually, in the kind of "biopower" that Michel Foucault names as the characteristic of modern democracies. Reform involved the making over of an entire society to higher standards, principally by ensuring that people had similar beliefs, were subject to plainer and more instrumental truths, and kept under better surveillance. Crucially, this meant the elimination of folk practices, superstitions, celebrations, and feasts. Reform did not target religion specifically; it was not first of all a doctrinal or theological innovation but a worldly one, indeed something much closer to what Foucault calls "governmentality" than to our textbook assumptions about religious reformers setting the landscape ablaze in service to fanatical convictions.[21]

This is a simple but crucial fact, one often forgotten or ignored amid the so-called "turn to religion" in the literary humanities: that *secularism is not first and foremost about religion* but concerns instead power—its consolidation and streamlining, its dispersal and diffusion. Within this framework, religion is often a useful counter in a complex series of worldly maneuvers.

Part I of this book, then, tracks the figure of King Henry VIII: in the first chapter he is the historical actor who changed the landscape of England and tried to remake the sensory capacities of his subjects; in the second and third chapters he is a figure for the melancholy and ambivalence that by the eighteenth century surrounds the very changes with which he is linked. One connecting thread is Shakespeare's play *Henry VIII*, immensely popular throughout the eighteenth century, a literary production that brilliantly highlights the great difficulty in saying just exactly what Henry's reforms *did* mean for the nation. I take up this question in Chapter 2, "The Melancholy of the Secular," which turns to Horace Walpole's 1764 gothic novel *The Castle of Otranto*—a book clearly modeled on Shakespeare's play (just as Horace's father, Robert Walpole, was frequently compared to Cardinal Wolsey, Henry's lord chancellor). I interpret the note of melancholy on which the book concludes as a rejection of the manliness officially celebrated at the close of *Henry VIII*. Rather than helping to consolidate the link between family and nation, Walpole's hero Theodore opts out of heterosexual reproduction altogether, suggesting that Henrician Reform, far from setting the nation on a smooth path toward Protestantism and prosperity, yields instead an iterated series of succession crises. In its resistance to the marriage plot and to the notion of an unproblematic destiny, Theodore's melancholy is an example of the "unquiet things" created by the very process of Reform itself.

In Chapter 3, "Wishing for Nothing: *Emma* and the Dissolution," I follow the long arc of reforming pressure into the early years of the nineteenth century. In Jane Austen's 1815 novel it is of course Donwell Abbey itself, home of Mr. Knightley and the ideological center of the narrative, that reactivates the history of Reform. To grasp this is to grasp also the politics of the novel's generic argument against romance, for though Mr. Knightley is in many ways the ideal landowner in his attention to detail, he adamantly refuses any hint of the festive—not only Mrs. Elton's silly plans for donkeys and picnics, but also Frank's love of dancing, Emma's high spirits, Harriet's overactive libido, and whatever lingering residue of free movement is left to the rural populace. "Quiet" is Mr. Knightley's watchword, and he is so effective in carrying out his reforms that there seems, by the end of the novel, very little to do and hardly any place to go. To learn to be content with nowhere to go and "nothing" to do, Austen's narrator continually reminds us, is to learn how to read a realist novel.

Foucault has taught us to look for power in its effects, and scholars have applied that idea to the secular, which is "best approached indirectly," as

Talal Asad remarks.[22] I, too, argue that secularism is not primarily about religion but about the reform (or regulation, if you like) of what I call here "unquiet things." But I also make a particular kind of claim for literary representation: that a play like *Henry VIII* complicates the *telos* of a reforming narrative posited as inevitable; that in so doing it enables us to tune in the voices of a secular age; that otherwise those voices would be hard to hear because of their tendency to slip quietly into the background. This background or ambience is what Taylor calls the "immanent frame" of the modern secular with its celebration of ordinary life, or what Coleridge in "Frost at Midnight" calls "all the numberless goings-on of life, / Inaudible as dreams!" (lines 12–13). Coleridge's poem works hard to count those goings-on and to make them audible, chiefly by registering their effects on him as he sits before the fire. The unquiet film at which the speaker gazes can also serve, then, as an example of my method here: the film moves not because of any observable contact but because of the invisible movements of air and heat in the surrounding environment. Call that surrounding environment *the secular*, and call the film *literature*. In this book the air currents that move the film are varied: governmental power, travel narratives, literary realism, close reading, metaphor, atheism. Yet within the static, the ambient noise, the alternative frequency, or what the poem names the "puny flaps and freaks" created by the moving air, we can hear the particular kind of unquiet that is my theme.[23]

The dominant mood of this first section is melancholy. Like Thomas Pfau, I think that attention to moods, to climates of feeling, allows criticism to address "the deep-structural situatedness of individuals within history as something never actually intelligible to them in fully coherent, timely, and definitive form."[24] Like secularism, then, the historical content of a mood must be traced in its effects. Melancholy is a particularly complex mood since it seems to have no origin and no solution. Yet in his study of baroque tragic drama, Walter Benjamin identifies three elements that lead to its characteristic melancholy. First, baroque tragedy is simultaneously worldly and uncertain: "The religious man of the baroque era clings so tightly to the world because of the feeling that he is being driven along to a cataract with it."[25] The era may have invented absolutism as compensation for this lack of discernable order, yet baroque tragedy returns again and again to the indecisive tyrant and the "sheer arbitrariness of the constantly shifting emotional storm" that characterizes his inactions (66). Second, while classical tragedy does not require an audience, baroque tragedy does. It is ceremonial and ostentatious, and marked by a certain extravagance: "The spectator of tragedy is summoned, and is justified, by the tragedy itself; the *Trauerspiel*, in contrast, has to be understood from the point of view of the onlooker" (119). And third, baroque tragedy is characterized by *acedia* (boredom, "world-sadness"), a restlessness that does not permit one to settle on any one thing, even though the world is full of things to which one might commit oneself. Together these aspects create the *Trauerspiel*'s dominant melancholic mood.

Such melancholy, with its component parts of indecisiveness, ostentation, and boredom, may seem like the polar opposite to a Foucaultian narrative of ever more effective and minutely adjusted Reforming power that I have been emphasizing. And yet we can see how the one might produce the other: the narrative of Henrician Reform highlights an increase in state power, but Henry himself, especially as figured by Shakespeare and Walpole, looks more like a mystified baroque prince than a decisive leader; meanwhile the ostentatious showiness, bordering on camp, that characterizes the worlds of Shakespeare and Walpole has less to do with governmentality than with a compensation for the loss of passageways between heaven and earth. Finally, Theodore's melancholy and Emma's *acedia* become the dominant moods of Walpole's and Austen's novels. In books that end by re-writing the eschatology of the marriage-plot into bleakly reiterative reminders that nothing more is needed, melancholy is the primary objection to the various eschatological and teleological plots to which these characters find themselves bound. Benjamin captures the dialectical and class-based nature of this mood when he writes that "by making the secular-political sphere a testing ground for a life that was only indirectly religious" the baroque might "instill into the people a strict sense of obedience to duty, but in its great men it produced melancholy" (138). Melancholy is not the same thing as nostalgia; as the imaginative postulation of a fullness already foreclosed upon, its discontent is temporally and emotionally complex. Secularism-as-governmentality is all too real in this first section of the book, then, but so too is discontent with that formation—and this is the other half of the story I wish to tell.

In a very literal sense Henry VIII imposed *secularization* on England. He removed property, power, and authority from the church and put them in worldly hands. And his reforms also prepared the ground for *secularism*, a set of opinions, beliefs, and institutional protocols involving the proper relation of church and state. But it is to the *secular* itself that I wish first to draw attention: to a pretheoretical way of life that bequeathed to modernity a particular phenomenology. Something of that phenomenology is captured in this book's cover image, Caspar David Friedrich's painting *Monk by the Sea* (1810), which shows a lone figure, his back to the viewer, contemplating a rough ocean and an ominous sky. The monk, set low in the frame, is diminished by the vast landscape and seascape, which are in turn immense without being sublime; they are simply omnipresent, as though foreground and background have slipped away into a kind of middle distance, while the energy of the painting is itself distributed horizontally rather than vertically. The familiar romantic association between art and religion remains intact here, but the monk/artist figure looks out at the world neither in mastery nor in worship, but rather with something more akin to *anomie* or melancholy.

We live in the secular before we cogitate about it. To ask what kinds of experiences—in particular what bodily experiences—the secular facilitates is to shift the focus from what the secular is to what it does, and to the powers and possibilities it both permits and prevents. In "Frost at Midnight," it is the "stern . . . face" (line 37) of the teacher—easily read as a figure of Reform—that first encourages the poem's speaker to turn to the fluttering film for solace; later, when he is an adult who has supposedly put away such childish fancies, the dream somehow remains, and the flickering, moving film still figures the "unquiet things" of a folk superstition that will not die, even in the midst of an overwhelming silence. Indeed, the speaker describes the stillness of midnight and the steady breathing of his sleeping child as "strange / And extreme" (lines 9–10), as though order holds within itself the potential for disorder. Here, the pitch and frequency of the secular age are transmitted from the very center of a culture.

❧

While Part I of *Unquiet Things* attends to discontent with the pretheoretical background of the secular, Part II turns to discontent with the theory itself. We all know the familiar story: beginning in the seventeenth century and accelerating throughout the eighteenth, political liberalism and the discourses of toleration slowly brought peace to a war-torn Europe by privatizing religion and subsuming it beneath the sovereign power of the modern state. "[A]lmost all those tragical revolutions which have exercised Christendom these many years have turned upon this hinge, that there hath been no design so wicked which hath not worn the vizor of religion," wrote John Locke in 1660. "All those flames that have made such havoc and desolation in Europe, and have not been quenched but with the blood of so many millions, have been at first kindled with coals from the altar."[26] Locke was thinking most

immediately of the English Civil War but also reflecting on the bloodshed of
the prior 150 years. Apparently the reorganized religious landscape of the early
modern period led not to peace but to havoc and desolation. Locke blames
religion for this: people are more likely to be duped into violent acts if someone is blowing on the coals. Thus "religious violence" is the problem that
the nation-state and its slowly developing discourses of liberalism and tolerance will be called on to solve. "[N]one ever went about to ruin the *state* but
with pretense to build the *temple*," is how Locke pithily phrases it, as though
religion were the innovation, and the state the neutral ground on which it
imposed.[27] This remains the dominant assumption of liberal political theory.
"First, and central, were the problems caused by religion" writes Ross Harrison of the early modern period.[28] And for John Rawls, political liberalism
begins "in the Reformation and its aftermath, with the long controversies
over religious toleration in the sixteenth and seventeenth centuries."[29]
Although modern commentators may differently imagine the relationship
between religion and the state, they tend to agree with Locke that religion is
intrinsically divisive. Henceforth peace will be a secular business, presided
over by a secular state—peace here meaning simply the absence of war.

In the past decade, however, a revisionist alternative to this liberal story
has gained some traction. Inspired by earlier critiques of liberalism as a form of
governmentality (Foucault) or violence (Benjamin, Derrida), the revisionists
propose that the directional arrow actually runs the other way: it is not the
nation-state that brings a halt to religious violence, but religious violence that
is the *result* of the nation-state. Religion, on such an account, is thus contin-
gently rather than necessarily divisive. This narrative has come from two directions. Stanley Hauerwas, John Milbank, and William Cavanaugh, basing their
arguments on a theological tradition oriented toward peace rather than conflict,
have argued that the nation-state is at best a manager of violence, the most
successful player in a Machiavellian world where force is primary and must be
met with counterforce.[30] In a more Foucauldian vein, meanwhile, scholars like
Talal Asad and Wendy Brown have analyzed the violence that adheres even in
liberal practices of lawmaking. Religion in its modern form, they note, is in
fact a creation of the liberal state.[31] Both groups of critics converge on the claim
that the nation-state, usually presented as a savior from religious violence, is
actually part of the problem. From time to time political interests, particularly
in trade and finance, may be more efficiently advanced through peace, but it is
the violence of war, or the threat of violence embodied in the law, that preserves
identity, territory, and sovereignty.

Is the modern state a bringer of peace, then, or a site of violence (even if that violence is sometimes presented as toleration)? In the middle section of the book I discuss three authors—Samuel Taylor Coleridge, Walter Scott, and James Hogg—who took up the challenge of measuring the new, secular arrangement of religion and state made possible by the work of Reform and by new arrangements of power. Writing in the early years of the nineteenth century, they each begin their thinking from the turning point of 1688/1689, the so-called Glorious Revolution, when England chased out its Catholic king, welcomed William and Mary to the throne, and ushered in a tolerant, latitudinarian regime that set the nation on a secular course of peace and prosperity. Much of Coleridge's prose, particularly his defense of the established church as an instrument of toleration, seems to continue this project into the nineteenth century. But in Chapter 4, "Coleridge at Sea," I argue that his great poem "Kubla Khan," far from aligning seamlessly with the progressive narrative of 1688, in fact reaches back over the eighteenth century into the more unsettled seventeenth. The poem's supposed source in *Purchas's Pilgrimage*, the most popular travel book of the seventeenth century, has long been a critical commonplace, but Coleridge uses Purchas for more than a few impressive images. In my account, "Kubla Khan" is best read as a report of the modern invention of "religion" itself—its invention, that is to say, as something dark and irrational that sits uneasily, if at all, within the tolerant confines of the liberal nation-state.

Chapter 5, "Hippogriffs in the Library," continues to explore the legitimacy of eighteenth-century toleration discourse. It begins with a discussion of David Hume and William Warburton, combatants in the polite world of eighteenth-century letters. Though they officially disagreed on much, the skeptical Hume and the orthodox Warburton agree that the movements of history foreclose on any return to the world before 1688. This progressive narrative, however, consistently produces its spectral negation, a revolutionary possibility that becomes increasingly fantastic over the course of the eighteenth century. What to do with such possibilities is a question taken up by the historical novel and especially by Walter Scott, an enthusiastic proponent of toleration who uses his novels to narrate the settling of possibility into probability, romance into history, the enchantments of unrealistic fantasy into the enchantments of worldly life. Yet even *Waverley* (1814), the novel that inaugurated this tradition so powerfully, registers its hero's lingering "sigh" for a life that cannot be his. Waverley is sighing in particular for the Jacobite rebellion, the dream or fantasy of a great reversal that haunted

Britain's progressive and prosperous eighteenth century. So long as it remains possible to imagine the return of the Stuart monarchs and the final undoing of the 1688 consensus, just so long does history remain alive as a field of contested and contingent forces rather than simply the site of a teleological unfolding. By the time of *Rob Roy* (1817), Scott's narrator seems to have taken this argument to heart, for in this novel modernity itself is a curious mixture of magical thinking and instrumental rationality. Rather than pitching Jacobitism against the present moment, this retelling of the 1715 rebellion suggests that Jacobitism is one of the ways that Scotland has of *being* modern.[32] Even rebellion becomes, in this handling, less an example of romantic nostalgia than a particularly compelling way to oppose the realist impulse to organize and manage change.

   This is the logic of minoritization, and it is the dominant theme of the middle chapters of this book. Chapter 6, "The Creation of Religious Minorities," turns to Scottish Presbyterianism in the seventeenth and eighteenth centuries, and to James Hogg's remarkable novel about those years, *The Private Memoirs and Confessions of a Justified Sinner* (1824). Hogg's treatment of religious history showcases a different kind of resistance to the moderate Enlightenment, one that takes its inspiration from the political covenantalism of seventeenth-century Calvinism rather than the monarchism of the Jacobite rebellions. Hogg's novel traces the career of a Scottish Covenanting family in the years 1687 to 1712, in the aftermath of the so-called Killing Times, when Presbyterian sectaries were harassed and murdered in a campaign of terror licensed by an English government intent on subduing anticolonial resistance. The novel presents the same story twice, first in the voice of a nineteenth-century "editor" and then in the voice of Robert Wringhim, a young Covenanter who embarks on a reign of terror and mayhem. Though it is typically read as an indictment of the Calvinist doctrine of predestination, *Justified Sinner* is also a powerful condemnation of the violence of the state—what Walter Benjamin called "mythic violence," the violence that is administrative and law-establishing. Benjamin insists that such violence is more than metaphorical; like actual physical violence, it wields power over mere life for its own sake. Both Hogg and Benjamin suggest that the majority/minority dynamics of the modern state have a tendency to produce rather than suppress religious violence; and in their shared fascination with temporalities that loop or double rather than progress in a linear fashion, both writers point to ways of organizing a life that interrupt the "empty, homogeneous time" of the secular nation-state.[33]

In her remarkable study *Outside the Fold*, Gauri Viswanathan shows how conversion, especially to minority religious positions, serves as a form of resistance to the official (and frequently colonial) state. Treating conversion at one remove (the visionary poet, the Jacobite, the Covenanter), the texts by Coleridge, Scott, and Hogg that I examine here all show how, in Viswanathan's words, "In much the same way that religious belief is placed outside public discourse, it is also evident that, in a parallel historical process, the content of minority religions is placed outside the space of national culture."[34] This process, she goes on, makes it difficult to grasp the worldliness of those minority positions: they seem to reside in a premodern or nonmodern space, set apart from the shared social world. The middle section of *Unquiet Things* describes the way in which the worldliness of these minority positions unsettles settled arrangements of power and self-assured declarations of historical progress.

❦

In *A Secular Age*, Charles Taylor describes the modern self as a "buffered self," for whom "the only locus of thoughts, feelings, spiritual élan is what we call minds; the only minds in the cosmos are those of humans; and minds are bounded, so that these thoughts, feelings, etc. are situated 'inside' them."[35] He contrasts this to a premodern "porous self" open to the powerful forces of a spiritual or magical realm not necessarily isomorphic with Christianity. Taylor proposes that a buffered self relates to religion mostly as a belief that it owns, or that it has lost, or from which it can opt out. Indeed, the felt sense that we *can* opt out is, for Taylor, the central phenomenological fact of the secular age, and accounts for both the intensity and the fragility of religious faith in the modern age: we feel how many other people there are, very like us in numerous ways, whom we like or respect or feel close to, yet who believe differently than we do. Taylor writes that this is now a condition of our lived experience: reflexive distance even from those things that seem to us most intimate.

This may seem like speculative or conjectural history.[36] Indeed, the real story is a good deal messier than Taylor implies, and the seventeenth and eighteenth centuries were in fact home to a variety of creative struggles—intellectual, aesthetic, and political—within and against the developing modern order. But whatever its problems, Taylor's history shares with the writers considered in the final section of this book a sense that we now confront a domain of buffered selves, of minds set apart from the world in a distinct way. The construal of religion as a set of cognitive beliefs, the political development known as confessionalization, the intellectual innovations that Stephen Toulmin calls the "quest for certainty," and the social transformation that Philip Gorski calls the "disciplinary revolution," had, by the early years of the nineteenth century, made possible a new set of intimate relations among individual subjects, their religion, and the nation-state.[37] And so the writers and critics of the romantic era felt themselves to be confronting a world uniquely inhospitable to alternative ways of organizing bodily and spiritual life. It was against the political and social consequences of the buffered self that many of them understood themselves to be writing—and this is why their interventions can look so very much like an alternative religion.[38]

The final section of the book explores the paradoxes and contradictions of this picture of the buffered self. Chapter 7, "Byron and the Paradox of Reading," turns to *The Giaour*, Lord Byron's poetic romance about the confrontation between romantic pluralism and the kind of antimodernism that we know as fundamentalism (and that the eighteenth century knew as fanaticism). Picking up on some of the threads already woven through my discussion of Hogg's *Justified Sinner*, I interpret Byron's poem as an acute meditation on the mutually constitutive character of fanaticism and pluralism. This is not because pluralism is unable to muster a sustained critique of fanaticism, as many on both the left and right argue today, but for the very opposite reason: in Byron's poem, pluralism harbors at its core a violence indistinguishable from that of its fanatical rival. The stateless and nameless Giaour thinks of himself as a cosmopolitan citizen of a world utterly different from that of Hassan, his stereotypical Muslim adversary; and yet the poem insists that the two men share a great deal, especially their indifference to the plight of Leila, the woman each claims as his own.

Multicultural pluralism may be limited by its philosophical roots in a romantic cultural relativism, then, but *The Giaour* suggests that the cosmopolitan alternative has its own limitations and its own, largely disavowed, violence. Chapter 8, "The Constellations of Romantic Religion," continues to explore this problematic by tracing the career of what I call "romantic religion"—a nondoctrinal spirituality simultaneously everywhere and nowhere—from its development in the eighteenth-century linguistic theories of Robert Lowth and J. G. Herder to its full-blown essentialization in Friedrich Schleiermacher's *On Religion* and then to its critique in Friedrich Schlegel's meditations on the fragment. I end the chapter with Percy Shelley's *Revolt of Islam*, highlighting the moment when the heroine Cythna learns to forgo her dreams of secular freedom in place of a different and more vexed practice that she describes as a "subtler language within language." With this phrase, politically modest but theoretically sophisticated, Cythna finds the voice that Leila, the dead woman of *The Giaour*, is never granted.

Conceptually, these two chapters work together to explore some of the complicated issues surrounding the politics of secularism in the context of a world that for all our talk of globalization remains nonetheless strongly tied to both the idea and the institutional power of the nation-state. Byron's poem offers an internal critique of its own fantasy of a cosmopolitan life able to transcend the limitations of a traditional culture; the career of romantic religion likewise points to the way that global and local interpenetrate.[39] Both chapters, then, argue against the tendency to locate "culture" within the boundaries of the nation-state.[40] This is because the nation-state is the prime carrier of secular modernity, and so resistance will have to come from someplace other than alternatives already theorized in advance as private: those activities constructed as religious, to be sure, but also the remnants of the carnivalesque itself, understood today largely as a zone of personal self-exploration, artistic creation, and spiritual experimentation held securely within the container of a state whose boundaries are porous to capital but buffered to everything else.[41]

I locate that "someplace other" at the confluence of *metaphor* and *becoming-minor*, the two terms that define the final third of the book. Theories of metaphor are legion, of course, but most definitions recognize the surprising coincidence or juxtaposition of unlike things, and the process by which language makes new meanings by carrying one set of referents across to another. "Becoming-minor," meanwhile, is a term developed by Gilles Deleuze and Felix Guattari to describe the way Kafka worked within the interstices of German to bring out a hidden or occluded story vibrating within the confines of a dominant language.[42] "Unquiet," as I develop it over the course of this book, is a similarly interstitial or immanent critique of the surrounding secular quiet, a way of marking things that exceed the spaces marked out for them. As registers of resistance and as theoretical interventions, unquiet things reject the distinction between politics, on the one hand, and aesthetic or spiritual self-fashioning, on the other. In this respect, Cythna's subtler language offers a sophisticated and conceptually rich theorization of an alternative, what I describe in Chapter 8 as a practice of making room for others while eschewing the political languages of "freedom" to which resistance had been traditionally committed. It is, crucially, a language that arises through a process of self-criticism, but self-criticism made possible in this case by its transposition out of Europe and into an exotic, Orientalized clime.

In this age of globalized public religion it has become fashionable in some quarters to plead for a return of the Enlightenment. We need another Hobbes, or another Voltaire. Joined to that thought is generally another one: that what came after the Enlightenment—that is, romanticism—is in some indirect way responsible for what currently ails us: our reflexive obeisance to identity, difference, and cultural autonomy, and our collective failure of nerve when it comes time to stand up for universal values.[43] One encounters this thought across the ideological spectrum. For liberals like Mark Lilla, the broad romantic tradition stretching from Rousseau through Schleiermacher to nineteenth-century German theology discovered the power of individual consciousness and wedded it to notions of cultural and national difference, thereby unleashing a series of political messianisms—nationalism, communism, fascism, and fundamentalism—that it was unequipped to handle.[44] Neoconservatives have sounded a similar theme at a higher frequency. Thus Samuel Huntington, Ayaan Hirsi Ali, Niall Ferguson, and policy institutes such as the Rand Corporation have argued in recent years that the defense of the Enlightenment and the defeat of terrorism require that we repudiate our romantic impulses in favor of a militant—and military-backed—secularism. For them, the line from romanticism to "Islamo-fascism" is apparently easy to see, and the Enlightenment our only hope for combatting it.[45] Even elements of the academic Left have begun calling for a critique of multiculturalism from the standpoint of a democratic universalism.[46] Ideological differences aside, these parallel movements share a structure according to which romanticism is a stalking horse for ethnic tribalism and the Enlightenment is the only alternative way to model our increasingly connected world. In these accounts Enlightenment means a secularized Christianity—self-evidently so on the right, but also on the left, where Alain Badiou, to take a prominent example, though he has "never really connected Paul with religion," nonetheless turns to Saint Paul as a model for what he calls the "fidelity to the event" that grounds the Christian community in the aftermath of Christ's resurrection and for which the French Revolution serves as the primary modern correlative.[47]

But it is precisely the enlightened secular language of the French Revolution that Cythna, trapped in her cave in *The Revolt of Islam*, forgoes. In instructing his readers to think beyond the Revolution and its failures, Shelley offers perhaps the most resolute and ambitious version of romanticism's political project: a countermodernity that not only refuses the too easy solace of nostalgia for the way things used to be but also refuses to accept the revolutionary model as the only possible way of thinking the future. Organized religion plays a vexed role in this endeavor: Shelley's thinking is clearly indebted to Christianity at numerous points; equally clear, though, is his self-professed atheism and support for the secular ideals of the French Revolution and the tradition of radical Enlightenment thinking on which the revolutionaries drew. This makes Shelley an essential thinker for our own age, caught as we are, conceptually and politically, between the impulses of an enlightened universalism (figured now as the reign of both global capital and human rights) and a cultural particularism (whether construed as identity politics, ethnic conflict, or as forms of traditional knowledge, indigenous ontology, or diasporic community). As I argue in "Shelley After Atheism," the ninth and final chapter, Shelley's poetic thinking helps us to see these oppositions as products of secularism itself. Shelley recognized that the Revolution's anticlericalism was deeply embedded in a politics of secularism that led first to terrible violence, then to Napoleon, and finally to the restoration of monarchies across Europe. In repeating the secularizing gesture of the Jacobins, then, supporters of enlightened universalism reiterate their primary mistake.

My test case for this claim is Shelley's great poem *Mont Blanc*. This poem is often read as an expression of its author's atheism; I argue, by contrast, that to view the poem as "expressing" any kind of content at all, even the negative content of a-theism, badly misconstrues the sophisticated conceptual project of Shelley's middle period—a project better understood as a critique not of organized religion but of the discourses, especially the radical Enlightenment and the French Revolution, that have made organized religion their primary target. To think of religion as something from which secularism will save us is to misunderstand how secularism helped to create religion in the first place, and to forget how political and military intervention continues to shape the forms that "religion" assumes. By placing Shelley "after atheism," rather than within it, my aim is to demonstrate that Shelley himself recognized the practical and philosophical limitations of the modern secular order.

The book's final section is called "After the Secular." Though the term "postsecular" has become popular for describing much recent work in the humanities and social sciences, I avoid it for good reason.[48] It seems to me too simple and linear a description of the complex sociological and theoretical realities of our present moment. It is also frustratingly imprecise about the very term—*secular*—whose passing it understands itself to be narrating.

The term "postsecular" might mean that we were once secular, but are no longer. In this case, the "post" in "postsecular" would be like the "post" in postmodern. One response is that just as we have never been modern (purely rational, purely instrumental, purely scientific, and so on), so we have never been secular. For in this case, "secular" presupposes a narrative of religious decline, and this is at minimum a debatable assumption, since it is not clear that religion ever went away. To be sure, academics in the North Atlantic regions have paid it less attention in the past half-century, and socio-logical data suggest that levels of participation have ebbed and flowed over the past centuries. But the trajectories are varied enough to cast doubt on any simple decline-and-return narrative. To cite only the most obvious examples, Christianity has declined markedly in Western Europe, held steady or declined only slowly in the United States, revived in parts of Eastern Europe, and grown strikingly in much of the Southern Hemisphere. Religion contin-ues to be a primary fault line in the Middle East and Southeast Asia; many East Asian societies, by contrast, have long been predominantly irreligious. And just as the evidence of decline is mixed, so too is the evidence of return. Many sociologists continue to insist that the overall trend for religious partic-ipation remains downward, and if this is correct it casts doubt on the "return" part of the decline-and-return narrative. Moreover, the continual and dramatic movements of peoples, driven by the churning of global capital, by environmental calamity, and by political conflicts that are themselves often related to questions of the legacy of secularism, means the ebb and flow of religious participation is now truly a global question. It seems quite simplistic, for example, to assert that the presence of large communities of Turkish Muslims in Germany, with all the attendant social questions and tensions, is evidence that we are living in a postsecular world. If anything, those questions and tensions are evidence of the continuing salience of *secu-larism*. And this leads finally to the crucial point already mentioned above and developed at length in the second section of this book: that "secularism" does not follow "religion" in any straightforward sense because the two notions are bound up together: without secularism, there is no religion as we know it today.

The "secular" in postsecular might, by contrast, mean a political doc-trine involving the separation of religion and the state. In this second instance, we can remain agnostic about religious decline, and focus instead on religion's privatization and depoliticization. Again, the terrain is remarkably varied, from officially secular states within religious societies (Turkey, Egypt,

India, the USA, all in different ways the legacies of the colonial era) to nomi-
nally secular states within religiously indifferent societies (the northern band
of Western Europe). Tying together such disparate cases, however, is the
notion that the political doctrine of secularism is itself a comprehensive theory of the good. In his well-known 2008 lecture "Notes on a Post-Secular
Society," Jürgen Habermas puts it like this: "To the extent that the government assumed a secular character, step by step the religious minorities (initially only tolerated) received further rights—first the freedom to practice
their own religion at home, then the right of religious expression and finally
equal rights to exercise their religion in public. An historical glance at this
tortuous process, and it reached into the 20th century, can tell us something
about the preconditions for this precious achievement, the inclusive religious
freedom that is extended to all citizens alike." As this process starts to come
apart, Habermas argues, we enter the domain of the postsecular. Importantly,
this is less a matter of governance itself than it is of citizen's ideational commitment to the ideal of secularism. "The description of modern societies as
'post-secular' refers to a change in consciousness," Habermas concludes.[49]

It is hard to know what to make of this claim. Various multicultural or
communitarian initiatives notwithstanding, there does not appear to be
much evidence for a widespread turn away from secular governance. Habermas's formulation in fact seems to smuggle in the first definition of "postsecular" (the return of religion) as evidence for the demise of the second
(the breakdown of a secular polity). But there is no logically necessary relation between the two. Indeed, the very thing that makes political secularism
so precious, in Habermas's words, is precisely its religious inclusivity—in
theory, one could have a secular state in a society of complete religious
participation. The "change in consciousness" to which Habermas refers
might therefore be a result of religion's de-privatization, a phenomenon
remarked on by Jose Casanova already in 1994.[50] Irreligious citizens may
thus feel themselves to be surrounded by religious discourse of surprising
intensity. But does the feeling that one is living in a postsecular society make
it so? This ignores the fact that religion is easily used by secular formations,
particularly the state in search of its own agenda. To take an example from
the United States: each session of the House of Representatives opens with
a prayer offered by the House Chaplain. Is this evidence of postsecularism,
or evidence of the way that religion can be interpellated? As James A. Beckford notes, religious identities can be summoned at moments like this
one; even largely secular citizens may take comfort in the thought of such

gestures.[51] Therefore the mere invocation of religious values does not by itself indicate the emergence of the postsecular.

Finally, "postsecular" is sometimes taken to mean a primarily theoretical development in the humanities and interpretive social sciences, highlighting the intellectual resources offered by the Christian tradition. The references here range from Radical Orthodox theology to Marxist and post-Marxist political theory to the revival of interest in political theology. With few exceptions, these movements have addressed themselves specifically to the Christian legacy, perhaps without fully recognizing that Christianity itself bears a special relationship to the secular. This was a theme developed by Weber, of course, and it has been picked up and modified by a range of more recent writers, including Charles Taylor, Talal Asad, and Tomoko Masuzawa. Those three offer quite divergent genealogies of the secular (from the viewpoints of, respectively, European social history, post-colonial theory, and religious studies), but they all agree that one cannot tell the story of the secular without also telling a story of the transformation of Christianity during the modern age. From this perspective, the assertion that we are living in a postsecular age would entail the claim that we are also living in a post-Christian age. This seems a highly debatable assertion, especially insofar as Christianity remains entangled in foreign policy and international relations. Even in western Europe, "Christianity" encompasses not only levels of participation or subjective belief but also influences how we think about practices of the self, of governance, of social collectives, and of aesthetics.

It is notable, finally, that each of the versions of "postsecular" offered above are in tension with one another. This is because they begin with different implicit definitions of the secular itself: as a real narrative of religious decline (sense one), as a political theory that encodes its own comprehensive notion of the good (sense two), and as a concept requiring a particular genealogy (sense three). One cannot be postsecular in all three senses simultaneously without changing the definition of the term itself, nor can one be simultaneously skeptical of all three senses of the term without also changing the definition. The cluster secular/secularism/secularity simply has too many connotations to be stabilized in this way without distortion.

In place of "postsecular" I therefore propose a different term: *after the secular*. The word *after* connotes a richer set of possibilities than *post*: one might *come after* the secular in a temporal sense; one might also *pursue* the secular, in the way that one pursues an aspiration or a model; and one might, finally, *take after* the secular, in the way a child takes after a parent, manifesting basic genetic similarities while at the same time developing her capacities in new and different ways. "After the secular" may not have the aphoristic ring of "postsecular," but it does a better job of capturing the multivalent meanings of the term, and the variety of relations one might have to it.

To be after the secular, then, is to start one's thinking from a romantic insight: a cautious, ambivalent recognition that the religious and the secular constitute each other, and that the attempt to pull them apart leads to a level of harm that is (or ought to be) morally intolerable. This is a simple theme, though its manifestations are legion. I do not claim that Shelley and Byron would be especially happy with this conclusion—any more than James Hogg would be happy about it. But some of the great poems and novels of the romantic era nonetheless leave us with the difficult thought that although it may be emotionally satisfying to eliminate the voice of "religion" from the modern conversation, or to assign it labels (religious, secular, postsecular), the cost of such satisfaction is steep. Better, they suggest, to let the unquiet things remain, a constant reminder that modernity has not yet delivered on its promises. To be "after the secular" in this sense means that one is, simultaneously, positioned chronologically after it, that one pursues it, and that one takes after it, carrying it forward while living into a different future than any it might have imagined.

℘

Readers may have noticed a set of tonal shifts in my summary of the book's argument so far. Part I of *Unquiet Things* employs a definition of the secular as a form of governmentality. Its characteristic mood is *melancholy*. By contrast, Part II highlights those figures and characters who disrupt or otherwise trouble the quiet. It is characterized by what I call *minoritization*. Part III, meanwhile, begins to construct an image of the secular as a normative posture toward the world. It is characterized by the tension between *metaphor* and *becoming-minor*. These shifts are deliberate.

The first section of the book offers a version of the claim that religion is privatized under the conditions of modernity; by emphasizing secularism rather than religion, though, I show how "unquiet things" register the secular quiet that surrounds them. The story I tell in this section is one of increasingly effective control. At the same time, authority is bought at the expense of a considerable narrowing. (In Austen's oeuvre, both *Mansfield Park* and

Emma demonstrate this double movement: at the end of these novels, there is a larger world that the principal characters simply turn away from.) My goal in this section is not to offer a history that takes in every aspect of Henrician reform but instead to track a problematic particular to that reform and posed in figural terms: a recurrent opposition between the forces of order and consolidated governmental power on the one hand, and on the other the increasingly marginalized forces of disorder, disruption, and disquiet associated initially with traditional Catholicism but by the eighteenth century simply free-floating signifiers of discontent.

My approach here shares something with that of Jon Mee, whose book *Romanticism, Enthusiasm, and Regulation* (2003) has done much to call attention to modes of expression that "transgress the boundaries of the emergent bourgeois public sphere" during the late eighteenth and early nineteenth centuries. Mee shows how vulgar religious enthusiasm became an object of concern in the aftermath of the English Civil War; polite culture well into the nineteenth century, he notes, was "haunted by the fear of combustible matter within both the individual and the body politic."[52] Romanticism, in this accounting, is the culmination of a long eighteenth-century process of stabilizing and regularizing enthusiasm so that it could be used. "To transform enthusiasm into art was to make it relatively safe," as Mee puts it.

I, too, am interested in "combustible matter," and I share Mee's supposition that modern power works through production rather than repression.[53] But my approach has been to emphasize less the stabilizing function of literature than its sensitivity to instability and disorder: the unquiet things of "Frost at Midnight," for instance, whose "puny flaps and freaks" continue to inspire "dim sympathies" within the living.[54] It is of course true, as Mee notes, that romantic writers were to varying degrees concerned with their professional status and relationship to official culture. But it does not automatically follow that their literary productions speak in the voice of that culture. "Kubla Khan," for example, gives us two models of literary activity: the more familiar high visionary argument, what the poem names a "miracle of rare device," that somehow transforms and organizes the tumult of voices that go before it; and another model, lower and more bodily but in its own way every bit as ambitious, that I term an "addiction to history" and that remains resolutely unreformed. In Hogg's novel of Scottish fanaticism, too, the haunted and haunting character of modernity already nascent in "Kubla Khan" and in Scott's novels of rebellion—and indeed in the abiding desire in "Frost at Midnight" for a "stranger"—becomes fully instantiated: not merely in its doublings and Satanic presence but in the historical and physical environment that surrounds the novel's characters themselves, who, like the unquiet film in Coleridge's grate, experience modern life not as the power to move but as the inevitability of being moved by larger forces.[55]

The religious identities in the book's middle section stretch from visionary Anglican poets to superstitious Catholic rebels to fanatic Presbyterian Dissenters. The range here is deliberate, for my goal is to identify a shared recognition among different texts and differing doctrines: by shifting the nation's self-identity, I argue, the 1688 consensus also off-loaded basic questions of peace and justice onto a discourse of religious toleration and capitalist prosperity that was, by the early years of the nineteenth century, no longer adequate to its unleashed energies. Scott's affection for Jacobitical anachronism is certainly patronizing, yet his need to renarrate its demise hints that the possibility of great reversals remains strangely alive even in the early nineteenth century, an era filled with revolutions of a decidedly different kind. I am therefore less interested in the contrasts between enthusiasm and superstition (the twin evils of religious extremism, according to Hume, the one intrinsically Protestant, the other Catholic) than in what both have in common: the shared sense that modern life has somehow passed them by, that they are out of place and out of time.[56]

This makes the present book quite different from my previous study *The Book of God* (2007), which addressed questions of romanticism and secularization by keeping its focus resolutely on the mainstream Anglican tradition of natural theology. In that book I was concerned to emphasize writers who in various ways managed to adjust themselves to modernity, and who in so doing revealed it to be considerably less secular than we might have thought. In *Unquiet Things*, by contrast, I turn my attention to those who have for different reasons been unable to adjust. In this I join other scholars who have brought religion back into circulation as a disruptive political force. A recent example is Jasper Cragwall's *Lake Methodism*, which convincingly argues for a two-way traffic between the "high arguments" of the lake school poets and the "disreputable Christianity" of Methodism. Cragwall demonstrates that Methodism was not, in the eyes of its detractors, so much a doctrine as it was a "language and performance" of enthusiasm, prophesy, and sentiment that sat uncomfortably close to the canonical statements of early romanticism.[57] I certainly share with Cragwall an interest in the power of plebeian or nonelite discontent. But Cragwall focuses on the tension between Anglican authority and Methodist revolt, and on how that tension informed the literature of the period. As such, his concern is explicitly with religion and religious dispute. My objects of analysis, by contrast, are more general. I am more interested in secularism than in religion per se, both because the former sets the conditions for any discussion of the latter, and because it is secularism rather than religion that offers the best analytical window on modernity. I am concerned, that is to say, less with religious dispute than with the atmosphere in which that dispute takes place—less with Coleridge's flickering film than with the air currents that push it around. This licenses the ideological range of the writers I study and the longer historical sweep of the book. By the same token, I avoid categorizing the flickers of discontent that the book isolates as intrinsically or necessarily religious: especially in the third section of the book, the "unquiet things" of my title are interpreted as a development from within the secular itself.

As a way of suggesting how this works, let me appeal to a brief essay by Isabelle Stengers. In "The Cosmopolitical Proposal," Stengers constructs a politics and an ethics that begin with the figure of what she calls the "idiot" (she is thinking of Dostoevsky), the one who "always slows the others down, who resists the consensual way."[58] Stengers does not romanticize this figure: s/he is not the repository of some hidden knowledge or sensibility that the world desperately needs, but is simply someone who does not understand and who is deaf to the legitimacy of the larger forces that run things. Stengers's "cosmopolitical proposal" is simply to work out how a politics might proceed *in the presence* of such figures. She choses an example from the current rhetoric of just-in-time capitalism. What if, she wonders, all the workers who have been laid off in the name of flexibility and overseas competition were treated with the honor that war veterans receive: parades, commemorations, benefits, and medical care that would keep them from "falling into oblivion and indifference" (998)? If that ever were to happen, she concludes, perhaps the "fact that we are caught in a war with no conceivable prospect of peace might become intolerable" (998). This sort of proposal has several qualities. First, it literalizes the metaphor of economic war: if the world of commerce is really a battlefield, as its proponents insist when justifying their difficult decisions, then that metaphor should be taken all the way, and its veterans honored. Second, it cuts the Gordian knot of necessity that tends to hamstring discussions of economic justice, the argument that runs thusly: if we don't lay off some workers now, all the jobs will eventually be shipped overseas at some indeterminate future time. Finally, the proposal does not offer an alternative. The spectacle of the jobless as war victims "does not concern a program for another world" but is rather a diagnosis and critique of our "stable acceptance of economic war as framing our common fate" (998).

In this book, the figures and attitudes variously marginalized by modern life are Stengers's "idiots." I am less interested in the affects attached to such figures—nostalgia, sentimentality, wise passiveness—than I am in literary work that confronts history's winners with the continued and stubborn presence of its losers. I find an ally in Jerome Christensen, who writes of the "insistently ethical and potentially political import" of romantic anachronism as "a place where the excluded and extinct can make common cause, eternally renewing their claims in effective apposition to the verdicts rendered by history and achieving thereby a plaintiff immortality."[59] This is not, of course, the same as believing that history could be, or ought to be, simply rolled back. It may even be the case, as the defeated Flora Mac-Ivor declares at the end of *Waverley*, that it was "impossible that it could end otherwise than this."[60] But as Stengers writes in addressing such arguments, "we may agree . . . , but we have to make sure you are fully exposed to their consequences" (997). In the case of literary art, the consequence is an imaginative construction of modernity in the presence of those who stand to lose the most. I do not assert that this is the only story to be told about the literary culture of the romantic era. Moreover, for the themes I wish to explore, and the general lessons I wish to draw, there is nothing *inevitable* about the particular texts I have chosen; others—other poems, other novels—might have served. Though not so well, in my view, for I am concerned with the way that certain canonical and quasi-canonical texts construct their arguments in proximity to those who have the most to lose if those arguments succeed.

Here Taylor's distinction between porous and buffered selves becomes useful less as a marker of a historical change from premodern to modern than as a way of distinguishing between kinds of literary work. The buffered self may comport well with a cultural world that seeks to regularize unquiet things, but the porous self suggests a different kind of relation between person and world, closer to what Schlegel celebrated as the ironic self not "fixed" or "classified" but "still in the process of becoming."[61] Taylor insists that there is a politics implicit in these selves, and a politics as well to the institutionally mandated triumph of the one over the other, and this insistence allows us to connect literary "becoming" to the flickering unquiet that is my theme here.

In making this connection, the first point to emphasize is that secularism struggles to recognize the legitimacy of subjective phenomenologies, comportments, and experiences that are not already secular. This is an argument made by Ashis Nandy in "The Politics of Secularism," a well-known essay that distinguishes between religion as an ideology (inflexible, keyed to authoritative interpretations of certain texts, and therefore complicit with models of secular politics that see religion in exactly those terms) and religion as a "confederation of a number of ways of life, linked by a common faith and with some theological space for heterogeneity."[62] In making this distinction, Nandy joins those who see the rise of fundamentalism as a *result* of modernity rather than a development intrinsic to religion itself. As a political doctrine, secularism (especially as it has been exported around the world) articulates well with models of the self that are bounded and individuated, in possession of their own thoughts and beliefs and relating contractually to other, similarly bounded selves. Such selves can be aligned with secular governments or, if they are more recalcitrant, articulated as minorities. But secularism comports much less well with what Nandy describes as the "somewhat fluid definitions of the self with which many South Asian cultures live [and] which can be conceptually viewed as configurations of selves" (324–25). This looks a great deal like Taylor's premodern porous self, yet while Taylor tends to describe the porous self as open to the world of gods and spirits, Nandy avoids that teleological schema by emphasizing that it is open *to other people*: "Traditional ways of life have, over the centuries, developed internal principles of tolerance," he writes; "religious communities in traditional societies *have* known how to live with each other" (336). It is the advent of colonial modernity, he argues, imported from Europe to South Asia and riding piggyback on the individuated self and on secular governance, that has hardened communitarianism into ideology and created the conditions for religious violence. Strong religion is the only religion secularism can recognize, which it does by trying to contain it; the kind of deep toleration or understanding that Nandy finds intrinsic to fluid conceptions of the self makes modern secularism uneasy.

Nandy's defense of tradition has been controversial.[63] And my appeal to him here should not, of course, be taken to mean that secularism and colonialism are the same thing.[64] The point is a more basic one: that some ways of life are fluid in a fashion that is hard to recognize from the standpoint of the buffered self. A buffered self may "tolerate" others, in the same way that a state may learn to tolerate minorities; but the mark of a fluid self is that it not only tolerates others but *imputes tolerance to them*. It is that ethic of generosity, fluid, porous, and open to the world, that Schlegel described when he modeled the romantic self on the fragment.[65] Indeed, I read Schlegel's argument as a brief for a particularly literary kind of self, one in which porosity (Taylor) or fluidity (Nandy) has been retrofitted for the modern age and that shows up consistently in my account as the possibility that one is never entirely alone: the hoped-for stranger in "Frost at Midnight," the haunted libraries and byways of Scott and Hogg, Hassan's inscrutable face, the multiple worlds and multiple selves envisioned by Schlegel and Schleiermacher, the transporting power of metaphor, indeed of language itself, variously characterized by Cythna and by "Kubla Khan."[66] There is, in other words, nothing *intrinsically* premodern, or merely traditional or religious, about this way of thinking of selfhood—it can be, rather, another way of being modern.

This connection between literary becoming and porous selfhood highlights a second point as well. I have remarked already that in my account literature is more than a normalizing device. In this book it chronicles discontent with a developing modern secular order; it is the frequency, as I put it earlier, at which one can hear the strange and sometimes melancholy stillness of the secular age. But the final section of *Unquiet Things* defends a further claim as well: that some romantic-era literature models kinds of thinking about alternative social arrangements that do not depend on an a priori distinction between religious and secular, private and public, nor on models of public discourse installed by secular arrangements of power and left in place by contemporary religious revivalism. One thing that romantic-era literature can do is deterritorialize such discourses. Stengers's "idiot," the figure who slows down mobilization in the name of something more or of something else, returns here not as a figure of abjection but of possibility.[67] The modern phenomenon of belief as something inert—something that you hold or have—may emerge with great intensity in romantic writing, but as Robert Miles nicely phrases it in a review of Taylor's book, "Romanticism is not a rescue operation mounted on behalf of intellectuals alarmed and enthralled by the spillage resulting from secularization, but rather . . . a constant, proliferating, mutual fragilization of immanence and transcendence, desacralized nature and inchoate fullness."[68] Moving back and forth between discomfiting modes of secularism and the life that chafes against them, *Unquiet Things* places that romantic motion within a history that runs from the early modern period to the present. My goal is to analyze an order with which secularism is largely complicit *and* to highlight models for preserving secularism's entirely laudable ambition to promote human diversity and human flourishing in a world increasingly interconnected. There are, to my mind, few better examples of that ambition than the writings of the romantics and their contemporaries during the early years of the nineteenth century, when our current economic and social arrangements were still unsettled enough to admit of other possibilities.

PART I

Reform

I, Roger, abbot of the monastery of Furness, knowing the misorder and evil life both unto God and our Prince of the brethren of the said monastery, in discharging of my conscience do freely and wholly surrender, give, and grant unto the King's Highness, and to his heirs and assigns for evermore, all such interest and title as I have had, have, or may have, of and in the said monastery of Furness, and of and in the lands, rents, possessions, revenues, services both spiritual and temporal, and of and in all goods and chattels and all other thing whatsoever it be, belonging or in any wise appertaining to the said monastery and every part and parcel thereof, in as large and ample manner and form as ever I had or ought to have, of and in the same or any part or parcel thereof by any manner of means, title, interest, gift, grant, or otherwise, permitting and binding myself by these presents that from henceforth I shall at all times and in all places, whensoever I shall be called upon, be ready and glad to confirm, ratify, and establish this my deed, purpose, mind, and intent, as shall be devised by the learned Council of the King's said Highness, which cometh freely of myself and without any enforcement.
—"Abbot Pyle's Surrender of Furness Abbey" (5 April 1537)

Farewell, rewards and fairies.
—Richard Corbet, "A Proper New Ballad" (1647)

FIVE HUNDRED YEARS ago, "belief" meant something rather different than it does now. The word's original sense implies passionate longing and relationship; its etymological ties to the German *belieben* (beloved), the Latin *libet* (it pleases) and *libido* (pleasure), and the Old English *leof* (dear) suggest as much. To "believe" in someone was to put your trust in that person, and therefore to presuppose a relationship and a certain posture or orientation— commitment, cherishing—toward that relationship, something partly captured in the Latin *credo*, also often translated as "believe." Consequently, to lose one's belief was a moral and emotional failing more than an epistemological one.[1] Today we sometimes try to capture this wider sense of belief with the word "faith," understood to encompass a range of experiences, faculties, and dispositions, as well as cognitive "beliefs."

But in the early modern period, in line with the development of modern science, *belief* took on an increasingly epistemological charge. Religion began to be thought of as a set of propositions in which one professed belief. The relevant question became whether a particular mental state was *true*, and salvation turned increasingly on believing in the correct package of propositions—about the substance of the Eucharist, the possibility of miracles, the precise mechanisms of salvation, the nature of free will, and so on.[2] This epistemologizing of belief, as a body of information about where salvation was to be found, placed a different kind of burden on the individual, who now had to grasp precisely what it was he was professing to believe. "[T]he traditional view," writes Peter Harrison, "had been that in the process of revelation God reveals himself. Now God reveals saving knowledge." This was a new understanding of what it might mean to "believe" in God: instead of focusing on a relationship, belief now focused on *content*. Perhaps, with sufficient rigor, certain knowledge of God's will could be constructed on epistemological foundations, and systematic doubt could yield clear and distinct ideas: new, decontextualized foundations for a solid belief. Modern religion, writes Harrison, thus involves tests, theories, comparisons, "in short a whole set of rules which governed the manner in which the nascent concept was to be deployed"—much, indeed, like the modern scientific experiment.[3]

Robert Boyle became the most influential of the era's many experimenters through his effort to detach "matters of fact" from the histories, regimes, and norms in which they had been embedded. As Steven Shapin and Simon Schaffer have famously argued, Boyle's air pump was a decontextualization machine: within the artificial environment of the laboratory it made "nature" appear whole and entire, a kernel of truth stripped of the husk of convention, creed, and ideology.[4] The early modern machinery of belief—creeds, confessions, inquisitions, and the like—might be considered the functional equivalent of Boyle's air pump, separating truth from its historical and ideological frames through a rigorous focus on fact and method. Meanwhile, other forms of knowledge could be refashioned or simply excluded by the search for rational certainty as a neutral base on which to build an experimental program.

If "religion" was *essentially* about belief, then it was *not* essentially about a lot of other things. This is of course partly to make a point about the differentiation that characterizes modern life: the Westphalian model of the modern nation-state created, at least in theory, a concept of a privatized, personal religion "without direct political relevance."[5] But it also imparted a distinct "feel" to a whole variety of human experiences simply by altering their relationship to the religious. For Thomas Aquinas, God revealed himself by revealing his plans and purposes, and the church was the corporate experience of that revelation. But as God withdrew from a world that ran more and more according to rules that did not seem to require divine attention, revelation came to seem like a violation of natural laws. Under the pressure of the quest for a knowledge purified of judgments of value, revelation acquired its more modern sense of *information* about the supernatural.[6] Thus when toward the end of the seventeenth century Locke famously defined the church as a voluntary association, he was building on a cognitive and explicitly voluntarist model of belief, and deliberately trying to imagine ways of bringing people together around a shared set of mental opinions rather than around a shared experience—of habit, space, posture, ritual, or bodily display—that tacitly infused all of life. In this sense the secular is not merely the lack of "religion"; rather, it inaugurates one sensory and emotional repertoire by displacing another one.

If the secular is a way of apprehending the world—imagining the future, feeling for the nation, picturing oneself as an agent, experiencing love, hatred, and desire—then it involves the act of perception itself. When Thomas Harding, professor of Hebrew at Oxford in the middle of the sixteenth century, worried that hearing the scripture in the vernacular rather than in Latin would change his parishioners' relationship to the Bible, he was certainly fighting a rearguard battle on behalf of tradition, but he was also recognizing the sensory power of language itself.[7] As Harding and many others realized, using everyday language in church would encourage a more analytic and cognitive relationship to religion—a more *secular* relationship, even if its topic remained religious.

What, then, is the phenomenology of the secular? What does it feel like? In order to grasp the secular at this level, we need not only a history of the state but also an account of how changes in official policy made new kinds of experiences possible. What are the attitudes toward time and space assumed by the secular? What new political forms does it make suddenly relevant?[8]

CHAPTER I

The Power of the Prince: Henry VIII
and *Henry VIII*

Thomas Cobb was a tenant of the archbishop of Canterbury. Elizabeth Barton was his servant. In 1525 she became severely ill with fits and a swollen throat. Soon thereafter she began to have visions, then mystical trances. She prophesied the imminent death of a local child and was able to tell onlookers of events taking place far away, particularly in other churches. In her trances, her throat would close up so that God's sweet voice would speak through her, apparently "within her belly."[1] Her body would contort, shake, and change color. Sometimes her legs gave way, and she flailed around on the floor, with her eyes protruding.[2] But her voice, when she spoke of the joys of heaven, sounded so sweet "that every man was ravished with the hearing therof."[3] Indeed, many of her prophecies and revelations poured forth in rhyme; William Tyndale, no friend to her notions, described her as a "goodly poetess."[4] The Holy Maid of Kent, as she came to be called, prophesied that she would be cured at the chapel of Court-at-Street on Annunciation Day, 1526. According to contemporary accounts, several thousand people witnessed her miraculous cure.

After some time, the Holy Maid revealed that it was God's will that she withdraw from the world and become a nun at St. Sepulchre's convent in Canterbury. There she named as her confessor and spiritual guide the monk Edward Bocking. William Warham, the archbishop of Canterbury, agreed to the arrangement after examining her and finding her to be orthodox. From St. Sepulchre's, the Holy Maid offered revelations and demonstrations of second sight; she encouraged her hearers toward orthodoxy, praised confession and the Mass, recommended pilgrimages and the worship of images, and warned her audience against the errors of Lutheranism. She would also identify and denounce, in considerable detail, the sins and failings of her hearers, encouraging them to repent.[5] Edward Bocking read to the Holy Maid about earlier female mystics, particularly Saint Bridget and Saint Catherine of Siena. And he compiled an account of her prophecies and miracles, known as the "Nun's Book," which circulated in manuscript but does not survive.

Popular prophets had been known to cause political unrest, and so the realigning of the Holy Maid's enthusiastic and charismatic voice with the masculine structures and hierarchies of the church—her withdrawal to the convent, her recommendation of confession, mass, and pilgrimage—might have seemed the end of the threat she embodied.[6] Such things were not unknown in the fifteenth and early sixteenth centuries. Yet England was about to undergo a momentous religious change, in which this illiterate young woman would play a small but significant role. For in 1526 King Henry VIII fell in love with Anne Boleyn, and approached Pope Clement VII about a divorce from Catherine of Aragon. Through Clement's ambassadors, the Holy Maid of Kent wrote letters to Rome, revealing that God would send plagues if Clement supported Henry.[7] She told Archbishop Warham and Cardinal Wolsey that God would punish them if they backed the king. An angel told the Holy Maid to go to the king and command him to change his life; if he married Anne Boleyn, she said, God's vengeance would plague him, and he would "die a villain's death."[8] (Alas, there are no eyewitness accounts of the Maid's two meetings with Henry.) In another vision the Maid saw Anne Boleyn and her father talking with the devil. Once, she was magically transported to Calais in order to prevent Henry's taking Communion there: she snatched the Host just before it got to his mouth. And she reported that she had seen the exact spot prepared for Henry in hell; he was "abominable in sight of God," she said.[9]

By 1531 the group gathered around the Holy Maid of Kent included some of King Henry VIII's most powerful opponents: John Fisher, bishop of Rochester, chancellor of Cambridge University, and the spiritual leader of the resistance to Henry's divorce; Archbishop Warham; the Marquis and Marchioness of Exeter, concerned that the rise of the Boleyn faction would lessen their influence with the king; the countess of Salisbury; and Agnes Jordon, abbess of Syon Abbey. The clerics who circulated the Maid's messages also preached her piety and connected her to these powerful people. This combination of popular and elite support clearly concerned the Crown: Joan of Arc, too, had been a "popular peasant visionary" with powerful clerical supporters.[10]

And so in September 1533 Henry sent his attorney general Christopher Hales down to Canterbury to investigate. In an exceptional show of judicial procedure, Hales spent several months gathering evidence. He searched chapels and monks' cells; he imprisoned and interrogated those who had special charge over the Holy Maid. Finally, on November 12, the Crown arrested the Maid and several of her associates.

Remarkably, Henry spent three days meeting with the bishops of the realm, the nobles, and all the principal judges of the kingdom before determining Elizabeth Barton's fate. On 23 November 1533, she was made to undergo public penance, together with Bocking, Henry Gold (a parson accused of putting her in contact with the papal ambassadors), and six others. According to the statute of attainder that had authorized her arrest, Barton had "infected a great number" of the people with her "false and feigned hypocrisy."[11] John Salcot, bishop-elect of Bangor, followed up this line of attack, denouncing Barton for her "false miracles, false visions and revelations" in a fiery sermon at the public penance.[12] Salcot claimed that Barton had greatly impeded the king's long-desired marriage—not because an illiterate servant girl had foiled the monarch of all England, but because she had in fact been manipulated by a scheming cabal of opposition to the king led by Fisher and Exeter, whose ground troops were Bocking, Gold, and the clerics and monks who preached up her piety, spread her messages, circulated the manuscript of the treasonous "Nun's Book" and introduced her to the most powerful of Henry's opponents. Under interrogation, Salcot said, Barton admitted that she had made the whole thing up and had been manipulated by the "learned men" around her, who found her useful for their political scheming. Bocking, her spiritual director, would taunt her if she did not produce a new vision daily. A letter that the Holy Maid had received from Mary Magdalene turned out to be written by a monk named William Hawkhurst. Barton claimed to be visited nightly by the devil, but she actually used a "paper full of brimstone, arcefetida, and other stinking gums and powders" to make "great stinking smokes . . . at such times as she feigned the devil to have been with her in her cell."[13] Actually, Salcot added, this was just a ploy to keep the other nuns in their cells so that she could meet Bocking for sex. She had "never had vision in all her life," wrote Thomas Cranmer, Henry's new archbishop of Canterbury, several years later.[14]

Yet the king was not content to stop here, for Elizabeth Barton would be useful to him one last time. By now Henry was married to Anne Boleyn, and the time had come to cement his hold over conservative resistance and put Catherine of Aragon away once and for all. This would be formalized in the Act of Succession of April 1534, which reduced Catherine's rank, bastardized her daughter Mary, and required all adult male subjects to take an oath of loyalty to the new dynastic settlement. And so on 20 April 1534, Elizabeth Barton and five associates were hanged at Tyburn and then decapitated. Their heads were set on the gates of the city.[15] That very same day, the good citizens of London were presented with the Act of Succession and required to swear an oath to it. There was little resistance.

Disjecta Membra Poetae

Elizabeth Barton was one piece of a long political campaign that aimed at nothing less than remaking the monarchy itself. The Act of Succession, imposed with the help of Barton's severed head, was itself part of the run-up to the Act of Supremacy of November 1534, which gave Henry the new title of "Supreme Head of the Church of England." The Act subordinated canon law to common law, placed the ecclesiastical courts in a state of limbo, and implicitly declared that divine law would be henceforth revealed by scripture rather than the church. If the church had spent the Middle Ages dictating to the monarchy, that relationship now reversed; henceforth, power flowed toward the central monarch and his unprecedented claim that within his realm he was both temporal and spiritual head.[16]

Political prophecy of the sort practiced by Elizabeth Barton tends to emerge at moments of historical crisis, and England in the early 1530s certainly fits that description. But Henry's extraordinary reaction to her— "suggestive of a government bent on denouncing a plot for which it had little hard evidence" according to one historian—also changed the landscape in which such political prophecies could emerge.[17] Because the Henrician revolution was promulgated in a series of acts of state, each one designed to increase the power, wealth, influence, and prestige of the Crown, it pressed with particular force on forms of populist and lay piety. Its technique, repeated at various levels, was to expose hypocrisy, and thereby to demystify or disenchant the world to which popular devotion stubbornly clung.

Those historians who have written about the Holy Maid of Kent often speculate about the degree to which she was or was not a tool for factional forces.[18] Discussions of modern sovereignty and state power, meanwhile, have focused largely on Lockean individualism and the liberal state. This chapter, by contrast, traces a history of sovereignty that could be said to "begin" in the clash between Elizabeth Barton and Henry VIII.

Consider John Donne's poem "An Anatomy of the World" (1611), whose speaker bemoans a world breaking apart some eighty years later:

'Tis all in pieces, all coherence gone;
All just supply, and all relation.[19]

Donne is speaking here of the Copernican revolution (a "new philosophy" that "calls all in doubt"), but he does so by describing a world slowly breaking up into its constituent pieces (or "atomies," as he calls them). According to the poem's conceit, Elizabeth Drury, the fourteen-year-old girl in whose honor it is written, might have put the world back together again, but her death removes all possibility of "coherence." The speaker finally takes refuge in the thought that the world is only a "carcase" (line 439) anyway; if its vital coherence is gone, that is only because it can now be found more completely in heaven. In this way the bits and pieces of the world, like Elizabeth Drury's own body and like the severed, floating head of Orpheus in Milton's "Lycidas" (1638), "Whom universal nature did lament," mark the passing away of a world in which nature is enchanted and spirit-infused.[20] Now there are simply material bodies whose spirits flee to heaven. Not coincidentally, the passage between these different thought-worlds is littered with the torn bodies of poets and figures for poets, to whose ranks we can perhaps add the dismembered limbs of the "goodly poetess" otherwise known as the Holy Maid of Kent, otherwise known as Elizabeth Barton, an illiterate servant girl who for a brief time commanded the attention of powerful people.

Sensory Politics

The Henrician revolution was a constitutional revolution, but Henry also set out to remake the religious lives of his subjects. Various elements of lay piety were immediate objects of reform. The 1532 Act reducing feast days and holy days, for example, took aim at the parish-based ritual year, its multiple local festivals, and the opportunities for camaraderie and mischief such days offered.[21] Fewer feast days meant a more regular calendar and a more productive work week; rather than the punctuated chronologies of festivals and feasts, time became more uniform and predictable. Visuals and rituals had organized medieval Catholicism; salvation in the next world was important, but so, too, were health, fertility, and healing. These goals made for tangible forms of devotion: the veneration of Mary and of Christ, of holy men and women, candles, crosses, holy water, the consecrated Host, the popularity of shrines and pilgrimages.[22] During the 1530s Thomas Cromwell and his ministers reclassified such rites and rituals as superstitions, and took aim at public shrines, images, and such "para-liturgical" practices as pilgrimage.[23] Of course, Cromwell had his eye on the vast wealth of the church. But his proscription on physical interaction (no kissing and licking of images, no public gathering and feasting, no pilgrimage) suggests he was concerned also with populist bodies now understood as potential sources of disorder.

If the common body is to be contained, the common mind must be engaged: Cromwell's 1536 injunctions declared that rather than celebrating feast days or telling over beads, the people should be instructed in acts of charity, mercy, and faith, and catechized in "the Creed, the Lord's Prayer, and the Ten Commandments in English."[24] The Bishops' Book of 1537 clarified that religious images, while important, were to be worshipped as representatives of absent things, not things in themselves. Throughout, Cromwell and his men aimed at a better-educated laity: literate, focused on scripture rather than the church, and able to say what they believed. Salvation depended neither on sacraments nor on locations of power, neither on special times and places nor on saints, angels, intercessors, and martyrs. God's sanctifying power spread rather to every facet of ordinary life. And this process depended on an inner transformation of a self who could now recognize God's sovereignty in the most mundane of events.[25]

These various orderings of body and mind are part of a concerted across-the-board effort to discipline and remake common life, a "deliberate [attempt] by élites," writes Charles Taylor, "to make over the whole society, to change the lives of the mass of people" through administrative and bureaucratic efforts.[26] The church raised its own internal standards by improving clerical education and discipline, and through education and rationalization it tried to bring the laity up to speed as well. This movement of Reform involved the streamlining of the sensory experiences of the medieval church, to be sure, but it went beyond the church to the disciplining and organizing of plebeian bodies, to an emphasis on education, literacy, and vernacular devotional literature—and, as a necessary part of this rationalizing process, the redirection of sacred energies toward the monarch, something perfected by Henry's daughter Elizabeth.

At the center of this more uniform culture stood the officially sanctioned English translation of the Bible. Early in the fifteenth century the church had ruled that translating scripture into English was heresy, at least in part because addressing the laity in their own language would encourage them to become involved in religious debate. By contrast, Henry VIII enthusiastically supported the production and dissemination of a Bible in the vernacular.[27] His goal was to exert authority over the ecclesiastical sphere, and he found his opportunity in the so-called Great Bible, produced in 1537 in Antwerp. In 1538 Cromwell instructed the bishops to make this Bible available in every parish church, and to encourage the laity to read it. The title page of the 1540 edition shows Henry, seated on his throne, distributing copies to both clergy and laity.[28] The message could not be clearer: all believers are welcome, but authority is singular. By stripping away an oral culture and replacing it with one based on the written word, Henry consolidated royal power, establishing his centrality in all aspects of national, social, and personal life: in place of the cacophony of traditional piety, he offered uniformity of belief and practice, carried out in the vernacular, and guaranteed by princely absolutism.

The Work of Reform

In the sixteenth century, writes Lucien Febvre in his classic account of the early modern period, "Christianity . . . was the atmosphere in which a man lived out his entire life—not just his intellectual life, but his private life in a multitude of activities, his public life in a variety of occupations. . . . Today we make a choice to be a Christian or not. There was no choice in the sixteenth century."[29] In the deeply embedded world that Febvre describes, the church had a monopoly on technology and education, Christian rules organized society, and Christian rituals marked the passage of time. Baptism, Communion, marriage, and burial blended religion and society together. Since Christianity was the substance of social life, sin and penance were matters not only for the individual but for the entire community. Deviance invited social disorder; pride and envy were offenses against charity; heretics, blasphemers, and unbelievers endangered not only their own salvation but the social fabric of their communities.[30]

But the temporal power of institutions is only a part of the story. A world in which the church holds such sway is also one in which spiritual forces bear on mundane existence. The enchanted world of magic and ritual, of spirits and saints and sacred spaces, widely taken for granted in late medie-val Europe, was "open and porous and vulnerable" to powers intruding from elsewhere.[31] And thus one could not simply rely on oneself, one's own thoughts or abilities, to keep darkness and evil at bay. One needed some kind of higher power. People might not "believe" in the doctrine of the virgin birth, or might have no opinion about it one way or the other, but they had faith in the power of holy water, in the healing power of a saint's relics, and in the importance of joining the whole community to beat the bounds. This-worldly goals, like keeping healthy and protecting one's crops, were thereby placed within a wider, enchanted context, tacitly understood to be more important than esoteric bits of theology. People participated in an entire set of actions, rituals, and habits simply by virtue of having been born when and where they were. Far from a coherent system, these were syncretistic blends of traditional Christian doctrine and folk belief, whose actions, rituals, and habits themselves presupposed a certain kind of world—a mundane world in which spiritual and magical forces impinged or potentially impinged in a variety of ways.[32]

In this context, Henry's reforms were part of a widespread, Pan-European effort throughout the early modern period to cleanse Christianity of traditional folk beliefs, to purge it of the heterodox, the magical, and the festive, and to "make over the whole society to higher standards."[33] This quest for order, clarity, and sobriety was about more than "religion," and it came from several directions simultaneously. The constitutional piece, with its drive toward absolutist power centered in the monarch, worked together with a more widespread elite project of taking the masses in hand, educating and organizing them, tabulating and measuring their movements. Codes of civility changed; certain activities were condemned or privatized; feasts and festivals were better regulated or abolished altogether. Just as Cromwell banned the kissing and licking of relics, so other bodily practices were brought into enclosed spaces, sealed off from public view in the name of civility and good order: defecation, spitting and nose-blowing, sleeping, sex, insanity, corporal punishment—even dying became more private and confi-dential, "watched only by intimates."[34] Many of these transformed activities, spaces, and mentalities eventually helped to shape the domesticated nuclear family—and a concomitant zone of privacy to be contrasted with a "public" world.[35]

Cutting across the theological differences of Reformation and Counter-Reformation, then, the "work of Reform" is an effort at social control in which the laity were either encouraged or forced to accept a more rigorous moral discipline and a more rational and less folk-influenced faith.[36] As elites withdrew from popular practices in favor of the more polished style and self-conscious behavior that came to define the sixteenth-century courtier, they were more willing to countenance such reform movements. For there were both social and religious reasons to police sexuality, control prostitution, and increase worker productivity: tightening up the rules yielded a more reliable and stable social order and brought a community closer to a God increasingly understood to be pleased by good order and sober industriousness.[37]

None of this would have been possible, of course, without a corresponding revolution in printing that made texts widely available, in particular vernacular translations of the New Testament based on the earliest known manuscripts rather than on the Latin Vulgate. In 1516 Erasmus produced the first Greek New Testament, the primary influence on William Tyndale's English New Testament. By 1543 there were thirteen editions of the entire Bible in English, and many more of the New Testament. The humanist desire to get as close as possible to the world of the biblical authors (*ad fontes*) began to transform what it meant to live a religious life. The Vulgate, for example, had translated Matthew 4:17 as "do penance, for the Kingdom of heaven is at hand." Erasmus pointed out that the Greek original should in fact be translated as "repent, for the Kingdom of heaven is at hand." The emphasis thus falls not on a particular activity sanctioned by the church (penance) but on a mental and emotional attitude (repentance). Reading a more accurate scripture in the right way might thus work an internal transformation in the life of the believer. Like the first Christians, the newly liberated reader could meet the risen Christ.[38]

But this meant that one read alone: spiritually alone, if not in actual solitude. As James Simpson describes it in *Burning to Read*, the "dark, energizing paradox" of such Protestant reading practices meant that one searched the scriptures for evidence of one's salvation, while also acknowledging that reading had little effect on a salvation that had already been decided one way or the other by God.[39] It may have been liberating to strip away the accumulated tradition of Catholic interpretation and the historical communities that gave those interpretations meaning, then, but without those supporting contexts a certain brittle quality also emerged, which Simpson locates particularly in Tyndale's "fragile, distrustful, and philologically aggressive" scholarly demeanor. Protestant reading may circumvent the traditional structures and institutions of authority and thus manifest a certain interpretive freedom, but it also "imposed punishing pressure on those who adopted it"—its own kind of discipline, now understood to be a strictly internal affair.[40]

The kind of mental anguish that Simpson describes may not have been terribly widespread in an era where literacy rates remained fairly low; but even among less scrupulous early modern readers, the wider availability of texts and indeed the very appearance of the written word validated certain kinds of sensory experiences while denigrating others. The translation of all things into the vernacular highlighted the surface of the text. Printing itself, with its multiplication of identical images in place of the "individual and erratic scribal 'hands' of the past," offered a new kind of relationship to Biblical truths. [41] In place of the oral and visual culture centered on the late medieval parish and on practices of popular piety like pilgrimages, the printed page is impersonal, suggesting that knowledge is "out there," waiting to be mapped and accessed. The ideal Christian was now an individual believer and a reader, prodded toward sobriety and self-examination. And if Christianity was becoming more personal, meditative, self-conscious, and interior, it was also developing a certain kind of intensity that, in retrospect, tended to make earlier and more participatory forms of communal worship look lax and luke- warm. One example of such privatization was the devotional closet that became popular in the seventeenth century. This "certain secret Chappel for my self," as Edward Wettenhall described it, was a literal example of the accelerating distinction between the superficial "forms" of devotion and the authentic depths of the heart where one worked out one's salvation.[42]

Alongside such private devotions, sermons too became more important. Not only did the preaching of the Word confirm iconoclastic tendencies within Protestant culture, but one's experience of that Word in both sermon and—if one were literate—private devotion became the primary means of grace, for it called the believer to repent and to turn toward a renewed and more intense relationship with God. Thomas Cranmer's "Preface" to the 1540 English Bible recommended that parishioners supplement the service by privately reading the passages preached on Sundays: "every man should read by himself at home in the mean days and time, between sermon and ser- mon," in order to "more profoundly fix in their minds and memories" what had been said on Sunday.[43] Minds and memories, worked on by a Word read and spoken, became piety's appropriate location.

The emphasis on self-control, explicit knowledge, and uniformity of belief across the board is striking, and it suggests that Renaissance humanism bequeathed not just texts and technology but also cultures of civility, order, good manners, taste, self-control, and self-development that accompanied and surrounded these new developments. The reformed subject did not just let things be; he worked on himself, reshaped himself in accord with a higher standard.[44] This cross-fertilization between the cultures of Renaissance humanism and religious reform is an important correction to familiar historical accounts, like those offered by Stephen Toulmin and Michael Hardt and Antonio Negri, that pit an imminent sixteenth-century humanist Renaissance against a transcendentalizing seventeenth-century absolutist reaction.[45] As inspiring as this story may be, its sharp contrast between literary humanism and state sovereignty tends to place religious uniformity solely on the reactive side of the ledger, making it something that holds back a modernity understood as a teleological inevitability.[46] In fact, the many and varied links between humanism and the Protestant Reformation are crucial for development of the secular as I understand it here—not, that is, as overt hostility to religion, nor as a set of ideas that are anti- or nonreligious, but as the redefining and reformulation of religion within the context of a newly emergent political formation that is about many things other than "religion." For Calvin and Luther, but also for Erasmus, Cromwell, and the Council of Trent, the reforming impulse is institutional, social, and ethical, carried out by means of better printing, better and more authoritative editions, the wider dissemination of texts alongside more effective censorship, better networks of information, and a clearer pedagogical program.

None of this means that Henry always got his way. Folk practices and feast days were hard to stamp out, the confession booth remained largely immune even to Cromwell's network of spies, and in an age of uneven education a religion of the preached and written word made slow headway.[47] Nevertheless, the iconography and the aims remain: less a matter of replacing Catholicism with Protestantism, the English revolution stands as an example of a remarkable effort to reform and remake a society, to take a people in hand and alter their very way of being in the world, and along the way to change the kinds of sensory experiences they could have.

Carnival

A good way to make sense of the narratives surrounding Henrician Reform is to turn to one of its most influential literary interpretations: William Shakespeare's *The Famous History of the Life of King Henry VIII*.[48] During that play's first recorded performance, in June 1613, the Globe Theatre burned to the ground. At least one contemporary observer, Sir Henry Wotton, had no doubt that the play's histrionic ambitions were to blame. He noted its "extraordinary circumstances of Pomp and Majesty," including "the Knights of the Order, with their Georges and garters, the Guards with their embroidered coats, and the like": "Now, King Henry making a masque at the Cardinal Wolsey's house, and certain chambers being shot off at his entry, some of the paper . . . did light on the thatch, where being thought at first but an idle smoke, and their eyes more attentive to the show, it kindled inwardly, and ran round like a train, consuming within less than an hour the whole house to the very grounds."[49] The play's "Pomp and Majesty" causes the fire *and* distracts anybody from noticing until it is too late. On this reading, royalist ceremony is a dangerous distraction from reality, and *Henry VIII* is less about the trials of a Protestant conscience than the power and hubris of the Renaissance state, whose grand ambitions bring on the fiery Reformation it deserves. So far, Wotton's commentary reads like an anticipation of the more emotionally serious and less spectacular productions of the play that would emerge only at the end of the eighteenth century.

Yet after this rather severe interpretation, Wotton finishes his account in a different mood. Although no one perished in the blaze, he writes, "one man had his breeches set on fire, that would perhaps have broiled him, if he had not by the benefit of a provident wit put it out with bottle ale." A carnivalesque conclusion like this upends not only the pompous theatricality of the play on the stage but also the pompous moralism of the voice that condemns it.

Riotousness likewise bubbles just below the surface of the play itself. These are, after all, times when almost anything can happen, as Stephen Gardiner, the play's Catholic killjoy, notes with concern when he complains that the king is playing cards while great doings are afoot: "These should be hours for necessities," he says, "Not for delights" (5.1.2–3). Theologically, Gardiner dislikes Anne because of her Lutheranism, but the dislike actually seems temperamental, for wherever Anne appears unruliness follows. Linked explicitly with her sexual availability, such boisterousness is neither "Catholic" nor "Protestant" but seems rather to harness another kind of power altogether. At her coronation, for example, she displays herself to the crowd, "opposing freely / The beauty of her person to the people" (4.1.67–68):

> which when the people
> Had the full view of, such a noise arose

As the shrouds make at sea in a stiff tempest,
As loud and to as many tunes. Hats, cloaks—
Doublets, I think—flew up, and had their faces
Been loose, this day they had been lost. Such joy
I never saw before. Great-bellied women
That had not half a week to go, like rams
In the old time of war, would shake the press
And make 'em reel before 'em. No man living
Could say 'This is my wife' there, all were woven
So strangely in one piece. (4.1.70–81)

Here dissolution of the self and dissolution of property are linked specifically to sensual joy. Apparently a similar kind of celebration happens at
Elizabeth's christening. "Do you look for ale and cakes here, you rude ras-
cals?" demands the Porter (5.3.9), chastising the crowd for treating the day as
a church festival. "Bless me, what a fry of fornication is at door!" he goes on
(5.3.33–34). We might recall Sir Toby Belch, in *Twelfth Night*, mocking the
puritanical Malvolio during an equally riotous scene: "Dost thou think,
because thou art virtuous, there shall be no more cakes and ale?"[50] In *Twelfth
Night* sexual objects become confused, to hilarious effect. *King Henry VIII*,
too, highlights the potential disruption that accompanies desire's inconvenient vectors. Within the obvious constraints marked out by the structures
of divorce from one wife and marriage to another, and where the larger
political aim is to shift the entire nation from Catholic to Protestant *without*
threatening royalist power, another, alternative mode of social life struggles
to break free, one that turns on the inability to distinguish, organize, and
control the individual body: clothes fly off of their own accord, bodies weave
together "strangely in one piece," and none of the onlookers can securely
pick out his own property. Here, the distinction between Protestant and
Catholic seems minor compared to the distinction between decorum and
carnival.

The meanings of carnivals and festivals in the premodern world have
long been a source of debate. Some historians have emphasized their basically
conservative function, as a way to relieve pressure before the restoration of
order, while others have emphasized their utopian aspect.[51] Most agree, however, on the felt need during the premodern era for both the energy of carnival and the restoration of order in its wake, an interplay of the official code
and its transgression. That sense of complementarity is no longer with us:

unlike their earlier counterparts, modern carnivals or festivals do not oppose the dominant code so much as foster identification with it, as in the fêtes of the French Revolution, or the spectacle of contemporary Mardi Gras celebrations.

Traditional Catholicism, with its feasts and holy days, pilgrimages and miracles, seemed to invite insubordination, at least temporarily. Feast days encouraged idleness and drunkenness ("cakes and ale"); more worryingly, many people outside the parish would come to participate in the festivities, and this made it hard to know who belonged where. The 1532 Convocation reduced the number of feast days, noting that not only were crops going unharvested, but that people were "entysed by the lycencyous vacacyon and lybertye of those holydayes."[52] But Protestantism, too, was a potentially disruptive power. "Are not riots commőn among this evangelical people?" asked Erasmus. "Do they not for small causes betake themselves to force?"[53] Cranmer, in his "Preface" to the 1540 English Bible, addressed a similar concern: "every man that cometh to the reading of this holy book ought to bring with him first and foremost this fear of almighty God, and then next a firm and stable purpose to reform his own self according thereunto; and so to continue, proceed, and prosper from time to time, showing himself to be a sober and fruitful hearer and learner."[54] Despite its focus on inwardness and on private acts of devotion, Protestantism, too, had to be harnessed to the new order. Recall again the title page of the Bible to which Cranmer refers, showing Henry in the center, distributing copies. The insight captured there is that a change in the religious and social sensorium will strengthen the hand of the sovereign if it is managed well; centralized power and the reformed citizen go hand in glove. Rather than taking carnivalesque energies as a necessary part of the give-and-take of the community, early modern elites began to perceive those energies as a threat that needed to be realigned with the prevailing order.[55]

Historical Questions

I have been emphasizing the competing narratives surrounding the English Reformation, brilliantly captured in Shakespeare's play as a carnival always barely contained. Until quite recently, however, the history of the English Reformation has largely followed a different interpretation, one begun by

Foxe's *Acts and Monuments* (1563), which contrasted Catholic tyranny, corruption, and superstition with the God-fearing piety of a populace eager for reform. In this account the English people, pious and sincere in their belief and horrified by clerical abuses, were Protestants before their institutions were. In standard histories from the eighteenth through the twentieth centuries, this Protestant history of a Protestant Reformation was easily joined to a Whig/nationalist reading whereby the Reformation became a "joyous national rejection of outmoded superstition."[56]

Since the 1980s, however, a revisionist interpretation of the English Reformation has stressed continuity over change and social factors over religious ones. According to this argument one cannot deduce from the fact of the Reformation a widespread *desire* for religious change. Rather than emphasizing the decadence and abuse of the church so that the Reformation becomes God's (or history's) own plan, the revisionists have argued that the church that Henry attacked was strong, with a vigorous lay piety movement and a hierarchy filled with competent and dutiful priests. Instead of superstition, these historians find a widespread and broadly coherent set of practices, distributed among elites and commoners alike, that took for granted the efficacy of saints, pilgrimages, intercession, and the Host. And the common people seemed willing to defend these things—most famously, for example, during the Pilgrimage of Grace, begun in October 1536 in Lincolnshire after a sermon inspired parishioners to defend their church against a scheduled visitation by Henry's agents. It spread to Yorkshire and much of the north country by the end of the month, eventually attracting an "army" of some 40,000.[57] Uprisings of this sort help to make sense of the lack of evidence of antipopery before the 1530s, among either laity or clergy, suggesting that the Reformation did not so much latch onto a preexisting anti-Catholicism as invent it.[58] And indeed, the Reformation was slow to take hold: in England at the time of the Elizabethan settlement in 1559, Protestantism was still the minority faith. On this reading, the Reformation has less to do with the king's fabled "conscience" or the sincere proto-Protestant piety of his subjects than with political gamesmanship in the context of a Renaissance court.[59]

This is a powerful claim, and not without controversy; it means that religious change is a *result* of political change rather than the other way around. But if it holds, and historians emphasize the vitality of a traditional religious culture, then it becomes hard to explain the Reformation at all. How was a "manifestly unpopular and unwanted policy . . . imposed so successfully?"[60] And why would Henry attack the popular religion of his subjects so systematically in the first place? Scholars concerned with this "post-revisionist" conundrum have tended to respond to it by questioning the very notion of a coherent Reformation. Rather than a single thing, they view the English Reformation as a "succession of contingent events," a series of discreet happenings undertaken for reasons of expediency rather than as part of a larger plan.[61]

From this perspective, *King Henry VIII*'s dramatic failure, frequently remarked on by contemporary critics, is its historical success. Its radically compressed time frame, which runs together events that took place as early as 1521 (Buckingham's fall) and as late as 1536 (Cranmer's near imprisonment), contributes to the principal character's bewilderment about what is happening. And the play itself is curiously reticent about actions and causes. It is not even clear who its protagonists are: though Wolsey dominates the early scenes, Katherine is in many ways the emotional center of the play; meanwhile Elizabeth receives Cranmer's final prophecy of greatness, which makes Anne Bullen, a relatively minor character, an agent of divine destiny. In all this Henry himself, the supposedly powerful Renaissance prince, looks by turns weak, vacillating, uninformed, and irrelevant. In this he is closer to the tyrants of the baroque tragedy, of whose indecisiveness Benjamin writes: "The prince . . . reveals, at the first opportunity, that he is almost incapable of making a decision . . . . [his] actions are determined not by thought, but by changing physical impulses" (71). Without a central agent, things simply *happen*, and while this may give the play an incoherent feel, we might defend it on those very grounds: its sheer contingency and unpredictability are a gloss on the chaotic history of the English Reformation itself.

This, again, is to set history's discreet and hard-to-synthesize events against the dominant Protestant narrative, or what Benjamin would call its "eschatology," voiced in the play by Cranmer and handed down by Foxe to historians of the Reformation, that seeks to locate the unity of providence and conscience within chaotic historical material. According to that narrative it is the king's proto-protestant "conscience" that causes him to divorce Katherine and marry Anne and in this way bring on the events that will together make up the Reformation. Yet *King Henry VIII* itself suggests that Henry's suddenly discovered conscience is a convenient screen for his sexual appetite:

Chamberlain:
It seems the marriage with his brother's wife
Has crept too near his conscience.

Suffolk:
No, his conscience
Has crept too near another lady. (2.2.15–17)

During the early stages of his divorce Henry made a great show of collecting opinions about the proper interpretation of biblical texts, in particular Leviticus 18:16 and 20:21, which seemed to forbid a marriage like his, and Deuteronomy 25:5, which seemed not only to permit it but to require it. These actions accentuated the great importance the Reformers placed on reading and proper scriptural interpretation, yet it has long been possible to construe such reading as a ruse. *King Henry VIII* shows Henry "reading pensively" (2.2.60), but the scene ends with an obviously self-justifying appeal to "conscience," and cuts immediately to a spicy conversation between Anne Bullen and a female attendant, who punningly recommends that Anne learn to "stretch" both her maidenhead and her conscience (2.3.33). From such scenes the readiest conclusion is that all interpretation is self-interested, and that there is no such thing as a "conscience" divorced from the desires of the body.

Henry VIII was first performed under the title *All Is True*, and as Gordon McMullan notes, the play "is obsessed with truth."[62] The word *truth* and its cognates appear fifty times in the text. "On my soul, I'll speak but truth," declares the Surveyor (1.2.177), in the midst of giving his perjured testimony against Buckingham. "Truth shall nurse her," predicts Cranmer of Elizabeth, during the play's most obviously ideological moment (5.4.28). Yet much of the information dispensed in the play comes at second or third hand, filtered through the various agendas of the tellers. As a result, what was once a slander "Is found a truth now" (2.1.153), and the audience is forced to confront the incommensurability of both experience and testimony in the face of unprecedented happenings. The play's jumble of events and self-interested interpretations suggests that we are never getting all the truth—or, conversely, that "all is true," namely that any interpretation is as true as any other.

When after his fall Wolsey announces that he has at last gotten his priorities straight, he becomes the most striking and powerful evidence for the possibility that this retrospective narrative will redeem questionable backstage dealings:

I know myself now, and I feel within me
A peace above all earthly dignities,
A still and quiet conscience. The King has cured me. (3.2.378–80)

In view of the persistent ironization of "conscience" within the play, it is hard to take these lines seriously. And yet Wolsey is here anticipating the moral of the drama itself, offered by Cranmer's closing prophecy that Elizabeth will bring "Upon this land a thousand thousand blessings" (5.4.19). "O Lord Archbishop," says Henry when he hears Cranmer's prophecy, "Thou hast made me now a man" (5.4.62–63). If the king cures Wolsey, then, he also cures himself by begetting Elizabeth, thus creating a powerful link between upright godly manhood and a Reformed, peaceful, and powerful nation. And yet, of course, the audience knows that this is far from the truth—that Henry's various appetites will remain largely ungovernable, and that close to a century later the Protestant settlement would still seem less than secure. Notwithstanding, then, Cranmer's overt appeal to the "truth" of his prophecy (5.4.15–16), the audience is left with the tricky task of balancing this kind of truth, with all the weight of dramaturgy behind it, with what they have learned about truth throughout the course of the play.

Like the tendency to read backward from the present, Cranmer's closing speech imparts a unity and coherence to events that were not felt by anyone who has actually sat through the action on stage. An example of the truism that history is written by the winners, the speech stretches the truth in order to make the play's events fit a preconceived providential pattern. In this it anticipates the kind of Protestant history of the Reformation that has largely shaped its reception until recent years. Meanwhile, those who are paying more careful attention will note a different pattern: all the major characters in *Henry VIII* collude in the task of containing populist energy, irrespective of confessional allegiances. The objects of their attention are not just the rabble but Anne and especially Henry himself, whose appetites and enthusiasms seem to place him somewhere between an absolute ruler and a lord of misrule.

In fact, *Henry VIII* is held together on stage neither by its characters nor by its thematics of truth, but by the pageantry of royalism itself: Anne's coronation, Elizabeth's christening, and a variety of other processions and set pieces that visually consolidate an otherwise chaotic narrative. The play opens, for example, with a second-hand account of royal pomp: the Duke of Norfolk's extravagant description of the Field of the Cloth of Gold meeting between the kings of England and France, an event planned and carried off by Wolsey, and which Norfolk himself refers to as a masque—absolutism prepared for mass consumption (1.1.26). Sutured to Cranmer's closing prophecy of a Reformed Elizabethan England, this association with royalist spectacle has lent the play a distinctively nationalist tone, particularly in performance. And this means that the drama's glittering surfaces tend to pull away from the play's various and contradictory discussions of truth and conscience.

The masque is indeed a fitting image of the kind of transition I have been stressing in this chapter, caught between secularized eschatology and real-time impulsiveness. Whatever else it may have done, the English Reformation consolidated royal power less in a person than in an institution. Sometimes reform was relatively direct, as in the case of Elizabeth Barton; at other times it worked at one or two removes, employing and arranging the sensory experiences of individual lives through networks of influence and authority, through the written word, the printing press, and a less festive calendar. The next chapter traces this work in the middle years of the eighteenth century. By then the populist energy that Shakespeare quarried had been largely put to work building a new order. And yet the question of the legitimacy of that new order remained—a question taken up, as we shall see, by the new literary mode of the gothic.

CHAPTER 2

The Melancholy of the Secular

Horace Walpole's astonishing literary debut, *The Castle of Otranto* (1764), is widely considered the first gothic novel, the original in a lineage stretching from the late eighteenth century to the present. Yet it ends not with fecundity but its opposite. The final words of the novel are these: "Frederic offered his daughter [Isabella] to the new prince . . . but Theodore's grief was too fresh to admit the thought of another love; and it was not till after frequent discourses with Isabella, of his dear Matilda, that he was persuaded he could know no happiness but in the society of one with whom he could forever indulge the melancholy that had taken possession of his soul" (110).

In this chapter I will work my way toward this melancholy ending, and its claim that the future, inevitable as it may be, will contain nothing that compares to the rich possibilities of what has already gone by. Theodore's lack of enthusiasm for his new bride is a result of his straitened circumstances, and his sexual and emotional situation—his lack of prospects and consequent melancholy—should be understood as part of the larger movement of Reform that Charles Taylor places at the origin of the secular age. For Taylor, one consequence of the secular is that we experience what he calls "fullness" differently—the rich sense of possibility that is the phenomenological root of religious as well as aesthetic experience has, he proposes, shifted as the background conditions for its articulation have become more secular. We are more likely now to engage in individual projects of self-fashioning than we are to experience deeply rooted communal richness. Here, though, I am less interested in fullness, and whether we experience it differently now, than I am in its opposite: melancholy, understood not simply as a closing down of options but as a recognition of possibilities glimpsed only as impossible, untried experiences encountered as irrecoverable, losses ungrievable because fullness was never there to begin with.

A New Species of Romance

Historians of the eighteenth century have alerted us to a gradually developing contrast between the self-determination of the rising commercial classes and the tradition and stability of the landed gentry, and scholars of the Gothic have described the genre as the mode through which the ascendant middle classes represented their political and social contradictions, particularly the desire to both overthrow and preserve the lineaments of state power.[1] Walpole's novel certainly seems to align itself with the old guard, for it tells a story of restoration and renewal: the usurper and tyrant Manfred is eventually made to give way to Theodore, the true heir of Otranto who has returned in disguise. Yet *Otranto*'s backward-looking plot depends on sensational techniques made available by the uncertain world of inflationary capitalism. This paradox, in which value is restored to land and to heritable wealth only after its liquidation by capital, sets the pattern for many gothic novels written in *Otranto*'s wake, and serves as something of an allegory for a period in economic transition. Specters, ghosts, and hauntings, like the rumor and speculation that drive finance capital, testified to possible experiences cut loose from landed traditions, available to anyone with an imagination and the desire for excitement, risk, and stimulation.[2] Despite the window dressing of absolutism that hangs over the novel, then, *Otranto* seems less concerned with theories of divine right than with defending the land-based wealth being threatened in the eighteenth century by a new economic order organized around speculation, credit, and capitalism.

Can such sensational means serve the ends of stability, good order, and landed wealth? The question emerges implicitly at the novel's end, when Theodore's identity is revealed for all to see:

> the walls of the castle behind Manfred were thrown down with a mighty force, and the form of Alfonso, dilated to an immense magnitude, appeared in the centre of the ruins. Behold in Theodore, the true heir of Alfonso! said the vision: and having pronounced those words, accompanied by a clap of thunder, it ascended solemnly towards heaven, where the clouds parting asunder, the form of saint Nicholas was seen; and receiving Alfonso's shade, they were soon wrapt from mortal eyes in a blaze of glory.[3]

Narratologically, this is the culmination of what Manfred's daughter Matilda had earlier referred to as "destiny" (39). It not only predicts the future but retrospectively clarifies and organizes events that had seemed confusing and contradictory at the time. Its supernatural machinery notwithstanding, this destiny is a progressive, secularizing force: divine power, having set things to rights, withdraws from the world as Alfonso's form ascends into heaven and disappears from sight. (The appearance of Saint Nicholas here is a typically Walpolean joke, since the book was published on Christmas Eve.) This closing vision contrasts with the more local superstitions that pervade the novel and which its narrative ruthlessly undercuts. Pictures move, skeletons walk, doors slam shut mysteriously; the servants and domestics are always credulous, and the elites often superstitious as well; all the characters shriek and faint with regularity. When it comes to such irrationality, the novel goes in for naturalistic explanations: figures appear and disappear, to be sure, but this is due to a network of underground tunnels; Theodore looks like Alfonso because he is Alfonso's grandson and not because he is the spirit of Alfonso returned from the dead. But the final apparition of Alfonso and Nicholas does not get this treatment; it is the only vision fully endorsed by the narrative.[4]

In sorting out true visions from false superstitions, then, Walpole grounds his allegory of eighteenth-century speculative economies in the reforms of an earlier era. According to both Michel Foucault and Charles Taylor, the early modern period was one of intensified discipline, an orderliness aligned with godliness, and a hoped-for end to "drunkenness, fornication, unbridled speech, immoderate laughter, fights" and other manifestations of social chaos.[5] Here Walpole's reference to Saint Nicholas takes on a different signification. That saint, the great giver of gifts, was linked throughout the middle ages to the "boy bishop" ceremonies, when from December 6 to December 28, a single boy would assume the role of bishop or parish priest, blessing the people and presiding over all offices except for Mass. Henry VII banned these boy bishop ceremonies—one more example of the shift from a premodern social world characterized by reciprocity and surprising gifts to the more rational and orderly arrangements of the early modern period.

In the second Preface to his novel, Walpole acknowledged this historical positioning in terms of genre: his "new species of romance," he wrote, had been modeled on Shakespeare.[6] *Otranto's* plot of usurpation and restoration certainly borrows from *Macbeth*, its supernatural elements and intimations of incest recall *Hamlet*, and Walpole learned from Shakespeare how to blend the low comedy of servants and domestics with the appearance of moral seriousness. But there is a more consistent, though unremarked, *historical* reference to the person of Henry VIII. For the novel's succession crisis turns on the tyrant Manfred's wish to divorce his wife Hippolita and marry the younger Isabella. And as if this plot device were not clear enough, Walpole twice has Manfred claim that he has developed "scruples on the legality of [his] union" with Hippolita.[7]

In the novel's second edition, questions of genre (the "new species of romance") seem to subsume these historical references. But in the first edition, published pseudonymously in 1764, historical reference—and argument—is closer to the surface. For Walpole had initially presented the novel as a translation of an Italian text, printed in 1529 and recently discovered "in the library of an ancient catholic family in the north of England" (3). That date places the text at the heart of the English Protestant Reformation and the debates it engendered. The year 1529 is also the year of Wolsey's fall and Henry's definitive break from Rome. These resonances inspire the editor to try out a reading of his own: perhaps, he speculates, *Otranto* is a product of the Counter-Reformation, the work of an "artful priest" trying to "confirm the populace in their ancient errors and superstitions" (3). Perhaps, that is, the humanist weapons of the Reformation, especially print, can be turned back against it.

And yet, the editor continues, the contemporary reader finds himself far removed from such intrigues:

> Miracles, visions, necromancy, dreams, and other preternatural events, are exploded now even from romances. That was not the case when our author wrote; much less when the story itself was supposed to have happened. Belief in every kind of prodigy was so established in those dark ages, that an author would not be faithful to the *manners* of the times who should omit all mention of them. He is not bound to believe them himself, but he must represent his actors as believing them. (4)

This found text, in other words, flatters its audience while entertaining it. The world it presents is an enchanted one, the editor is a medium or translator between the enchanted and modern worlds, and the reader who is asked to excuse the "*air* of the *miraculous*" has the power to suspend her disbelief at will (4). The first Preface thus offers its readers a remarkably compact version of modernization as secularization: in the beginning we lived in an enchanted, largely static universe; various developments—modern science, the growth of literacy, and so on—gradually disenchanted the world; by the time of the Reformation certain elites had broken with folk piety but continued to manipulate the credulousness of the populace; now, with the process of disenchantment complete, humanity is freed from the bonds of tradition, and the tale can be read as a comforting narrative of progress and freedom. In taking in all these levels simultaneously, the reader comes to appreciate how far humanity has come.[8] In this sense the novel must endorse its final inflationary vision, even as it fantasizes that this bubble-style economy ("dilated to an immense magnitude"), having done its work, has now, like Wolsey, vanished for good.

It is one thing, however, to posit a transcendent "economy" that expands, sets everything to rights, and then disappears. It is another thing to narrate *how* European society moved away from the era of absolutism, confessionalization, and the framework of territorial sovereignty, into a new regime of economy and management associated most immediately in England with Horace Walpole's own father Robert, de facto prime minister from 1721 to 1742. Neither *Otranto*'s Preface nor the novel itself offers much in the way of historical explanation, but in its casual way the first Preface does suggest that things are a little more complicated than the novel's closing vision suggests. The presence of the "artful priest," for example, whose rhetorical efforts in the service of the Counter-Reformation actually helped bring about the end of the age of faith, implies that modernity may have been built, even if inadvertently, rather than simply discovered.

Recent scholarship on the Counter-Reformation, in fact, has described it as part of the movement toward explicitation that characterized the age of Reform and the confessional period in general—has emphasized, that is to say, not its doctrinal distinction from the Reformation but its institutional similarity.[9] The Council of Trent, for example, though directed specifically against Protestant critics of Catholicism and devoted to containing their revolutionary energy, was largely an organizational rather than doctrinal innovation. The founding of the Roman Inquisition and the rejuvenation of the papacy centralized power, increased efficiency, ensured doctrinal conformity, and made provision for better education of both clergy and laity; despite the antimodern cast of its theology, then, Trent was a modernizing and streamlining movement. The age of "confessional Catholicism," that is, was neither merely atavistic nor reactionary; it actually helped build the secular state.[10]

One of the council's decrees seems particularly appropriate to *Otranto*'s stressed absolutism. "On the Invocation, Veneration, and Relics of Saints and on Sacred Images" (1563) commended the veneration of images but drew a clear distinction between such veneration and idolatry. Relics and images did not have any virtue in them, nor could trust be placed in them; rather, according to the council, such things "represented" Christ and the saints. The council goes on to worry, however, that the distinction between a likeness of the thing and the thing itself may escape the unlettered, who might think that "divinity represented in pictures" is the same thing as that which "can be seen with bodily eyes or expressed in colors and figures." For social order depends on keeping these things separate:

> in the invocation of the saints, the veneration of relics and the sacred
> use of images, all superstition shall be removed, all filthy quest for
> gain eliminated, and all lasciviousness avoided, so that the images
> shall not be painted or adorned with a seductive charm, or the cele-
> bration of saints and the visitation of relics be perverted by the peo-
> ple into boisterous festivities and drunkenness, as if the festivals in
> honor of the saints are to be celebrated with revelry and with no
> sense of decency.[11]

Implicitly distinguishing itself from the Protestant Reformers with their emphasis on the ear, the council does allow the kissing and veneration of objects. But their emphasis nevertheless falls largely on the worshipper's frame of mind as the means by which to regularize a tactile relationship with devotional things. According to the logic of the passage, lasciviousness, drunkenness, and revelry flow from a mental mistake, a failure to grasp the proper theory of representation. This suspicion of embodied boisterousness carves out a distinct secular domain in which reformed civility can do its pedagogical work.

In Walpole's novel, this Counter-Reformation effort to harness art to an orthodox but nonsuperstitious sensory modality fails. On the one hand, relics and images really *do* seem to come to life. A skeleton appears to Frederic, the plumes of the colossal helmet shake, and the form of Alfonso inflates to enormous size over the course of the narrative. More pertinently, both Matilda and Isabella have a hard time following the council decree to keep thing and representation distinct as they gaze lovestruck at a portrait of Alfonso the Good. The portrait itself even comes to life at crucial moments, bleeding from the nose during one of Manfred's outrageous speeches, sighing mournfully, and eventually leaving the frame altogether to lead Manfred down a passageway. The general disorientation of the tale and its characters suggests that disenchantment, exemplified here by the artful priest who wields superstition in the service of worldly power, cannot restore the desired "sense of decency." That can only be done by the progressive narrative that the text labels "Providence." The larger point is that Walpole's gothic novel is a straightforward tale of neither disenchantment nor reenchantment; it is an experiment rather with the institutional forms such processes can take.

Walpole's second Preface, published with the novel's second edition in spring 1765, abandoned any pretense to historical narrative. Here Walpole revealed what almost everybody already knew: that he was the author of the book, not simply the translator of a found manuscript. He writes that *Otranto* had been from the beginning an experiment in genre, "an attempt to blend two kinds of romance, the ancient and the modern" (7). The modern novel—Walpole is thinking of both Richardson and Fielding—had the virtue of realism, but it was limited by "a strict adherence to common life" (7). The ancient romance, by contrast, may have been unbelievable, but it also freed the imagination. *Otranto* is an attempt to combine the two, to place real people in unreal situations: the characters react the way real people would react if they saw a ghost, "according," Walpole writes, "to the rules of probability" (7–8).

The two editions, then, offer two very different accounts of secularization. The first edition positions the characters as enchanted, the author as a mediating editor, and the reader as an enlightened observer of the progress of human reason and its gradual emancipation. Its moral purpose is clear: to assure readers that they are on the proper side of a progressive history. It does this by narrating a historical shift away from a festive folk culture, and locates that shift historically through the consistent references to Henry VIII. The second edition, by contrast, positions the author as reflexive and experimental, the reader as a passive observer of his experiment, and the characters' world as obviously fictive. In consequence, the moral purpose of the novel becomes less clear: according to the second edition, the past is not a record of human emancipation but merely a laboratory for formal experiments. It makes superstition available as entertainment without harnessing it to an obvious exemplary function.

Such superfluity turned contemporary reviewers against *Otranto*. The *Monthly Review*, which had approved of the first edition of the novel, noted that while it "could readily excuse . . . preposterous phenomena" had the text been authentic, it could not do the same for a "false tale in a cultivated period of learning. It is, indeed, more than strange that an Author, of a refined and polished genius, should be an advocate for re-establishing the barbarous superstitions of Gothic devilism!"[12]

Of course, this objection misses the point, and in a symptomatic way: Walpole's novel is less an exercise in barbarism than it is an experiment in authorial control over a public more gullible than enlightened.[13] In the second edition power flows to the center—toward the author, away from the reader, and away from the historical validity of the characters—as if the author claims for himself the power that the tyrant Manfred can no longer claim, the power to position the viewer or reader, organize his sensory experience, even reach into his mind and shape his beliefs. In moving from the first to the second edition, then, the reader trades a narrative of progress—we must have advanced beyond them, because we can recognize irrationality for what it is—for something else, the creation of a space for aesthetic experiments and the transformation of the supernatural into the spectacular.[14] If before it was the artful priest who unintentionally helped build the secular age, now it is the artful novelist who does so, and with full knowledge of what he is doing. This combination of factors is worth underlining: the author, not the monarch or priest, is the authority, and this means that power is more fully distributed and harder to locate. Rather than marching under the banner of secularization and disenchantment, the secular becomes a background condition, a presence palpable but not localizable.

In keeping with this secular picture of power, the Preface to the second edition serves to emphasize that despite its supposed setting during the age of the crusades, the novel's vertiginous spaces, which open and close, change direction, entrap and disorient, are the spaces of the baroque. Florid and visceral, baroque architecture, with its turns, reversals, paradoxes, and bodies flying through space, disoriented the viewer in a process that Susan Stewart suggestively links to vertigo: "this art constantly unsettles the stance of the receiver, providing experiences that are analogues of ecstasy"—but ecstasy methodized, harnessed to earthly authority.[15] This emphasis on spectacle and worldly power characterized the Counter-Reformation Catholic aesthetic, when the church encouraged a more direct and self-confident style as a way of doing battle with Protestantism; art and architecture increasingly aimed to impress and perhaps disorient the masses. The paradoxical result, as Walter Benjamin remarked in his own study of German baroque drama and its characteristic melancholy, is that despite its overtly religious content and

wealth of sacred architecture, the baroque is in fact obsessed with the precari-
ousness of *this* world. Seventeenth-century court life, centered around the
figure of the monarch, was radically uncertain; baroque style, despite its
flourishes and embellishments, points always toward the king.[16] Replace
"king" with "author," and we can glimpse how Walpole's project in the
second edition seeks to join an eighteenth-century progressive narrative of
secularization to a seventeenth-century narrative of aestheticized power, retrofitted, in this case, to the inflationary narrative of speculative capital.

Walpole writes that he modeled this new species of romance on Shakespeare. And indeed it is worth recalling, now, that *The Famous History of the
Life of King Henry VIII* was one of the most popular Shakespeare plays of the
eighteenth century. Performed for George I at Hampton Court (Wolsey's
former seat, appropriately enough) in 1717, it was revived virtually every year
in the middle part of the century. At the end of the play, after the chaos
and uncertainty that have dominated it, Cranmer produces a prophecy of
Elizabeth's future greatness that imposes an order and direction missing from
the events themselves:

> This royal infant—heaven still move about her—
> Though in her cradle, yet now promises
> Upon this land a thousand thousand blessings,
> Which time shall bring to ripeness. (5.4.17–20)

Cranmer's picture of Elizabeth consolidating the blessings of the English
Reformation sets the pattern for a retrospective history whose partiality
would have been evident to anyone who had watched the disjointed events
depicted in the play itself. Even Henry is bewildered by the history whose
instrument Cranmer reveals him to be. His response to the speech is remarkable: "O lord Archbishop," he says, "Thou has made me now a man. Never
before / This happy child did I get anything" (5.4.62–64). The suggestion is
that the progressive forces of history grant to Henry his proper role as father
to a nation. In the familiar story, this is the moment when Henry centralizes
power; in Shakespeare's telling, it is the moment that power dissipates into
providential history, procreation, and "the future." Shakespeare thus narrates
the birth of absolutism as if it were the death of absolutism. Perhaps this is
why the play spoke so powerfully to eighteenth-century audiences—not
merely through its spectacle and pageantry, but also because it served as an

allegory for a crucial transformation from the individual conscience of a sovereign to the collective moral consciences of middle-class reformers, who were, in the early years of the eighteenth century, still trying to clean up and organize a resistant popular and folk culture.[17]

Good and Bad Fathers

Shakespeare's closing image of Henry as, at last, a good father suggests what is at stake for Walpole when he corrals the secularizing energies of a progressive narrative into the figure of the author. In Shakespeare's play the bewilderment of the supposedly central figure invites a reading that favors the baroque and the spectacular over the providential and reproductive. Walpole takes that idea further: like Henry, Manfred and his aging wife cannot produce a viable heir; unlike Henry, Manfred will not be granted an Elizabeth to retroactively make a man of him. In Walpole's version of the story there is no real future to look forward to—only a past of foreclosed possibilities for which the creative powers of the author serve as a rather melancholy substitute.

The operative model here is the analogy between state and family known as *patriarchalism*. "The whole worlde is noethinge but a greate state; a state is no other than a great familie; and a familie is no other than a greate bodye. As one God ruleth the worlde, one maister the familie," remarked John Hayward in 1603.[18] The analogy between state and family suggests that as we are born into a preexistent family and into a natural condition of dependency, so subjects are born into a preexistent state and into a natural condition of subjection. The political structure preexists the subject: just as one cannot imagine being born of a different father, so one cannot imagine being under a different ruler, or no ruler at all.[19]

It is of course the novel, and especially the gothic novel, that *does* imagine what it might be like to be born of a different father, or the wrong father.[20] Indeed *Otranto* might be read as an allegory of the shifting role of the family as absolutism slowly withers away. Manfred is a figure for someone living through this transition who still behaves as if he is a Renaissance prince of the Machiavellian type—or more specifically, given the references, of the Henry VIII type. In the patriarchal model, a good father works hard because he considers himself to be in the service of the family; a good monarch, likewise, has the interests of his people at heart. What makes the father-king analogy work is a picture of the traditional household as itself a well-managed economic entity. But Manfred is a spectacularly bad father, and in precisely those terms: rather than serve his family, he concerns himself solely with holding on to power and territory.[21] This makes him a baroque prince, whose fascination is in Benjamin's words "rooted in the conflict between the impotence and depravity of his person [and] . . . the sacrosanct power of his role" (72). With a bad father/king and a household in disarray, the patriarchal model was no longer tenable, and, as historians of the family have demonstrated, a new, more impersonal kind of economic thinking emerged, with a conjugal "private" family now held separate from economic activity itself understood to belong to a bourgeois public sphere and to such impersonal abstractions as the market.[22]

This is to say that *Otranto*, its irony and playfulness notwithstanding, is a sober meditation on the various processes that make up what we call "modernity." Where the medieval church once owned a monopoly on education, health care, law enforcement, and charity, self-directed autonomous institutions gradually assumed those functions. The demise of a single moral universe in which all persons and occupations have an assigned place greatly multiplied individual social and professional options. This indeed is the original meaning of "secularization," which refers to the transfer of land, property, or persons from the domain of the church to the domain of the world.[23] As the career of Henry VIII suggests, that transfer initially strengthened the state. But it eventually weakened the very absolutism it was invoked to support.

Scholars have emphasized different aspects of this paradoxical development. Charles Taylor has for example written of an enlightened intellectual world understood to be "governed by universal causal laws," and a consequent "moral distaste" for an interventionist God.[24] The result was a disengaged and impersonal cosmos, offset in the eighteenth century by the increased prominence of human sociability. This is the age of commercial activity, finance capital, and social theory modeled on interpersonal relations. Less concerned with sovereignty, war, and territory, the state took an increasing interest in commerce and finance. These are the origins of what Michel Foucault has termed the governmental state, "essentially defined no longer in terms of its territoriality, of its surface area, but in terms of the mass of its population with its volume and density."[25] For Foucault the crucial change was the introduction of economy into political practice. Sovereignty may have meant the administration of territory, but the art of modern governance was now the administration of *things*: their arrangement, ordering, tabulation, and management. The concept of a population, in its modern sense, emerged.[26]

The separating out of public from private and economy from family, moreover, introduced what Habermas has called a "process of self-clarification," wherein private people reflected on the novel experience of their privateness and eventually gave birth to the "public sphere of the world of letters."[27] More and more of the world came under the control, or apparent control, of instrumental reason. As the process of differentiation accelerated, for instance, a burgeoning insurance industry, the science of weather prediction, an industry of critics, writers, printers, and booksellers, and a "growing culture of quantification" that tabulated mortality and disease statistics further rationalized and autonomized what had once been a single social domain.[28] And if order was something that could be imposed on things through the effort of human will and sustained labor, then humanity's natural state seemed less an instantiation of divine form than a terrain on which to work. God may have designed everything according to a plan, but it was up to human actors to put that plan into action.

Providential deism, governmentality, and rational self-clarification: it was Horace Walpole's father Robert who made these intellectual innovations into social policy. Known as "the fat old squire of Norfolk," the gifted, wealthy, and corpulent prime minister of England was first elected to Parliament in 1701 and stepped forward decisively with the collapse of the South Sea Bubble. For twenty years he was arguably the most powerful man in the kingdom. Ruthless and systematic, an administrative genius and a man of earthly appetites, Walpole used his power to enrich himself, filling his small palace at Houghton with paintings and furnishings purchased at astronomical prices. But he also made government run more efficiently than it ever had before. Rationalization, efficiency, and trade, he believed, would smooth over otherwise intractable ideological differences. His aims were simple and clear: avoid war, increase trade, reduce taxes. Take care of the economy, and the rest would take care of itself.[29]

Not everyone was thrilled. Within a few years of the Hampton Court performance of *Henry VIII*, the opposition press began linking Walpole with Cardinal Wolsey, Henry VIII's lord chancellor.[30] The link made sense: like Walpole, Wolsey was fat, rich, hugely skilled, and detested by the courtier class. From humble origins (he was a butcher's son) Wolsey had risen to become a cardinal and, in 1515, the lord chancellor of England.[31] If Walpole's own rapid rise was an obvious point of comparison, then Wolsey's eventual fate offered opposition writers of the eighteenth century the chance to speculate on Walpole's own future. In 1727 *The Craftsman* described Wolsey's greed and ambition and then noted archly that "Reflecting people may observe from this Picture how like human Nature is in her Workings at all Times."[32] Awful as he was, Wolsey was better than Walpole, as *The Craftsman* opined the following year when it compared the two men more overtly:

> Learned Himself, to Learning was a Friend;
> Himself, adorn'd with Arts, did Arts defend;
> Whilst all Thy [Walpole's] Knowledge is confin'd to GAIN;
> To funds, and Stocks, and Bribes, thy Country's Bane.[33]

And the anonymous writer of the *Authentick memoirs of the life and infamous actions of Cardinal Wolsey* (1731) went so far as to refer to Wolsey anachronistically as a "prime minister" and to note darkly: "But to the Terror of future evil Ministers it will be seen, that their [sic] is no Power so very great as to be always able to skreen [sic] him from the Vengeance of an *injured People*."[34]

Wolsey's fall was easily read in the eighteenth century as an allegory of the failure of an upwardly mobile professionalization narrative. But in *Henry VIII* this does not mean the restoration of traditional sovereignty. In the play Wolsey serves a useful purpose in helping to get rid of Katherine, but the future he has made possible is an uncertain one. The play is held together on stage by royalist pageantry, which is why the eighteenth-century tendency to frame it as an exercise in spectacle seems so apposite: it is less about individuals (sovereign or otherwise) than it is about forces, and particularly the problem of their management by an increasingly abstract entity known as "the government." Walpole too may be eclipsed, but one lesson of *Henry VIII* is that the changes associated with modernity cannot be located in a single person.

In recent years, both Robert Miles and Diane Long Hoeveler have written of the gothic mode as "poised" on the cusp of these transitions—an agent of Reform, or, as Hoeveler writes, a "part of the ambivalent secularization process itself."[35] Both critics seek to complicate arguments like E. J. Clery's that see the gothic as spectacle, a merely aesthetic reaction to the confluence of enlightenment, secularization, and capitalism.[36] I agree with them, but I view *Otranto*, at least, less as a pluralizing instrument for human flourishing within the immanent frame than as a prescient *critique* of that frame, a meditation less on the options immanence opens up than on the possibilities it closes down. In this I am inspired by E. P. Thompson's argument that early modern English society held "customs in common"—that both elites and plebeians were committed to the maintenance of a reciprocal culture that balanced the demands of the different orders through well-developed but informal mechanisms, ranging from carnival to food riot, which together ensured that elite and plebeian forces remained in rough equilibrium. David Collings, in a recent application of this idea, argues that modernization was the steady withdrawal of elite commitment from such mutual give-and-take; in its place came the belief that society does fundamentally cohere, or *would* cohere were it not for some illegitimate or unpalatable element that must be expelled. Cast out of proper society, reciprocity thus returned in monstrous form, in the fevered imaginations of social reformers during the revolutionary era and in the mobs and monsters of the gothic novel.[37]

Reform and its symbolic economy allow us to place a novel like *Otranto* into this timeline, beginning with the early modern "rage for order" that swept across sixteenth- and seventeenth-century Europe. In this example, the ideals of Reform—discipline, order, efficiency, sobriety, right belief— produce the very political uncanny they claim to banish. This paradox, which I take to be central to secularism itself, illuminates the persistence of the gothic alternative to official culture. This is one reason that gothic novels and the realist novels that owe so much to them continued to treat Catholicism symbolically well into the nineteenth century—as part neither, that is to say, of a theological conflict (Catholic versus Protestant) nor of an economic one (landed aristocracy versus rising bourgeoise), but as a particularly secular form of haunting, the result of a reforming elite's withdrawal from a social compact that had once upon a time made space for popular culture. As we will see shortly, the gothic possibilities that circle around the edges of Jane Austen's novel *Emma*—its various fantasies, love affairs, charades, and mysterious coincidences—should be read not simply generically (as debased romance plots), but historically, as the illegitimate progeny of Henrician reform itself, possibilities made marginal by the same process that fathered them. The issue is, once again, not so much a matter of doctrine or belief as it is a conduit to a rambunctious and decidedly *different* world of folk practices that by the early years of the nineteenth century lie within the realm of what the narrator of *Emma* will insist upon calling "impossible things."

Heterosexual Melancholy

Eighteenth-century conversations and clarifications structured the public sphere, but they also reached into the more private zones of sexuality and the family. Unlike patriarchal theory, contract theory (favored throughout the seventeenth century by religious and political dissenters, and in the eighteenth century by the liberal Anglican mainstream) "entails the explicit consent of its participants" rather than their merely tacit acceptance.[38] Foucault has noted, too, that the development of statistics revealed populations as entities with their own cycles—growth, retraction, epidemic, productivity— not always reducible to the cycles of the family.[39] Thus the family became newly instrumental and paradoxically irrelevant: where its role had once been the patriarchal one of providing a model of the well-run state in microcosm, its symbolic and biological functions now began to pull apart: it would "contribute" to a population that didn't need it. Such contradictory imperatives cleared room for a literary public sphere that limned the contours of bourgeois procreativity, creating new ways of imagining a social whole.

While *Otranto*'s first edition may comport well with the general outlines of the public sphere as a mode of secularization and self-clarification (we were once in thrall to outside forces, but now we have self-determination), the second edition repudiates that ideal; in place of a comforting narrative of religious privatization and eventual irrelevance, Walpole offers an experimental, campy, and differently "irrelevant" literary confection. In the opening scene a giant helmet falls from the sky and crushes Manfred's heir; soon Frederic arrives carrying a giant sword; later, other colossal pieces of armor will accumulate, as if the scattered body parts of the legitimate heir are being slowly reassembled. The only official point of this parade of comically larger-than-life items may be that such a burlesque (replete with vibrating feathers) is a new thing in the world, but the reassembled body of Alfonso suggests nevertheless that the process of Reform is now far enough along to be available for literary reflection: the dis-membered, re-membered, and inflated figure registers, though in oblique and ridiculous form, the real violence done to people like Elizabeth Barton.

It remains, however, to specify the relationship between the secularity of Reform and the manliness achieved with such labor in Shakespeare's play and achieved not at all in Walpole's novel. For *Otranto*'s closing sentences seem to reject a normative model of the private conjugal family, and to reject

in consequence the imperative of heterosexual coupling and the literary public sphere that depends upon it. Here is the closing passage again:

> Frederic offered his daughter to the new prince . . . but Theodore's
> grief was too fresh to admit the thought of another love; and it was
> not till after frequent discourses with Isabella, of his dear Matilda,
> that he was persuaded he could know no happiness but in the society
> of one with whom he could forever indulge the melancholy that had
> taken possession of his soul. (110)

Now restored to the throne and bestowed with a wife, Theodore is the novel's
most obvious representative of the future—a role established for him
moments earlier by the giant Alfonso and his closing commands. Yet Walpole
avoids the device that would be rapidly categorized as the marriage plot.
Remarkably, he lets the problem of paternity and inheritance, already an
issue in Shakespeare's *Henry VIII* and in Manfred's family, linger beyond the
end of the text. Theodore's melancholy and his decided lack of enthusiasm
for heterosexual union suggests that another succession crisis is in the offing.

The world of *Otranto* is a world full of things that have lost their significance, and the prospect of boredom and consequent sensationalism in this
text is less the direct result of market society and its appetite for stimulation
than it is of the restlessness and *acedia* of characters unable to attach themselves to anything in particular. To be sure, believing in impossible things is
easily coded as backward-looking, credulous, or irredeemably aestheticized—
modes very unlike Habermas's conception of the clarifying effects of the
literary public sphere. But the novel's melancholy also looks backward like
Benjamin's angel of history, who helplessly views the wreckage of the past as
he is propelled into a future he cannot face.[40] Some critics have interpreted
Walpole, together with near contemporaries like William Beckford and Matthew Lewis, as early examples of what would eventually be codified as male
homosexuality.[41] But this is to focus on questions of sexual identity rather
than on the queerness of *Otranto* itself, particularly how at odds it seems with
the eighteenth-century public sphere—either in its Habermasian version as a
process of "self-clarification," or in the more nuanced model of the "conversable world" for which Jon Mee has argued. If Shakespeare had staged the
birth of absolutism as already dissipating into a familial and procreative
future structured by the division between the private conjugal family and the

public sphere of self-clarification and conversation, then Walpole's innovation is to suggest that this "future" forecloses upon a past that never was. The novel seems determined to hold public-sphere formations at arm's length. Its melancholic rejection of the public world and appeal to another kind of discourse is not simple nostalgia for an enchanted world but rather the thing that binds together the politics of sexuality and secularity in this novel, marking a relation to plenitude located in a past not so much superseded as never available in the first place.

This is true historically as well as psychologically. For melancholy is one of a range of bodily experiences that is itself secularized over the course of the early modern period. Taylor writes of this process in terms of medical history in particular. The premodern link between black bile and melancholy is intimate: black bile doesn't *cause* melancholy, it *is* melancholy, and so being told that my mood comes from black bile isn't reassuring but rather confirms that I am in the grip of something malevolent. By contrast, learning that my depression is the result of something particular to my body chemistry allows me some distance on the feeling: the feeling doesn't "mean" anything in itself but is rather the effect of a set of causes that are in principle analyzable from the outside. In this sense a wholly different set of meanings accrues to the feeling: even if its phenomenology is the same, I have a different relationship to my embodied experience of it.[42]

Robert Burton's famous *Anatomy of Melancholy* (1621) suggests something of the array of possibilities within this schematic shift, for Burton explores his topic through such an exhaustive range of texts and authorities that melancholy becomes not a single thing but a window into the seemingly infinite nature of knowledge itself, both supernatural (devils, witches, and the stars may cause melancholy) and natural (old age, genetic inheritance, diet, bad air, and insufficient exercise are also culprits). Finally Burton arrives at what he calls the "passions and perturbations of the mind," particularly sorrow itself, an "inseparable companion, *the mother and daughter of Melancholy, her Epitome, Symptome, and chiefe cause: as Hippocrates hath it, They beget one another and tread in a ring, for Sorrow is both cause and Symptome of this Disease.*"[43] Especially in the context of Theodore's lack of interest in his new wife, Burton's mutual begetting of sorrow and melancholy suggests the circular and self-fulfilling nature of this mood, its entropic or simply exhausted repertoire of feeling. The community of rational and deliberative individuals whom public sphere theory invokes seems here to depend on a prior act of self-alienation, its circular treading a mark of its difference both from itself and the world in which it now finds itself.[44]

Something of this alienated self-founding remains in Freud's definition of melancholia as the unfinished process of grieving. But for Freud the mutual self-constitution of sorrow and melancholy now marks not only difference but loss: when a "person has to give up a sexual object, there quite often ensues an alteration of his ego which can only be described as a setting up of the object inside the ego."[45] This is why the grieving is never complete: the subject preserves the object psychically, even if it is, in reality, gone. On this reading, the most obvious cause of Theodore's melancholy would be the dead Matilda. And yet the tenuousness of gender is very much at issue in both *Henry VIII* and *Otranto*. In both texts becoming a man is an "accomplishment," to use Judith Butler's term—something achieved or attained partly in despite of other options, necessary as those choices may be for the maintenance of an always precarious sexual order coded as "destiny." That this contingency must be disavowed means that heterosexuality is structured by its loss of what Butler calls "unlived possibilities."[46] Her reading thus returns to a pre-Freudian notion of melancholy as less invested in a particular sexual object than in the constitutive relation between selfhood and self-alienation. Heterosexuality is melancholic by definition: the loved object does not have to die or disappear in order for gender identification to be structured by an "unlivable passion and ungrievable loss" (135). Melancholy is simply the sign of disenchantment, of a plentitude forgone.

We can glimpse the secular dimensions of this kind of psychological melancholy if we appeal to Ashis Nandy's assertion of a "homology between sexual and political dominance" that characterized the colonial situation in nineteenth-century India. In *The Intimate Enemy*, Nandy examines a dynamic of identification in which colonial Indians "saw their salvation in becoming more like the British, whether in friendship or in enmity."[47] When it came to anticolonial resistance, he continues, "the search for martial Indianness underwrote one of the most powerful collaborationist strands within Indian society," the collaboration in this case between colonial aggressors and the anticolonial Indians who, in identifying with a picture of virile masculinity, unintentionally propped up colonial dynamics of power (7). Nandy argues that this martial picture of masculinity, competitive and aggressive, unwittingly led to a flattening out of other gendered possibilities that had always existed in India. Under colonial rule, he writes, there was "an attempt to lump together all forms of androgyny and counterpoise them against undifferentiated masculinity" (8). Nandy wrote these words some years before the advent of queer theory, but his discussion of how "femininity-in-masculinity" came to be perceived by Indians themselves as "a pathology more dangerous than femininity itself" (8) resonates with Butler's more recent insistence that, precisely because gendered identification is an accomplishment that depends upon the renunciation of other options, it must defend itself militantly against anything that threatens the categories it has worked so hard to achieve.[48] Some years later, when Nandy himself turned his attention to the place where secular and sexual politics meet, he made the link to what he had called "androgyny" and what Butler called gender performance explicit: secularism, he wrote, is "uncomfortable with the somewhat fluid definitions of the self with which many live."[49]

The range of premodern and early modern sexual possibilities and experiences remains difficult to specify, but there is a widespread consensus among historians that it was at least some of the time more fluid than our modern categories can easily accommodate. In traditional societies procreation was an important but far from exclusive purpose of sexual contact, which involved a range of practices and a variety of bodily interactions.[50] By the seventeenth century, however, a growing emphasis on procreative coupling as an activity distinct in kind from other activities had begun to emerge. Those other practices could now be distinguished, sorted, and often condemned: fondling, masturbation, fornication, sodomy, and so on.[51] The codification of a homosexual identity that Walpole variously anticipates is thus a relatively late development in the much longer process of Reform. It is part of the same series of civilizing and reforming imperatives that cleaned up unruly common practices, privatized devotion, death, and other bodily activities, and narrowed and deepened the experience of (religious and sexual) privacy. Theodore, the clever but melancholy young man forced into a marriage for which he has little inclination, is in this analysis the latest subject of that reforming and disciplining work that had begun with the policing of public bodies (festivals and carnivals, icon worship, prostitution) and now, by the middle years of the eighteenth century, began to take the family too in its purview.

Theodore's melancholy highlights these processes of Reform, especially as their weight bears disproportionately on heterosexual marriage. To be "made a man," as Henry is by Cranmer at the conclusion of *Henry VIII*, is to be rushed headlong into a future where procreation and the family will be marshaled toward certain ends. Henry's bewilderment at this moment marks it as a sudden loss of possibilities that he didn't know he had until they were gone; the loss is in this sense ungrievable, even if the compensatory gain—a nation, the future—seems worth it. *Otranto* takes this dynamic a step further, highlighting the way Reform produces melancholy as an unquiet *refusal* of a future destiny imagined in terms of a biological contribution to such things as "economy" and "population." One cannot mourn for a possibility that was never anything other than impossible. One can, however, speak of it— and so the novel's conclusion, wherein "frequent discourse" leads not to Habermasian self-clarification but to yet more melancholy, hints that the only resistance to such an arrangement is simply to call it what it is. If Cranmer's closing speech makes a man of Henry VIII, then, Theodore refuses to let Alfonso's speech make a man out of him. Coleridge, in a nasty mood, once remarked that Walpole had no "spark of true *manliness.*"[52] It was meant as an insult, of course. But if we read "manliness" less as a matter of personal identification than as a mark of how identities and desires are enfolded into the destinies of nations, then Coleridge was more right than perhaps he knew.

CHAPTER 3

Wishing for Nothing: *Emma*
and the Dissolution

In a pivotal scene in Jane Austen's 1814 novel *Mansfield Park*, Henry Crawford reads some passages from *The Famous History of the Life of King Henry VIII* to a rapt audience. Fanny Price, whom Henry is courting, is impressed despite herself: "in Mr. Crawford's reading there was a variety of excellence beyond what she had ever met with. The King, the Queen, Buckingham, Wolsey, Cromwell, all were given in turn. . . . It was truly dramatic."[1]

Henry VIII was performed virtually every year in the middle part of the eighteenth century, and remained popular well into the nineteenth. Productions marking the coronations of both George II and George III cemented its reputation as a drama celebrating spectacle, pageantry, and power. Yet the play's dominant sensibility changed with the times, and when John Philip Kemble revived the play at Drury Lane in 1788, he cut the coronation scene and placed new emphasis on the parts of Wolsey and Katherine. His sister Sarah Siddons, the most famous tragic actress of her day, gave the part of Katherine a new emotional intensity, and sent the entire play off in a more earnest and dramatic direction that provided a model for the nineteenth century. Kemble mounted the play a number of times after his move to Covent Garden, each time with Siddons as Katherine, and it is presumably one of these performances that Henry Crawford saw, or at least heard about: "I once saw Henry the 8th acted.—Or I have heard about it from somebody who did—I am not certain which," he casually remarks after his own reading performance.[2] In earlier eighteenth-century performances, the play's emphases on royal pageantry and on Cranmer's closing prophecy of Elizabeth's greatness muted the contrast between its "Protestant" and "Catholic" themes. But that contrast became acute once Katherine was felt to be the emotional center of the play. For it is hard to reconcile her unjust fate with the glorious future of English Protestantism that Cranmer predicts.

It is surely no accident that the Siddons/Katherine version of *Henry VIII* appeared only after the likelihood of an actual Catholic restoration had faded. Indeed, Fanny's own desire for the "arches, inscriptions, and banners" that populate the world of medieval romance is easily written off by *Mansfield Park*'s narrator as mere nostalgia, picked up from too much reading.[3] Austen's intertextual use of *Henry VIII* thus acknowledges the romance of Fanny's pre-Reformation fantasy (the "Katherine plot," as it were) while containing it within a providential, Whiggish view of history.

Such containment is the very thing analyzed and critiqued in Walpole's *Castle of Otranto*. Corralling the various possibilities of the pre-Reformation world into a destiny formalized by marriage and family led, there, to what Walpole called "melancholy," a loss that is not simply nostalgia for an enchanted world but an identification with some world of possibility never fully available. Emma Woodhouse, the titular heroine of the novel to which Austen turned after completing *Mansfield Park*, also suffers from this kind of melancholy. When we meet her at the beginning of the novel, she is mourning the loss of her governess: "Emma could not but sigh over it, and wish for impossible things" (7), the impossible things in this case being not simply the undoing of the marriage that takes her governess away but a world in which such things need not happen—in which single young women need not marry if they choose not to. Emma, that is to say, is sighing not for Miss Taylor but for herself, and in the face of a narrative that will, by its end, have prepared her so thoroughly for marriage that she can say, with all apparent honesty, that far from wishing for impossible things she now "wishes for nothing" (373). My argument in this chapter is that the inevitable destiny that causes Emma to sigh, formalized here as in Walpole through marriage and family, also like Walpole's novel opens onto the wider horizon of Reform. For in the stability and fixity of Donwell Abbey, the home of Mr. Knightley and the ideological center of the narrative even though it is almost entirely offstage, Austen depicts one possible terminus of the process begun by King Henry VIII so many years earlier. Critics have noted that Mr. Knightley and the narrator collude to school, shape, and contain Emma's overactive imagination so that she is finally worthy of Donwell. Generally unremarked, however, is that in training Emma for Donwell the novel is also aligning her with the Reform narrative Donwell embodies, a history of literal

secularization and emotional straitening written into every view, walk, and
prospect that the place offers. To be worthy of Donwell is, as Emma reflects,
to wish for nothing—or, as we can rewrite that sentiment, to turn impossible
things into no things as if by magic, so that losing them feels like an
achievement.

Just What It Ought to Be

In *Emma*, things serve as a mark of social ambition and arrival. Mrs. Perry
has begun to long for a carriage; when Miss Taylor becomes Mrs. Weston,
she gets a horse and carriage along with a husband; Jane Fairfax gets a mysterious piano; the Coles too get a piano, though none of them can play; and
everybody goes to Ford's store. The village of Highbury, close enough to
London to feel the force of the expanding metropolis, witnesses the rise of
the professional classes: lawyers and doctors are on their way up, while Miss
Bates, a "gentleman's daughter," is on her way down. The novel's plot, such
as it is, turns on Emma's comic efforts to discern the social positions of those
people around her who do not bear the familiar markers of class distinction.[4]
Her misreading of this changing world is the subject of much tedious scholarship on the novel, which typically fails to point out that Emma is *right* to
distrust appearances and to suspect that there is more going on than meets
the eye. The plot bears her out in this: Jane Fairfax *is* keeping secrets; the
mysterious piano *does* indeed possess a hidden meaning; Frank Churchill and
Mr. Elton *do* have romantic intentions. Most of what matters in Highbury
in fact takes place behind the scenes: Emma misreads the signs, but she
correctly intuits the symbolic slippage all around her. Even Mr. Knightley
turns out to have a secret.

If the social world of Highbury is full of interpretive difficulties, Donwell
Abbey stands alone as a site of hermeneutic stability. Indeed, the place is
virtually self-referential: "It was just what it ought to be, and it looked what
it was," declares the narrator, or Emma, or both.[5] As elsewhere in Austen,
the figure for such honesty is resistance to improvement: much is made of
Donwell's "neglect of prospect, . . . and its abundance of timber in rows and
avenues, which neither fashion nor extravagance had rooted up" (281).
Against the phony Mrs. Elton, with her beribboned picnic basket and fantasies of rusticity ("I wish we had a donkey. The thing would be for us all to
come on donkies" [279]), Mr. Knightley and his home are easily read as

representatives of the true nature of things: there is no deception here, no pretending to be something else, no playing with surfaces to hide what is beneath, none of the false naturalization of rustic picnics and improvement.[6]

Donwell's walls and gates, its timber, its resistance to fashion—these things abide, along with their ability to link questions of morality ("it was just what it ought to be") to those of epistemology ("it looked what it was") without any slip or stutter between inward state and outward representation. In a novel that continually thematizes deception and misreading, then, the Abbey becomes a kind of ideal-type, an organizing principle for Highbury society itself. It is what Lacan calls the *point de capiton*, the "quilting point" that intervenes to stop the sliding signifiers of the rest of the novel and fix their meaning.[7]

But the quilt itself has been pieced together over many hundreds of years. In 1534, when Henry became supreme head of the Church of England, some 750 monasteries, priories, and convents dotted the landscape of England and Wales. Between 1538 and 1540, Henry's ministers, led and orga-nized by Cromwell, suppressed 450 of them, turning 8,000 monks, nuns, and friars out into the world, and carting off most of the valuables to the royal coffers in London. A number of the old monastic cathedrals, including Canterbury, Ely, and Durham, were suppressed and then refounded. Many others were dismantled or torn down altogether. And some were preserved and then given, together with their lands, to the nobles who had supported Henry. Indeed, after the first Act of Suppression, in spring 1536, which aimed at the smaller and less prosperous houses, Cromwell's mail was full of requests for the spoils. "[N]o policy of his reign had so direct an impact on so many people or on so much of the English landscape and skyline," writes Richard Rex (58). David Knowles is even more dramatic, calling the dissolution "the most sudden and wholesale transformation that English social life has ever undergone between the Norman conquest and our own day."[8] And this "wholesale transformation" is how Donwell Abbey came, years later, to be the home of Mr. Knightley.

A Girl Taught a Lesson

Like his residence, Mr. Knightley is eminently legible: he has a direct way of speaking, a "downright, decided, commanding sort of manner" (28), he never prevaricates or lies ("You hear nothing but truth from me," he tells Emma

[338]), and he dislikes mystery and intrigue. "You might not see one in a hundred, with gentleman so plainly written as in Mr. Knightley," says Emma—punning perhaps too obviously on his name itself.[9] Clearly Mr. Knightley is meant to be representative of something: he has "English delicacy toward the feelings of other people" (118), a "true English style" (79), and he speaks "plain, unaffected, gentleman-like English" (352).

Emma herself will bear the brunt of this English style, as Mr. Knightley scolds and cajoles her into the wife whom he can finally marry at the novel's close. Readers have had a hard time not following Mr. Knightley's lead in this; as Eve Sedgwick noted some years ago, Austen criticism "is notable mostly, not just for its timidity and banality, but for its unresting exaction of the spectacle of a Girl Being Taught a Lesson—for the vengefulness it vents on the heroines whom it purports to love."[10] Emma, the most recalcitrant of Austen's heroines, is also the toughest to remodel; but Mr. Knightley, the novel's prime agent of reform, is up to the task, gradually turning her from a desiring young woman to a fixed object of desire. "This is my wife," we can imagine Mr. Knightley saying by novel's end, in implicit repudiation of the carnivalesque licentiousness and bodily confusion that surrounds Anne in Shakespeare's play.

Marriage, indeed, is the figure for just this sort of lesson. The novel opens with Miss Taylor's marriage to Mr. Weston, which introduces an unwelcome change at Hartfield. Mr. Woodhouse, we are told, is "fond of every body that he was used to, and hating to part with them; hating change of every kind. Matrimony, as the origin of change, was always disagreeable" (7). The joke, of course, will be on Mr. Woodhouse: when Miss Taylor becomes Mrs. Weston she moves only half a mile from Hartfield, and the family continues to see her almost daily; even more to the point, when Mr. Knightley marries Emma, he agrees to move in at Hartfield, rather than removing Emma to Donwell, so that Mr. Woodhouse will not even feel the change. In this novel, marriage is the way things change in order to stay the same.

Along the way to this deflating conclusion, however, alternative possibilities and voices surface now and again. Some of these are heavily ironized: the gypsies that "threaten" Harriet, the turkey thieves that frighten Mr. Woodhouse. Yet even those incidents point to a larger world in which "change" might really mean something. Considering the historical moment in which Austen wrote her novels, Claudia Johnson has argued that "the Revolution in France gave rise to the novel of crisis in England, . . . in which the structures of daily life are called into doubt and in which the unthinkable just keeps happening." These themes are a concern for writers of all political persuasions; for the women novelists of the 1790s, in particular, Johnson continues, "the moral as well as aesthetic center has ceased to hold, and despair, confusion, weariness, and apocalyptic dread or yearning strain the fabric of their narratives."[11] Austen is more decorous than some of her contemporaries. But the closing pages of *Emma*, with its "small band of true friends" (381) huddled together, points to a larger and unmanageably chaotic world beyond the shrubbery. Of all Austen's novels, this is most a "novel of crisis" insofar as it continually raises, if only to defuse, the possibility of real change.

The most dramatic example of how things might be otherwise is associated, reflexively, with those debased romance fictions that provide the literary context for Austen's practice. Emma, plenty smart but indifferently educated, is particularly susceptible to the stock elements of fantastical romance-plots: the obscure birth, the chivalric rescue, the class mobility fantasy. This last and horrifying possibility finally brings on Emma's own crisis of self-recognition: "It darted through her, with the speed of an arrow, that Mr. Knightley must marry no one but herself!" (320). Austen is too accomplished a stylist, and one too sparing of figurative language, for this hackneyed image to be anything but deliberate—as if to mark, at the level of style, how conventional and predictable is the romance genre, even when it finally delivers the "truth."[12] Austen herself loved Charlotte Lennox's *Female Quixote*, whose ludicrous heroine has her head stuffed full of French romances. And in *Northanger Abbey*, the novel that confronts the legacy of the gothic romance directly, the narrator remarks that Henry Tilney falls in love with Catherine Morland largely out of gratitude, "a new circumstance in romance, I acknowledge, . . . but if it be as new in common life, the credit of a wild imagination will at least be all my own."[13] Continually and wittily pointing out the difference between the world of romance and the real world is this narrator's stock-in-trade.[14]

Yet Highbury is a world in which things are not always what they seem, and Emma, along with the rest of the village, is forced into habitually mistaking appearance for reality as much by the plot as by her own recalcitrant willfulness. Beneath the bland exterior, things are in motion. In ways surprisingly like Walpole's treatment of an inflated economy in *Otranto*, the mysteries of the commodity form help to generate the world of romance that is the heroine's greatest temptation.

The most striking example occurs, appropriately enough, in Ford's store. While Emma is questioning him rather closely about Jane Fairfax, Frank distracts her by declaring his sudden intention to make a purchase:

> "Ha! this must be the very shop that every body attends every day of their lives. . . . I must buy something at Fords. It will be taking out my freedom.—I dare say they sell gloves."
>
> "Oh! yes, gloves and every thing. I do admire your patriotism. You will be adored in Highbury. You were very popular before you came, because you were Mr. Weston's son—but lay out half-a-guinea at Ford's, and your popularity will stand upon your own virtues."
>
> They went in; and while the sleek, well-tied parcels of "Men's Beavers" and "York Tan" were bringing down and displaying on the counter, he said—"But I beg your pardon, Miss Woodhouse, you were speaking to me." (157)

The freedom Frank is actually "taking out" is the freedom to move around Highbury so that he can meet Jane Fairfax from time to time, keep her spirits up, and make sure she is still in love with him. In order to do this, he starts several alternative plots going. His own romance with Emma is the most plausible of these; somewhat less plausible, but equally important, is the Jane Fairfax-Mr. Dixon plot. And so when Frank invites Emma to ask her question again, he is ready with an answer: "Then I will speak the truth, and nothing suits me so well. I met her frequently at Weymouth. I had known the Campbells a little in town; and at Weymouth we were very much in the same set" (158).

This half-truth, which effectively leads Emma away from the full truth by inviting her to speculate that Mr. Dixon is in love with Jane, is presented as the gloves are circulating, as the narrator's curious language suggests, literally under their own agency, "well-tied parcels . . . bringing down and displaying on the counter." The message is clear: commodities engage in half-truths (which is why, like Frank, they are so appealing) by inviting speculation that leads the mind astray, and distracting Emma from noticing "real" relations of cause and effect. Things move about as if under their own power, which makes it difficult to trace agency back to individual actors. From a generic point of view, Frank's deception effectively prevents the romance plot of his engagement with Jane from entering the realist world of the novel; he manages this by inventing an even more unlikely romance-plot involving Mr. Dixon. In this way romance disguises itself by posing as romance—by pretending to be itself, and hiding in plain sight. The Frank Churchill-Jane Fairfax plot, complete with a secret engagement and its elaborate arrangements, is itself a familiar novelistic convention of the period, from Frances Burney's *Cecilia* to Charlotte Smith's *The Old Manor House*. The frequent observation that not very much happens in *Emma* can thus be understood as an acknowledgment that things *are* happening in the unwritten Frank and Jane romance novel that circulates rather brazenly within this realist text.[15]

The scene at Ford's tells us something else as well: to educate Emma out of romance and into a real world in which nothing much happens and things change only to stay the same is also to inoculate her against the speculative force of commodity culture and retrain her for the land-based economy that, through marriage to Mr. Knightley, she will eventually join. Part of "the younger branch of a very ancient family," Emma indeed is particularly vulnerable to monetary and romantic speculation. Resident in Highbury only for several generations, the Woodhouses own no land: their considerable wealth comes "from other sources" (108). Mr. Knightley, by contrast, has "little spare money" (167) and a lot of land; Emma's home at Hartfield, in fact, is "but a sort of notch in the Donwell Abbey estate, to which all the rest of Highbury belonged" (108). Here economy, morality, and plot match perfectly: marriage to Mr. Knightley will redeem Emma from her addiction to speculative romance, and it will allow him to smooth out a notch in his estate and give him access to ready money.[16]

In *Emma* as in *Otranto*, however, the connection between a wildly speculative economy and the improbabilities of the gothic romance can be grasped only within the context of the longer history of Reform:[17]

> Again and again, semi-refractory masses were forced to shape up to a new regime, sometimes rudely, sometimes by gentle persuasion. . . . They are dealt with by being organized, taken in hand, disciplined, sometimes semi-incarcerated.
>
> This is only one facet of the new "police state," which undertakes to organize the lives of its citizens in rational ways; ensure that they are properly educated, that they belong to churches, that they lead sober and productive economic lives.[18]

This is what Charles Taylor calls the "Work of Reform." It is the perspective of the narrator, of Knightley/Donwell, and of those readers who take pleasure in Emma's reeducation. This perspective cuts across confessional divides; its goal is to make an entire culture over to higher standards. Among other things this means teaching the heroine and the reader to make do with, indeed to take pleasure in, much less than they had before.[19] It is not, then, commodity culture itself that the narrator condemns; indeed, the economic stability of Austen's minor gentry relies to a great extent on that culture. It is, rather, the speculative habit of mind *associated* with commodification that the narrator has in her sights, for it is this imaginative tendency that leads away from the sobriety that Mr. Knightley stands for and that Emma will discover, by novel's end, to be the termination of all her desires. It is Frank Churchill, of course, who stands opposite Mr. Knightley in this regard—Frank who, in John Wiltshire's apt description, "presents the possibility of seeing things another way—one that allows much more to impetuosity and surprise, to passion and risk-taking."[20]

Technically speaking, *Emma* is Austen's most accomplished novel. It was issued by John Murray, a serious house better known as the publisher of Lord Byron and Sir Walter Scott. In his own review of *Emma*, which appeared in Murray's *Quarterly Review*, Scott argued that *Emma* was the kind of novel that could be written only in the present age, when the possibility of seeing things "another way" can be placed within a world of common experience. Novels may have sprung from romance, Scott wrote, but they now claim the new territory of everyday probability, "of such common occurrences as may have fallen under the observation of most folks; and her dramatis personae conduct themselves upon the motives and principles which the readers may recognize as ruling their own and that of most of their contemporaries."[21] Thus when Emma discovers that Mr. Knightley in fact loves her, she "felt for Harriet, with pain and with contrition; but no flight of generosity run mad, opposing all that could be probable or reasonable, entered her brain" (338). To banish a romance plot (a "flight of generosity run mad") in favor of the probable and reasonable, as the narrator continually does in *Emma*, means that much of the novel consists in plots, incidents, or happenings resisted, denied, or deliberately foreclosed on. "I have escaped," Emma tells Mrs. Weston (312), and she means she has escaped from involvement with Frank Churchill, and his belief in "anything, everything," in "time, chance, circumstances, slow effects, sudden bursts" (343).

But if this is what Emma has escaped *from*, it is less clear what she has escaped *into*. Indeed, given everything that might have happened, it is extraordinary how little *actually* happens in this novel. Scott remarks that

Emma has "even less story" than *Sense and Sensibility* and *Pride and Prejudice* (65), and his contemporaries concurred: "There was no story in it," declared Maria Edgeworth; "There is no story whatever," wrote Susan Ferrier; "There is so little to remember," agreed Anne Romily.[22] Emma begins as an "imaginist," a fantasist, seeing things that aren't there, generating plots that do not materialize. By the end, she has given all that up:

> When it came to such a pitch as this, she was not able to refrain
> from a start, or a heavy sigh, or even from walking about the room
> for a few seconds—and the only source whence any thing like conso-
> lation or composure could be drawn, was in the resolution of her
> own better conduct, and the hope that, however inferior in spirit
> and gaiety might be the following and every future winter of her life
> to the past, it would yet find her more rational, more acquainted
> with herself, and leave her less to regret when it were gone. (332)

Emma, at twenty, is now contemplating the "winter of her life." She is being too dramatic, of course, but this is still a long way from the young woman of the opening pages, who wishes for impossible things and revels in the serial erotic attachments of Harriet Smith. Such radically diminished expectations are the price of progress in this novel. Emma's "escape" into a life without plot, her new view of the present as something for which the best that can be hoped is that it leaves her less to regret when it is gone, is properly read as part of the larger narrative of Reform for which, again, Donwell Abbey stands as an omnipresent historical marker.

So Placed as to See Them All

The importance of riddles and word games in Highbury's social circles has been often remarked on; even more striking is the importance assigned to the sending, receiving, and interpreting of letters. Jane Fairfax makes daily trips to the post office; Frank Churchill sends his father a "highly-prized" letter in place of himself, which remains a subject of comment for weeks; Emma complains to Harriet that "every letter from [Jane Fairfax] is read forty times over" (70). And Robert Martin's letter of proposal to Harriet "would not have disgraced a gentleman; the language, though plain, was strong and unaffected, and the sentiments it conveyed very much to the credit of the writer"

(40). Consider the contrast between this plain, direct, and unadorned letter of proposal—a realist novel writ small—and one of Mr. Elton's charades, which also amounts to a proposal. The charade is in verse, of course, and also sardonically described by the narrator as "the only literary pursuit which engaged Harriet at present" (56). Predictably, Elton's charade is a collection of clichés, and though Emma recognizes how hackneyed they are, and also guesses the riddle easily, she misses the obvious fact that the charade is addressed not to Harriet but to her. The implicit contrast developed here between good plain prose, almost irresistible in its force, and the kind of "literary" writing that flatters the receiver into willful misinterpretation is at last cemented when the foolish Harriet endorses its exact opposite: "'It is one thing,' said she, presently—her cheeks in a glow—'to have very good sense in a common way, like every body else, and . . . to sit down and write a letter, and say just what you must, in a short way; and another, to write verses and charades like this'" (62). The value of saying "just what you must, in a short way," is of course associated with Mr. Knightley, with his plain, direct way of speaking, and with Donwell Abbey, which does not prevaricate or dissemble but simply looks like what it is. And it is, too, the value of the narrator's practice, and its quest to foreclose the sort of unlikely romantic events introduced by charades and word games.[23]

The narrator's proxy in this, as in so much else, is Mr. Knightley, who almost invisibly oversees the business of the parish, making sure that carriages and gifts are sent around to the Bateses when necessary, consulting with his tenant farmer and steward, disbursing advice and aid. Such are the tasks of the responsible landholder as Austen conceives them. Yet Mr. Knightley's oversight also intrudes into the drawing room: he designs and eventually brings off the marriage of Robert Martin and Harriet Smith; through careful observation he discerns the attachment between Frank Churchill and Jane Fairfax; and he hovers over even the light amusements of Highbury's citizens: "Frank Churchill placed a word before Miss Fairfax. She gave a slight glance round the table, and applied herself to it. Frank was next to Emma, Jane opposite to them—and *Mr. Knightley so placed as to see them all*; and it was his object to see as much as he could, with as little apparent observation" (273, emphasis added). Mr. Knightley's status as the unwatched watcher reaches its apotheosis, of course, in the love plot with Emma. At the novel's opening, we learn that Emma is nearly twenty-one, while Mr. Knightley is "a sensible man about seven or eight-and-thirty" (8). The plot works to diminish the importance of this age gap, and while it perhaps feels insignificant now that both are adults, we also learn that he is "an old and very intimate friend of the family" (8), and has been in the regular habit of visiting Hartfield and correcting Emma's faults for a number of years: "I could not think about you so much without doating on you, faults and all; and . . . have been in love with you ever since you were thirteen at least," he confesses (363). This may be the lighthearted banter of lovers, but we are nevertheless faced with the rather disconcerting picture of Mr. Knightley, age thirty, contemplating a thirteen-year-old girl who has no adults to protect her (her mother is dead, her father is an invalid, and even Emma admits her governess had no authority over her). He watches her, thinks about her, appears regularly at her house, waits until the moment seems right. Even the proposal scene has a faintly sinister air about it: it takes place away from the house, after Mr. Knightley "follows her into the shrubbery" (339). Small wonder, in any case, that when Mr. Knightley finally speaks his love he finds it returned, as it were, beforehand: "The affection, which he had been asking to be allowed to create if he could, was already his!" (339). His apparent surprise (sutured by free indirect style to the narrator's "surprise") that she loves him already does not convince: he has been "creating" her affection since she was a girl.

Emma's own selfish efforts to improve Harriet Smith tend to distract readers from the fact that Emma has all along been, in her turn, a project of Mr. Knightley's. Indeed, her answer to the proposal echoes Mr. Knightley's own values back to him: "What did she say?—Just what she ought, of course. A lady always does" (339). With this response Emma and the Hartfield "notch" are ready to be incorporated into the symbolic economy of Donwell, where everything is "just what it ought to be, and it looked what it was." She has, in a very real sense, been made for it.[24]

If Emma cannot finally escape the force of Donwell's truth, however, the novel that bears her name does allow us to sketch its genealogy. By connecting Donwell to the process of monastic dissolution we have already begun to do that. For the networks of information, reorganization of land, appropriation of resources, and general rationalization of procedure—in short, the bureaucratic reforms introduced by Cromwell and intended to give the new dispensation a monopoly on truth—are values industriously carried forward by Mr. Knightley, who consults maps and moves paths and has a "plan of a drain" in the works (80). We know, too, that Mr. Knightley has only one tenant on his estate. Robert Martin may be the model of a prosperous and enlightened tenant farmer, but the fact that he is the only one indicates that he is the sole survivor of the consolidating and rationalizing practices known as enclosure and engrossment.[25] Robert's prosperity notwithstanding, the long-term legacy of enclosure was rural poverty and depopulation, as the widespread food riots of 1810, the Luddite rebellion of 1812, and the passage of the Corn Laws in 1815 all indicate. There are only hints of this darker history in *Emma*, but Robert Martin's success within a remade agricultural landscape contrasts markedly with those who are less fortunate: the impoverished family whom Emma visits, the gypsies who frighten Harriet, the turkey thieves who close out the novel—in short, the hungry people who ring the margins of Highbury society.

These developments—a modernizing and rationalizing overclass, a small but growing middle class, and a rural underclass sinking into political irrelevance—signal the end of the reciprocal relations between elite and common that had structured early modern life in England: "Plebeians," writes David Collings, "accepted gentry power over local political and economic affairs on the condition that the gentry protected the interests of their charges, safeguarded their traditional rights, and recognized them as fellow human beings in festivals and communal rituals."[26] Reciprocity might thus lead to a mutually affirmative exchange, but it might also be the site of social contest if the gentry failed to hold up their end of the bargain. By the end of the eighteenth century such reciprocity had come under repeated and concerted attack from elites across the ideological spectrum. We can therefore see the social world of Austen's novel, including the discontent that surrounds the comfortable lives of its protagonists, as the result of the thing that Austen places at its very center. Mr. Knightley's values are those of his residence; together, man and house quilt together a genre—realism—and a historical narrative—Reform—according to which a popular culture corrupted by superstition, characterized by free movement, and marked by lax discipline needed intervention in order to save it from itself.

If, however, we appeal to a different historical picture, according to which lay piety was not in need of reform and Cromwell's men largely created the "superstition" that they claimed to find, then another possibility comes into focus. In this picture, the reformers deliberately refused to recognize the degree to which relics, shrines, and pilgrimages were woven into the fabric of lay religious life; their aim was not to transform doctrine but to break apart a traditional culture whose "preoccupation with the communal," "sense of the intimate interweaving of this world and the next," and relative lack of interest in sorting out the distinctions between prayers, invocations, and charms combined to create a world in which selves were porous rather than buffered, and individual life was embedded in a social order that was itself part of a divinely ordered cosmos.[27]

Indeed, the visitations of Cromwell's men offer remarkable evidence of how that world was differentiating, and thus how the distinction between true religion and mere superstition came to be elaborated during these tumultuous years. The visitors sent back lengthy reports of the superstitious practices they discovered, and eventually began sending back the objects themselves—staffs and girdles and saints' fingers, Saint Margaret's comb and Thomas Becket's boots.[28] Sometimes the visitations read like early attempts at the gothic novel: salacious rumors about the sexual activities of the monks and nuns combine with accounts of relics, superstitions, and arcane beliefs.[29] Cromwell even organized a few representative exposures—the Rood of Boxley, for example, with its movable eyes. The reformers sometimes seemed as superstitious about the power of these objects as their opponents. "[I]dolatrie will neaver be left till the said images be taken awaie," noted the bishop of Rochester approvingly when Cromwell ordered the Boxley Rood burned.[30]

It is worth stressing once again that these activities were not aimed primarily at doctrinal or theological "errors" but rather at resources, both material and ideological, that had until now escaped the control of the Crown. Alongside collating superstitious practices the visitors also assessed the value of the monastic houses—their rents, debts, ready money, valuables, timber, cattle, and servants. This process introduced into church affairs a newly rationalized organizational scheme, involving the collection and distribution of information and the centralization of command. And Cromwell's extraordinary network of spies and informers tracked down those individuals or houses who resisted this new and more open dispensation.[31]

However lacking *Emma* is in historical detail, then, its insistently endorsed narrative values of truth, sincerity, openness, and naturalness are there to be read in the history of Donwell Abbey itself, which looks the way it does thanks to the literal process of secularization that saw vast wealth, and land, transferred from the church to private citizens. Within the novel, any resistance to those principles is largely located in unlikable or morally compromised characters: in Miss Bates's tiresome narratives of irrelevant minutiae, for example, or in Harriet's libido and her superstitious relationship to objects, especially the treasure box that constitutes something of a shrine to

Mr. Elton and whose relics—a piece of court plaister and a pencil stub—she significantly burns in order to destroy their power over her. Frank's machinations, too, begin to look positively gothic by the end: "What has it been but a system of hypocrisy and deceit,—espionage, and treachery?" demands the newly enlightened Emma, with a hyperbole bordering on hysteria (314). And then, of course, there is Mrs. Elton's obsession with finery, her love of accessories, and her obnoxious pursuit of pageantry, which is everywhere mocked in the novel, right up to the final description of Emma and Mr. Knightley's wedding:

> The wedding was very much like other weddings, where the parties have no taste for finery or parade; and Mrs. Elton, from the particulars detailed by her husband, thought it all extremely shabby, and very inferior to her own.—'Very little white satin, very few lace veils; a most pitiful business! . . .'—But, in spite of these deficiencies, the wishes, the hopes, the confidence, the predictions of the small band of true friends who witnessed the ceremony, were fully answered in the perfect happiness of the union. (381)

It matters, here, that Mrs. Elton's opinion is not rendered in the free indirect style of which Austen is a master; it is made to stick out, rather, against the background voices that proclaim in unison the perfect happiness of the union. Based around heartfelt sincerity and lack of "parade," and invested with the political symbolism of the various acts of union that between 1530 and 1800 would gradually neutralize opposition by making political differences into matters of aesthetic taste, the purity for which this conclusion strives must be set against the image of the "small band of true friends" who gather in its name. More even than the other novels, *Emma* barricades itself against an array of unknown forces beyond the confines of village life. We are told early in the novel that Mr. Woodhouse rarely ventures beyond the shrubbery surrounding Hartfield, which for him delineates the known and safe world. His fear of open windows and inclement weather seems to infect the entire population of Highbury: a few inches of snow on Christmas Eve induce a major crisis; an expedition to Box Hill, seven miles away, is a historic event; Harriet is "attacked" by gypsies after wandering out of town half a mile. Whatever this closing union portends for the future, then, it seems a pinched vision at this moment, with its small circle of friends drawn together in mutual fear and incomprehension of the world outside, where reside the carping Eltons, the vulgar new gentry, the gypsies, and the turkey thieves.

There are bound to be problems, after all, with a narrative that depends so heavily on sincerity, openness, and teleological inevitability, but that roots those things in a history beginning with Henrician reform. "'My Emma, does not every thing serve to prove more and more the beauty of truth and sincerity in all our dealings with each other?'" asks Mr. Knightley, rhetorically, near the novel's end. "Emma agreed to it," adds the narrator, unnecessarily (350). Emma may be eventually badgered into self-knowledge, but it still remains unclear what the relationship between self-knowledge and truth amounts to, and whether inside and outside can be made to match in the way that Donwell's official stance implies they can.[32] It is curious, for example, that "truth" in this novel often emerges in the vicinity of another word—*nothing*—so as to suggest how very few people within its pages actually tell the truth.[33] We have already observed Frank Churchill's deceptive half-truth in Ford's: "Then I will speak the truth, and nothing suits me so well" (158). Jane Fairfax, too, dissembles under the sign of truth: "her account to her aunt contained nothing but truth, though there might be some truths not told" (130). That same construction returns again at the novel's climax, when Mr. Knightley tells Emma, "You hear nothing but truth from me" (338). On the evidence of Jane Fairfax, "nothing but truth" is not the same as the whole truth, and so we might wonder what truths Mr. Knightley is withholding even at this moment of self-revelation. In these passages, "nothing" marks the absence of the "somethings," the fantasies and plots and imaginative happenings, that have filled up Emma's days and have been shown, over and over, to be wrong. To say, as Mr. Knightley does, that he offers nothing but truth is to say that he does not deal in empty words but in a somehow contentless full disclosure: "I cannot make speeches, Emma. . . . If I loved you less, I might be able to talk about it more" (338).

D. A. Miller has written brilliantly about this kind of reserve as harboring a plentitude foreclosed on and yet available nonetheless for contemplation. For Miller, Emma's fullness and invention are distinct from the severity that the narrator imposes on herself.[34] My own reading of this novel's many "nothings," by contrast, is more melancholy, and interprets Emma herself as more fully interpellated by the joint authority of the narrator and Mr. Knightley. For to use "nothing" in this way is also to suggest that the truth itself *is* nothing—that the narrator's realist practice has here become so stringent that plot disappears entirely.[35] That is what Austen's earliest readers were sensing when they said that *Emma* had "no story." And so when Emma contemplates her future as Knightley's wife, her voice becomes indistinguishable from the narrator's masterful free indirect style: "What had she to wish for? Nothing, but to grow more worthy of him, whose intentions and judgment had been ever so superior to her own. Nothing, but that the lessons of her past folly might teach her humility and circumspection in future" (373). At the novel's opening Emma had wished for "impossible things" (7). Now she wishes for nothing.

It Led to Nothing

And so we return to Donwell Abbey, the "nothing" at the center of *Emma's* truth. In a novel where the "something" of plot arises from the gap between being and looking, Donwell Abbey, which is "just what it ought to be, and . . . looked what it was," cannot by definition have any story attached to it. It is about nothing—an ideal-type toward which Highbury, and the heroine, even the novel itself, may be seen to strive.

This desire is a powerful one, as we learn during the novel's only visit to Donwell. The strawberry-picking party itself begins in high spirits, but eventually the heat begins to tell, and the general goodwill deteriorates until finally Jane requests a tour of the grounds in order to escape Mrs. Elton's pestering:

> It was hot; and after walking some time over the gardens in a scattered, dispersed way, scarcely any three together, they insensibly followed one another to the delicious shade of a broad short avenue of limes, which stretching beyond the garden at an equal distance from the river, seemed the finish of the pleasure grounds.—*It led to nothing*; nothing but a view at the end over a low stone wall with high pillars, which seemed intended, in their erection, to give the appearance of an approach to the house, which never had been there. Disputable, however, as might be the taste of such a termination, it was in itself a charming walk, and the view which closed it extremely pretty. (283; emphasis added)

The "view" is of the Abbey-Mill farm, "with all its appendages of prosperity and beauty, its rich pastures, spreading flocks, orchard in blossom, and light column of smoke ascending" (283).[36] The orderly but "natural" arrangement, the unity-in-variety, even the gentle column of smoke—this composition is meant to suggest everything that good management might accomplish. It looks like an exercise in the picturesque, of the sort Austen might have learned from William Gilpin.[37] Yet the narrator's interpretation of the view goes well beyond the picturesque: "It was a sweet view—sweet to the eye and the mind. English verdure, English culture, English comfort, seen under a sun bright, without being oppressive" (283). As so often in this novel, it is impossible to say just who is speaking here. It seems to be one of those "interior monologues that somebody, although it is never clear whom, over-hears."[38] Despite the impression of universal agreement given by the free indirect style, it cannot really be the voice of the strawberry pickers them-selves, for it is too unlike their own experience. From where the strawberry pickers stand, the sun *is* oppressive. The heat is the reason for the general crossness and stickiness that has usurped the earlier gaiety, and the reason that the group has sought the shade of the lime avenue. Indeed, the characters insist on this: Emma tries to dissuade Jane Fairfax from walking home because "The heat . . . would be a danger" (285); "The heat was excessive," reports Frank Churchill a few minutes later (286). Yet the narrator, floating in an airier place, seems insensible to the temperature: while her characters remain trapped behind a wall on a path that leads nowhere, largely unmoved by what they are said to have seen, the narrator's confident voice invites the reader to a "view" that comes to stand for England itself.

With its dynamics of obstruction and transcendence the scene at Don-well recalls aspects of the sublime. Typically, sublime blockage accompanies a crisis, a felt discontinuity in the mind's relationship to the transcendent that is suddenly, in a moment of dialectical reversal, overcome by the mind's ability to apprehend such discontinuity: the subject stands in awe and emo-tional satisfaction before a supersensible destiny she discovers in herself.[39] At Donwell, that supersensible destiny is England itself, or rather an *idea* of England, a unity whose apprehension suggests the transformation of the par-ticular and contingent (this view, these trees, this sun) into the whole and necessary (English views, English trees, English sun). Thus culminates a proc-ess whereby everything associated with Donwell, from the Knightley brothers with their "true English style," to the view of "English culture" from the Abbey itself, has become associated with the nation's own self-understanding as a frictionless place where appearance matches reality, where things look like what they are, where what you see is what you get, where outside ("sweet to the eye") matches inside ("and the mind"). Such closure avoids the danger of endless interpretation that is understood to lurk everywhere that is not "England": in the commodity, in the romance, in the evidence of increasing rural desperation, in Emma's overactive imagination and in Harriet's overactive libido. For if the novel's insistently thematized temptation is that of endless interpretation, of making something out of nothing, then it is the synecdochic linkage of Donwell and England itself that puts a stop to such excessive signification by drawing a series of discrete impressions into a comprehensible whole, which is both "nothing" and also somehow everything that anyone might want.

The sublime has long been linked to secularization; as Thomas Weiskel noted some years ago, "the sublime revives as God withdraws from an immediate participation in the experience of men. . . . [It] is pervaded by the nostalgia and the uncertainty of minds involuntarily secular."[40] But this moment's expressive subjectivism does not simply bear a formal analogy to secularization. It *is* secularization, in the literal sense that what secures the meaning of this event, and licenses the confidence of the narrative voice, is the history of Donwell Abbey itself, removed from the hands of the church and turned over to private, worldly interest. Despite the profoundly ahistorical manner of its presentation, this sweet view is historical through and through. So that the entire sequence can "lead to nothing," however, the histories that have brought the Abbey into being in its present form must be rendered invisible, absorbed into a prospect that overwrites anything that might identify the Abbey as itself the product of a particular and contingent history. Instead, Donwell's sublime preserves and transforms the authority of the past so effectively that there seems to be nothing here at all, only a brightness as far as the eye can see.

Nothing But

Robert Aske had been a leader of the Pilgrimage of Grace, the rising in the north inspired by the first round of monastic dissolutions. Before his execution in 1537, he offered this description of England's new landscape: "the temple of God . . . pulled down, the ornaments and relics of the church unreverent[ly] used, the tombs and sepulchers of honourable and noble men pulled down and sold, none hospitality now in those places kept, but the farmers for the most part let . . . out the farms of the same houses to other farmers for lucre and advantage to themselves."[41] Aske focuses here on the destruction of an older, reciprocal economic order, which he describes as "hospitality." Now, after the dissolution, farmers are on their own: if they own something, they rent it out "for lucre."

This is not the view of things to which Austen's narrator invites us with her picture of Robert Martin's prosperous tenant farm, for the economic realities of Robert's success do not figure into the view. Yet the strain at Donwell is clear. Why insist that politics has no place here, that the sun is not oppressive but only bright, when in fact the characters clearly *are* oppressed, by the heat and by a great deal else besides? And why the nervousness of the grammar, with the initial "it led to nothing" revised to "nothing but a view," as if in implicit acknowledgment that a sentence leading nowhere will fail to satisfy? Syntactically, "nothing but a view" recalls the "nothing but truth" of which both Jane Fairfax and Mr. Knightley speak. And just as in that earlier case there are some truths that might not be spoken, so here there are some views that are not seen. The truth of Donwell may be a prospect of a reformed and improved England, but this scene offers not the cool nothing of a novel that has no plot, but a "hot" and vaguely uncomfortable supplement ("nothing but") that points in other directions: toward a different England characterized by "hospitality" rather than a rentier economy, toward stories not yet activated, toward possibilities foreclosed before they ever even registered, or perhaps simply toward a contingency of historical experience that can be made to conform to a providential narrative only through strategic acts of forgetting, reordering, and reforming.[42]

In *Emma,* Austen had set out to create a heroine "whom no one but myself will much like," and in that she largely succeeded.[43] Emma is "handsome, clever, and rich," as the novel's first sentence informs us, but she is also snobbish, self-satisfied, and manipulative (5). Her habit of imagining things that are not there binds these qualities together: she is an "imaginist" (263), a "fanciful, troublesome creature" (9) who will "never submit to any thing requiring industry and patience" (30), without "steadiness" (35) or application. When Emma is around, exclaims the bewildered Harriet Smith, "the strangest things do take place!" (60). And yet very little actually happens to Emma herself. Even by the standards of Austen heroines, her daily life is remarkably tedious.

She has never seen the sea, nor visited Box Hill; "She goes so seldom from home" and has "so few opportunities of dancing" (33, 206). And she has no friends. Ennui and loneliness are at the root of her manipulation of

Harriet and her cruelty to Miss Bates; perhaps desperation, too, at the equally daunting prospects of spinsterhood or a marriage that condemns her to adolescence. If it is a novel about nothing, then, that observation also means that it is a novel about what happens, or does not happen, when there is very little in your life.

Like the "nothing" that becomes a "nothing but," however, the debts of history have a way of reemerging. And the early years of the nineteenth century offered yet another example of the structuring power of Henry VIII and the events attached to his name. I refer to what became known as the "Delicate Investigation": the prince regent's long-standing effort to divorce his wife, Caroline of Brunswick. Kemble's 1811 version of *Henry VIII*, with the emotionally powerful Siddons as Katherine, was immediately understood in this context, with the prince regent as Henry, eager to rid himself of an older wife in order to move on to greener pastures. Jane Austen sided with Caroline: "Poor woman, I shall support her as long as I can, because she *is* a woman, & because I hate her Husband," she wrote in 1813.[44] And yet it was only a year later than the prince's librarian, James Stanier Clarke, let Austen know that the prince regent enjoyed her novels and would not take it amiss if the next one were dedicated to him. Austen at first refused, and yet when *Emma* appeared at the end of 1815 it bore the requested dedication: "To His Royal Highness the Prince Regent, this work is, by His Royal Highness's Permission Most Respectfully Dedicated, by His Royal Highness's Dutiful and Obedient Humble Servant, the Author." It is not clear why she changed her mind; Murray, her publisher, may have insisted on it. Still, one cannot help but notice a difference between Austen's own emotional sympathies and the professional advantages to be had from tethering her realist practice to the fate of a man currently reenacting the role of Henry VIII. Her grudging dedication points in two directions at once: toward a demonstration of how constraint and reform yield stylistic brilliance, and toward her own novel's tendency to throw off, as if by accident, hints of a fuller, more plentiful, more rambunctious world.

PART II

Sounding the Quiet

I esteem it above all things necessary to distinguish exactly the
Busines of Civil Government from that of Religion, and to settle the
just Bounds that lie between the one and the other.
　　　　　—John Locke, *A Letter Concerning Toleration* (1689)

IN THE SIXTEENTH and seventeenth centuries it seemed to many observers
that religious uniformity was the only cure for England's social and political turmoil. Thus the question for Queen Elizabeth I and her advisers "was
not whether there should be one religion in England, but what that religion
should be."[1] In the ensuing century the nation would try out several possibilities, backed by varying degrees of state power. Yet a trend remains visible:
Henry VIII executed 51 heretics, while Mary dispatched 284; during her long
reign, by contrast, Elizabeth executed only five people for heresy; and after
the Restoration, the religious policies introduced by Charles II aimed not
at the reformation or correction of Nonconformists but at their political
neutralization. As C. John Sommerville pithily phrases it, in a little more
than one hundred years "England moved from the extermination of heresy
to the harassment of nonconformity."[2] The conceptual shift from "heresy"
to "nonconformity" is a profound one: it makes dissent a *political* rather than
a theological category. The various government acts of the Restoration period
thus made religion a matter of state power even as they tacitly acknowledged
that national religious conformity was no longer a practicable goal in
England.[3] After the Restoration, England was a collection of more-or-less
private believers (Nonconformist, Catholic, and Anglican), held together by
a state apparatus forced willy-nilly to recognize their existence.

Voltaire's eighteenth-century observation, quoted at the beginning of
this book, that "If there were only one religion in England, there would be
danger of despotism, if there were only two they would cut each other's
throats; but there are thirty, and they live in peace," actually shares a good
deal with the Elizabethan demand for religious uniformity.[4] Both take for
granted the modern idea that you ought to be able to choose your religion.
The difference is that before 1660, religious difference was externalized:
England existed in a religiously diverse world but did not understand itself as
a place of religious diversity; by the mid-eighteenth century, in comparison,

religious difference had become internal to the nation itself, and even received the credit for England's increasing global and financial success.

There is no better symbol of the transition from absolutism to a modern arrangement of state power, economic growth, and religious diversity than two ships that sailed from Holland to England at the end of the 1680s. The first carried Prince William of Orange at the head of the biggest armada Europe had yet seen: 463 vessels, 40,000 men, and 4,000 horses sailed through the English Channel in November 1688 and landed at Torbay. By the middle of December William was in London, and by the end of January he was king. His ship, full of statesmen and printing presses and backed by armies and weapons, brought the modern state to England. The second ship, a few months later, brought the Enlightenment: it carried the philosopher John Locke and the new Queen Mary.

For William and for the Dutch merchants who supported him, the invasion of England was a means to strike a blow at France and Louis XVI, whose policies threatened to destroy the Dutch overseas trading system. From a European perspective, then, the invasion was a delicate matter of trade, finance, and war, in which religious alliances were merely instrumental. William needed Protestant Hanoverian troops to guard the Dutch Republic's eastern flank against a threatened invasion from France, yet since the Dutch trading empire depended on good relations with Catholic Austria and Spain, he could not risk having his invasion of England interpreted as an attempt to save Protestantism from the predations of a Catholic English king. This delicate situation led to a Janus-faced foreign policy during the months leading up to the invasion: William simultaneously assured English Anglicans that he was committed to a state church and would not tolerate Catholics (in other words, that he was fighting a religious war), and assured continental Europe that he was committed to Catholic toleration (in other words, that he was *not* fighting a religious war).[5] Thus a revolution widely interpreted inside England as a religious transformation appeared, from a European perspective, to be a matter of power and trade in which religion was an inconvenience to be neutralized or a tool to be used.

These differing interpretations of the same event are worth dwelling on for a moment. As a theory, secularism motivates discourses of human rights, religious toleration, and the separation of church and state; it is the thing that is at issue whenever the courts debate prayer, evolution, veils in public schools, crèches on the statehouse lawn, or evangelism in prisons. Although secularism of this sort tends to dominate much current debate, its roots must be sought elsewhere: before theories of secularism, there were *practices* of the secular—for example in early modern Europe, more concerned with state-craft than with "new ideas." Intellectual developments tend to lag behind cultural and political ones: in large part, the secular was something felt and experienced before it was articulated.

So too with toleration, which in the case of England became official doctrine with the Toleration Act, issued in May 1689. The act, wrote Gilbert Burnet, "gave the King great content. He in his own opinion always thought, that Conscience was God's Province, and that it ought not to be imposed on. . . . [H]e restrained the heat of some, who were proposing severe Acts against Papists. He made them apprehend the advantage, which that would give the *French*, to alienate all the Papists of *Europe* from us."[6] Burnet thus began with a familiar argument about freedom of conscience, but interna-tional diplomacy quickly dominated the discussion. Toleration as England came to experience it was thus bound intimately to matters of statecraft. This is a good example of how the enterprise of toleration involves things other than religion, even entailing, in this case, the analytical separation of a nation (France) and a religion (Catholicism).

Some historians interpret the rise of toleration as a tacit admission by the seventeenth-century state that it could not police its own subjects. It was an answer, in other words, to the breakup Donne mourned in "Anatomy of the World" when he wrote that "all coherence" was "gone."[7] In the absence of social uniformity, religion had become tribal and blinkered; state-sanctioned toleration, born of the desire to be free from interference about matters that ought to be private, was the best solution. And the primary practical concern was how far such toleration could be stretched before national unity began to fray.

There is truth in this account. Yet toleration did not simply arise from below; it was also imposed from above. It was a *tool* of the modern nation-state itself—and political power was central to its development, both at its point of origin and in its continued maintenance.[8] The creation of politicians and statesmen committed to stability, trade, and the management of popula-tions, toleration was not automatically the sign of an enlightened state, but it *was* a sign of a confident one. And so the new King William, with one eye turned outward toward the networks of mutual hostility and mutual dependence that had been redrawing the map of Europe, recognized the advantages of limited internal dissent. The Toleration Act did not protect heterodoxy for its own sake, but for the greater good of the state; rather than a breakdown of social control, it was really a new form of social control, a way to ensure what John Dryden, writing a few years earlier, had called "Common quiet."[9]

Given these origins in raison d'état arguments, it is not surprising that toleration has never quite managed to realize its announced intentions. Statesmen are less bothered than philosophers by contradiction, so it is no real wonder that religious tolerance would come to rest on a larger intolerance—of Jews, Muslims, Catholics, freethinkers, or atheists. One or another group will fall outside the bounding line, wherever that line is drawn. Quiet, as Coleridge's speaker notes in "Frost at Midnight," can vex meditation as well as enable it: "'Tis calm indeed! So calm, it disturbs / And vexes meditation with its strange / And extreme silentness" (lines 8–10). The following three chapters of this book pursue the idea that extreme quiet can itself be a form of vexation. This may seem a paradox by the time that Coleridge is writing, but its origin is to be found in the settlement with modernity marked by the Glorious Revolution of 1688/89 and the latitudinarian Anglican consensus it ushered in. Toleration was the primary mechanism of "common quiet" in the aftermath of Reform, and yet its vexing and minoritizing logic tends to amplify rather than lessen any disturbances in the atmosphere. To insist on quiet is actually to turn up the volume, as we shall see first in a canonical romantic poem by Coleridge, then in a debate in Walter Scott's novels about how to tell the history of Jacobitism, and finally in James Hogg's anticolonial novel of the Scottish Covenanters. All three writers show that what seems an irony is actually intrinsic to toleration's logic: it *creates* minorities.

CHAPTER 4

Coleridge at Sea: "Kubla Khan"
and the Invention of Religion

I found myself all afloat.
—Samuel Taylor Coleridge, *Biographia Literaria*, Chapter 10 (1817)

In the Preface attached to "Kubla Khan" when it was finally published in 1816, Samuel Taylor Coleridge wrote that he took an "anodyne" and then fell asleep in his chair as he was reading some lines from a seventeenth-century travel book called *Purchas His Pilgrimage*. He reported that he "continued for about three hours in a profound sleep, at least of the external senses, during which time he had the most vivid confidence, that he could not have composed less than from two to three hundred lines; . . . without any sensation or consciousness of effort."[1] When he woke up, he "instantly and eagerly" started writing down the lines given him in his dream. Before long, though, a "person on business from Porlock" interrupted him, and when he returned to his desk all that remained was a "vague and dim recollection of the general purpose of the vision" together with a few scattered images.

The likely fabrication of this entire episode notwithstanding, "Kubla Khan" has long stood as *the* archetypal example of the visionary imagination interrupted by the business of mundane life. The goal of this chapter is to reconstruct the import and meaning of this event, in particular its appeal to Purchas as the context of its visionary dreaming. The Purchas encounter, I shall argue, is an intervention in the two liberal models of secularism bequeathed by the eighteenth century: toleration on the one hand, and on the other the literary interpretations that would eventually yield textual criticism of the Bible and the so-called Higher Criticism. The first of these is quintessentially English, the second quintessentially German. By turning to Purchas, Coleridge avoided both options, reaching back instead to the seventeenth century, when the definition of "religion" was still in flux, and the settled complacency of the post-1688 consensus had not yet taken hold. "Kubla Khan" invites an interpretation of its speaker as a kind of visionary, trying to rebuild Kubla's dome within his soul or mind. But the medium for that rebuilding is a song sung by an Abyssinian maid, and a reading of Purchas's comments on Abyssinia reveals not an idealized utopia but a textual paradise made up of books that encompass all the religions of the world. Thus an interpretation of "Kubla Khan" in the context of the whole of Purchas's text—its mission and development, rather than simply its imagery— will reveal a different picture of religion, one worldly rather than other-worldly, less a floating dome than a room full of books. And thus the poem's final image, of a prophetic singer encircled by a fearful and uncomprehending crowd, is in my interpretation not an endorsement of the visionary mode but rather an anticipation of the kind of misreading that characterizes the liberal tradition. Thinkers in this tradition, from Locke to Habermas, stress exactly what the 1688 consensus established: that it is necessary to "settle the just Bounds that lie between" religion and the state. That penchant for boundary drawing, I hope to show, misrecognizes the very thing it would claim to manage.

A Word About Politics

Chapter 10 of the *Biographia Literaria* (1817) is mostly taken up with Coleridge's retrospective account of his efforts twenty years earlier to construct an independent literary career. In 1797 this was a perilous business. Trying to drum up support for his short-lived periodical, *The Watchman*, Coleridge encountered the same kind of obsessive focus on business that had supposedly derailed "Kubla Khan." The first potential subscriber, a "rigid Calvinist . . . in whom length was so predominant over breadth that he might almost have been borrowed for a foundry-poker," told him that he did not have time to read anything except the Bible. The second, a Manchester cotton merchant, asked for a "bill or invoice," glanced at it, crumpled it up, and "without another syllable retired into his counting-house."[2] Together, the Calvinist and cotton merchant anticipate the kind of argument Weber was to make some one hundred years later about the secularizing spirit of the Protestant ethic. In such a world, Coleridge seems to assert, making a living from writing was impossible. Earlier in the chapter he had already advised aspiring writers to sell their copyrights, for it was simply too financially and emotionally risky to be both author and publisher: "fifty pounds and ease of mind are of more real advantage to a literary man, than the chance of five hundred with the certainty of insult and degrading anxieties" (243). Anxious to present his youthful self as more than a hack waiting for the next royalty check, Coleridge writes that he eventually disclaimed all political interests and retired to a drafty cottage at Nether Stowey in December 1796. Anxious and depressed, the only breadwinner in a crowded house that included his pregnant and unhappy wife, Sarah, he turned more frequently to laudanum.[3] "I saw plainly," he writes, "that literature was not a profession by which I could expect to live" (250).

Coleridge's plan at Nether Stowey was to devote himself "to poetry and to the study of ethics and psychology" (250). Yet politics intruded here, too, in the shape of problematic friends. By July 1797 Charles Lamb and John Thelwall were staying at Nether Stowey, and William and Dorothy Wordsworth had moved into a nearby cottage. Coleridge's anxiety about what he called "party zeal," and especially about the radical Thelwall's presence among them, reached its doubtful apotheosis in the famous "Spy Nozy" episode, during which a Home Office spy tailed the group and finally reported that although they were not in fact scouting the coastline for a possible French invasion site, they were nevertheless "a mischievous gang of disaffected Englishmen."[4]

Coleridge's uneven relationship with the truth has received plenty of attention, but I am more interested here in the different models of literary activity that the Coleridge of 1817 is retrospectively constructing for his younger self. To be a "mere literary man" (278) at this moment was to be a partisan of one side or another, and so to "pursue literature as a trade" (274). This brought him too near to the spirit of capitalism, not to mention too near the partisan spirit of the times. To study "poetry, . . . ethics and psychology," by contrast, was to renounce such immediate concerns, and thus avoid both the countinghouse and the prison house: "Our talk ran most upon books," writes Coleridge of his rambles with his friends, "and we were perpetually desiring each other to look at this, and to listen to that; but [the spy] could not catch a word about politics" (254). Then, after a rapid history of religious conflict during the seventeenth century, the *Biographia* passage culminates with an invocation of a decidedly depoliticized model of institutional toleration. Coleridge celebrates 1688/89 as the beginning of a new peace: "A wise Government followed; and the established Church became, and now is, not only the brightest example, but our best and only sure bulwark, of toleration! The true and indispensable bank against a new inundation of persecuting zeal—*Esto perpetua* [May it last forever]!" (257).

Despite appearances to the contrary, there is an internal logic to the way that Coleridge runs together religious history, Spinoza, the French Revolution, and institutional toleration. But we need to look back again at the latitudinarian consensus of 1688 in order to understand why one might tell the story in this fashion. Once in power, William largely left the care of the Anglican Church to his wife, whose preferred inner circle included men of formidable learning and liberal inclination. John Locke, Gilbert Burnet (like Locke an exile living in Holland during the years of James II), and John Tillotson (the new archbishop of Canterbury), together with Edward Stillingfleet, Samuel Clark, and Richard Bentley, made up the intellectual core of English latitudinarianism. Despite some important differences of opinion,[5] their commitment to reason and their connections with Cambridge aligned them with the generally Newtonian sensibility that would come to dominate intellectual discussion in the early years of the eighteenth century. They shared a tone and a manner, one dedicated to intellectual and social moderation and comfortable and successful within the structures of Whig patronage.

Convinced that Enlightenment and Anglicanism were fellow travelers, these men found themselves in the right place at the right time, at the "conjunction of political crisis and intellectual revolution, buoyed up by the stimulating social atmosphere provided by swarms of refugees, pamphlet wars, coffee houses and clubs, and the international web of the republic of letters."[6] Reinforcing positions already established by the Royal Society, they aimed to preserve a civilized public against sectarianism and enthusiasm of all kinds, not only Catholic and absolutist "mystery" but also Puritan antinomianism and the rumblings of Continental republicanism.[7] Though there remained a radical Enlightenment culture (deists, freethinkers, republicans) off to one side, the English Enlightenment was in general a more moderate affair than its Continental cousins. A broadly liberal consensus came to power with William, and after some back-and-forth, secured its hegemony following

George I's ascension in 1714. Unlike those in other European nations, therefore, England's progressive thinkers were establishment rather than oppositional figures. The post-1688 Anglican Church and the philosophical Enlightenment were thus not merely intellectual compatriots; there was a stronger, mutually reinforcing unity of purpose in their outlook, aims, and sensibilities.[8]

It is hardly a surprise, then, that the Toleration Act was a cautious document. It permitted Dissenters to worship in their own meetinghouses, so long as they were registered and kept the doors unlocked. Dissenting ministers still had to subscribe to some of the Thirty-Nine Articles; all had to swear loyalty to the king and deny transubstantiation, and the civil disabilities established in the 1660s still applied to them. Although something like half a million citizens had legal protection for the first time, then, others, particularly Catholics, remained outside the protection of the law. The very moderation of the law, which institutionalized what Roy Porter nicely calls an "unshakeable commitment to . . . freedom, Protestantism, patriotism and prosperity," meant that even conservative High Churchmen would henceforth be playing by rules established by Whigs and latitudinarians.[9]

Having brought matters up to the present day, having drawn a firm line between literary-philosophical talk and political sedition, and having finally described the established church's policy of toleration as a bulwark and bank against the floods of persecuting zeal now emanating from France, Coleridge strangely renarrates his retreat to Stowey: "I retired to a cottage in Somersetshire," he writes, "and devoted my thoughts and studies to the foundations of religion and morals" (258). The first time around, he had written of his desire to study poetry, ethics, and psychology. Now, after the Spy-Nozy episode indicates that poetry was too easily mistaken for the radical Enlightenment, he turns to engineering: to foundations, bulwarks, and embankments. Yet he finds none of these, but rather an ocean of textual sources that immediately overwhelms him:

> Here I found myself all afloat. Doubts rushed in; broke upon me "from the fountains of the great deep," and fell "from the windows of heaven." The fontal truths of natural religion and the books of Revelation alike contributed to the flood; and it was long ere my ark touched on an Ararat, and rested. (258)

This extraordinary passage, resonant with the account of the flood in Genesis, raises immediate questions about the strength of the earthworks that Coleridge had thrown up only two paragraphs earlier. Coleridge's biographer Richard Holmes refers to this moment as a "crisis in his imaginative powers."[10] In order to protect himself from the charge of sedition Coleridge had removed poetry to its own apolitical domain: the spy could not catch "a word about politics." Now sequestered, poetry was no longer available to aid the search for the foundations of religion and morals, nor, consisting as it did entirely of the limited latitude of the established church, could it be part of the bulwark against persecuting zeal. This opens Coleridge to the flood of biblical criticism that had been shaking foundations and overflowing embankments, at least in elite intellectual circles, for a generation. Suddenly, the prosaic institutional toleration of the Anglican Church looked rather feeble.

No wonder Coleridge found himself afloat. Walking with his friends and speaking of poetry looked like French Jacobinism; the prosy toleration of the official English church looked too much like business; and the floodwaters of textual criticism were rising. And no wonder, then, that he writes with evident relief, "While my mind was thus perplexed, by a gracious providence for which I can never be sufficiently grateful, the generous and munificent patronage of Mr Josiah, and Mr Thomas Wedgwood enabled me to finish my education in Germany" (262). We know, of course, what finishing his education in Germany meant for Coleridge. It meant Kant. It meant Eichhorn's lectures on the Bible, and the historicist tradition of Michaelis and Herder that stood behind those lectures.[11] And it meant reattaching the historical and poetic qualities of scripture (the tradition of Herder) to questions of epistemology and morals by means of a transcendental argument (the tradition of Kant). It meant, in short, a search for "foundations," theoretically robust, historically informed, and poetically sensitive, that the prosaic English model of institutional toleration apparently could not provide.[12]

Could I Revive Within Me

As Coleridge knew all too well, scripture changed in the eighteenth century. Especially in Germany, a new method of reading the Bible as a form of literature definitively shifted textual interpretation onto the historical-critical ground now familiar to literary scholars. This story—of a new method of biblical interpretation and its gradual infiltration of elite and middle-brow literate culture throughout the North Atlantic—is a complex one.[13] But of the many and tangled strands of this intellectual web, I wish to emphasize here the unique way that German philosopher-theologians like Herder, Michaelis, and Eichhorn knit together historicism and universalism, two structures of feeling traditionally at odds with one another, by means of what they called "poetry." Freed from the weight of interpretive tradition, the Bible in Herder's hands could be received as its first readers and hearers received it, a record of the idioms, styles, and thought patterns of its time and place of origin. Following this impulse, Michaelis, Eichhorn, and eventually Coleridge learned to treat scriptural texts historically and culturally—as examples of the literature of a Semitic people, to be sympathetically interpreted according to their particular mind and spirit.[14] This is the dream of "Kubla Khan" as the poem draws near its lyrical conclusion:

> A damsel with a dulcimer
> In a vision once I saw
> It was an Abyssinian maid
> And on her dulcimer she play'd,
> Singing of Mount Abora.
> Could I revive within me
> Her symphony and song . . . (lines 37–43)

On the one hand, such "revivals" undertaken within the mind of the sympathetic interpreter undermined the uniqueness of Scripture and humanized its interpretation, shifting the focus from a timeless message of salvation to the conditions of religious experience and the historical circumstances that informed the texts. On the other hand, this method produced a Christianity that was once again universal. The Old Testament might be only the literary expression of a particular people and a particular time, freshly revealed now as a historical document pieced together "from a diversity of culturally uprooted mythologies." But this in turn positioned Christianity as "the culmination and expression of the whole range of human religious demands."[15] As Coleridge's speaker imagines it, his internal revival would allow him to rebuild Kubla's dome, but now in a visionary mode, in the air, where all could see it. Christianity was the true universalism—not because it was true while other religions were false, but because it recognized and synthesized into a grander whole the inner truth those other religions contained.

Of course, it is hard not to be skeptical about a solution like this one. Rather than facing the facts—that the Bible was a human document, written long after the events it claimed to describe, and full of inconsistencies—the school of Herder, Michaelis, and Eichhorn declared that the facts did not matter very much. Whether Moses really wrote the Pentateuch, or Noah's flood really covered the whole earth, whether John of Patmos was really John the Evangelist, or whether either of them were the disciple whom Jesus loved best—these things mattered less than the visionary character of the accounts in which they appeared, which expressed and exemplified a kind of truth that surpassed questions of empirical evidence. This opened the door to a certain kind of relativism but extracted from it not a radical *philosophe*-style critique of priestcraft but a new and hugely influential form of Christian universalism. By making faith and culture largely coterminous, the mythological critics preserved both.[16] They got to be in the intellectual vanguard and yet felt no existential threat.

There is no question that we can read "Kubla Khan" in exactly this context; forty years ago Elinor Shaffer did so, and brilliantly. For Shaffer the poem was a poetic investigation of the conditions of religious experience, a meditation on how to handle a new set of intellectual tools that were historicist and relativist on the one hand, and timeless and universal on the other. She reconstructs the argument of "Kubla Khan" this way: to be asleep in the West is not to be nodding over our hymnbooks but to be awake to new kinds of spiritual possibilities. And this is why it finally does not matter whether Coleridge's dream actually happened, or whether he was where he said he was, or whether he was really interrupted by a man from Porlock. Such literal-mindedness is exactly what the new biblical criticism pushes aside: the vagueness of the whole "person from Porlock" episode is a performative instance of exactly this new intellectual reality. The visionary sleep of "Kubla Khan," in other words, *just is* the condition of religious experience and biblical truth in a historicizing age.[17]

In this short set of passages in the heart of the *Biographia Literaria*, then, amid typically Coleridgean digression, pedantry, and self-doubt, we encounter a basic question about the fate of British romanticism and the narrative of European modernity: will it be English (institutional, liberal) or will it be German (philosophical, conservative)? That apparent choice has structured, even at many removes, most of the criticism of the era's literature. Less remarked on is that both of these possibilities depend on a secularization narrative: in the English case, that Anglican latitudinarianism, officially born

in 1688 but with roots in the middle of the seventeenth century, can be
secularized sufficiently to promote tolerance beyond its own sectarian genealogy; in the German case, that the spiritual rewriting of religious tradition will
prove sufficiently capacious for all. However we choose, then, one thing
seems certain: the future will be secular.

And perhaps it will be, but for a twenty-first-century reader trying to
make sense of the continuing salience of religion, that choice seems to foreclose on a great deal of contemporary experience. Is there a third path? I
believe that there is, but it requires first that we return to Purchas in order to
reconstruct a different, seventeenth-century discourse of religion as neither
Lockean belief nor Herderian spirituality but rather as an always-already-
worldly phenomenon.

Addiction

I know not by what naturall inclination . . . (Purchas, "To the
Reader")

If Coleridge did indeed read Purchas's introductory note ("To the Reader")
when he turned to his book in late 1797 or early 1798, he would have found
there a relevant example of the tension between the business of literature and
the business of life that occupied him in Chapter 10 of the *Biographia Literaria* and, supposedly, in the Preface to "Kubla Khan." Samuel Purchas was an
Anglican minister, first in Essex and later in London. In his leisure time he
collected and organized lengthy travel narratives, which he assembled into
two massive, and very popular, books. While Purchas notes in a somewhat
perfunctory way that his researches showcase the superiority of Protestant
Christianity, one might nevertheless wonder why a minister should devote so
much time and energy to studying other religions. Indeed Purchas himself
seems rather uncertain about this. "Being," he writes in his address to the
reader, "I know not by what naturall inclination, addicted to the studie of
Historie, my heart would sometimes object a selfe-love, in following my
private delights in that kind. At last, I resolved to turne the pleasures of my
studies into studious paines, that others might againe, by delightful studie,
turn my paines into their pleasure."[18] The faintly masturbatory crossing of
pleasure with pain may look back to Spenser, but in the context of a self-
confessed "addiction" it also looks forward to Coleridge.

When he says that he is "addicted to history" Purchas means that he has given himself to it fully and unreservedly, that he is attached to history to the point of surrendering his freedom, and that this inclination is itself something of a mystery to him. This is the standard meaning of "addiction" by the late seventeenth century, when the word completed its transition from legal discourse—in Roman law an *addicens* is one who authoritatively transfers a thing, and to be addicted to someone was to be legally made over to him—to a description of a subjective condition that implies a weakness of the will: one *gives oneself* over rather than *being given* over. Although addiction was always opposed to free will, then, it was now opposed in a new way: from being bound to another through no will of one's own, to being bound to one's own base desires because of insufficient willpower.[19] There is something immoderate or compulsive about addiction in this sense, "an ouermoche addiction to priuate appetites," in the words of the *OED*'s initial 1532 citation of the new term.

This gradual shift from external to internal bondage, and from legal to moral constraint, mirrors other transitions in the early modern period, among them those of religion itself. This is the transition discussed earlier in this book: that "religion" in our modern sense depends on a new understanding of what it might mean to "believe" in God. In a departure from medieval conceptions of "belief" as a relationship of trust, belief in sixteenth-century Europe took on an increasingly epistemological charge. The question of religion came more and more to depend on what people believed and whether those beliefs were true, while the thing called "religion" became the sum total of the propositions in which one professed belief.[20] Because salvation meant believing in the correct package of propositions, it became increasingly important for believers to reflexively grasp what it was they were professing to believe. Accordingly, the content of those beliefs was construed epistemologically, as a body of information about where salvation was to be found. Subjected to tests, confessions, documentation, and other mechanisms of control, comparison, and standardization, modern religion entered the domain of modern knowledge.

These discursive transformations of both religion and addiction are best understood against the background of an epistemological revolution that takes in Cartesian dualism, the development of modern science, and the efforts of reformers and counter-reformers to make religion into an object of cognition. Intellectual historians describe this change in various ways—Stephen Toulmin calls it the "quest for certainty," Charles Taylor calls it "disembedding," and Michael McKeon terms it "explicitation"—but all agree that something fundamental shifted in the western European mind, first at the elite level and then, gradually and as part and parcel of widespread political and social transformations, across a wider section of the populace.[21] We can call it, as Taylor does elsewhere, *reflexivity*: the idea that mental states (beliefs, feelings, attitudes) are accompanied by their own construal, so that we take up a third-person perspective in relation to them.

Taylor describes this change in largely intellectual terms, but it plays out most significantly in institutional and historical settings. In England, the process of reflexivity did not reach its culmination until the events of 1688/89 and the installation of an official state policy that beliefs were things to be tolerated. After 1688, the Anglican Church became a player in a political field rather than a definer of that field. Though the bishops retained their traditional landed independence, they increasingly found themselves split along party lines and involved in current political debates.[22] And though religion remained central to the nation's identity, the increased attention to "religion" as an entity in itself pointed not to the political strength of the church but to its developing weakness. All political partisans, from Tories like Francis Atterbury to Whigs like Benjamin Hoadly, addressed the question of religion with a self-consciousness indicative of its new legal and conceptual footing; "religion" had become an object of attention, of debate, and of knowledge. From now on, it was a "matter to be defined, limited, or encouraged—by powers of another character."[23]

This need to be explicit about "religion" affected not only the church's political fate but also its internal sense of itself. Whig centrism altered the look and feel of religion in England. Thanks to the Toleration Act, the government licensed 2,536 meetinghouses in the years between 1691 and 1710. The act also made it difficult for parish constables and churchwardens to enforce attendance, and the simple fact that on a given Sunday parishioners might choose to go to a different church—or, perhaps, not to go to church at all—helped to drive home the fact of religious diversity at an everyday level. Anglican clergy now had to face, as never before, the reality of religious competition. Freshly conscious of its audience, and of needing to persuade rather than coerce them, the church began to emphasize pastoral training, pastoral care, and the orthodoxy of the universities.[24] This gave rise in turn to a different kind of religious expertise, what Mark Goldie calls "a new type of churchmanship which sought to seize the pastoral initiative" within a diversified religious landscape.[25] As newspaper editors were discovering at

about the same time, authority took a different form once the concept of an
audience began to matter.

Historians of the period have described a noticeable uptick in lay piety
and an "astonishing market for devotional literature," much of it based on
the Book of Common Prayer.[26] As the century progressed, the Methodist,
Evangelical, and Sunday School movements absorbed and fostered much of
this popular piety. Yet modern-day historians, like their eighteenth-century
clerical counterparts, struggle to get an accurate picture of the religious landscape of the age. They can track print runs and sales figures, perhaps, and to
a certain extent the numbers of bodies in the pews. But how were those
bodies spending their time away from church? And even *in* church, what
were they thinking about? What did they believe? These questions achieved
new visibility and new import in the aftermath of the Toleration Act, when
English religion took on its distinctively modern character as something that
people "have"—and thus what they might potentially lose. Defining it was
hugely important, yet the new belief-based descriptions turned upon internal
states that were impossible to verify. The potential gap between the positioning and disposal of the body (increasingly the domain of the state) and the
contents of the mind (increasingly the domain of "religion") thus created a
new kind of conflict. We might say that the body was secularized in the sense
that its needs, behaviors, and performances increasingly became the business
of differentiated social spheres: the state, the economy, the medical professions, and so on.

Finally, although the epistemological turn may have made early modern
religious belief more secure (less relational and less public, more cognitive
and more private), it also created the new problem of other people's beliefs.
We might think of this as an international relations problem, in contrast to
the national and pastoral problem of what was happening in local congregations. For if belief named a set of ideas that might be false rather than a
participation in something tacitly known to be true, and beliefs became
things that *other people had*, then it was a short step to understanding alternative beliefs as different religion*s*, in the plural, to be ranged against the "true
religion" (that is, Christianity). This suggests a methodology for handling
the plethora of information that travelers and explorers were bringing back.
The new science of religion could adopt a methodology like that of the
natural sciences, making comparative religion possible for the first time.
Newly equipped with qualities understood to belong properly to it, religion
thus became an "outsider's term," part and parcel of a developing science of

religion designed to accord with the new natural sciences.[27] A fourfold division of the world's religions into Christianity, Judaism, Islam, and Idolatry became the standard taxonomy.[28]

When Purchas speaks of his "addiction" to history, the word anticipates all of these changes. To begin with, the shift toward cognitive definitions of religion accentuates a growing conflict between mind and body widely distributed across early modern intellectual culture. If addiction was once a discourse concerned with the ownership of the body, in the early modern period it became the site of a contest between mind and body: to be addicted was to be in thrall not to someone else but to one's own body, and even more, to the weakness of one's own will. Thus, although the automatic connection between addiction and drug use did not enter medical discourse until the early twentieth century, its possibility was circulating much earlier: the *OED* lists 1716 as the earliest mention of substance addiction in this sense, citing a doctor's "too great Addiction to the Bottle"—a physical bondage that signifies a moral failure.

We can use this medical sense of addiction to open up another kind of reading as well: not just the developing conflict between mind and body, but the developing conflict between home and abroad, center and periphery, religion and religions—conflicts that can be mapped, though none too neatly, onto the mind/body opposition. As Nigel Leask and John Barrell have pointed out, opium use by romantic writers like Coleridge and Thomas De Quincey was a technology for delivering panoramic knowledge: exotic, well traveled, and powerful, but never separable from its material conditions. In "Kubla Khan," a travel book carried into a dream generates a poem that cannot be written down because it is interrupted by business. That dialectic of unity and breakdown, of dreams and business, is central to the experience of opium, itself both commodity and conduit of a composite Orient.[29] And if "Kubla Khan" is a celebration of the synthetic mind of the romantic artist/ genius, able to grasp all at once the basic and underlying unity of the fragments of human experience, it also documents that fragmentation itself. Opium is a release from the world of business, and it *is* the world of business. No wonder that dynamic sometimes yielded not a visionary dream but a nightmare. As Coleridge himself put it in *The Pains of Sleep*,

The third night, when my own loud scream
Had waked me from the fiendish dream,

O'ercome with sufferings strange and wild,
I wept as I had been a child.[30]

The opium context of "Kubla Khan," then, reminds us that long before
the narcopolitics of our own moment, addiction was a global phenomenon.
Beneath the poem's superficial poetry versus business contrast is a deeper
one, born of colonialism, travel, international finance, and the quest for certainty, or what Coleridge called "foundations," in the midst of it all. "Addiction" names the anxieties and confusions of a modern subject before whom
the world was opening up in frightening but intoxicating ways.

Religions Gone Global

I here bring Religion from Paradise to the Arke, and thence follow
her round about the World, and (for her sake) observe the World it
selfe, with the several Countries and peoples therein. (Purchas, "To
the Reader")

I stress this point because the presence of opium in "Kubla Khan" allegorizes
something plotted more clearly by Purchas's own book and the manner of its
arrangement, with its own complex connections to the loss and recovery of
autonomy, to sleeping, pleasure, and pain. The poem's visionary or mythic
character, that is to say, responds not only to the world of "business" but
also to a central but little-noticed quality of Purchas's own text: it was the
first important English book to use the word "religions," in the plural, in its
title.

The book's full title is this: *Purchas His pilgrimage. Or Relations of the
World and the Religions Observed in All Ages and Places Discovered, from the
Creation unto This Present.* If this title is not daunting enough, a glance at
the table of contents immediately confirms how futile it would be to read the
book straight through. Even the first and shortest edition of 1613 runs to
752 pages; the fourth edition of 1626 is "much enlarged with additions, and
illustrated with mappes through the whole worke"—it is over 1,000 pages
long.[31] Perhaps such unrestrained growth is to be expected from an early
seventeenth-century text that aims to describe "all ages and places
discovered."

Yet it is not merely the sheer size of Purchas's undertaking that makes it such a daunting read. Purchas believed himself to be doing something new, "an enterprise never yet (to my knowledge) by any, in any language, attempted."[32] In pursuit of this ambition, the book's lengthy subtitle concludes with a significant addendum: *With briefe descriptions of the countries, nations, states, discoveries, private and publike customes, and the most remarkable rarities of nature, or humane industrie, in the same.* "Religion," Purchas assures the reader, "is my more proper aime."[33] Yet the subtitle promises nothing less than the whole world. Or rather, it promises "the world and the religions." Although he is far from clear here, Purchas seems to mean that while religions, in the plural, can be analytically folded into culture (which he like most other seventeenth-century writers calls "customes"), religion, in the singular, cannot. True religion may involve the mind not the body, but it is for that very reason relatively inaccessible to the travel writer. Most of Purchas's survey therefore betrays little interest in what the many denizens of the globe "believe." Their various religions are largely indistinguishable from the detailed, indeed almost endless histories and contemporary cultural practices that Purchas calls, simply, "the world." This world, in all its variety, is the addiction of Purchas's leisure hours, while the true religion of Christianity remains his professional responsibility—his business. From this perspective, the opium dream of "Kubla Khan" simply follows Purchas's own half realization that addiction and true religion, like leisure and business, pleasure and pain, arrive on the scene together.

For true religion needs propping up. Everywhere he turns, Purchas sees divine judgment against the sorry state of Western Christianity. His account of Mohammed, for instance, stresses the schisms that afflicted Christianity, the "Soule thereof being . . . torne and rent by the Sects and Heresies of the Arrians, Donatists, Nestorians, Pelagians, and others" (202). The rise of Islam is consequently a "secret and just judgement of GOD" (193). And Purchas is less than impressed with "not-preaching Ministers, especially in Countrievillages" who "onely read the service, and never studie for more." "[E]ven the Heathen shall rise up in judgment against them," he writes, for his literary pilgrimage shows that most of the world's religions involve the doing of many things.[34] In the passage that Coleridge was supposedly reading when he fell asleep, for example, Purchas reports that Cublai Can owns 10,000 horses, "as white as snow." "According to the direction of his Astrologers or Magicians, he . . . spendeth and powreth forth with his owne hands the Milke of these Mares in the Aire, and on the Earth, to give drinke to the spirits and Idols which they worship" (350). Perhaps the spectacle of these bizarre "customes" taking place elsewhere will inspire the sleeping guardians of the true religion at home: "Likewise our Ministers may bee incited unto all godly labours in their function of preaching the Gospell, seeing [as] otherwise, for outward and bodily ceremonies, the Turkes and Jewes in their manifold devotions . . . would convince us of Idlenesse" (2). "I subscribe with hand and practise to our Liturgie, but not to such Lethargie," he concludes (2).

Thus does Samuel Purchas confront, and half realize, the degree to which true religion requires religions. His title pages, in their almost endless taxonomy and their range from Asia to Africa to the Americas, implicitly come to terms with this new historical reality. Like almost all of his contemporaries, Purchas finds that atheism is unnatural and religion ubiquitous. Religion is "the soule of the world," the "law of Nature having written in the practice of all men (as we here in the particulars doe shew) the profession of some Religion."[35] And to acknowledge that there are many religions in the world, rather than simply a taxonomy of heresies, paradoxically enough makes it possible to distinguish the true religion from all the others on offer. However fleetingly, then, Purchas entertains the possibility that true religion has something to learn from the fact that religion is everywhere. The care of one's internal state, the real genius of Protestant Christianity and the soul of true religion, needs a prod from the global cultures within which it suddenly finds itself situated. As Purchas seems to recognize but cannot quite say, addiction is true religion's other—its disavowed but necessary condition in the new global marketplace of religion.

Delight

We are now in a position to mount another kind of defense of the visionary mode of "Kubla Khan," one that depends not on its synthetic power but on the remarkable historical facts that Purchas registers almost without noticing them: that religion, however Christian a category, is also a worldly phenomenon; that it becomes an object of analysis at a moment of global consciousness that can be found more or less across the board in seventeenth-century Europe; that despite the culturalist insight that jump-starts German biblical criticism, the "enabling milieu" that makes a people and a religion was never limited to the nation.[36]

Here is where the poem's own account of things can help us. Its two primary geographic sites, China and Abyssinia, are not really susceptible to the kind of imaginative syncretism that Shaffer hopes to find. As Nigel Leask demonstrates in an important essay, English radicals of the 1790s associated Kubla's Chinese garden with the corruptions and imperial arrogance of the ancien régime. By contrast, Abyssinia (the origin of the poem's "maid" and her visionary song) had long denoted an ancient and uncorrupted Christian culture. The Mount Abora of which Coleridge's maid sings is Mount Amara, fabled home of the Ethiopian kings and possible seat of Prester John, the mythical Christian king of the East.[37] The idea that the maid's song is the means for a visionary rebuilding of Kubla's dome ignores this important distinction between old corruption and primitive purity—a distinction that would have mattered very much to Coleridge in 1797, even if he downplayed it by the time of the poem's eventual 1816 publication.[38]

As befits a fantasy of a truly global Christianity, accounts of Prester John vary widely. Many of the sources Purchas had available to him, however, converge on the general idea that Prester John was part of a dynasty of Asian kings who converted to Christianity and ruled over huge sections of India and China until the Tartars drove them into Africa, where they eventually retreated to the hills of Amara in Ethiopia and were henceforth falsely believed to be African.[39] Although he is clearly nervous about disagreeing with this narrative, Purchas nevertheless offers a different and more skeptical account. Considering the many texts arrayed before him, he remarks that "such a multitude of Fables could not but have some truth for their ground" (560). He suggests that there must have been several Johns, Christian kings of varying powers, ruling over different parts of the globe at different periods. The confusion of names and languages, and the migration of peoples between India, Egypt, and Ethiopia, have caused even careful historians to group all these into one vast Christian kingdom of the East.

As Purchas sifts laboriously through the sources, analyzes the reports, and weighs the evidence, the figure of Prester John, and thus by extension the possibility of a Christianity both pure and universal, becomes more and more bookish.[40] The invention of "religions" may very well be, as some have argued, a "projection of Christian disunity onto the world," but already here one senses the beginnings of the "solution" to this disunity in the remarkable wealth of the textual record to which Purchas had, at the beginning of his own book, confessed his addiction.[41] We are deep in a library rather than deep in someone's imagination.

The textuality at the heart of his account becomes clear when Purchas in fact turns to the remarkable library, larger than that at either Constantinople or Alexandria, that Amara is said to house. "There are three great Halls, each above two hundred paces large, with Bookes of all Sciences, written in fine parchment, with much curiositie of golden letters, and other workes, and cost in the writing, binding, and covers: some on the floore, some on shelves about the sides." Among these books are the lost writings of Enoch, Noah, Abraham, Solomon, and Job, and a variety of gospels "ascribed to Bartholomew, Thomas, Andrew, and many others," writings of the Queen of Sheba, the Greek Fathers, texts from "Syria, Egypt, Africa, and the Latine Fathers translated, with others innumerable in the Greeke, Hebrew, Arabike, Abissine, Egyptian, Syrian, Chaldee, . . . Saint Augustines workes are in Arabike: Poets, Philosophers, Physicians, Rabbines, Talmudists, Cabalists, Hieroglyphikes, and others [who] would be too tedious to relate" (567). The account, greatly abbreviated here, speaks for itself. In this fantasy library are all the books relevant to Christianity as a world religion, in conversation and conflict with Judaism and Islam. Remarkably, the knowledge continues to flow in: "When Jerusalem was destroyed by Titus; when the Saracens over-ranne the Christian world; many Bookes were conveyed out of the Easterne parts into Ethiopia; when Ferdinand and Isabella expelled the Jewes out of Spaine, many of them entered into Ethiopia, and . . . enriched the . . . Library with their books."[42] Everywhere Purchas turns, books are on the move. Amara is so beautiful that some have mistaken it for paradise, but when Purchas imagines an earthly paradise, he imagines room after room of books. Those volumes do not all say the same thing—indeed, they say many different things, but that matters less than the sublime experience of being in the presence of texts that flow endlessly like waters: "It is a Sea, that every yeare receiveth new rivers, never running out" (567).

Faced with this textual flood, Coleridge had described himself in the *Biographia* as floating, searching in vain for a solid foundation for "religion and morals" on which to rest. "The fontal truths of natural religion and the books of Revelation alike contributed to the flood; and it was long ere my ark touched on an Ararat, and rested," he writes (258). Purchas, by contrast, seems at home on the sea, and thrilled to be floating on a sublime tide of manuscripts. Unlike Coleridge's established church, a now ineffective "bulwark" of toleration against the rising waters of textual criticism, Purchas needs no barrier: his fantastic library will expand infinitely, absorbing all in a gesture that the speaker in "Kubla Khan" calls "deep delight":

Could I revive within me
Her symphony and song
To such deep delight 'twould win me
That with music loud and long,
I would build that dome in air,
That sunny dome! Those caves of ice! (lines 42–47)

"Kubla Khan" thus grasps as an opportunity one of the stranger aspects of Purchas's text: it is a travel book written by a man who never traveled but simply read a lot of books. This banal fact tells us something about what it means to say that an abstraction like "religion" gets invented at a particular historical juncture. Inventions require a medium, and they require a technology. For Purchas, the book is the medium, and addiction is the technology. The result is what Purchas labels "pleasure" and Coleridge terms "delight," an affect that for both men involves a complex alchemy of addiction by which pain becomes joy. What the poem names as the "ancestral voices prophesying war" have not been banished from this delight—indeed, some of the books of which Purchas dreams arrive only because of conflict. But the meaning of "war" has shifted. This is not the clash of civilizations, nor a religious conflict against which established institutions must throw up a hasty embankment of toleration. Nor is it an imaginative or visionary overcoming of conflict in the name of an underlying and heretofore hidden universalism. It is rather, as Purchas says on his title page, "the world *and* the religions." For to "sing of Mount Abora" with the maid is to sing of books, to sing of a textual paradise.[43] Long before anyone thought to put it in such terms, religion is a media event. This is not a theory of religion, of the kind on offer in Germany. Nor is it a critique of religion, of the kind on offer in France. Nor is it, again, an attempt to manage religion, of the kind on offer in England after 1688. It is rather a reminder that the history of religion is also the history of the things that are not religion—which to say, the history of the world.

Weaving the Circle

John Locke owned a copy of *Purchas His Pilgrimes*, the follow-up volume to the *Pilgrimage*. And though he complained of its length, he also found it useful. It was a point of pride for Locke that his political principles were based not on theory but on empirical evidence; this was the basis of his attack not just on Filmer's patriarchal theory but on Lord Herbert's deist argument for the universality of religious experience. Herbert's *De Religione Laici* (1645) had grounded its universalism in faculty psychology; the claim "*That there is one Supreme God . . . [who] ought to be worshipped*" dominated the deist debates until the 1680s.[44] Locke's attack on this idea is a winsome one. In the first book of the *Essay Concerning Human Understanding*, he has great fun listing all the nations and cultures he can think of where atheism is the order of the day, and makes much too of the fact that "Men have far different, nay, often contrary and inconsistent Ideas" about God.[45] Although religion is clearly spread all over the world, then, Locke claims that the empirical evidence cannot support the deist's argument that we all share an innate sense of the divine. The diversity is just too great, as Purchas himself had demonstrated at such length.

When Locke began to formulate toleration as a theoretical program in its own right, then, it was natural that he start with the premise that because salvation was a personal matter, no human being should dictate its forms to another.[46] The sheer fact of the world's diversity made any other position the height of arrogance. That this seems so uncontroversial now is a testament to Locke's influence, for at the time it was a remarkable place to begin, even despite the widespread circulation of travel narratives in the seventeenth century. After Locke, conceptually at least, it became possible to detach "religion" from political and social structures, and make it an object in its own right—a matter, in particular, for each person to meditate on in private. "[T]he care of each mans Soul, and of the things of Heaven," as Locke put it, "is left entirely to every mans self."[47] In the vision of the world laid out in the first *Letter Concerning Toleration*, the state cannot coerce religious belief, but neither can the church. Locke, that is to say, helped to articulate what would eventually become known as political liberalism: for him, individuals were bearers of rights (freedom of thought, freedom of expression, freedom to own property), and the role of the state was to foster and—up to a point— protect those rights by drawing a line around them. By limiting its remit to the care of souls, the discourse of toleration thus makes religion political in a new way: it becomes a delimited object existing within the larger realm of the polity. In order to distinguish religion from the state, moreover, the state must know what religion was: toleration thus entailed the thorny issue of defining the thing that it would tolerate. In a remarkable and influential move, Locke thus took the empirical evidence of religion's varied distribution across the globe and turned it into a reason for detaching it from the world and installing it in the conscience of the individual, its true and only home.

That particular solution, what we might describe as an *unworlding* of religion, is alive and well today. Thus Jürgen Habermas, in a well-known 2006 essay entitled "Religion in the Public Sphere," comes to terms with the continuing salience of religion simply by making it unknowable. Like many of our leading public intellectuals, Habermas had long argued that the Enlightenment made religion culturally superfluous.[48] His 2006 essay was notable, then, because it marked a shift in his thinking, and set the parameters for his ongoing effort to grapple with what world events were clearly revealing as the inadequacy of his earlier analysis. Habermas's essay takes itself to be sympathetic to the needs of religious citizens, particularly their presumed sense of loss or displacement in the modern world. And in a number of ways the essay is remarkable and even moving. Most striking, however, is that Habermas reproduces the very terms that made religion such a problem for the liberal tradition in the first place. He insists on seeing "religious citizens" not only as a monolithic category but as an unworldly one, enclosed in a sphere of their own making. The problem for liberal democracies, accordingly, is how to accommodate "them" without compromising core democratic principles. What seems unimaginable to Habermas, just as it seemed unimaginable to Locke, is a religion that is also, essentially and legitimately, a part of our shared world.

Near the end of his essay, Habermas produces a striking description. "At best," he writes, "philosophy *circles* the opaque core of religious experience when reflecting on the intrinsic meaning of faith. This core must remain so abysmally alien to discursive thought as does the core of aesthetic experience, which can likewise only be circled but not penetrated by philosophical reflection."[49] A potent force, resistant to explanation and opaque to its core, religion, like the aesthetic, turns in on itself. All we can do is draw a line around it, and say, in effect, "There it is; it cannot be penetrated." Lines demarcate, and sometimes protect; they also contain and limit, and produce an object where before there may have been a more fluid set of relations. The gendered nature of this description scarcely requires comment, but it bears thinking about in the context of Coleridge's fantasized Abyssinian maid, playing and singing of Amara. For I have argued in this chapter for a different way of picturing the relation of religion and the public sphere—one rooted in Abora/Amara and its library, one less alien than simply mediated, worldly, and on occasion surprisingly delightful: not a line in the sand but a voyage on the sea.

The poem ends, though, not with the hopeful image of the singing maid and her library but with a visionary poet, circled round by fearful and uncomprehending voices that seem to come from elsewhere:

> And all should cry, Beware! Beware!
> His flashing eyes, his floating hair!
> Weave a circle round him thrice,
> And close your eyes with holy dread,
> For he on honey-dew hath fed,
> And drunk the milk of Paradise. (lines 49–54)

This is a public sphere organized by its incomprehension of the abyssal being in its midst. The unworlding of religion wins the day, at least in this poem. For though the poet may be singing of books, what the public sees is something else: opaque, holy, flashing, dangerous.

CHAPTER 5

Hippogriffs in the Library: Realism and Opposition from Hume to Scott

Superstition is a considerable ingredient in almost all religions, there being nothing but philosophy able entirely to conquer these unaccountable terrors.

—David Hume, "Of Superstition and Enthusiasm" (1741)

It was his object to draw such a picture of domestic life and manners, during the feudal times, as might actually have existed.

—Walter Scott, on Walpole's *Castle of Otranto* (1811)

The events of 1688 may have cemented England's Protestant character, but in the exiled Stuart court they also created a Jacobite alternative that would haunt the nation for the next sixty years. The 1707 Act of Union abolished the Scottish Parliament and incorporated Scotland into an expanded Great Britain, but it did not so much thwart a Stuart return as tie that return to the question of Scotland itself. And so in the eighteenth century, Scotland—or more accurately, a certain idea of Scotland—fixed an unrealistic desire for a Stuart restoration and, even more, for a reversal of the 1688 settlement and all that it had come to represent: improvement, reason, capitalism, moderate Enlightenment, empire.[1] Formalized as Jacobitism, such discontent seemed for a time potent enough to actually undo the recent history of the nation. Even after the failure of the 1745 Rebellion, which came closest to achieving that dream, Jacobitism's combustible mixture of discontent and nostalgia remained an object of concern. Jacobitism was an unquiet thing, then—perhaps the primary unquiet thing during the middle years of the eighteenth century. Its plot was a gothic one, turning on the restoration of social and religious mandates both familiar and superseded; its possible return was therefore uncanny, threatening not just peace and stability but the very ordering of history.

This chapter moves between the idea of the Jacobite threat and a social and literary mode developed to contain it. From David Hume's philosophy in the middle of the eighteenth century to Walter Scott's historical fiction in the early years of the nineteenth century, an affable middle way emerges and then culminates in the thing that Scott calls "history" and that literary studies recognizes as novelistic realism. This is the argument traced, *in nuce*, in the two epigraphs to this chapter. When Hume claims that it is only "philosophy" that is able to countermand superstition, he means not only reason but a certain style of living marked by sociable equipoise and an immersion in the common pursuits of life. As Hume is all too aware, this is itself a kind of fiction—but one, he assures his readers, worth believing in. Scott, in his review of Walpole's *Castle of Otranto*, will claim that the best means for cultivating this regimen is not the fiction of philosophy but what we now recognize as the chief quality of historical fiction, or what Scott will simply call "history": life as it might actually have existed, and characters who react to it as real people might be expected to react, no matter how unlikely the events taking place. The best antidote to superstition, according to Scott, is another kind of fiction altogether.

James Chandler, in *England in 1819*, and Ian Duncan, in *Scott's Shadow*, have done much to trace the history of Hume's influence on Scott and thereby on the tradition of nineteenth-century historical realism itself.[2] Duncan is particularly committed to Hume's influence. "It was Hume," he writes, "who provided the philosophical justification for Scott's combination of history and romance. The Humean trajectory of enlightenment traces a skeptical dismantling of the metaphysical foundations of reality and their replacement with a sentimental investment in 'common life,' intermittently recognized as an imaginary construction of reality ratified by custom" (29). Duncan offers this trajectory as a complication of now-familiar arguments about Scott's conservatism. Whatever Scott's personal politics, his novels according to Duncan expose the fictive or contingent nature of the social order they officially celebrate. Scott's romantic dreamers may return, chastened, to common life, but their reattachment is necessarily an ironic one, customary rather than foundational. This is a compelling argument, and readers will feel its force in both this chapter and the next. But I am a bit less sanguine than is Duncan about the potency of skepticism (or irony, as he romantically renames it). My position is closer to that of Paul Hamilton, who finds in Scott a "progressiveness frozen in skepticism" and thus a "failure to represent . . . history."[3] There is in Scott, Hamilton argues, a skeptical turning away from the consequences—the real consequences, not the fictional ones—of his skeptical narrative technique. Scott's conservatism, on this analysis, is a real force in the real world, not just a performance within an already performative world.

Thus, whereas Duncan focuses his attention on the literary field that Scott does so much to shape, I remain attentive to the situation that constructs Scott's skepticism. I find an oppositional voice not in the novel's ironic play between events and the textual apparatus (frame narratives, editorial prefaces, footnotes) that mediates them, but rather in their exposure of the power differentials that structures these elements. I am interested less in ironic reattachment than in the figures and persons that irony leaves behind. In my reading, *Waverley* (1814) and especially *Rob Roy* (1817) offer accounts of Jacobitism that are Humean in outline but oddly reiterative in their specifics. Limning a history less progressive and teleological than repetitive and spectral, *Rob Roy* in particular is a remarkable exploration of a possible resistance to Scott's own ironically realist practice, and thus, by implication, to Hume's probabilistic calculus. Here Scott picks up on a submerged strand of Hume's own thinking, namely his reluctant admission that however appealing the joys of common life and sociable pursuits, the "hippogriffs of romance" (Scott's phrase) do not disappear simply because no one believes in them any longer. They remain, rather, as sites where we might sound and measure the silence surrounding accounts of historical progress.

Waverley's Sigh

Waverley describes the adventures of the Englishman Edward Waverley, Scott's eponymous and rather blank hero, who gets caught up in the 1745 Jacobite Rebellion, falls in with the charismatic Highland chieftain and Jacobite leader Fergus Mac-Ivor, loses his heart to Fergus's beautiful and exotic sister Flora, pledges allegiance to Bonnie Prince Charlie, and along the way endangers his family, his country, and everything that matters to him. With the rebellion in tatters, Flora in exile, Fergus executed, and the prince on the run, Waverley comes to his senses, returns to England and his appropriate station, and is rewarded with the right girl and a prosperous future within a rapidly modernizing Great Britain. Scott's point is that sentimental nationalism can be extended from "England" to "Great Britain," but only on the understanding that Jacobite intrigue and the Highland culture to which it is linked give up their claim on the present and submit to becoming colorful curiosities of the past. What's done is done.

The ideological center of the novel thus seems to reside in a painting unveiled in its final chapter: "It was a large and spirited painting, representing Fergus Mac-Ivor and Waverley in their Highland dress; the scene a wild, rocky, and mountainous pass, down which the clan were descending in the background. . . . The ardent, fiery, and impetuous character of the unfortunate Chief of Glennaquoich was finely contrasted with the contemplative, fanciful, and enthusiastic expression of his happier friend."[4] The way that rebellion and Highland culture are aestheticized in the scene, made over into a kind of style to be admired and hung on the wall, has drawn comparison to George IV's visit to Edinburgh in 1822, which Scott himself stage-managed as what Ian Duncan terms a "gaudy tartan pageant."[5] Divorced from a strongly held revolutionary identity, Highland garb becomes something to be picked up and put down as the mood suits. Scott himself drives home the point when, late in the novel, Waverley wanders from Fergus and his comrades and exchanges his Highland plaid for something less conspicuous. After this costume change, Waverley "felt himself entitled to say firmly, though perhaps with a sigh, that the romance of his life was ended, and that its real history had now commenced." Like Emma's sigh, this reflexive moment marks Waverley's resumption of historical responsibility.[6] It is all that is left of the imaginative, romance-tinged possibility represented by Jacobitism.

A few years later, Scott obliged his publisher John Murray by reviewing *Emma* for the *Quarterly Review*. He began in a similar vein. "In its first appearance," he wrote, "the novel was the legitimate child of the romance." Even with the fading away of the enchanted world, he continued, the reader turned to novels expecting something other than everyday life: not giants and fair maidens, perhaps, but still "adventures of a nature more interesting and extraordinary than those which occur in his own life, or that of his next-door neighbors."[7] But Austen's books, Scott concluded, were something newer yet: they "draw . . . characters and incidents . . . from the current of ordinary life." Indeed, Scott praised Austen in language that seems deliberately Humean: "common occurrences," "common life," and the "ordinary business of life" are her domain; her writing, Scott concluded, "affords to those who frequent it a pleasure nearly allied with the experience of their own social habits," and with these words one can almost see the companionable philosopher himself, playing backgammon and enjoying the company of his friends.[8]

An even more normalizing reading of Austen came from Richard Whately's 1821 account of her work, one of the most influential of the early reviews. "Virtue must be represented as producing, at the long run, happiness; and vice, misery," wrote Whately: "and the accidental events, that in real life interrupt this tendency, are anomalies which, though true individually, are as false generally as the accidental deformities which vary the average outline of the human figure."[9] Here, though, Whately inadvertently stumbled on a problem for his method. For however benevolent the overall pattern may be said to be, such reassurance has little existential purchase in the face of its interruption. Accidents do happen. And deformity may be "false generally," but it is true in particular cases, and therein lies a challenge for any method that would seek to keep our attention on the big picture.

Jacobitism is exactly this kind of accident. It threatens to interrupt regular and predictable historical progress; it is a "deformity" in the social body that seeks to establish a new norm for that body; and for these reasons, as Whately's own language unintentionally makes clear, its possibilities tend to reside in anomalous figures. This makes Jacobitism, as Scott understood very well, an intrinsically "literary" event. But to see why it takes this figurative and disturbing form, we need to return to debates over language and clarity that occupied the defenders of the 1688 settlement.

If We Would Speak of Things as They Are

The intellectuals and churchmen who had gone into self-imposed exile during James's reign held to a broadly Newtonian metaphysics and a latitudinarian polity. When these men returned to England early in 1689, they were given influential positions and immediately got to work interpreting and justifying the new order.[10] Despite important differences, the members of the moderate Enlightenment unanimously emphasized clarity and simplicity in both thinking and writing. In tune with the gradually sharpening antithesis between natural and supernatural during the seventeenth century, they viewed mystery as the antithesis of understanding. The "hot and superstitious part of mankind," wrote Isaac Newton in his commentary on the Gospel of

John, "like best what they understand least. Such men may use the Apostle John as they please; but I have that honor for him, as to believe that he wrote good sense; and therefore take that sense to be his, which is best."[11] By good sense Newton meant language that was consistent and unequivocal.

In their influential book *Leviathan and the Air-Pump*, Steven Shapin and Simon Schaffer describe how Newton's colleagues in the Royal Society likewise celebrated clear language and reliable testimony. Robert Boyle, for instance, conducted his scientific experiments in a manner designed to maximize transparency. The credibility of his method depended on an accurate and clear account of what had happened: a description that could create in the reader's imagination the feeling that he was actually in the room while the experiment was taking place. Shapin and Schaffer call this "virtual witnessing": in order to create trust in the reader and encourage him to picture the experiment in his mind, Boyle developed a "literary technology" whose characteristics included prolixity, a plain rather than "florid" style, and the use of naturalistic engravings. It was all written up as an essay or letter—forms more appropriate to scientific induction than a book-length philosophical system. In each case, from the details of the drawings to the wordiness of the prose, the aim was to produce what Shapin and Schaffer call a "density of circumstantial detail."[12]

Methodologically, the modern scientific experiment strove to isolate its objects from the accumulated weight of personality, context, and tradition. And yet, because most citizens had neither the means nor the ability to reproduce experiments themselves, the propagation of scientific knowledge really depended on writers and readers. Complexity, expelled from nature, reasserted itself in the domain of representation, and this was one reason that the predictability and stability of language became so important.[13] If the "best sense" was to win out against mystery and fanaticism, it would require referential stability. Michel de Certeau calls this the "deontologizing of language," according to which "the experiment stood opposite language as that which guaranteed and verified the latter."[14] Truth was now a set of propositional statements, and to "believe" in a scientific experiment was to have already adopted a particular notion of language itself. This involved both believing that the requisite authority had firsthand access to the truth, *and* believing that the truth could be communicated in language, without distortion or loss of meaning. The goal was to reduce the noise in the transmission and minimize the gap between first- and second-order observations, so that the reader perused the report of an experiment as if he were right there in the laboratory.

It is not hard to see how language that is vague, layered, ambiguous, or metaphorical would run into trouble in this new regime. And indeed, across the ideological spectrum, influential divines of the late seventeenth and early eighteenth centuries argued that everything needful in scripture was right there on the surface; figurative murkiness, along with the allegorical methods developed to make sense of it, was simply Catholic obscurantism, linked to a reactionary politics out of step with the reasonable *telos* of the moderate Enlightenment. In the *Essay Concerning Human Understanding*, Locke remarked that "if we would speak of Things as they are, we must allow, that all Art of Rhetorick, besides Order and Clearness, all the artificial and figurative application of Words Eloquence hath invented, are for nothing else but to insinuate wrong *Ideas*, move the Passions, and thereby mislead the Judgment"; among the wrong ideas that rhetoric might urge on us is a habit of unthinking obedience to arbitrary authority, and it is largely for this reason that Locke urges parents whose children showed an interest in poetry to "have it stifled and suppressed as much as may be; and I know not what reason a father can have to wish his son a poet."[15]

So Studious an Obscurity

Nowhere are the virtues and limitations of this enlightened linguistic program more evident than in William Warburton's multivolume *Divine Legation of Moses*. Warburton was an ambitious and successful Whig, eventually bishop of Gloucester, an enthusiastic controversialist and man of letters. *The Divine Legation* first appeared in two volumes between 1738 and 1741, but Warburton labored on it his entire life and left it uncompleted on his death in 1779.

The book confronted a problem raised by those whom Warburton calls "free-thinkers" (apparently Bolingbroke and Shaftesbury): that the Hebrew Scriptures betray little interest in the afterlife. If God had indeed revealed the early chapters of the Bible to Moses, he would surely have mentioned the possibility of eternal life. That he had not done so suggested that the texts were of human origin. The usual orthodox response to this argument had turned on a few key passages. Genesis 5:24, for example: "And Enoch walked with God: and he was not; for God took him." And Psalm 16:9: "Therefore my heart is glad, and my glory rejoiceth: my flesh also shall rest in hope."

Such passages could be interpreted as anticipations of a Christian doctrine of life after death.

Warburton takes the opposite tack. He agrees that the Old Testament does not develop a theory of future rewards and punishments, but argues counterintuitively that this is evidence *in favor* of a divine revelation. All pagan societies, he proposes, *did* depend for their stability on a doctrine of the afterlife; elite rulers did not themselves believe in such a doctrine, but they found it highly useful for manipulating their people. The fact that Moses *does not* appeal to such a doctrine, then, is for Warburton proof that the Jewish nation is something different and set apart, for surely if Moses had been driven only by motives of instrumental governance, he would have appealed to a notion as politically serviceable as an afterlife. In the passage about Enoch, he writes, "there is so studious an Obscurity" that Moses must have "purposely designed to hide" the doctrine of eternal life.[16] Scriptural silence about the afterlife is thus evidence of a hidden or secret agreement between God and Moses; God must have privately assured Moses that he would look out for Israel in a special way.[17] And so we arrive at the surprising idea that belief in a future state, loudly proclaimed in pagan societies, is for that very reason false; while belief in a future state, kept hidden in the Jewish polity, is for that very reason true.

Armed with this paradoxical reading, Warburton's Moses leads his people out of the state, with its manipulations and cynical politics, and into an uncertain future that requires faith in the obscure pronouncements of a monotheistic divinity. Corrupted by their long sojourn in Egypt, the Israelites must be constantly called away into a novel and intense relationship with a new God. In contrast to the kind of comparative analysis of religion practiced by the deists, which threatens (or promises) to relativize all religious expressions, Warburton's account of Jewish monotheism emphasizes that it is not a refinement of an earlier polytheism but something decidedly different and unique. Indeed, it is so unique that it purposely omits any doctrine that would make it *more like* its pagan competitors. Christianity is then the completing or fulfillment of Judaism precisely because it offers as a positive knowledge what Moses had kept "out of sight." And because God waits so long to reveal this truth, Christianity escapes the charge of priestcraft.[18]

As Warburton had already made clear in *The Alliance Betwixt Church and State* (1736), he understood an established religion, confirmed and maintained by religious tests, as central to civil society and social order; at the same time, as a good post-Lockean Whig, he argued for full toleration for those who dissented from the established church. This halfway strategy is typical of the moderate Enlightenment strand of Anglican Christianity: English intellectuals from Boyle to Newton to Locke were willing to go a certain distance with the new thinking sweeping across the Continent in the aftermath of the Cartesian revolution. To be sure, Jonathan Israel is right to point out that within this English tradition, toleration is understood "theologically," insofar as it extends only to competing Christian sects; it is therefore distinct from the nontheistic doctrines of toleration emanating from such Continental theorists as Grotius and Spinoza.[19] Yet Warburton, for his part, gets to this halfway point through means that are extraordinarily, and symptomatically, circuitous. For in order to deploy a materialist analysis of pagan religious mystification while insulating Judaism and Christianity from the same kind of analysis, he must employ a "deist" reading practice according to which linguistic obscurity is a deliberate attempt to hide something, rather than a good-faith effort to represent a real complexity.[20] And to further complicate things, Warburton thinks that what is being hidden is the *truth*, not—as for the deists—its absence. Clear yet cryptic, literal yet figurative, the Hebrew scriptures' "studious obscurity" matters politically but not theologically: it is the distinguishing feature of an entire nation's bond with its God, but not of any one individual's relationship to the divine.

Job and the '45: Too Sublime, or Dark

Warburton's readers were particularly struck by his treatment of Job, where the themes of obscurity and the afterlife merge. The controversy turned on Job 19: "For I know that my redeemer liveth, and that he shall stand at the latter day upon the earth: And though after my skin worms destroy this body, yet in my flesh shall I see God: Whom I shall see for myself, and mine eyes shall behold, and not another; though my reins be consumed within me" (19: 25–27). Job's statement of faith comes in response to the arguments of his three friends, who variously try to explain, or explain away, his suffering, telling him he must somehow deserve the punishment being inflicted on him. In a similar fashion, orthodox interpreters generally made sense of Job's suffering by referring to his rewards in a future state. Warburton, by contrast, held that Job was referring not to some resurrected future state but to the restoration of his earthly fortunes.[21] Job's suffering is so extreme, Warburton writes, that he would have taken refuge in a doctrine of future rewards had it been available to him. And though the obscure passage in Chapter 19 *might* be so interpreted, Warburton is struck by the fact that Job doesn't return to it; rather, he writes, Job "sticks to the Argument he *first* set out with; and, though he found it gave them little Satisfaction, repeats it again and again" (547).

The questions surrounding the proper interpretation of Job 19 exemplify a larger mid-century worry about suffering—one shortly to be given new urgency by the disastrous Lisbon earthquake of 1755. In his marvelous study *The Rhetoric of Suffering*, Jonathan Lamb finds in the Job controversy a "mid-century crisis of confidence in the value of consolations and vindications."[22] Against the impulse to rationalize it through a deeper "meaning"—whether his own culpability or God's mysterious purposes—Job insists on the magnitude and incomprehensibility of his suffering; he simply "repeats it again and again," as Warburton notes. He makes no headway with his friends, refuses to be comforted, and rebuffs efforts to draw him again into the circle of sociable human society. He seems to speak a language that only he can understand.[23]

In the middle years of the eighteenth century David Hume made a similar discovery. Hume's notorious essay on miracles acknowledged that testimony to miraculous happenings violated all the rules laid down by Boyle for the production of matters of fact: details were often sketchy, the witnesses unreliable, the evidence of a preconceived system too transparent. But Hume went even farther. Miracles were by definition improbable events, he wrote: "There must be a uniform experience against every miraculous event, otherwise the event would not merit that appellation."[24] So testimony to a miracle required belief in two contrary things: first, as Boyle had made clear, that it was accurate, lucid, and detailed—in short, probable; and second, that it described something exceedingly *im*probable. Even if the testimony could be made to fulfill all the criteria of the early modern virtuosi, it would *still* not be able to overcome the probability argument. The better the science, the more unlikely the event.

If Hume seemed at first to be simply following out the arguments of the moderate scientific Enlightenment to their logical conclusion, it became clear by the end of the essay that he had taken those reasons somewhere else entirely. By defining warranted belief in miracles solely on the basis of testimony, and defining testimony as the retelling of sensory experience, Hume did not show that miracles never happened, but rather that, if they *did* happen, there was little chance of ever telling anyone about them. "Our most holy religion," Hume wrote with wry humor, "is founded on *Faith*, not on

reason . . . and whoever is moved by Faith to assent to it, is conscious of a
continued miracle in his own person, which . . . gives him a determination
to believe what is most contrary to custom and experience" (*E* 130–31). Not
only is religion here defined as a set of propositional truths; more radically,
those truths are defined entirely by a personal language. On this definition,
religion *just is* lonely testimony to oneself. Like Job, the man of faith is the
man at the margins of society, repeating his own arguments to himself.

The point to stress here is that for both Hume and Warburton, the
dogma of clarity in effect creates the obscure, dark, and literary spaces that it
had been invoked to expel: were it not for the assumption that language was
a transparent medium, neither Job nor the modern miracle-believer would
be so isolated. As it is, such figures are difficult to place within the ideological
landscape, in part because nobody quite knows what they are saying. Hume's
miracle-believer is a particularly dramatic example. But Warburton's technique in the *Divine Legation* is equally counterintuitive. In his account Jewish
monotheism is radically distinct from pagan Egyptian culture because it is
silent about what matters most. Here Warburton's strategy feels remarkably
modern: that something is *not* said becomes evidence of its central importance. The very thing that distinguishes the Jews from pagan societies is
wrapped up in the obscurity of that which cannot be explicitly said. Even
Warburton's sympathetic friend and biographer, Richard Hurd, calls his
strategy "new and paradoxical."[25]

For broad-minded establishment Whigs like Warburton, the most
immediate historical referent for such unaccountable lacunae in the sociable
world was the Jacobite Rebellion of 1745. This attempt to restore the Stuarts
to the throne was not only a repudiation of the 1688 Glorious Revolution,
the latitudinarian Lockean/Newtonian intellectual regime it had ushered in,
and the reasonable narratives of progress that provided its ideological justification; it also drew on a different conception of time itself. For a rebellion in
the name of the Catholic Stuarts seemed also a rebellion in the name of
repetition rather than forward movement, of a temporality more punctuated
than progressive: a figurative history, in short, that refused assimilation to the
tolerant, linear historical narrative to which the moderate Enlightenment had
committed itself.

Warburton preached two sermons on the Jacobite Rebellion of 1745.
Though both were implicitly meditations on the politics of historiography,
the second is of particular interest because it focuses like Job's friends on the
meaning of the rebellion.[26] Against those who would interpret the events of

1745 as a divine judgment against a nation that had wandered too far away from a biblical polity, Warburton's sermon made a sharp distinction between the politics of Judaism and the politics of Protestant Christianity. In good Lockean fashion he argued that unlike ancient Judaism, "the *Christian* Religion has no public Part; has not the State, as such, but Individuals only, for its Subject. Hence Vice and Impiety are not now public, but private Crimes."[27] We know the rebellion will fail, insisted Warburton, not because there were exact precedents in the Scripture for what was happening in 1745 (there were not) but rather because we have general knowledge of the way that God works: we "infer from the Nature of eternal Justice and Mercy" that "the same merciful Providence" will enable England to triumph over "this Northern Army of Locusts" (6). The point is that God's providence is *generalizable*: while it is wrong to interpret Protestant liberty of conscience as if it were a continuation of Hebrew polity ("This hath been the Source of numberless Superstitions, hurtful both to Religion and Government" [7]), it is right to search for an *overall* coherence. Indeed, "the greatest Part of the Old Testament is historical, and chiefly written for our Information concerning the general Oeconomy of God's Dispensation to Mankind" (10). The contrast is stark: on the one hand, a Whiggish "general Oeconomy," instantiated in civil society, susceptible to reason and probability, manifested in plain language, politically grounded in the events of 1688/89 and 1707, and for these reasons properly "historical"; on the other, a rhetoric of obscure portents and direct divine intervention, a sublimity that disrupts temporal progress through a logic of anachronism and rebellion. Whatever their official politics, those who search the Old Testament for historical precedent are methodologically complicit with those who wish to restore the Stuarts; they are on the side of superstition rather than history.

Hume himself suffered from occasional Job-like bouts of paranoia, most notably when he abandoned law in pursuit of a life in letters, and then again when the *Treatise* failed to impress the learned establishment. Hume's famous comment that the book "fell still-born from the press," and his consequent conviction that the fault lay in the book's style, rather than its argument, makes the problem of language *the* problem of the literary life as Hume practiced it. Hurd, Warburton's biographer, rather acidly remarked on Hume's "super-subtle lucubrations of the metaphysical kind; which, however, did no great mischief to religion; and what chagrined him almost as much, contributed but little to his own fame, being too sublime, or dark, for the apprehensions of his readers."[28]

Hurd's comment might be taken as a gloss on the most famous passage of Hume's *Treatise*, when the narrator falls into skeptical despair at the end of Book I: "I am first affrighted and confounded with that forelorn solitude, in which I am plac'd in my philosophy, and fancy myself some strange uncouth monster, who not being able to mingle and unite in society, has been expell'd all human commerce, and left utterly abandoned and disconsolate."[29] Readers of the "Miracles" essay will recognize this pose as that of the miracle-believer. Severed from social intercourse by their uncouth beliefs, both the skeptical philosopher and the miracle-believer can testify only to themselves.[30] Leaving pleasant social intercourse for the sublime loneliness of personal conviction, both betray a preference for minor details rather than general economies, for lonely rhetorical extravagance rather than the conversable world, for intellectual and social disorder rather than clarity and probability. People muttering to themselves on the sidelines could be muttering about all manner of things, and they are scattered unpredictably on the social and political landscape; they might be uncouth inner-light Protestants, they might be Christian Tories with a particularly literary sensibility, they might be Tory atheists with a libertine bent. Hume himself defied every label—atheist, deist, freethinker, skeptic—with which his contemporaries tried to describe him. And though that protean quality is usually a social advantage, in the *Treatise* it seems to have become the opposite: unable to muster the language that would reconnect him with the general economy of the social whole, the narrator is alone on the sea, borne aloft in his forlorn solitude on waves of rhetoric.

We can detect this, indirectly, even in Warburton's clumsy response to Hume's miracles essay, which lurches from heavy irony to a very pertinent anxiety about the politics of reviewing. "I am strongly tempted too to have a stroke at Hume in parting," Warburton wrote to Richard Hurd in 1749. "But does he deserve notice? Is he known amongst you? Pray answer me these questions. For if his own weight keeps him down, I should be sorry to contribute to his advancement to any place but the pillory."[31] If the philosophical skeptic is as forlorn and unnatural as the religious enthusiast, then neither of them can harm the reasonable public sphere that has worked so hard to banish all forms of poetic enthusiasm. Unsure whether Hume's arguments were so dark that they would have no effect, or whether their darkness suggested a kind of power of which one must beware, Warburton at one point referred to Hume as "an atheistical Jacobite, a monster as rare with us as a hippogriff."[32]

This may have been, unintentionally, Warburton's most accurate remark. For during the 1745 rebellion Hume was a Scotsman living in England, and he had several close friends who supported the Jacobite cause. Had he received the Edinburgh professorship he was seeking at the time, moreover, he would have taken up residence in an occupied city. For obvious reasons, then, he kept his opinions on the rebellion largely to himself. "Of the Protestant Succession," an essay he apparently wrote during the uprising, remained unpublished until 1752, probably on the advice of his friends. "[S]ome People," he wrote to Charles Erskine, thought the piece "extremely dangerous."[33] The essay itself is remarkable for bringing the Humean value of proportion to bear on a heated topic. Observing that the world is a complicated place, Hume notes that both the House of Stuart and the House of Hanover have their advantages and their disadvantages. In such a situation, "Hesitation, and reserve, and suspense, are, therefore, the only sentiments [the philosopher] brings to this essay or trial."[34] He then notes that when the Stuarts ruled, England was in turmoil; when the Hanoverians took over, peace reigned at home, accompanied by military success abroad: "So long and so glorious a period no nation almost can boast of" (508). In this situation, Hume comes out in favor of not rocking the boat. He admits that anyone living during 1688/89 might have had a hard time determining which was the best course. But a course has been chosen, "the settlement in the House of Hanover has actually taken place" (511), and presumption is always in favor of the present order, particularly if it has been a relatively good one.

From one perspective, this argument demotes the Glorious Revolution, making it simply one event among others. Hume seemed to argue that it was not England's destiny to become securely Protestant, nor to incorporate Scotland into an expanded "Great Britain" that remained essentially English—but since that is what *had* happened, there was little point in trying to turn back the clock. Hume's technique rendered the Stuarts, particularly Bonnie Prince Charlie, as sublime figures, initially inspiring but eventually abandoned by their friends and doomed to live out their years as the chief actors of a history that never happened—a history "possible but not probable," in Hume's parlance. Cut off from any actually existing history, the Stuarts remain a formal principle of interruption that may periodically tear the social fabric: "the claims of the banished family, I fear, are not yet antiquated; and who can foretel, that their future attempts will produce no greater disorder?" (508). On this reading, the Stuarts do not stand *for* anything; they are a code for something else, and bear more than a passing likeness to those other monstrous figures—the skeptic, the miracle-believer—scattered through the Humean corpus.

The recurrence of these figures may account for Warburton's unease when he calls Hume a "monster as rare with us as a hippogriff." His heterodox opinions notwithstanding, Hume in fact offers very little real threat to the mainstream of orthodox Anglican thought; he is certainly not a Jacobite in terms of the content of his political opinions. Yet Hume's literary flourishes, so obscure and dark, suggest how closely disruption shadows the easy, sociable world of union and progress. Somewhere, in the darkness, beat the wings of a hippogriff, turning unpredictably from skeptical antinomianism to Tory sublimity and taking in Jacobitism and atheism along the way. Should such creatures be faced or ignored?[35]

From Backgammon to Novels

In his "Miracles" essay Hume had conceded that there might "possibly be miracles" (127), but he insisted that there could be no probable testimony to them. Both the debate over Job and the debate over the 1745 Rebellion likewise turned on this distinction between probability and possibility, between a general truth and a historical particular. History may be tending in one direction, there may be a "general economy" behind suffering, but those abstract truths cannot explain the sudden, heterogeneous appearance of a counterhistory, or the dramatic eruption of suffering in the here and now. The attempt to fold such events into a larger narrative structure is false comfort: all that Job can do is report what has happened to him. By the same token, the historian must acknowledge, however tentatively, the continued possible "disorder" of the exiled Stuarts; the Whig narrative of progress is a contingent one, the result more of good fortune than of divine dispensation.

To be sure, Hume does leave the skeptical persona of the *Treatise* an escape clause: "Most fortunately it happens, that since reason is incapable of dispelling these clouds, nature herself suffices to that purpose, and cures me of this philosophical melancholy and delirium. . . . I dine, I play a game of back-gammon, I converse, and am merry with my friends."[36] Soon, indeed, the narrator is feeling so much better that he resolves not to "torture [his] brain with subtilties and sophistries" but rather to enjoy the "commerce and society of men." Such common life, its rituals and norms built up over time, becomes Hume's most important philosophical resource.[37]

Hume's choice of backgammon to illustrate this position is not accidental. An ancient game and a favorite in England during the Middle Ages (when
it was known as "tables"), backgammon appears in both *The Canterbury Tales*
and *The Faerie Queene*. But in 1526 Cardinal Wolsey banned all games involving dice and cards, inspiring a black market in backgammon boards disguised
as books. By Hume's time backgammon was back in favor as one of polite
society's most popular games. Hoyle's *A Short Treatise on the Game of Back-
Gammon* (1743), often bound together with the same author's treatise on
whist, cemented its status. Backgammon playing was associated in particular
with the clergy; when Hume pictures himself playing a game of backgammon
and being merry with his friends, then, some of those friends are presumably
the miracle-believing clergymen who were part of his social circle.

Backgammon was also the subject of theoretical interest. In the early
years of the eighteenth century, games of chance and hazard had begun to
receive serious attention from mathematicians, thanks in particular to the
development of probability theory and the distribution curve.[38] A game that
blends luck and skill, backgammon generally rewards those with a good grasp
of probability, and punishes those who take large risks. From an interdicted
game of chance to a polite pastime subject to increasingly codifiable rules,
then, backgammon's social history matches exactly the kind of progressive
philosophical narrative Hume constructed in his own passage from "delirium" to sociability.

The successful backgammon player must weigh not only his opponent's
skill and experience but also the probability of the die rolling a certain way
and the likelihood of particular responses to those rolls. Probability values
repeated experience: the expected or the common trumps the surprising or
unusual. What *actually* happened exerts a normative force; what *might* have
happened does not. Sometimes this yields the contingent conservatism of
Hume's essay on the 1745 Rebellion, with its presumption against disorder.
Sometimes, as in the miracles essay, it yields a kind of radical conservatism.
But in either case, Hume's technique diminishes the power of testimony. If
Boyle had marshaled testimony in the service of probability, Hume's account
of miracles and rebellions suggests that the philosophical principle of probability will trump the literary technology of testimony whenever the two come
into conflict. Indeed, we might understand Hume's career, *in nuce*, as an
effort to create a literary technology more adequate to probability, and
thereby join together "philosophy" and "literature" more securely than Boyle
was able to do.

Perhaps Hume should have tried his hand at writing novels. As Jonathan Lamb demonstrates with great subtlety, novels were the eighteenth-century technology that took probability as their defining philosophical challenge.[39] In Humean terms, writers of fiction cannot dogmatically appeal to the "false reason" of theodicy, but neither can they adopt the extreme skepticism of simply narrating contingent happenings as if there were no connection among them. This is the problem of what we now call novelistic realism: how to contextualize possibility within the larger confines of probability. Probability may be the principle that ties events together, but it needs to be understood loosely enough to make room for the occasional unexpected happening without allowing such things to destroy the coherence of the narrative or tip them into the debased genres of fantasy and romance.

Here Scott does indeed appear as Hume's greatest disciple. For even more than a backgammon board disguised as a book, Scott's historical novels enact probability by disguising fiction as history. In his review of *Emma* Scott wrote that Austen's novel does not make the reader discontented with his own prosaic existence: "the youthful wanderer may return from his promenade to the ordinary business of life, without any chance of having his head turned by the recollection of the scene through which he has been wandering."[40] This is Scott's interpretation of Austen's stringent narrative practice, which works to make Emma's wish for impossible things seem contentless, a mere sigh.

Yet like Hume himself, Scott's narratives discover the limits of this vision. Edward Waverley, that most archetypal of youthful wanderers, *does* turn his head as he leaves the romance of 1745 for the history of "Great Britain," and the gesture is not an entirely empty one. As he quits the castle of Carlisle, where the Highland chieftain and Jacobite leader Fergus Mac-Ivor has been executed, Waverley "dared hardly look back towards the Gothic battlements of the fortified gate under which he passed (for the place was surrounded with an old wall). 'They're no there,' said Alick Polwarth, who guessed the cause of the dubious look which Waverley cast backward."[41] Waverley is looking for Fergus's head, which after his execution will be impaled on the battlements for all to see. But he does not see it, for the head has been stuck on the northern gate, the so-called Scotch gate, while Edward is exiting south, toward England and the properly historical future. That unseen revolutionary head, looking north toward Scotland and a future that has failed to arrive yet again, thus stands in implicit counterpoint to the stylized rebellion offered by the painting of Waverley and Fergus shortly to be unveiled.

Suffering, whether mental or physical, marks the limits of the subject's ability to act. Those familiar with it may desire a connection to the wider world, but they are isolated by their experience and by a language unable to adequately represent their plight. Suffering is in this sense a sign of the world and of its material presence, but it also invites the kind of ameliorative agency that puts "the center of gravity of goodness in ordinary living, production and the family." This is the outlook that Charles Taylor calls the "affirmation of ordinary life," a focus on human flourishing central to his story of the making of the secular age. "It belongs to this spiritual outlook," writes Taylor, "that our first concern ought to be to increase life, relieve suffering, foster prosperity."[42] Such affirmations, manifested in habits of discipline and self-control and in the overall tendencies that Warburton termed the "general oeconomies" of history, serve to isolate those figures whom Whately calls deformed: the skeptical philosopher, the miracle-believer, Fergus's severed head, the hippogriff, Job. When Waverley turns and does not see Fergus's head because Fergus is looking elsewhere, sublime suffering and improbable romance interrupt the teleology of a general economy and the theodicy of modernization. And yet the details of such romantic suffering do not figure into the general scheme.

In Waverley's "dubious look," then, Hume's formal tension between testimony and probability reappears. This "Scottish problem," initiated by the events of 1688, threads its way through the eighteenth century, from the opposition Stuart court in exile and the Rebellions of 1715 and 1745 to the various literary and philosophical attempts, from Warburton and Hume to Scott, to grasp just what this all amounts to. A political order committed to minimal tolerance and legitimated by an intellectual regime suspicious of figurative language has trouble finding a place for ambiguity, obscurity, deformity, or the "fables and fictions" that have come to denote an old order addicted to secrecy and absolute power. Resistance to what Locke (and Godwin after him) called "Things as they are" thus finds refuge in a sensibility or mood—a sigh, a look, a restless disquiet—whose source is hard to locate but whose effects are there to be read.

Above All, Divinity

Waverley attempts to refine Jacobite opposition into a single sigh and a dubious backward glance. When Scott revisits Jacobite and Highland culture in *Rob Roy* (1817), his goal seems to be a historical novel more adequate to the challenges posed by Jacobitism's history of potential disorder—a novel that, in effect, *encourages* the reader to turn her head, though without allowing her to wander too far.

Rob Roy's early chapters find Frank Osbaldistone, the naive Waverley-like hero, sojourning at his uncle's ancestral home in Northumbria. London-bred and Protestant, Frank is thoroughly out of place in the Catholic, Jacobite, priest-haunted and mystery-laden Osbaldistone Hall. Indeed, northern England seems an anachronism in this novel, stuck somewhere in the seventeenth century, stagnating in unceasing rounds of drinking and hunting ("the mode of life at Osbaldistone Hall was too uniform to admit of description," reports Frank) and literally unable to reproduce itself: in one comic paragraph near the novel's close, five sons and heirs are dispatched in rapid succession.[43]

When Frank eventually arrives in Glasgow, he meets Nicol Jarvie, a representative of Scotland's rising commercial class, who tutors him informally in political economy. Jarvie's various speeches draw directly on a group of post-Humean Scottish thinkers—Adam Smith, John Millar, William Robertson, Dugald Stewart—who advanced a theory of history whereby societies move through a series of stages, advancing from the primitive to the modern, but do so *unevenly*, at a pace determined not by a universal historical teleology but by contingent, local, factors.[44] The most famous of Scott's many references to such uneven development comes in the final chapter of *Waverley*, when the narrator remarks that "The gradual influx of wealth, and extension of commerce, have . . . united to render the present people of Scotland a class of beings as different from their grandfathers as the existing English are from those of Queen Elizabeth's time." Scott's point is that the historical novel is the literary technology best suited to the theory of uneven development, or what he calls "complete . . . change." Such a novel can affectionately describe those who "still cherished a lingering . . . attachment to the House of Stuart" while simultaneously narrating "the progress we have made," thus inviting the reader to witness and admire the rate of Scottish modernization as it rapidly closes the developmental gap with England.[45]

Scotland may be amenable to such development, but northern England is another story. And it is particularly the library of Osbaldistone Hall, eventually revealed as a key center of Jacobite intrigue, that comes to stand for all that is backward and recalcitrant:

> The library . . . was a gloomy room, whose antique oaken shelves
> bent beneath the weight of the ponderous folios so dear to the seven-
> teenth century. . . . The collection was chiefly of the classics, as well

foreign as ancient history, and, above all, divinity. It was in wretched
order. . . . [A]n air of dilapidation, as obvious as it was uncomfortable, pervaded the large apartment, and announced the neglect from
which the knowledge which its walls contained had not been able
to exempt it. The tattered tapestry, the worm-eaten shelves, the huge
and clumsy, yet tottering, tables, desks, and chairs, the rusty grate,
seldom gladdened by either sea-coal or faggots, intimated the con-
tempt of the lords of Osbaldistone Hall for learning, and for the
volumes which record its treasures.[46]

The literary technology of the historical novel and its narrative of uneven
development have no place here. So how does one apply its lessons to such a
place? Perhaps we can appeal not to political economy per se but to its ideological wing. For libraries like this one are set pieces in the gothic genre. Not
only a refuge and place of discovery for the hero or (more often) heroine, the
gothic library functions metafictionally as an arena for self-consciousness,
what Deirdre Lynch calls an "interrogation of literary reading" that forces
the reader to consider the relationship between the book he or she is perusing
and the books tucked away on the shelves. When, for example, the eponymous heroine of Charlotte Smith's *Emmeline* (1788) salvages from the dust
and decay of a castle library "Spencer and Milton, two or three volumes of
the *Spectator*, an old edition of Shakespeare, and an odd volume or two of
Pope," her canon making, writes Lynch, "prefigures the manner in which
Smith throughout the novel will align questions of pedigree, the disposition
of property, and nationality."[47] In the library, the relation of reader to book
transforms into a relation of book to book; mirroring the gothic genre's more
overt obsession with the inheritance of real property, the library links past to
present by means of a literary heritage that also transfers cultural capital. In
this manner a tradition is retrospectively created, the canon of English literature born as a family history one of whose functions is to create a feeling for
the nation at the very moment that the nation itself expands via colonial
endeavors both at home (Scotland and Ireland) and abroad (Asia and the
Americas). But why is the specifically *gothic* library the site of this imaginative
creation? Because, Lynch argues, such acts of canon creation are poised
between the desire for the dead to be safely dead so that they can be smoothly
incorporated into a national heritage, and the need to reanimate the dead,
bring them back to life, so that the living will be haunted by the power of
the dead writers in whose tradition they stand. On this reading the business

of "literature," as Scott perfects it, is the connecting tissue between the gothic library and the modernizing urban center of Glasgow; by bringing the dead back to life in the form of a cultural inheritance, literature magically knits together the twin impulses, commercial and historical, of modernity.

Placing the library alongside Nicole Jarvie's lessons on political economy makes it possible, then, to read gothic supernaturalism as a symptom of modernity's progress. Modernization may be inevitable, but it is distributed unevenly, and this means that there will inevitably remain eddies and backwaters where enchantment lingers. On this interpretation a lingering belief in the enchanted world is not the binary opposite of modernity but its dialectical other, and an indicator that no matter how disenchanted it takes itself to be, modern life remains the site of various mystifications that require further analysis.[48] Marx would speak in *Capital* of the "metaphysical subtleties and theological whimsies" of the commodity form before subjecting those subtleties and whimsies to stringent critique, and plenty of literary critics have followed his lead, noting that, like the fabulous resourcefulness of capital itself, the canon keeps on giving.[49] A literary classic is marvelously renewable: it lives and breathes from beyond the grave—or, in a more gothic register, it is in some mysterious way *undead*. "[T]he strangely fearful modes of canon-loving at work within the Gothic library," Lynch concludes, "seems to me a good way to become alerted to the mystifications at work in that nationalist idea of a cultural capital *given* to all." The critical presupposition here is that supernaturalism is an epiphenomenon of material forces like the economy and the nation. The "alarming reenchantment of the late capitalist world" is thus, in the words of Terry Eagleton, a "pathological symptom of what is awry with us," since we prefer supernatural distraction to critical thought.[50]

And yet, however widespread such cultural work in Scott, in the gothic genre, or indeed in "literature" itself, the library at Osbaldistone Hall is doing something else. Indeed, literary inheritance and "canon love" *try* to make themselves felt here, but an obstinate negation, never fully explained, blocks their way. This becomes clear when Frank, busy translating Ludovico Ariosto's *Orlando Furioso*, gets up the courage to show his verses to the lovely Diana Vernon. He asks her to meet him in the library after supper, "to which arrangement Miss Vernon . . . refused her consent, alleging some apology which I thought frivolous at the time." When, later that evening, Frank sees lights in the library and realizes that Diana is engaged there in a tête-à-tête with someone else, his jealousy overcomes him: " 'Silly, romping, incorrigible girl!' said I to myself. . . . 'I suppose, notwithstanding the excellence of her understanding, the society of half a dozen of clowns to play at whisk and swabbers would give her more pleasure than if Ariosto himself were to awake from the dead.'"[51] To waken Ariosto "from the dead" is of course exactly what Frank is trying to do with his translation: to join the progress of a literary canon in which the dead animate the living. That such literary haunting is specifically and "frivolously" blocked indicates that the library at Osbaldistone Hall attends to a different story than the story of literary inheritance and Scottish "progress" to which Frank—and perhaps the ideological work of the gothic itself—is willy-nilly committed.

Frank's choice of Ariosto's *Orlando Furioso* (1516, 1532) is not accidental. Set against the background of Charlemagne's campaign against the Saracens, *Orlando Furioso* is one of the longest poems in all of European literature, and one of the most influential (particularly on Spenser's *Faerie Queene*). In *Rob Roy* the poem is a generic marker of romance: "Ladies, and knights, and arms, and love's fair flame, / Deeds of emprize and courtesy, I sing." This is Frank's translation of the poem's opening lines, and it gives an accurate taste of the thousands to come: "There is a great deal of it," remarks Diana Vernon, shortly after beginning to read Frank's translation. In *The Origin of the Distinction of Ranks* (1771), an account of stadial theory that greatly influenced Scott's own university instructors, John Millar calls *Orlando Furioso* "a bundle of incoherent adventures, discovering neither unity of design, nor any selection of such objects as are fitted to excite admiration."[52] Blinded by love, though, Frank misconstrues Diana's tone: "Of what nature could those mysteries be with which she was surrounded as with an enchanter's spell . . . ?" he wonders, continuing to see her through the lens of *Orlando*'s romance-world.[53]

One of Ariosto's notable imaginative achievements was the hippogriff, an offspring of a griffin and a mare. It has the body of a horse, and the head, wings, and talons of an eagle. Many of Ariosto's knights accomplish their daring feats of bravery from the backs of these creatures. Though Ariosto is generally given credit for inventing the hippogriff, its roots go back to Virgil's *Eighth Eclogue*:

> The hopes of lovers
> Are wild and witless. Aye, griffins may
> Yet mate with mares, and the timorous she-deer
> May share a drinking trough with hounds, one day.[54]

Griffins and horses are enemies; Virgil's point is that in love impossible things become possible. In Scott, the hippogriff typically figures romance more generally—most famously in *Waverley*, when early in the novel the narrator apologizes for "plaguing" his readers with extensive discussions of "old-fashioned politics." "The truth is," he continues, "I do not invite my fair readers . . . into a flying chariot drawn by hippogriffs, or moved by enchantment. Mine is an humble English post-chaise, drawn upon four wheels, and keeping his Majesty's highway."[55] The kind of historian that Scott aspires to be must tell the story of Jacobitism with his feet on the ground; the horses pulling his post-chaise will certainly not mate with griffins.

This distinction between history and enchantment, horses and hippogriffs, offers a particularly telling gloss on the description of the library of Osbaldistone Hall, whose collection, we recall, "was chiefly of the classics, as well foreign as ancient history, and, *above all, divinity*" (my emphasis). "History" is of course the most overdetermined genre in Scott's writing, the place where his "humble English post-chaise" intervenes in the "foreign [and] ancient history" that had gone before. Given the Virgilian precedent that stands behind the hippogriff, we can read the library's "classics" as a reference to the hippogriffs that Frank attempts to introduce into the library via *Orlando Furioso*, or more generally to the kind of secularizing "canon love" with which the gothic library is typically associated, in which literature serves as cultural capital and an agent of an expanded feeling for the nation. As Scott renders the situation in *Waverley*, the hero must choose between the enchanted hippogriffs of literary romance and the smooth post-chaise of historical probability, even though both lead ultimately to Union—a nonchoice presented as a choice, whose emptiness is registered only in Waverley's sigh and in his furtive turn of the head.

But *Rob Roy* adds a third possibility to classics and history: "above all, divinity." As we learn toward the novel's close, the mysterious lights sometimes seen in the library, which Frank in his jealousy interprets as a rejection of both himself and his literary endeavors, come in fact from Sir Frederick Vernon, Diana's father and a Jacobite intriguer, who spends his days either hidden in secret passages behind the library's tapestry or posing as the family's priest. It may be that Sir Frederick comes closest to embodying the alternative contained in "divinity." For here Scott allows the political enchantments of Jacobitism to pull away from the literary enchantments—sighs, tartans, romance—to which he had so firmly tied them in *Waverley*. Jacobitism is

decidedly not a literary conceit in *Rob Roy*: indeed, it is Jacobitism that blocks
Frank's effort to share Ariosto with Diana.

It would be more accurate, perhaps, to say that Jacobitism is not literary
in the way that Lynch or Jon Mee describe the literary: as something that
contains enthusiasm or discontent, toning it down and making it presentable
for polite conversation. Jacobitism is, though, literary in another sense, namely
in the way that, like Purchas's rendering of addiction, it opens onto prospects
not yet entirely foreclosed. We could say that Jacobitism remains "unread" in
this novel—and not only because Frank is mostly unable to see the Jacobite
plot that is unfolding all around him. For Scott's narrator does his part, too,
inserting the library and its theological collection into a decidedly horsey historical narrative. From its ponderous seventeenth-century folios, he writes, "we
have distilled matter for our quartos and octavos, and which, once more subjected to the alembic, may, should our sons be yet more frivolous than ourselves, be still farther reduced into duodecimos and pamphlets" (153).

An alembic, Scott's metaphor for this frivolous reduction, is a pot used
for distilling spirits. The word had a certain charge in the period thanks to
Edmund Burke's use of it in *Reflections*, where it figures a temporary but
destructive atheism linked to revolution.[56] But when Scott picks up the figure
in *Waverley*, he uses it to rather different effect. In the novel's second chapter,
Sir Everard Waverley, a Tory and Jacobite, learns of his brother Richard's
rapid rise through the Whig government, and although "these events followed each other so closely . . . they came upon Sir Everard gradually, and
drop by drop, as it were, distilled through the cool and procrastinating alembic of Dyer's Weekly Letter" (39). Unlike the heat of what Burke calls the
revolutionary "alembick of hell," *Waverley*'s alembic is a cooling device; the
"slow succession of intelligence" prevents the shock of everything happening
"at once." Indeed the narrator humorously compares Richard's rise, and by
metonymy the rise of the bourgeois public sphere and its accelerating publication pace, with the slow fall of news in the Jacobite hinterlands, where a
single weekly paper, after passing from Sir Everard to his sister and thence to
his aged butler, "was regularly transferred from the Hall to the Rectory, from
the Rectory to Squire Stubbs' at the Grange, from the Squire to the Baronet's
steward at his neat white house on the heath, from the steward to the bailiff,
and from him through a huge circle of honest dames and gaffers, by whose
hard and horny hands it was generally worn to pieces in about a month after
its arrival." In thus comically tracking the social gradations celebrated by
Burke as "an entailed inheritance, derived to us from our forefathers, and to

be transmitted to our posterity," Scott's newspaper limns the very world that his novels will cautiously prod into a relationship with the rapidly modernizing metropole.[57]

What then of the alembic that Scott's narrator prospectively applied to the tomes gathering dust in the library of Osbaldistone Hall? Can it, too, cool overheated passions and gently bring the library into the modern world—gently enough to prevent an eruption of the "great disorder" that lurks somewhere within it? If so, the alembic might be the agent of uneven development, a role elsewhere assumed by the idea of a literary inheritance or a historical novel. But the alembic is a complex figure. Indeed it sits exactly on the border of the premodern and the properly modern, of the esoteric and the exoteric, of alchemy and chemistry.[58] It might indeed be an agent of secularization, containing just enough enchantment to ease the transition into a world where enchantments will have to take a different form, enabling "our sons to be yet more frivolous than ourselves." Yet the novel's plot gives voice to a more serious kind of frivolity when Diana refuses to met Frank in the library to hear his Ariosto translation and offers "some apology which I thought frivolous at the time" (200). Diana's frivolity, we eventually learn, was not frivolous at all: it was in fact a screen for her father and thus for the novel's Jacobite plot. Her frivolity is the sign, then, of a real change, even if a hopeless one. The mysterious lights and shadows in the library are not gothic ghosts but the actors of a potential counterhistory.

"Seventeenth century divinity had been massively learned," writes the historian G. V. Bennett. "Today its great tomes lie heavily on the shelves of old libraries and surprise the casual reader with closely printed columns, an array of ancient languages, and intricate reference to the authority of the traditional past. Theological argument was won or lost by appeal to the writings of the Fathers of the Early Church."[59] Bennett could almost have been thinking of *Rob Roy*, but it is more likely that he is thinking of descriptions like this one, from John Toland's *Christianity Not Mysterious* (1696):

How many voluminous Systems, infinitely more difficult than the Scriptures, must be read with great Attention by him that would be Master of the present Theology? What a prodigious Number of barbarous Words, (mysterious no doubt) what tedious and immethodical Directions, what ridiculous and discrepant Interpretations must you patiently learn and observe, before you can begin to understand a Professor of that Faculty?[60]

In seeking to simplify this intricate textual world, Toland would embrace Scott's alembic with alacrity—and though he may not represent the main-stream at the end of the seventeenth century, he nevertheless encapsulates the tendency of even the more moderate elements of the age: the search for a new, clearer basis on which to erect a multitude of things, from theology to science to statecraft to political economy to the writing of history. Charles Blount's indictment of the "crafty and covetous Sacerdotal Order; who . . . introduced Fables and Fictions of their own coining" is more blunt, but it makes much the same point as Locke's more cautious disparagement of the "artificial and figurative application of Words."[61] In the new world that these writers hail, it is hard to imagine a different fate for what Scott's narrator calls the "ponderous folios so dear to the seventeenth century."

Perhaps the most that can be said is that the meaning of "above all, divinity" is contained in the very folios that sit, moldering and unread, on the shelves of the library in Osbaldistone Hall. Whatever possibilities those volumes contain remain undeveloped yet present—unlike, then, the sighs that accompany the Waverley novel's various portrayals of historical inevita-bility, and more like the flickering film in Coleridge's grate, responding to the changes in air pressure as various historical actors come and go in pursuit of the numberless goings-on that make up everyday life. Scott's dialectical post-chaise of historical fiction seeks simultaneously to honor and surpass the past—to invent, in the name of everyday life, the tradition whose obsoles-cence it then narrates and redeems. Against such "progress" we may set the library at Osbaldistone Hall, still waiting for the reader who will dust off its ponderous volumes and begin to read.

Magic Politics

Allen Ginsberg noted, apropos of the 1968 Democratic convention, that "We need . . . magic politics to exorcise the police state."[62] An eschewal of "strat-egy" and indeed of propositional statements has characterized the countercul-ture since the 1960s. Yet Ginsberg's frivolity also served a serious purpose: to imagine how the world could be made anew. Thus the events, chanting, meditation, experiments with sound and with chemicals, that make up such magical politics aimed to let other kinds of "meanings" shine through. What one thinks about this will be largely determined by what one thinks about the relationship between "culture" and politics. For its critics, of course, such experimentalism was either self-indulgence or mere stylistic window-dressing: magic, by definition, has nothing to do with the daily grind of politics. Jacobitism is Scott's example of magic politics, and in *Waverley* he works hard to reduce it to a style or costume that bears little relation to the long, linear work of modifying institutions and effecting change.

Thomas Carlyle was correct when he wrote that for Scott, "the false, the semi-false, and the true were alike true in this, that they were there."[63] This is the power of realism: that it naturalizes and historicizes the improbable, reinforcing along the way modern distinctions between the supernatural and the natural, the miraculous and the ordinary. The technique of the historical novel is reflexive in this distinctively forward-looking way: it is less concerned with the truth of what people believed than in the fact that they believed it at all. As Scott put it in his own introduction to Ballantyne's 1811 edition of *The Castle of Otranto*, Walpole's generic experiment is groundbreaking because it "details supernatural incidents as they would have been readily believed and received in the eleventh or twelfth century." The reader, Scott continues, "understands precisely what is demanded of him."[64] Thus natural histories of enchantment, once the domain of writers like Hume, find their generic home in the novel. In a neat extension of Hume's essay on miracles, testimony to the fact that people once believed in extraordinary things serves to make that fact merely ordinary, part of the tapestry of a diverse human experience that has finally found its appropriate genre.

By general consensus the realist novel reached its high point in the nineteenth century. When, sixty years ago now, F. R. Leavis set out to explain why Jane Austen, George Eliot, Henry James, and Joseph Conrad were great in a way that distinguished them from all other English novelists, he wrote that their books gave readers an "awareness of the possibilities of life." The great novels, he continued, "are all distinguished by a vital capacity for experience, a kind of reverent openness before life," that Leavis saw as a transformed and secularized Christianity.[65] "Realism" is a term notoriously resistant to definition. But Leavis's "possibilities of life" comes close in the way that it balances fiction (what we're reading about didn't *actually* happen) with "life" (it *could* have happened). As George Levine describes the genre in his own field-defining study, realism belongs to an "affable and moderate tradition . . . and defines itself against the excesses, both stylistic and narrative, of various kinds of romantic, exotic, or sensational literatures."[66] The echoes of Hume and Scott ring loudly here. What "realism" tries to capture is the normative force of things as they are: it shows us the real, the actual,

the facts of the matter, the "way we do things around here"—but without
tying itself to a restrictive metaphysics of representation that demands one-to-
one correspondences. *Waverley* thus plays the probable off against the merely
possible in the service of a narrative that reminds us that Jacobitism is well
and truly finished, and for that very reason recoverable as a romantic dream.
The bet is that such dreams will in turn foster fidelity to the actual world, to
other people, to "life."

Such realism is today's most powerful carrier of the modern tendency
that Charles Taylor calls the "affirmation of ordinary life." From the Protestant critique of higher spirituality to raised standards of social behavior, from
Calvinist work to providentialist natural science, the series of transformations
that together make up modernity gradually revalued everyday life by infusing
it with spiritual meaning and ethical significance. Whether romanticism is
part of an immanent reaction to this affirmation, as Taylor thinks, or whether
it is part of the "ordinary" recovery from skepticism that Stanley Cavell finds
in Wordsworth, the everyday affirmations and enchantments that make up
these secular celebrations of "life" are the latest instance of the probabilistic
tradition whose political roots are to be found in the events of 1688 and
whose aesthetic zenith was the realist novel.[67]

One can of course admire the generous impulse behind such reverence for
the world and still wonder about its exclusions. Like Locke, realism desires to
"speak of things as they are," not as they could be or might have been. That
desire is itself a theodicy of modernity, with its own well-established record of
handling unexpected things—miracles, suffering, political rebellion—by historicizing and naturalizing them. "It was impossible that it could end otherwise
than thus," says the still-defiant Flora Mac-Ivor to Waverley, as though the
rebellion has always already failed.[68] Even though everybody knows the ending,
it is nevertheless remarkable that here, at the very moment of her generic defeat,
Flora's militancy gestures toward a rebellion whose staying power seems to
depend on its lack of obvious content. It only promises, without specifics, what
Hume called "disorder." So, too, the books of divinity in Osbaldistone Hall
remain closed, waiting for the reader who will reactivate their hidden message
in the present. Such enchantments, if that is what they are, do not "explain"
anything: they are not systems for generating meaning. They are, rather, the
magic politics of frivolity, silly and earnest in equal measure. Like Job's reiter-
ated sufferings, they do the only thing they can, which is simply to object to
explanation tout court, and so preserve a space of unquiet testimony to the
possibility that the world as it is may not be all there is.

CHAPTER 6

The Creation of Religious
Minorities: Hogg's *Justified Sinner*

From its very origin Christianity has struggled with how to read the Hebrew Scriptures, neither ignoring their literal content nor overemphasizing the importance of a tradition supposedly surpassed. This required a theory of reading that for most of Christian history proceeded allegorically. In *Burning to Read*, James Simpson calls allegory "a way of managing history" without being tied to it; it is "fundamentally a poetic system," he continues, "insofar as the allegorical connections between past and present are likenesses." In Simpson's telling Tyndale, Luther, and their Protestant followers stripped the poetry out of their interpretive models, favoring instead a "new confidence in the literal sense" that made "the figural scheme look suddenly rheumatic, laborious, and implausible."[1] With his implication that Protestant reading is literal in its very essence, Simpson joins those historians who have argued that the English Reformation was an attack on a lively tradition of lay piety rather than a reform of a decadent and corrupt religion. Cultural historians like Eamon Duffy have emphasized that the transition to Protestantism meant the loss of a vibrant popular culture. And intellectual historians like Stephen Toulmin have linked this transition to a context-independent "quest for certainty" that dominated seventeenth-century philosophy and science.[2]

Simpson, however, is focused neither on culture nor on metaphysics but on the demise of an elite reading practice that cherishes the richness and ambiguity of figurative language. And he provocatively links this to the growth of what he calls "fundamentalism," which in his account is little more than an agonized Protestant hermeneutics in which knowledge—of one's salvation, of the natural world—is simultaneously on the surface and hidden, obvious to all but also somehow clear only to a select few. Desperately search-ing the scriptures for evidence of salvation, Simpson's fundamentalist reader is at the mercy of these contradictory demands.

Near the end of Walter Scott's 1816 novel *Old Mortality*, the narrator shows us such a "fundamentalist." He is the talented Scottish military leader John Burley, literally gone to ground in a hidden cave, half-mad in his place of "almost unapproachable seclusion":

> Burley, only altered from what he had been formerly by the addition
> of a grisly beard, stood in the midst of the cave, with his clasped
> Bible in one hand, and his drawn sword in the other. His figure,
> dimly ruddied by the light of the red charcoal, seemed that of a
> fiend in the lurid atmosphere of Pandemonium, and his gestures
> and words, as far as they could be heard, seemed equally violent and
> irregular.[3]

Burley is a Covenanter, a particularly resolute group of Scottish Presbyterians who in the middle of the seventeenth century committed themselves to a radical version of the social contract and a resistance to Anglican polity. But more than that, with his Bible in one hand and his sword in the other, Burley is a figure for literal reading. In this chapter I trace one history of the literalist reader. The story is rather more complex than anachronistic charges of "fun-damentalism" might indicate.

Misapplication; or, Religion and Violence

The history that has brought Burley to his cave defies easy summary. From 1560 onward, the English had attempted to contain Scotland's growing Pres-byterianism by means of an Episcopalian church polity.[4] William Laud, arch-bishop of Canterbury from 1633 and an organizational genius, imposed a variety of High Church modifications on Scotland: kneeling for communion, a new prayer book, and a high altar moved to the east end of the chancel. To many on the Calvinist end of the spectrum, these changes looked like Catholicism through the back door. In this environment Scottish nation-alism and Calvinist theology became fused as a resistance to the Anglo-Arminianism through which Charles I and Laud seemed intent on colonizing their northern neighbor.

True to the spirit of this confessional age, the Scots responded with the National Covenant of 1638 and the Solemn League and Covenant of 1643. These documents cemented the alliance between English Parliamentarians and Scottish Presbyterians and pledged each to the extirpation of "Popery, Prelacie, (that is, Church-government, by Arch-Bishops, Bishops, their Chancellors and Commissaries . . . and all other Ecclesiasticall Officers depending on that Hierarchy) Superstition, Heresie, Schisms, Prophanenesse, and whatsoever shall be found to be contrary to sound Doctrine, and the power of Godlinesse."[5] This political covenantalism with its model of political power flowing from a God whose decrees were available to all, inaugurated a debate over the nature of power itself.[6] The English bishops whom Charles and James had been carefully placing as proxies for royal power were swept away, and Covenanting congregations elected their own boards of elders and appointed their own ministers. According to their version of contract theory, it was impossible to separate temporal and religious authority— not because religion was meddling with an autonomous "secular" domain but because the quasi-republicanism of Presbyterian governance directly opposed the temporal power of the Anglican Church.

The Covenanters, and all of Scotland, suffered greatly in the English Civil War.[7] Nor did matters improve with the Restoration: Charles II, like Laud before him, understood that the control and management of Scotland would be greatly facilitated by an Episcopal governance structure, or what the Covenanters called "Prelacie." The English state took no official position on matters of doctrine; the number of sacraments and the nature of salvation were considered matters of individual "conscience." But the state *did* take a position on temporal authority: it extended tolerance only to government-approved Presbyterian churches, those whose clergy had accepted a top-down Episcopal polity rather than a bottom-up Presbyterian one. In this political separation of temporal authority and religious doctrine we can recognize the origins of the Lockean model of tolerance that would shortly emerge.

Presbyterian ministers who refused to conform (about a third of the clergy) were forced from their livings. Many began preaching in open fields, sometimes to huge crowds. Because they were in more or less constant danger from government soldiers, they often posted armed guards and lookouts at the perimeter. Deprived of official toleration, members of these scattered congregations were harassed, imprisoned, tortured, and sometimes killed. In 1680 Richard Cameron, a Covenanting field preacher and military leader, marched with twenty armed men into the town square of Sanquhar and announced that "being under the standard of our Lord Jesus Christ, Captain of Salvation," he consequently declared war on Charles II, "a tyrant and usurper, and all the men of his practices, as enemies to our Lord Jesus Christ, and His cause and covenants."[8] Cameron did not last the year, but in death he lent his name to the underground remnant of the Covenanting tradition hounded throughout the so-called Killing Time from 1680 to 1688, when an increasingly nervous Stuart monarchy intensified its persecution of the Cameronians.

"Upon the 19 of February Captain Bruce with a Party of Soldiers surprised Six of the suffering Wanderers in Lochinkit-muir . . . and shot Four of them upon the Spot, without any further Process. . . . The other Two . . . the Captain carried with him to the Bridge of Orr. . . . And next day they carried them to the Parish of Irongray . . . and hanged them upon an Oak Tree, near the Kirk of Irongray."[9] One of the thousands collected in Robert Wodrow's massive *History of the Sufferings of the Church of Scotland* (1721), this account hints at the speed and vicissitude of government action, and the fear such acts provoke. The "suffering Wanderers" who had the bad luck to encounter government forces might be brought to trial; usually, however, they got a rougher kind of justice:

> finding Edward Kyan . . . who had fled in betwixt the Gavel of one House and the Side-wall of another, they dragged him out, and took him through a Yard. . . . When one of the Soldiers had him by the Arm dragging him away, without any Warning, further Questions, or permitting him to pray, the said Lieutenant . . . shot him through the Head, and presently discharged his other Pistol, and shot him again in the Head, when lying on the Ground struggling with Death; and one of the Soldiers of the Party coming up, pretended he saw some Motion in him still, and shot him a Third Time. . . . He was but a youth, and could not have been at Bothwel or any of the Risings, and they had indeed nothing to charge him with but his hiding himself.[10]

This is toleration as the Covenanters experienced it in the 1670s and 1680s. Those who refused the "choice" to accept a church polity that they rightly saw as a means for monitoring and supervising their activities were hounded out of their homes, kirks, and parishes. Living rough, relying on networks of friends and fellow congregants who risked their own lives to help them, they were vulnerable to all the vagaries of asymmetrical warfare. Around the time of Charles's death in 1685, Wodrow writes, "The deaths of the persecuted Wanderers are so numerous, in the Space of Three or Four Months Time, that I cannot give Accounts of them all."[11]

Occasionally the Covenanters struck back—most spectacularly in 1679, with the murder of James Sharp, the archbishop of St. Andrews. In Scott's fictional telling in *Old Mortality*, Burley had been the leader of the group who killed Sharp. But according to an anonymous 1679 pamphlet entitled *True Account of the Horrid Murther Committed upon His Grace*, the murder was really the result of a mistaken reading practice. The pamphlet identifies an earlier pamphlet, entitled *Naphtali, or, The wrestlings of the Church of Scotland for the kingdom of Christ* (1667), as the chief culprit. Something of a Covenanting sourcebook, *Naphtali* contained copies of both national Covenants, accounts of the speeches, testimonies, and sufferings of numerous Covenanters, and a history of the Reformation in Scotland. This pamphlet, writes the author of the *True Account*, "endeavoured to perswade all men to Massacre their Governours and Judges by the misapplyed Example of holy *Phineas*."[12] He refers here to the account in the book of Numbers, when Phinehas (as the name is usually rendered) resists the Midianite women who tempt the Israelites into idolatry:

> And, behold, one of the children of Israel came and brought unto his brethren a Midianitish woman in the sight of Moses, and in the sight of all the Congregation of the children of Israel, who wept before the door of the Tabernacle of the Congregation. And when Phinehas the son of Eleazar the son of Aaron the Priest saw it, he rose up from the midst of the Congregation, and took a spear in his hand, And followed the man of Israel into the tent, and thrust them both through, *to wit*, the man of Israel, and the woman, through her belly. So the plague ceased from the children of Israel. (Numbers 25:6–8; Geneva Bible)[13]

When the author of the *True Account* calls this a "misapplyed" example, he means that Phinehas ought to be a spiritual rather than a literal exemplar, a symbol of faithfulness rather than a model for action. He implies that because they miss this literary point, the Covenanters mistakenly match contemporary life to the template of Scripture. Their reading proceeds like this: we sojourn among a wicked people, just as the children of Israel did. Phinehas killed the unfaithful Israelite and was rewarded by God; Archbishop Sharp is like the unfaithful Israelite; if we kill him, we, too, will be rewarded.

This is literalism of the bluntest kind. It is the sort canvased in Simpson's *Burning to Read*, in which the reader searches Scripture for a particular kind of *knowledge* independent of the words in which it is clothed. The stakes could not be higher—eternal life hangs in the balance—but the reader has no way of knowing if he is reading properly because he has denied a priori the entire history of textual interpretation that has brought him to this point; he has nobody but himself to rely on. The agony of this moment seems overdetermined, the violence of "misapplication" inevitable.

Yet it is easy to overdraw the distinction between figurative and literal on which this charge of misapplication depends. What would be a better—that is, less literal—interpretation? For if Phinehas is merely a figure for faithfulness amid adversity, then he becomes difficult to distinguish from the weeping Israelites of the congregation. They, too, are faithful, as we know from their tears of sorrow. The power of the story in fact turns on the decisive manner in which Phinehas *separates himself* from the weeping congregation, strides into the tent, and with one thrust of his spear changes the narrative. Indeed there is no way to read this story that is not a "misapplication" in the sense meant by the *True Account*. Phinehas may be better read as a symbolic rather than a literal exemplar, but even that symbol involves a kind of precision and violence that retains its power to shock. The charge of misapplication thus seems to miss the way in which Phinehas is himself a sign—in the rather puerile way his spear thrusts through the belly of the Moabite woman, to be sure, but also because his gesture itself is less a part of a deliberately executed strategy than a sudden and dramatic way of empowering a disenfranchised community.[14] Phinehas *just is* misapplication, personified—which is to say that even in his literalism he is already a figure.

Even if we grant, therefore, that the Covenanters are modeling themselves on Phinehas, this is less a misapplication than an accurate *application* of what is already a figural action. To put it another way, the relevant issue here is not some distortion of a scriptural text, as if fanatics cannot read properly, but rather a dispute between a mode of reading that distinguishes a priori between religion (the domain of interpretation) and politics (the domain of action) and a mode of reading that refuses precisely that distinction, on the grounds that it so construes the intellectual terrain as to predetermine that certain kinds of reading practices will never count as legitimate. Without that distinction, there is no such thing as a misapplication: all action is both literal *and* figurative, historically located but also signifying beyond its immediate context.

In any event, *Naphtali*'s supposed misapplications were thought danger-ous enough to get the text condemned by the Privy Council soon after it appeared; in an act of symbolic disarmament, all Scottish citizens were instructed to turn in their copies to be publicly burned; those found to be still in possession of this "most treasonable and seditious Pamphlet" were fined 2,000 pounds, while those involved in its distribution were promised "pains and penalties" "inflicted without mercy."[15] Fascinated with the vio-lent reading practices it here condemned, the Privy Council does not bother to reflect on the state-sponsored violence with which it contravenes fanaticism.

Indeed, the charge of misapplication creates the space in which such official power can operate. "It is undeniable," according to the *True Account*, "that those of the same profession and Way, have lately wounded many of His Majesties Officers, for putting of the Uncontroverted Laws in[to] Executions."[16] Sir Mungo Murray, one of the government officers whose efforts to put "Uncontroverted Laws" into effect earn him several mentions in Wodrow, boiled the link between religion and violence down to a couplet when he concluded his elegy for Sharp with the following aphorism:

> *The first Protestant Bishop heard or read*
> *In Scotland for Religion Murdered.*[17]

Bishops are both temporal and religious authorities, and this fact allows Mur-ray to cement the link between violence and religion at the moment that religion intersects the state. For Murray as for the other progovernment writ-ers, when a servant of the state is killed, the violence is religiously motivated. Violence only becomes visible *as violence* when a persecuted religious minor-ity employs it. By contrast, when violence *serves* the state it is simply law, even if this means shooting teenagers in the head in an alleyway: far from misapplication, that is simply an application.

The Magic Rod of Fanaticism

How does one tell the story of the Covenanters? In *Old Mortality*, Scott skips over the Killing Times. He sends his hero Henry Morton to Holland for a

decade and then brings him back in 1689, as things are settling down. According to Scott's narrator, the new government intended to "tolerate all forms
of religion which were consistent with the safety of the state."[18] Always a
reluctant Covenanter, Morton finds in this new dispensation enough flexibility to effect a marriage to Edith Bellenden, the High Church Anglican he
has long loved. Mutual affection, rational self-interest, and the promises of
modernity conquer religious strife. Scott's majority account, like those of
Burnet and Tillotson and Locke, emphasizes the power of the secularizing
nation-state to prevent the wars of religion from beginning all over again.
Toleration creates room to maneuver; it brings about a marriage that represents a new, postconfessional beginning for Scotland. And like the author of
the *True Account* with his worries about "misapplication," Scott's narrator
argues that those who continue to murmur at this new order are tied to an
outdated way of reading: "The principles of indulgence . . . gave great offense
to the more violent party, who condemned them as diametrically contrary to
Scripture; for which narrow-spirited doctrine they cited various texts, all, *as
it may well be supposed*, detached from their context."[19]

The "as it may well be supposed" says a great deal about the shared
assumptions of narrator and reader. In *Old Mortality* we do not even need an
example of such context-free reading practices. The narrator simply brings us
to Burley's cave, and to the powerful image of a bearded man, bathed in red
light, a Bible in one hand and a sword in the other. To be sure, Burley still
has the support of the country people round about; the secret of his cave is
"carefully preserved by the few shepherds to whom it might be known."[20]
These tight-lipped folk are largely beneath the notice of the elite soldiers and
rising middle classes tasked with keeping an eye on them. But Burley's final
effort at reestablishing himself is pitiful and, more important, solitary. There
is no host to gather any more, no army to assemble, no Rising. In this novel,
toleration works, and the Covenanters sink "into the scattered remnant of
serious, scrupulous, and harmless enthusiasts."[21] Helped along by a theory of
uneven development learned from the thinkers of the Scottish Enlightenment, the Covenanters become striking but harmless reminders of the passions that once upon a time enflamed Scotland. No longer dangerous,
"misapplication" is now anachronism.[22]

To get a sense of how Scott understood the political stakes of this argument, we can turn to Coleridge's analogous account of Scottish religious
sectarianism in Chapter 10 of the *Biographia Literaria*, published a year after
Old Mortality. Coleridge's version seems an odd insertion in the midst of his

comments about toleration (discussed already in Chapter 4 of this book). Like Scott, Coleridge reads the French Revolution and radical agitation in England through the optics not of the continental Enlightenment but of a fraught religious history that centers on Scotland. The partisan "fervour" of the present moment, he writes, causes him to reflect that the "magic rod of fanaticism" always lurks in human history. He goes on to cite the Peasants' War in Germany, Anabaptism, and the English Revolution. After the Restoration one might have expected that the triumphant Royalists would show some mercy. "But no! The ball of persecution was taken up with undiminished vigour by the persecuted. The same fanatic principle, that under the solemn oath and covenant had turned cathedrals into stables . . . emptied its whole vial of wrath on the miserable Covenanters of Scotland." And then Coleridge adds, in a significant parentheses, "Laing's History of Scotland.—Walter Scott's bards, ballads, etc."[23]

The thinking behind the reference to Scott can be gleaned from Scott's own letter to Robert Southey in September of 1824: "By the way, did you ever observe how easy it would be for a good historian to run a par[a]llel betwixt the Great Rebellion and the French Revolution, just substituting the spirit of fanaticism for that of soi distant philosophy."[24] This is the argument laid out in great detail in Burke's *Reflections*—and it is Coleridge's argument in this *Biographia* passage as well when he concludes that the persecuting zeal of "democratic fanaticism" has now risen again: "the same principles dressed in the ostentatious garb of a fashionable philosophy once more rose triumphant and effected the French Revolution."[25] The final chapter of this story—the Coleridge-Scott extension of Burke, in effect—is the predicament of post-Waterloo England. Napoleon's defeat, Coleridge worries, may be the stimulus to "awaken the thunder and precipitate the lightning from the opposite quarter of the political heaven" (257). During the Napoleonic years, patriotism may have blunted the "democratic frenzy" of the revolutionary era, but now, with the demise of a common enemy, that frenzy threatens the social fabric of the nation once more. The fear that Coleridge shares with Scott, then, is that the republicanism of the revolution will reemerge, and that a nascent working class, repressed by law or co-opted by nationalist rhetoric during the past two decades, will once again begin to make demands.[26] This is one way to read *Old Mortality*'s conclusion: Burley's defeat is an allegory for the defeat of the political hopes of the laboring classes.

To understand the political effect of this argument, we need to reconnect it to the "Spy Nozy" episode earlier in the same chapter of the *Biographia*.

For by linking the French Enlightenment and French Revolution to seventeenth-century religious fanaticism, Coleridge managed to cut it off from a different seventeenth-century source, namely the Spinozism whose subterranean influence has been so impressively traced by Jonathan Israel in *Radical Enlightenment.* "By the mid-1670s," Israel writes in typically enthusiastic fashion, "Spinoza stood at the head of an underground radical philosophical movement rooted in the Netherlands but decidedly European in scope. His books were illegal but yet, paradoxically, excepting only Descartes, no other contemporary thinker had enjoyed, over the previous quarter of a century, so wide a European reception, even if in his case that reception was overwhelmingly (even if far from exclusively) hostile."[27] As Israel describes it, this Radical Enlightenment was a kind of determinate absence throughout the later seventeenth and eighteenth centuries, mostly identified in shadowy allusions, a feeling or possibility glimpsed only in certain moments—in the shops of radical booksellers, in the clandestine circulation of texts, in the court records and trials to which various members of this radical coterie were subjected. The movement, Israel goes on to argue, shaped the moderate English Enlightenment of Locke, Newton, and their contemporaries, who wished "to conquer ignorance and superstition, establish toleration, and revolutionize ideas, education, and attitudes by means of philosophy," but also wished to uphold traditional authority by safeguarding "essential elements of the older structures, effecting a viable synthesis of old and new, and of reason and faith" (11). By contrast, the Radical Enlightenment "sought to sweep away existing structures entirely, rejecting . . . the intervention of a providential God in human affairs, denying the possibility of miracles, . . . and refusing to accept that there is any God-ordained social hierarchy, concentration of privilege or land-ownership in noble hands, or religious sanction for monarchy" (11–12). It is this "uncompromising anti-monarchism and egalitarian tendency," Israel concludes, that "leads in direct line of descent to the revolutionary rhetoric of Robespierre and the French Jacobins" (22).

I am less interested in whether Israel overstates the actual importance of the Radical Enlightenment than I am in his description of the shadowy but very real anxiety that the movement clearly produced. It is this unease that so clearly registers in Coleridge's account in the *Biographia.* This is why, although he had been speaking enthusiastically of Spinoza on his rambles around the Quantock Hills with his friends, he insists that the spy "could not catch a word about politics." All he could learn was that Spinoza was a "man who had made a book and lived long ago" (254). This is the real genius of the "Spy Nozy" episode: it enables Coleridge to locate the origins of the

French Revolution not in the republicanism of the Radical Enlightenment but in the republicanism of religious sectarianism, thereby freeing poetry from the charge of political sedition and sinking Spinozism under a pile of books.

What matters here is the secularism of the method, its implicit assumption that the political content of religious sectarianism can be detached from its cultural expression, that questions of injustice are therefore distinct from enthusiasm in the same way that politics are distinct from religion, and thus that any attempt to think the two together amounts to what I have been calling a "misapplication." It is a remarkably efficient technique, for by refusing to face up to the political presence of the Radical Enlightenment, it also refuses to recognize the political potency of the religious disputes that were the seventeenth century's *other* legacy to modernity. Fanaticism was never solely about reading. It was also about justice. But one would be hard pressed to learn this from the standard accounts that stretch from Mungo Murray to Coleridge and Scott and down to discussions of fundamentalism in our own day. Scott insists in *Old Mortality* that time has rendered the Covenanters harmless; the real worry in the second decade of the nineteenth century is not religious sectaries but their figurative epigones, the "union men" and luddites, the marginalized working poor who like Burley's "hill people" have melted away into the landscape but not disappeared, awaiting what Coleridge calls the "concurrence of events" that will bring them forth once again. The magic rod of fanaticism, as Coleridge wrote, "needs only the re-exciting warmth of a master hand to bud forth afresh and produce the old fruits."[28] Or, as the fictitious editor of Hogg's *Private Memoirs and Confessions of a Justified Sinner* puts it, "we have heard much of the rage of fanaticism in former days, but nothing to this." Which could mean either that here is evidence of even greater former fanaticism, or that "this" is the present—in other words that the danger of fanaticism is now, in the 1820s, greater than it ever has been.[29] Perhaps the politics of the Covenanting tradition, that is to say, cannot be detached from its vision of a redeemed life *in the present*.

The Logic of Religious Minoritization: From Marriage to Toleration to Illegitimacy

The Private Memoirs and Confessions of a Justified Sinner (1824), James Hogg's bizarre masterpiece of a novel, is also a radical literary response to *Old Mortality*. It is a novel obsessed by questions of justice and injustice, and it works

hard to pry apart the tight links among religion, violence, and political insur-
rection that Coleridge and Scott jointly roll together and label fanaticism.
Hogg's simple point is that fanatics are made, not born, and that the novel
is the means by which to trace their genealogy. Stretched over the years from
the Glorious Revolution to the aftermath of the Act of Union, the *Memoirs
and Confessions* begins where Wodrow's *History of the Sufferings of the Church
of Scotland* leaves off. Its crucial formal innovation is to tell the same story
twice; we begin with an "editor's narrative," penned supposedly in 1823, that
presents the backstory and context for an extraordinary "confession," a found
document that covers the years 1703 to 1712 and makes up the second half of
the novel.

The novel's plot begins abruptly. For reasons nobody can fathom,
George Colwan, a morally flexible Cavalier and Royalist, marries a prudish
Presbyterian Covenanter, "the most severe and gloomy of all bigots to the
principles of the Reformation."[30] Within six months the parties have
retreated into a hostile truce: "The upper, or third story of the old mansion-
house, was awarded to the lady for her residence. She had a separate door, a
separate stair, a separate garden, and walks that in no instance intersected the
laird's; so that one would have thought the separation complete. They had
each their own parties, selected from their own sort of people" (56). If Scott's
marriages across the space of religious and political difference tend to cement
the ideological work of the Glorious Revolution and the Act of Union, Hogg
makes marriage the *beginning* of trouble rather than its resolution.[31] We open,
that is to say, with the failure of the toleration Scott had celebrated—an irony
unremarked by the editor, who continues to present himself as a product of
post-1688 "marriages" and turns his ire on Lady Dalcastle's intolerance:
"though the laird never once chafed himself about the lady's companies, it
was not long before she began to intermeddle about some of his."[32] This is
not strictly speaking true: the laird does indeed "chafe himself" regarding
his wife's acquaintances. His tolerance for her, moreover, is structured by a
governmental logic. Like the nonconforming Covenanters, Lady Dalcastle
can engage in all the theological controversy she wants (and Hogg has some
fun with her endless hair-splitting); what she may not do is upset the political
establishment of the Dalcastle home. She is allowed the private space of
the mind and conscience (allegorized by her placement on the top floor of the
mansion, her separate door and separate stair) while the laird represents the
family in public. Under these conditions, any attempt to leave the top floor
will count as disturbing the peace. Read against the background of what the

editor terms the "party spirit" (68) of the times, Covenanters on the move are a source of unrest.

Despite their mutual hostility and separate establishments, Lord and Lady Dalcastle manage to produce two sons. George, the eldest, takes after his father: "a generous and kind-hearted youth; always ready to oblige, and hardly ever dissatisfied with anybody" (61). His younger brother, Robert, is a different story. Named for his mother's spiritual adviser, a "flaming predestinarian divine" named Wringhim (50), young Robert is "an acute boy, an excellent learner, had ardent and ungovernable passions, and withal, a sternness of demeanour from which other boys shrunk" (62). Fanatical and self-justifying but also pitiable and needy, he dogs George's footsteps, taunting him at every turn, and eventually kills him. Increasingly bizarre and bloody events follow; aided by Gil-Martin, a remarkable companion who may be the devil or may be simply a product of his imagination, Robert runs wild. Debauched or unconscious for extended periods, he apparently also seduces and then murders a local village girl, kills his mother, and ends up on the run, with only the clothes on his back and a price on his head: "My state both of body and mind was now truly deplorable. I was hungry, wounded, and lame; an outcast and a vagabond in society; my life sought after with avidity. . . . Miserable, forlorn, and dreading every person that I saw, either behind or before me, I hasted on towards Edinburgh, taking all the bye and unfrequented paths" (206). Homeless and defenseless, Robert begins to inhabit the history of his people—those "suffering Wanderers" who fill the pages of Wodrow's volumes. Yet because he is ignorant of the history in which he participates, he suffers without context, and the editor supplies none. Oblivious to whatever larger political or social forces may be afoot, Robert retreats farther inward with every step, until he is moving through a landscape peopled entirely by his own delusions. He apparently ends by hanging himself, though the story is unclear on this point as on much else.

Robert's downward spiral is easily read as a satire on religious fanaticism, as though he is a late addition to the pantheon of anguished Protestant readers described by Simpson in *Burning to Read*: on the one hand, the demise of an allegorical universe and a mediated, hierarchical social order means that the significance of things must be directly grasped; on the other hand, because the contemplative ideal is replaced by an investigative one, the order of things that had once been manifest now seems inscrutable, so that the quest for knowledge takes on a forensic quality. Searching the Scriptures for evidence of their salvation while knowing all the while that the question had already been decided by God, people like Robert are pushed into antinomianism, madness, and mayhem. This is certainly the editor's position, for though he frames the second half of the novel as an effort of understanding, it quickly becomes clear that confronting a first-person account of fanaticism will not get the reader very far toward this goal. Indeed, as he moves through a succession of murders in which he can hardly recognize himself, Robert grows more and more bewildered at the forces arrayed against him. In fact, Robert thinks that he is home in bed when he is supposed to have committed his bloodiest crimes, as though fanaticism were an extended fugue state: "I was a being incomprehensible to myself. Either I had a second self, who transacted business in my likeness, or else my body was at times possessed by a spirit over which it had no control, and of whose actions my own soul was wholly unconscious. . . . [O]f dates I could make nothing: one-half, or two-thirds of my time, seemed to me to be totally lost" (179). Unable to understand himself, and lacking the historical context for understanding how he has become what he is, Robert's dark desires appear a form of madness or insanity subject to no explanation whatsoever. "What can this work be?" asks the editor at last. "I cannot tell" (222). Bewilderment, confusion, the inability to "adjust"—these become Robert's hallmarks as, in a dark parody of the Killing Times, he rampages across the countryside. He becomes incomprehensible to himself, and so it is no wonder that we wind up reading the diary of a madman.

Yet this interpretation, which sees in Calvinism or even in "religion" itself some dark core of fanaticism and potential violence, fails to account for the social and historical processes that have brought Robert to this pass. For example, Robert's first act under Gil-Martin's tutelage is to murder the Reverend Blanchard, "a worthy, pious divine, but quite of the moral cast" (141–42). Just before this murder Blanchard had remonstrated with Robert about his reading practices. He reads selectively, says Blanchard, "forcing" the principles of Calvinism "beyond their due bounds" (142). A sincere Presbyterian who nevertheless conforms to Episcopacy, Blanchard most obviously represents the possibility of a compromise with England, one that depends on a distinction between belief and politics and that will issue, if Scott's version of history stands, in a gradual diminution of sectarian strife within a new entity called Great Britain. Like the narrator of *Old Mortality*, Blanchard offers a path to modernity that depends on an "unforced" reading practice, in contrast to the scriptural wrenching and "pressing" in which Robert engages. But the question of force is a complicated one, since Blanchard's

notion of unforced religious reading presupposes the temporal forcing of
political conformity. Because his more liberal reading presupposes a *political*
arrangement whereby Presbyterianism gives up its version of the social contract in favor of episcopacy, Blanchard's tolerant and contextual practices are
less self-generated than they are "gifts" of modern sovereignty. When he kills
Blanchard, Robert in effect reverses the vector of these forces; he returns force
to his reading of Scripture, which means in this case resisting the force of
temporal authority when it appears *in the guise of unforced reading*. The point
is worth stressing: in his confused way Robert correctly senses that a Scotland
narrated into modernity by men like Blanchard will leave people behind—
particularly those who, like Robert, are educated, serious, but somehow *unfit*,
irregular, out of place.

A passage from Scott's *Old Mortality* can shed light on the significance
of Blanchard's murder. It recounts an argument between Morton and Burley
about whether particular passages can be applied directly to the Covenanters'
rebellion. "I revere the Scriptures," declares Morton. "I look into them with
humble hope of extracting a rule of conduct and a law of salvation. But I
expect to find this by an examination of their general tenor, and of the spirit
which they uniformly breathe, and not by wresting particular passages from
their context, or by the application of Scriptural phrases to circumstances
and events with which they have often very slender relation" (230). Morton's
language, particularly his talk of the "spirit" with which Scripture breathes,
is more at home in the early nineteenth century than the late seventeenth.
His is clearly, that is to say, also the voice of the narrator, who writes his own
historical fiction out of a comprehensive knowledge of the "general tenor" of
a period. Such knowledge worn lightly, rather than wrested or forced in its
application, is exactly what Georg Lukács celebrated about Scott's historical
technique. In *The Historical Novel*, Lukács wrote that "the deeper and more
genuinely historical a writer's knowledge of a period, the more freely will he
be able to move about inside his subject and the less tied will he feel to
individual historical data. Scott's extraordinary genius lay in the fact that
he gave the historical novel just such themes as would allow for this 'free
movement'."[33] By casting Scott's value in these terms, Lukács offered a perhaps unintentionally political interpretation of Scott's technique, for it is of
course exactly freedom of movement that characters like Morton, Blanchard,
and other "indulged" Presbyterians have—freedom of movement denied to
the Covenanters in ways that, again, Hogg allegorizes very early in his novel
when he sequesters Lady Dalcastle at the top of the house, where she is forced

to watch the comings and goings of others rather than moving about herself. Particularly during the decade of the Killing Times, as Wodrow's *History* details so tirelessly, all Covenanting movement was inherently political movement. Lukács's commentary thus allows us to track the translation of religious and political "freedom" into interpretive freedom: to move about freely inside one's subject is to control it, to be the master of a history rather than, like the Covenanters, to be continually mastered by it. To put it another way, Blanchard and Morton, as well as Scott's narrator, can *afford* to be free in their reading of Scripture, because history and the army are on their side. Robert has no such luxury.

Of course, the murder of Blanchard was doomed to fail as an attempt to recover a different Covenanting future or even just an expanded capacity for movement. But the reason for that failure is, again, surprising, because it springs from Robert's own experience of illegitimacy—of being outside the law, and therefore outside the domain in which movement is protected. For the editor hints strongly that Robert is the Reverend Wringhim's biological son. As so often with Hogg, the tone shifts from sophomoric innuendo about Wringhim and Lady Dalcastle getting "warm" in their doctrinal conversations (57) to the serious question of Lord Dalcastle's legal responsibilities to his second son:

> A brother he certainly was, in the eyes of the law, and it is more
> than probable that he was his brother in reality. But the laird
> thought otherwise; and, though he knew and acknowledged that he
> was obliged to support and provide for him, he refused to acknowl-
> edge him in other respects. He neither would countenance the ban-
> quet, nor take the baptismal vows on him in the child's name; of
> course, the poor boy had to live and remain an alien from the visible
> church for a year and a day; at which time, Mr. Wringhim, out of
> pity and kindness, took the lady herself as sponsor for the boy, and
> baptized him by the name of Robert Wringhim,—that being the
> noted divine's own name. (61)

When Robert says that he was "born an outcast in the world," then, he is speaking the simple truth (117). Consider the grudging nature of the legal arrangement here: like the earlier separation agreement of which it is the logical successor, it identifies a bare legal minimum and refuses to go beyond it. The result is that a son and family member is transformed first into a barely tolerated legal entity and then into what the editor calls a "religious maniac" outside the boundaries of law (232). The trauma this induces is sufficiently illustrated by fact that Wringhim senior spends years "struggling with the Almighty" (118) to ensure Robert's salvation. At the psychological level this struggle is clearly Wringhim's effort to expunge his own sexual guilt; but at the narrative level something different happens, since the day that the assurance finally comes is also the day that Robert meets Gil-Martin and begins his crime spree. Having sought and obtained an alternative form of legitimacy, Robert now takes his revenge on the system that had so casually tossed him aside.

Psychologically, covenanting Calvinism and its focus on original sin may mean guilt for something that happened before one was born; but in this the Covenanters are examples of what it means to be a religious minority in a modernizing nation-state. Calvinism's paranoid dynamics have a political valence, in other words: when the soldiers come, you run, and the running makes you guilty. In place of the modern aspiration of autonomy—the ability to move oneself—the Covenanters are moved by someone or something else: by soldiers, by the force of unforced reading, by the language of toleration, by the legal categories of marriage and illegitimacy. Like the film in "Frost at Midnight," flickering in response to invisible turbulence and change, the movement Robert experiences is not often directly caused. Usually it is indirect, the result of forces unseen until they are made manifest in their effects. Robert's illegitimacy thus stands in for a much larger question of the legal status of religious minorities, and in tracing the downward spiral from marriage to toleration to illegitimacy Hogg's novel is brilliantly counterintuitive in its suggestion that there are no religious minorities before their interpellation by the law. As Hogg tells the story, it is not that state power, in the form of a tolerant "marriage" between warring elements, works to contain an already existing religious fanaticism; rather, the power of the state *precedes and creates* religious fanaticism. Scott-style marriages, with their promise of toning down conflict and ushering Scotland into modernity, turn out to be disastrous for all parties. The fanatical product of such marriages, once born, refuses to die. Like the spirits and doubles and devils that people this novel, it keeps coming back, in increasingly violent forms.

Of all the texts considered in this book, then, Hogg's novel is the most ethically and politically pointed critique of secularism as a form of state-sponsored violence. It is not only that the editorial, third-person account cannot "know" fanaticism. That may be true, but it is merely a symptom of the kinds of systematically unrecognized "forces" that undergird the modern regime of which the editor is representative: read Scripture in an unforced way, yet under the guidance of government forces; believe what you want, but only *after* you have been forced into political conformity; no one forced you to run, so if you did run you must have done something wrong. The editor's own complicity with these forces-that-are-not-forces emerges every time he blurs the line between editorial narrative and first-person confession, and since he does this regularly, his claim to leave "everyone to judge for himself" (116) can be true only, like Colwan's acknowledgment of Robert's legitimacy, in the most narrow and technical sense.[34] In reality, "forces" shape the entire reading experience, though often invisibly: when he wonders whether he is "possessed by a spirit over which [his mind] had no control" (179), for example, Robert gives voice to the power of a narrator to put his characters through hell. Of course, this is true of any novel; the virtue of Hogg's novel is that its notional splitting into original document and editorial apparatus elevates this banal fact into an allegory of interpretive practice itself, by virtue of which religious fanaticism is posed as an example of forced and unnatural interpretation so that the editor's own interpretive intrusions can appear under the guise of unforced neutrality.

Covenanting bewilderment at this narrative power generally takes a sexual turn. The novel's misogyny, Wringhim senior's infidelity, and Robert's sadism, not to mention the text's obsessive doubling and the "strange sensations that thrilled [Robert's] whole frame" (131) when he first meets Gil-Martin led Eve Sedgwick years ago to interpret the novel as an expression of homosexual panic.[35] As she did throughout her book *Between Men*, Sedgwick resisted interpreting Robert as a representative of a minority queer identity that cannot be "expressed." Indeed, as she pointed out, misogyny is the overwhelming leitmotif here, and the novel's most strongly thematized fantasy is that of the all-male family: God, Robert Wringhim senior and Robert Wringhim junior, with Robert's mother, her problematic womb, and the stain of illegitimacy magically banished. Like other period texts such as *Vathek* and *Frankenstein*, Hogg's novel dreams of a world without the possibility of illegitimacy, dreams, that is to say, of a world without women—a dream structured by a disavowed homoeroticism that, wrote Sedgwick, projects the homosexual "as a failed but dangerous and repudiated version of itself."[36] The key is not homosexuality as such, then, but straight male fantasies of the domination of women. I would add to this a political claim: that Hogg links that fantasy to the fantasy of political resistance itself. Think again of Phinehas thrusting his spear into the belly of the Midianite woman: as if the power to rewrite the script of illegitimacy can be claimed by a desperate and persecuted community only if it turns violently on the proximate rather than ultimate cause—the womb standing in here for the legal violence of the state that makes the womb its business whenever it determines illegitimacy. Unable to combat the distributed forces of the state itself, Robert turns on his mother as a proxy for that force, the place where temporal power intersects with embodied life. Dead because she happened to be in the wrong place at the wrong time, Robert's mother is an example of a civilian death if ever there was one—a victim of illegitimate violence, to be sure, but before that a victim of the legitimate violence that brought illegitimacy into being.

This is not to say, of course, that identity does not matter, nor that the question of minorities and their treatment does not matter; as long as force is distributed unequally within a state, there will be majorities and minorities. It is, however, to call our attention *away* from the problem of how to tolerate minority expressions within a majority state, as if the fact of minority identities is just a given in the world, and *toward* the discourse that has made it seem as if the question of minorities and what we should do about them is the relevant question. Hogg's novel insists that such questions are not born but made, and made by the very structures—toleration, law, separation of politics and religion—that are then called on to deal, inadequately, with the half-crazed results. Just as homophobia depends on that which it perpetually disavows, so too secular power depends on the process here thematized as *illegitimacy*. Whenever the troops arrive, someone will be sure to run; and in that act, to suddenly find themselves "religious" in a way that takes them outside the law, outside the space in which recognition—of a child, of a way of being in the world—is even possible.

Measuring Religion

Near the end of the novel we read of a strange tale in *Blackwood's Magazine*. Apparently two local shepherds had partly dug up the body of a suicide, buried for some one hundred years: "One of the young men seized the rope and pulled by it, but the old enchantment of the devil remained,—it would not break; and so he pulled and pulled at it, till behold the body came up into a sitting posture, with a broad blue bonnet on its head, and its plaid around it, all as fresh as that day it was laid in!" (225). Intrigued, the editor and a chummy group of Edinburgh literary men head into the hills near Selkirk to investigate this strange tale. They borrow a horse from Walter Scott, find the spot, and dig up the entire body. By now the top half has begun to disintegrate, but the undisturbed bottom half is still in perfect condition. A lengthy, minute, and dispassionate account follows, as the editor makes a show of his keen observations and his deductive power. He describes the coat ("tweeled, milled, and thicker than a carpet"), the vest ("striped serge, such as I have often seen worn by country people"), and the shoes: "in the inside of one of the shoes there was a layer of cow's dung, about one eighth of an inch thick, and in the hollow of the sole fully one fourth of an inch. It was firm, green, and fresh, and proved that he had been working in a byre" (229).[37] All along, the editor has gone out of his way to broadcast his empiricist credentials. Much of his narrative is structured like a detective story; during an earlier description of a rainbow he had already signaled his affinity with Newtonian natural science; and now, when he digs up the body, he seems to channel Boyle himself: "I will describe every thing as I saw it before four respectable witnesses, whose names I shall publish at large if permitted," he writes (228), invoking the technology of virtual witnessing developed in the early modern laboratory.

Eventually the group finds the manuscript of Robert's confessions. But nothing about it conforms to the editor's forensic penchant for measuring and comparing. Though he repeats the several conflicting traditions about the location of the body and how it came to be there, he is really more interested in the weave of the cloth and the condition of the shoes, and anxious to carry away as many souvenirs as possible. As for the manuscript, though he acknowledges that the writer must have attached great importance to it and to its preservation, he concludes that he does not understand it. He has, after all, come to the place on Walter Scott's horse. The message may have been sent, in other words, but there is no one on the other side to receive it.

Compare this scene—a dead body, clothes, a curious crowd, a book—to a somewhat more famous literary encounter with a dead body:

Seeking I knew not what, I chanced to cross
One of those open fields, which, shaped like ears,
Make green peninsulas on Esthwaite's Lake:
Twilight was coming on; yet through the gloom

I saw distinctly on the opposite Shore
A heap of garments, left, as I supposed,
By one who there was bathing; long I watched,
But no one owned them; meanwhile the calm Lake
Grew dark, with all the shadows on its breast,
And, now and then, a fish up-leaping snapped
The breathless stillness. The succeeding day,
(Those unclaimed garments telling a plain Tale)
Went there a Company, and in their Boat
Sounded with grappling irons, and long poles.
At length, the dead Man, 'mid that beauteous scene
Of trees and hills and water, bolt upright
Rose with his ghastly face, a spectre shape
Of terror even! and yet no vulgar fear,
Young as I was, a Child not nine years old,
Possessed me, for my inner eye had seen
Such sights before, among the shining streams
Of Fairy Land, the Forests of Romance:
Thence came a spirit hallowing what I saw
With decoration and ideal grace;
A dignity, a smoothness, like the works
Of Grecian art, and purest Poesy.[38]

In Wordsworth's telling, the "heap of garments" had first indicated, in their speaking silence, that a body was missing. They tell a "plain tale." When, the following day, the dead man sits "bolt upright / . . . with his ghastly face, a spectre shape / Of terror even!" the speaker insists that he is not in fact terrorized because he has read of such things already in books. Among other things this is a lesson in how easily one might separate the body from its meaning, the letter from the spirit: a lesson, that is to say, in nonliteral reading. Hogg's scene plays with the same elements, but to radically different ends. There is no plain tale here: the body disintegrates, "shaken to pieces" by the officious editor (230), the clothes become collector's items, and the book that emerges from it all, rather than "hallowing" the scene with "decoration and ideal grace," remains impenetrable. Hogg's novel remakes fanaticism into something uncomprehendingly sampled, weighed, and measured by literary elites from elsewhere, but it also reminds us that the meaning of the tale is still wrapped up obscurely in the meaning of the body: letter and spirit will not be parted. More stridently and consistently than Walpole, Scott, or Wordsworth, Hogg insists that the gothic mode is not merely an intellectual transgression: its terror is stubbornly material, a sign of a political history that continues to structure the social reality of the present moment. And so it remains unhallowed, spectral, unquiet.

Living Together

When he insists that the dead man did not terrorize him because he had already read about such things in books, Wordsworth expresses one influential way of managing terror by means of historical and literary perspective. Compared to the editor's hyper-empirical claim that "nothing" compares to the terror that Robert visits on the countryside, Wordsworth's gentle and bookish relativism suggests that a great deal potentially compares to it, *if* we have read widely and in the right spirit. The speaker's reading prepares him to distinguish form from content, subsume the irregularities of terror into the dignity and smoothness of Grecian art, and so reestablish the boundaries between the human and the nonhuman that terror momentarily threatens. Thus the dead man has the "shape of terror," but he does not terrorize. To be sure, books are never for Wordsworth a way to escape death, but they *do* help us understand its significance; they suggest reasons for it, deepen its meaning, and enrich the proleptic encounters with it scattered throughout his poems. In this way books help us value life even if they point toward death. By contrast, terror cheapens human life by holding it to an ahistorical and nonhuman standard. (Wordsworth's original 1799 version of the scene lacks both the language of terror and the discussion of reading, as if one calls forth the other.)

And yet we might wonder just what examples of "Grecian art, and purest Poesy" Wordsworth has in mind. Presumably not the story of Niobe,

Whose twelve children were destroyed in her palace,
Six daughters, and six sons in the pride of their youth, whom Apollo
Killed with arrows from his silver bow, being angered
With Niobe, and shaft-showering Artemis killed the daughters;
. . . .
Nine days long they lay in their blood, nor was there anyone

To bury them. . . .
And now somewhere among the rocks, in the lonely mountains,
In Sipylos, . . . stone still, she broods on the sorrows that the gods
    gave her.[39]

In his essay "Critique of Violence" Walter Benjamin points to this episode as an example of what he terms "mythic violence," the violence central to the making and preserving of law. For Benjamin the point of the story is not the punishment meted out, horrific as that might be. The action of Apollo and Artemis, he writes, actually "*establishes* a law far more than it punishes the infringement of a law that already exists."[40] Niobe in her arrogance had challenged fate, and fate cannot afford to lose. As Benjamin reads the story, then, the violence of law, which is cyclical, boundary establishing, systematic, and often invisible, is also creative and secularizing. It places a "boundary stone on the frontier between men and gods."[41] Turned to stone, Niobe sits at the border and marks the impossibility of a human opening to the divine.

Niobe's children lie "in their blood" for nine days. Wordsworth and Hogg, by contrast, call attention to a body buried and unearthed. Wordsworth is certainly closer to the Niobe story: by hallowing the scene, he is able to rebury the body once again, although perhaps at some unremarked psychic cost passed off as a theory of reading. It is as if mythic violence has taken up residence in the relationship not between body and fate but between body and reader, who reads precisely in order to reestablish the border between humanity and the gods, between body and spirit. For Wordsworth such reading is life-affirming because it leaves literalism behind, rescuing the psychological significance of terrorism without actually terrorizing. Hogg's novel tells the same story from the other side, thereby highlighting how much terror loves the law: Robert's dreams of antinomian freedom notwithstanding, each of his violations in fact binds him more firmly to an organized brutality whose logical conclusion is suicide. Whether in the form of the managed violence brilliantly theorized in Wordsworth's spots of time or in the unregulated violence of Robert's antinomianism, then, mythic violence is power over mere life for its own sake.[42]

Yet if the only *theoretical* difference between the mythic violence of law and the mythic violence of Robert's terrorism is what side of the legal line they fall on, it is also clear that in the real world it matters a great deal where we draw that line. Though "terrorism" is a fuzzy category, all experts agree that terrorists are nonstate actors. Yet from revolutionary France to Germany,

Russia, El Salvador, Cambodia, Kosovo, and South Africa, the modern state has sponsored terror on a massive scale. Mythic violence falls differently on different kinds of populations. Sometimes it comes so suddenly and powerfully that it looks divine. At other times its spirit can be salvaged by reburying the body and hallowing the ground. And at still other times, as the dismembered minority body of Hogg's novel reminds us, its spirit will not be detached from the material world, sticking instead to the body like a needy lover. We might recall again the Covenanting bodies that pile up in Wodrow's *History*: "I cannot give Accounts of them all," he remarks, as if to say, "I do not have time to give each a proper burial." With the benefit of a hundred years' distance on the Glorious Revolution and the Act of Union, Hogg's readers know that unburied or improperly buried bodies are still to be found. Indeed, in 1715, only three years after the events of *Justified Sinner* supposedly conclude, the first of two Jacobite rebellions reanimated from another direction the specter of religious and nationalist fervor so recently buried.

Of course, those rebellions were unsuccessful, and the possibilities and fears they represented were themselves rewritten in the intervening century—rewritten most effectively, of course, by Walter Scott, Hogg's compatriot, rival, patron, and sometime friend. Scott's version of the majority story draws on theories of uneven development to redeem historical backwardness as evidence of progress. For many, this has been an attractive prospect, one worth aiming at; that is why Scott's technique of transmuting romance into real life is so magical.

Scott's mediocre heroes choose life—mere existence—over the possibilities of a just life. To his credit, Scott does not hide from the potential costs of this bargain. His penchant is for feckless, bored young men who find themselves in dicey situations largely because they have nothing better to do. For them, modernity *has* delivered on its promises, but those promises are rather thin stuff. For the sake of secular peace they have agreed to forgo what Charles Taylor calls "fullness," those moments when life seems richer and more worth living, when it takes on greater significance and meaning.[43] Taylor argues that the empty, homogeneous time of the modern nation-state has inflected our search for such moments; we seek for them now in practices of aesthetic self-fashioning, in expressive culture, or in immanent forms of authenticity. One of the more controversial parts of Taylor's account is the implication—one he has denied—that modern immanent and episodic modes of fullness are less satisfying than those deriving from religious traditions.[44] Scott, for his part, does not pretend to solve this problem. Having given up on fullness, his heroes simply fill their empty time with more things: they settle down, get married, have children, exchange romance for real life. Mood is not so much managed, as in Wordsworth, as simply dulled and regularized by a bourgeois life without risk or consequence. The resulting emptiness is worth it, or so Scott's narrator insists.

By making George Colwan and Robert Wringhim half-brothers, Hogg suggests that this opposition of romance and real life is a tendentious one. If George's life is pointless and empty, Robert's is much too full. Created by the discourse of illegitimacy and laid by Hogg largely at the door of so-called toleration, that contrast makes it impossible for the brothers to live together, but also impossible for them to live separately: "To whatever place of amusement [George] betook himself, . . . there was his brother Wringhim also, and always within a few yards of him" (75). Though the narrator is much too obtuse to notice, the terror of Hogg's novel flows from the way space is partitioned before George and Robert are even born; bound together by history, the brothers live out a drama whose deeper motivations and causes are never clear to them.

Benjamin writes that divine violence is the only exit from the "storm that we call progress," but the brothers' proximity suggests a different kind of exit. For there is a fractured quality to the identities in this novel, however stridently they are defended in theory. "I was a being incomprehensible to myself," says Robert. Wherever George turned, "there was his brother Wringhim also," the editor tells us. Just hinted at here is the possibility of a real and mutual connection *through*, rather than despite, the simple fact that neither brother is truly at home to himself. This goes well beyond the narrator's half-hearted gestures toward "tolerance." It reconceives difference as something internal to the subject, and thus as a tentative or performative common ground. Robert and George share a history of crisis, differentially distributed along the axis of the law, allegorized by the hauntings and doublings of the novel, and manifested at last in the body that emerges in its final pages: disintegrating and disturbed yet somehow also still with something to say, that body is less irrecuperably atavistic than a sign of a different modernity.[45]

It goes without saying that the possibilities of such a different modernity remain systematically undeveloped in the novel, just as the body's parts and accessories are randomly bestowed on the unimaginative representatives of the Edinburgh literary establishment. It will never give up its secrets to them. But a different kind of reader might focus instead on the brothers' shared history, and thus on the novel's stubborn faith in the ethical power of Robert's shadowing, despite his thoroughly unlikable character. "We fight on. And we keep saying, 'We're going to live together with you,'" Edward Said once remarked to an interviewer who suggested that the Palestinians might be running out of time. Said insisted to the end of his life that in the case of Israel and Palestine partition would never work. People will not be kept apart, and destinies are mutual, if only because such entanglements are simply what it means to be modern. "No matter what they do, we're a shadow," he concluded. Said's humanist readers hear in this call "an affirmation of unity rather than division," and though I hear that, I hear, too, the kind of attachment that Lauren Berlant has called "cruel optimism," a fantasy that sustains everyday life when everyday life has become unlivable.[46] Said spoke throughout his career of the need for self-alteration, even self-disintegration, as the precondition for connecting with the other, but he also insisted, wrongly in my view, that such mobility and mutability must be secular or worldly gestures if they were to avoid becoming contaminated by nationalism.[47] He does not sufficiently appreciate, I think, that the boundaries of the secular are as difficult and traumatizing to secure as are the boundaries among peoples. Niobe sits weeping at that boundary, and in this respect we are all her children.

PART III

After the Secular

And the Spirit of God moved upon the face of the waters.

—Genesis 1:2

Create the opposite dream. Know how to create a becoming-minor.

—Gilles Deleuze and Felix Guattari, "What Is a Minor Literature?"

WALTER SCOTT'S POST-CHAISE of history and his hippogriff-drawn chariot of romance share one important quality: they *move*. Images of literary activity in a world ordered by post-messianic historical time, post-chaise and chariot point to a particular kind of literary effect. We sometimes say that literature moves or inspires us, or we speak of being "carried away" by a story. Let us for a moment be literal about these moving pictures: does it matter that images of how writing moves us are themselves vehicles for transportation?

This is not an idle question. Consider another image of literary activity that we encountered in Scott's novels: the alembic. There, too, the question is how a spirit causes change in the material world. As the novel makes clear (and the background context of Burke's *Reflections on the Revolution* underlines), there are other uncertainties as well. How does spirit interact with body? Can a spirit move a vehicle? Can a spirit move us? These are questions raised by the gothic mode, and they are philosophical questions with an important origin in Descartes's mind-body dualism.

Long before Descartes, though, the writer of Ezekiel saw four fantastic creature-vehicles that ran on pure spirit: "Whithersoever the spirit was to go, they went, . . . ; and the wheels were lifted up over against them: for the spirit of the living creature was in the wheels" (Ezekiel 1: 20). These four living creatures, each with four wings and four sides, flashing lightning, are also the wheels wherewith they move. For them, spirit interacts seamlessly with matter.

When I. A. Richards turned his attention to metaphor in *The Philosophy of Rhetoric* (1936), he distinguished between its *tenor* (the object referred to) and its *vehicle* (the object whose qualities are being borrowed). A metaphor moves: it moves itself, it moves language, and perhaps a good one moves us. The word means "to carry over" or "to transfer." Yet its motions remain at the same time elusive, spiritual, ethereal. How does it interact with the physical world? What does it mean to be moved by a word? And what does it mean to be moved at a distance—not by the touch or push that Hume took as a model of causation but by subtler pressures and changes in the air, in the surrounding environment, in the mood of a place or of an age? These questions confront the speaker in "Frost at Midnight," gazing at the film, the "sole unquiet thing" in his midnight world, whose flickering motions alert him to the air currents moving about the room. The pun may be accidental, yet questions of the soul are clearly in the air whenever we confront such action at a distance. It is probably *not* accidental that the speaker compares such action to his memory of church bells, sounds that "stirred and haunted [him] / With a wild pleasure" (lines 31–32). Though they may be silent now, the bells continue to haunt indirectly, just as the unquiet film allows the speaker to register how much the silence of his environment disturbs and stirs his thought.

Metaphors are not only vehicles; they are tethered by their tenor, by the thing that does not move but is rather augmented, as it were, *in place*, by the vehicle. In the previous section I explored several examples of this kind of metaphorical movement—movement, that is to say, wherein distant forces so change the surrounding atmosphere that they force a movement not so much because of direct contact but because of distributed and often invisible influence. My examples in the previous section were largely negative: Scott's interleaved discussions of horses and chariots, frivolity and alembics; the encircled poet of "Kubla Khan"; government troops traversing the Scottish countryside, whose presence forces a Covenanting movement that signifies as guilt. These, I argued, are images of life in a secular age. To be moved by worldly rather than otherwordly forces is part of the metaphysics of the secular age—and as we have seen, such movements can be painful. The word that I used for that process was *minoritization*: the process of being rendered minor, unimportant. In the case of someone like Robert, that rendering is traumatic.

Such spectral histories, with their gothic overtones, tend to construe the secular as a form of loss, and that indeed has been my primary though not exclusive emphasis so far—loss, however, not of religion nor enchantment per se but rather of varied possibilities for living, a loss visited most dramatically upon the already vulnerable. Still, the kind of motion figured by a creative spirit moving on the waters, by metaphor, or by Coleridge's church bells, can also be a pleasure of a distinctly human and worldly kind. The church bells, after all, are silent now, their wild pleasure transposed into other, more immanent kinds of human flourishing. In her recent book *The Future of Illusion*, Victoria Kahn reads such developments as positive and creative steps away from religion, enabled by what she calls *poiesis*, namely humanity's own self-recognition as creator in its own right. Criticizing the fascination with political theology in the recent work of Agamben, Žižek, and Badiou, Kahn argues that it was only by *breaking* from the theological legitimation of the state that Renaissance writers from Shakespeare to Hobbes to Spinoza cleared room for a purely immanent theory of creativity and made it possible for art and fiction to step into the space once occupied by religion. Against Taylor and Asad, she claims that the advances of the early modern period, from science to philosophy to governance to art, cannot be understood as developments from within Christianity but must rather be seen as examples of the human ability to "artfully construct the world of human interaction and political order."[1] We only know what we can make ourselves—that may be a limitation, but it is also an invitation.

Though I believe Kahn underestimates the messiness of the break from political theology, her account nevertheless reminds us that the *poiesis* of minoritization can sometimes be turned around, its line of flight not only a passive motion but a process of being pulled or pushed toward a conversion, toward the making of a new space, or at any rate toward a *change* from the status quo, from things as they are or were.[2] Scott's frivolity, and the strange "delights" of addiction in Purchas and Coleridge, would be cases of this—examples not so much of minoritization as of what Gilles Deleuze and Felix Guattari call "becoming-minor." This implies a creative agency missing from the passive construction of minoritization, an artful construction dedicated less to an end product than to the process of getting there.

A minor literature, according to Deleuze and Guattari, has three components. First, it "doesn't come from a minor language; it is rather that which a minority constructs within a major language." Second, a minor literature is intrinsically political, since "a whole other story is vibrating within it." And third, a minor literature is charged with the "role and function of collective, even revolutionary, activity."[3] Kafka, their main example, could have engaged in a symbolic "re-territorialization" by composing in either Czech or Yiddish rather than German, or indeed by writing in a German swelled up "through all the resources of symbolism." He does none of these, however, choosing instead to proceed by a "willed poverty, pushing deterritorialization to . . . an extreme." He "deliberately kills all metaphor, all symbolism, all signification."[4]

At certain moments in *Prometheus Unbound*, Percy Shelley may approach such decomposition—but Deleuze and Guattari are really extrapolating from a modernist aesthetic too quick to disparage figurative language as a form of bad faith. The writers in this final section are rightly cautious of such a gesture of negation. Attracted to the politics of a becoming-minor, they remain all too aware of the costs associated with absolute separations, and mistrustful too of the unforeseen consequences of human creativity. Shelley, for example, will make grand claims for the power of figure to change the world, but he does so by means of what his heroine Cythna in *The Revolt of Islam* (1817) calls a "subtler language":

Clear, elemental shapes, whose smallest change
A subtler language within language wrought.[5]

Such "language within language" shares a great deal with a minor literature, created "within the heart of what is called great (or established) literature" (18). But it realizes that impulse not by abandoning figurative resources but through what Shelley in his 1821 *Defense of Poetry* calls the "vitally metaphorical" quality of language, "which marks the before unapprehended relations of things."[6] Poetry creates relations where there were none before. Rather than a purely immanent innovation, a decisive and modern step away from the old enchantments, such *poiesis* serves as a reminder that modernity has not yet delivered on its promises. Metaphor, the crossing-over or traversing of a space, encapsulates a desire for change—but it also keeps one nearby, within range of the place where one has begun. One may long to fly farther, to become mere vehicle, but the tenor is still there, like Coleridge's church bells, holding one's feet to the ground through flights of memory or of imagination. It is in this sense what Shelley calls the "smallest change," though its effects may be magnified under the right conditions. This, too, is a way of becoming minor, to "be a sort of stranger within [one's] own language," as Deleuze and Guattari put it (26). Like Cythna in her cave, weaving a language open to unexpected arrivals, or like Coleridge's speaker, anticipating a surprising visit: "and still my heart leaped up, / For still I hoped to see the *stranger's* face," a stranger who seems already almost present in the "*strange* . . . silentness" that is the "sound" of the secular (lines 40–41, 10–11, emphasis added).

Thus the texts in this final section are poised between the metaphorical and the becoming-minor. There is here a developing argument that literature does not only register the governmental aspects of secularity but also mobilizes the secular for a constructive project. The writers in this section are attracted to the creative possibilities of a minor literature, to the way that such a literature can open up new pleasures, possibilities, and capacities. Yet it is in their characteristic hesitation or pause along this line of flight that they "express another possible community"—not through a willed linguistic poverty nor a decisive break, but rather through a small change or an arrested movement: the strange, atemporal pause of the Byronic hero, the metaphorical constellations theorized by Robert Lowth and Friedrich Schleiermacher, or the odd "vacancy" of Shelley's *Mont Blanc*.[7] In such spaces we encounter the potential for another, or for many others, to emerge. The arrival of such strangers alters the terrain. And that would be, not a becoming-poor, but a becoming-plentiful.

CHAPTER 7

Byron and the Paradox of Reading

To see this plainly will require a closer reading than most of us give
to poetry.
—Cleanth Brooks, "The Language of Paradox"

At one point in Mark Juergensmeyer's book *Terror in the Mind of God* (2003),
a definitive account of the rise of religious violence at the end of the millennium, we follow the author as he visits a maximum security prison in Lom-
poc, California, where Mahmud Abouhalima is serving a life sentence for his
role in the 1993 bombing of the World Trade Center. Even after all the legal
trials and newspaper articles, Abouhalima remarks, Americans "still did not
understand him and his colleagues." Why, Juergensmeyer asks him, was that?
"What was it that we did not understand?"

> "The soul," he said, "the soul of religion, that is what is missing."
> Without it, Abouhalima said, Western prosecutors, journalists, and
> scholars like myself "will never understand who I am. . . . I lived
> their life, but they didn't live my life, so they will never understand
> the way I live or the way I think."[1]

Why do people like Abouhalima do what they do? This question of motivation haunts Juergensmeyer's book. Is understanding possible, or is there an
inaccessible dark core to religious violence that resists all explanation?[2]
Though Juergensmeyer retains a sociologist's faith that third-person descriptions can get us pretty far in "reconstructing the terrorists' world views from
within," as he puts it (13), first-person experience remains something of a

black box nonetheless. Michael Bray, who torched seven abortion clinics in the 1980s, sips white wine in his suburban Maryland living room and tells Juergensmeyer that there is a "great war" for America's soul going on, though it "goes unseen largely because the enemy has imposed its control gradually and subtly" (153). The sociologist can follow such paranoia only so far; at some level Bray is simply a middle-class white man listening to the voices in his head. Perhaps there is not, after all, any terrorists' "world" for an academic observer to reconstruct: maybe they really are just crazy.

This is, again, the difficulty allegorized by the split narrative of Hogg's *Justified Sinner*. Robert Wringhim's account of his own life may have a certain internal coherence, but it resists editorial comprehension. When he introduces it, the editor calls the confession an "original document," distinguishing it from the "history, judiciary records, and tradition" that are the sources of his own knowledge and tacitly understood to be nearer the truth. And though the editor says he will present Robert's confession without comment, "leaving every one to judge for himself" (116), this pose of generous neutrality does not make it any easier to get "inside" Robert's fanaticism. "With regard to the work itself," the editor writes, "I dare not venture a judgment, for I do not understand it. I believe no person, man or woman, will ever peruse it with the same attention that I have done, and yet I confess that I do not comprehend the writer's drift" (232). Even reliable first-person testimony remains incomprehensible, just as Abouhalima tells Juergensmeyer that he will never understand "the way I live or the way I think." In the face of the insistence on the uniqueness of the vision in question, what chance does the observer have of reconstructing it "from within"?

Answering such questions with the help of Lord Byron's poem *The Giaour* (1813) may seem a surprising choice for any number of reasons. Yet at the heart of Byron's poem is an encounter very similar to the one relayed by Juergensmeyer: a meeting between the nameless title character and a fanatic. This encounter yields a fragile recognition—and if we read it carefully, we learn something not about the fanatic but about the one who seeks to understand him.

Paradox

One could do worse than read Byron's poem as an allegory of pluralism, in which truth is determined by context and presupposition, and whose larger textual apparatus strives to bring rational order to a world of competing loyalties and dispositions. For this reason, *The Giaour* can also serve as a document of pluralism's complications and exclusions.

The first part of the poem, set in a homogenized Eastern location, presents several different voices describing what the reader eventually understands to be the murder of a slave woman named Leila for running away from her master to join her lover. The master, Hassan, has her tied up in a bag and thrown overboard. Leila's lover, the Giaour, avenges her murder by killing Hassan. The second half of the poem is the Giaour's lengthy confession to a nameless monk in a Christian monastery, once again in an indeterminate location. The Giaour himself is a stateless and nameless man who operates on the borderlands of cultures, traditions, and beliefs. The poem named after him, meanwhile, is a collection of fragments apparently arranged by an editor, in which different and anonymous voices take up small bits of the story before themselves disappearing from it. The same fictive editor also provides footnotes to the fragments, and these footnotes vary in tone from scholarly and pedantic to wittily informative to a few in the first person that conflate the editor with Byron himself. Taken together, these various elements place a tremendous burden on the reader: it is difficult enough to figure out the plot, let alone who speaks, whom to trust, and whom, in the end, to believe.

Against this world of interpretive complexity and incomplete attempts to organize it through textual apparatus, the poem sets two examples of orthodoxy. The first is Hassan himself; the second is the monk to whom the Giaour confesses. Both fulfill the stereotypes of (Islamic and Christian) religious orthodoxy. And neither is of much interest to the editor, who goes so far as to excise a harangue that the monk delivers to the Giaour, telling us in a footnote that it will appeal to nobody: "The monk's sermon is omitted. It seems to have had so little effect upon the patient, that it could have no hopes from the reader. It may be sufficient to say, that it was of the customary length . . . and was delivered in the usual tone of all orthodox preachers."[3]

The poem, then, does not derive its energy from a clash of civilizations; indeed, Christian orthodoxy never meets Islamic orthodoxy, and in any case both are so emptied of content as to become literal invitations for readers to fill in the blanks for themselves. The poem concentrates rather on the complex space *between* orthodoxies, in which a curious kind of understanding seems to be possible. For when he makes his confession, the Giaour remarks that he and Hassan are not so very different:

Yet did he but what I had done
Had she been false to more than one.
Faithless to him, he gave the blow;
But true to me, I laid him low:
Howe'er deserved her doom might be,
Her treachery was truth to me. (lines 1062–67)

The Giaour says, in effect, that he would have killed her, too. He imagines
himself in Hassan's place, and from that perspective approves of what he has
done; he also imagines importing Hassan's perspective into his own, taking
it as a guide for his own future actions were Leila subsequently to betray him.
The Giaour's code and Hassan's code do not reduce to the same thing, and
yet, these lines suggest, Hassan's code might be rewritten in the Giaour's
language.

This may be simply a fantasy of liberal tolerance, but if so its act of
transposition depends on the alarming idea that Leila's fidelity to her lover
meant that she deserved to die. The translation is not symmetrical: Hassan
kills Leila because she is his property, but the Giaour would kill for love (that
is, he would kill Leila *because* he loves her). This difference is crucial to the
poem's project; by distinguishing between bondage and freedom it keeps
Hassan's code and the Giaour's code from collapsing into each other. Hassan
murders Leila from within his tradition; as the poem's "Advertisement" tells
us, she was "thrown, in the Mussulman manner, into the sea for infidelity"
(167). The Giaour, by contrast, imagines murdering Leila in the name of a
love described as unique and personal and thus deliberately counterposed to
all traditions. To murder in the name of love is to murder freely; as Gulnare
tells Conrad in *The Corsair*, "love dwells with—with the free" (2.502). Love,
or more specifically the death inevitably attached to it, is thus linked to a
freedom that orthodox tyrants like Hassan cannot understand, and for which
the poem's code word is "heart":

To me she gave her heart, that all
Which tyranny can ne'er enthrall. (lines 1068–69)

As the Giaour's sympathy for Hassan suggests, the heart can understand
tyranny. But tyranny can never understand the heart. When Leila chooses to
follow her heart rather than the dictates of her culture, she crosses from the

realm of orthodox subjection into an ambiguous space defined by its *distinction* from culture and tradition. Such movement, the poem implies, is deadly.

One result of this contrast between love and orthodoxy is that love itself comes to seem like a substitute religion. This is only incidentally because the Giaour uses religious language to describe his love; primarily, love looks like religion in this poem because it is not a feeling at all but an enacted discipline. The Giaour spends the remainder of his days in mourning for Leila, dedicated to her idea to the exclusion of all else, experiencing visions of her, and unable even to hear alternative creeds such as the orthodox sermon excised by the editor. The Giaour's goal, he tells the monk, is "To die—and know no second love" (line 1166). And he scorns inconstant men and what he calls their "varied joys" (line 1175). His constancy is predicated upon the utter hopelessness of his love. Because Leila deserves to die according to a tradition that neither she nor her lover can alter, and that the Giaour does not criticize, there is nothing for him to do but mourn her as the lost object whose very irrecoverability is the condition of his faithfulness toward her.[4]

Is the heart, then, in opposition to orthodoxy, or is it simply another kind of orthodoxy? More abstractly: is human love the opposite of religion or another version of it? Does the poem take love seriously, and treat religion as its foil? Or does it take religion seriously, finding in human love another image of it? The Giaour himself says both things. Or rather, he *says* that love is the opposite of orthodox tyranny, but the poem forces him to experience love as simply another and more complex kind of orthodox tyranny: the tyranny of that very tradition which he claims cannot "enthrall" the heart but which in killing Leila has melancholically bound him more firmly to it than it ever could have were she alive. At the level of plot, meanwhile, love and orthodoxy *must* be mutually exclusive—for if they were not, Leila would not have left Hassan, and so there would *be* no plot. Two paradoxes, then: the Giaour's liberal ability to understand religious orthodoxy depends on orthodoxy's power to kill those who would leave it—depends on, that is, its illiberalism; and the poem's own motivating distinction between love and religion is likewise a paradox, for if the poem is to proceed, that distinction must both exist (at the level of plot) and not exist (at the level of the Giaour's subsequent experience) at the same time.

Only now can we grasp Byron's complex handling of faithfulness and infidelity. The Giaour's name literally means "infidel"—that is, non-Muslim. At the same time, he is faithful—*fidelis*—to the dead Leila. Meanwhile Leila herself is killed for sexual infidelity, but her unfaithfulness to Hassan means fidelity to the Giaour and even more to the liberal notion of a freely given heart. The *OED* shows that infidelity as disloyalty to God and as disloyalty to a person both appear in English in the early sixteenth century, and these two meanings existed more or less in tandem well into the nineteenth century, though in modern usage the interpersonal and romantic connotations have gained the upper hand. Byron's poem certainly accentuates the tensions between love and religion, underlining the difficulty of holding both kinds of fidelity within the same thought-world. But those tensions are hardly new; indeed they are central to pastoral and theological discourse throughout the Christian tradition. As both Talal Asad and Wilfred Cantwell Smith have noted, for most of Christian history an "infidel" was someone in a moral rather than epistemological predicament. *Infidelis* had a wide range of meanings within Latin Christendom, but none of them emphasized internal or cognitive states (atheism, skepticism, unbelief, or the like). Infidelity had less to do with making a choice than it did with a threat to emotional, social, and political relationships.[5] The point to emphasize here is the wide spectrum of attitudes, habits, dispositions, and cultural locations ranged under the category of infidelity—a variety that Byron emphasizes by using *giaour*, the Turkish rather than Latin word. Here the poem's Orientalism gains some critical purchase: if Christianity in the aftermath of Reform is by this period too obsessed with the content of the mind, the nameless Muslim narrators of the first half of the tale are still thinking in terms of what people do rather than what they believe. They define the Giaour by where he is relationally located: among the infidels rather than the orthodox.

This relational connotation—the undercurrent of fidelity rather than institutionally protected belief—is why love and religion are so tightly bound in this poem: not because human love is "like" religion in its content, but because the two are indistinguishable *formally*. Earlier I used the word "paradox" to describe this complexity, and the word was chosen deliberately, for I mean to recall a central moment in the history of literary study. In his famous 1947 essay "The Language of Paradox" Cleanth Brooks undertakes a reading of Donne's poem "The Canonization," in which the paradox is precisely the one that appears in Byron's poem. Here is Brooks (at some length):

> The basic metaphor which underlies the poem (and which is
> reflected in the title) involves a sort of paradox. For the poet daringly
> treats profane love as if it were divine love. . . . The poem then is a
> parody of Christian sainthood; but it is an intensely serious parody

of a sort that modern man, habituated as he is to an easy yes or no, can hardly understand. He refuses to accept the paradox as a serious rhetorical device; and since he is able to accept it only as a cheap trick, he is forced into this dilemma. Either: Donne does not take love seriously; here he is merely sharpening his wit. . . . Or: Donne does not take sainthood seriously; here he is merely indulging in a cynical and bawdy parody.

Neither account is true; a reading of the poem will show that Donne takes both love and religion seriously; it will show, further, that the paradox is here his inevitable instrument. But to see this plainly will require a closer reading than most of us give to poetry.[6]

If the Giaour's philosophy of love is a paradox, then, so is he himself a paradox. More precisely, he is a figure for the very paradox that structures the poem's presentation of the conflict between love and religion. John Guillory, who has written intelligently about the theological resonances of Brooksian paradox, points out that Brooks carefully avoids naming or promulgating a particular orthodoxy. "[P]aradox names the very condition by which the poem does not *name* the truth to which it nevertheless gestures," Guillory writes.[7] What Guillory nicely terms "paradoxy" becomes for Brooks a means to skirt the irreconcilable religious differences on which competing versions of orthodoxy are predicated. The Giaour, likewise, lives between civilizations and is beholden to none; what Guillory calls "paradoxy" is what the poem's narrator calls the Giaour's "nameless spell, / Which speaks, itself unspeakable" (lines 838–39). He is the very figure of what he cannot say. And so his nameless spell offers up the possibility of a reading practice whose very elusiveness and indirection deflect cultural or ideological conflict into the realm of the aesthetic.

The name for that reading practice is of course largely coterminous with the New Criticism itself: close reading. Glance again at Brooks's final sentence: "But to see [paradox] plainly will require a closer reading than most of us give to poetry." The close reading of which "most of us" are incapable is a reading that begins by recognizing the highly nuanced way in which literary language gestures toward *doxa* rather than naming it. In this way, close reading displaces religious dispute, with its always-lurking potential for violence, into the interpretive arena. Where there was once the distinction between the orthodox and the heretical, there is now the distinction between those few who can read and the majority who cannot. Although New Critical

close reading has sometimes been labeled crypto-religious, then, it is important to understand that in replacing orthodoxy with paradox, close reading is
functionally congruent with a project that seeks to restrain religious violence
by making it the proper domain of hermeneutics.[8]

Readers will recall that Brooks's 1947 book, *The Well Wrought Urn*,
which opens with this celebration of paradox, closes with an essay entitled
"The Heresy of Paraphrase." Paraphrase, he argues there, is a heresy against
the paradoxical language of poetry itself. It simply extracts truths from a
poem, restating it in different words rather than attending to the movements
of its language. Paraphrase is thus functionally equivalent to orthodoxy,
which reduces the language of religion to its doctrinal content. And, in a
suitably paradoxical twist, Brooks declares such orthodoxy to be a heresy
against literature that must be resisted in the name of a secular reading practice. It is too simple to say that literature simply replaces religion in this
argument. Rather, close readers of the Brooksian variety must rescue literature from the ravages of naive readers who still want it to fight their cultural
battles for them, who wish to flatten paradox into the paraphrasable doctrine
of orthodoxy. Brooks thus stands in a line of cultural critics that includes
those Anglican opponents of the Covenanters who accused them of "misapplication" in their reading of biblical texts. By making Phinehas's actions the
direct model for contemporary practice, the argument goes, the simple and
violent reading practices of the Covenanters short-circuited all the rich and
affective literary qualities of the biblical text. Readers must be continually
reeducated in a different interpretive method, one not content to rest on
the surface of words, nor with an easy paraphrase, nor with an immediate
"application." This different method searches out that which is hidden—not
in order finally to say it, but rather to show how the text *does not* say it, for
the "it" here is precisely *doxa* itself, that which by definition goes without
saying. Translated from the political to the literary arena, religious violence is
thus remade into literary paradox. The final withholding of the "it" is what
makes literature *literature* and not orthodoxy.[9]

The Pause

Implicitly, this argument assumes that orthodoxy verges on violence while
paradox does not. Byron's poem—and indeed, his other "Turkish Tales"—
raises some questions about this assumption. We can grasp these questions

by noting that, taken as a group, the Turkish Tales obsessively thematize the figure we know as the Byronic hero: a dark, brooding character with some mysterious tragedy in his past; always alone, even in a crowd, he displays a world-weariness that nevertheless gathers itself into a reluctant heroism at moments of crisis. Most importantly, perhaps, he is an object of obsessive curiosity for the ignorant crowd, who speculate endlessly, and always incorrectly, about his inner life. Byron's heroes simultaneously invite close reading and repel it: there is always more to be grasped, though it is unlikely that the reader will be up to the challenge. As Selim tells Zuleika in *The Bride of Abydos* (1813), "I am not, love! what I appear." In *The Corsair* (1814), Conrad's face "attracted, yet perplex'd the view."[10] *The Giaour*, meanwhile, dwells at length on the Byronic hero as a site of interpretive complexity, in lines that strikingly anticipate Brooks's distinction between inattentive reading and close reading:

> The common crowd but see the gloom
> Of wayward deeds, and fitting doom;
> The close observer can espy
> A noble soul, and lineage high. (lines 866–69)

Translating such lines into Brooks's idiom, we can say that the "common" readers who see in the Byronic hero only "wayward deeds, and fitting doom" are lazy and casual; they wish to paraphrase the Giaour, and therefore miss the paradox that makes him what he is. Their focus on content ("wayward deeds, and fitting doom") leads necessarily to a picture of the Giaour as a cultural warrior. By contrast, the "close observers" who can pick out a "noble soul, and lineage high" are reading for paradox; these readers have no time for orthodoxy because they are striving to get to that mysterious and protean something against which orthodoxy can be made to seem a relatively shallow and culture-specific orientation. Of course that thing cannot be named: as the narrator says, its very essence is to be "unspeakable" (line 839); all that close reading can do is produce what the poem calls the "nameless spell," the evocation of mood, that *is* the essence of the Giaour's noble soul. The Giaour's truth is that he produces the feeling that one is in the presence of a depth that cannot be spoken because to speak it would be to render it superficial. His own ideal of fidelity to the dead Leila figures the fidelity of the close reader, who wants to get to the truth of things but is forced to acknowledge that "the truth of things" is at bottom the irreducible fact of paradox itself.

In these poems, the invitation to read closely is mounted most insistently around a characteristic *pause* that marks the hero. The pause arrives just before a moment of decisive action; it is a moment carved out of time during which the hero seems both to gather his strength and to review his entire life before diving once again into the flow of human events—a lyric moment in the midst of narrative time. In *The Giaour*, the pause comes almost as soon as we meet the man himself:

> A moment check'd his wheeling steed
> A moment breathed him from his speed
> ·
> His brow was bent, his eye was glazed;
> He raised his arm, and fiercely raised,
> And sternly shook his hand on high,
> As doubting to return or fly. (lines 218–19, 240–43)

And the narrator then reflects:

> 'Twas but an instant he restrain'd
> That fiery barb so sternly rein'd;
> 'Twas but a moment that he stood,
> Then sped as if by death pursued:
> But in that instant o'er his soul
> Winters of Memory seem'd to roll,
> And gather in that drop of time
> A life of pain, an age of crime.
> O'er him who loves, or hates, or fears,
> Such moment pours the grief of years:
> What felt *he* then, at once opprest
> By all that most distracts the breast?
> That pause, which ponder'd o'er his fate,
> Oh, who its dreary length shall date!
> Though in Time's record nearly nought,
> It was Eternity to Thought! (lines 257–72)

In its elusiveness, its stripping away of all manner of context, and its characteristic compression and stylization, the pause solicits close reading almost to the exclusion of all else.[11] Indeed, the pause that marks the Byronic hero becomes also the recommended procedure for the one who would read such a hero. "[W]ho paused to look again, / Saw more than marks the crowd of vulgar men," remarks *The Corsair*'s narrator of Conrad (1.199–200). When the Giaour invites the monk to read the characters on his brow, he cautions: "Still, ere thou does condemn me, pause; / Not mine the act, though I the cause" (lines 1060–61). And what follows immediately is the paradox with which we began, in which the Giaour claims to understand why Hassan killed Leila. The activity of close reading, characterized and made necessary by the pause, immediately leads the reader to confront the poem's central paradox regarding the relation of religion and human love.

If the pause characterizes close reading, it is also dangerous. For Selim, in *The Bride of Abydos*, the pause is "fatal" (2.565); Conrad, in *The Corsair*, pauses when he has unexpected forebodings about his latest adventure (1.309). Whether the hero pauses, or whether he instructs his reader to pause, such momentary stopping figures a richness of experience, memory, and history, and therefore trails death in its wake—not for the reader, but for the object being read. This is why the close reader, the reader who pauses and searches out paradox, must be unattached. Indeed her freedom of movement is the necessary condition of the cosmopolitan fantasy of the Byronic hero: the fantasy of never being tied down, of never having to "represent" anything in particular but of always being more than the sum of your parts, more than either the place you are from or the place that you are at the moment, *and* of having a reader willing to come along for the ride, a reader who understands the whole business as a series of acts or gestures—parodies, to recall Brooks, of an intensely serious sort. That reader is made to recognize how simultaneously necessary and deadly the characteristic pause is: necessary, because it is the condition of close reading; deadly, because we can get caught up in reading and forget the plot, which is the plot of clashing orthodoxies and civilizations, of dying for an "identity." As imaged in the Byronic hero's paradoxical, nameless spell, close reading seeks to deflect this kind of cultural and religious violence into the hermeneutic realm. Thus the strange and ultimately "unspeakable" commonality that the Giaour feels with his orthodox opponent. It is as if, could he be read in the right way, Hassan would die not for his "civilization," his culture, or his religion, but for love—he would die, as the Byronic hero aspires to die, as himself.

We are now in a position to appreciate what is at stake in the ideals of close reading (a method) and paradox (its object). Close reading may be a secular form, both in its relationship to the orthodox reading practices known as "paraphrase" and in the way it tries to blunt and divert religious passion while still acknowledging its power. But the *doxa* to which it points without naming is not the residue of religion but the everyday ebb and flow of secular time itself, brought to a sudden and remarkable pause in the lyrical and stylized figure of the Byronic hero. Like the speaker in "Frost at Midnight," numbering the otherwise numberless comings-and-goings that make up the secular affirmation of ordinary life, the Byronic hero arrested in medias res unveils not an exquisitely balanced paradox but an asymmetrical one. And because this is Byron, not Coleridge, the asymmetry leads more readily to violence. For in *The Giaour*, the method's condition of possibility is an intimacy between orthodoxy and freedom, forged over the body of a dead woman.

Byronism and the Wounded Mind

Readers typically associate Byron, particularly the Turkish Tales, with the stereotyped and licentious depictions of the East that we have learned to call "Orientalism."[12] Yet *The Giaour* is more than simply an exercise in Orientalism: it insists that Hassan and the Giaour share a great deal, even if their differences have the final word. The close reading of faces and figures may be central to *The Giaour*'s operation, but there is one moment in the poem when the hero, instead of being read, actually tries to do the reading. It comes after he has vanquished his fanatical opponent, who lies dying on the battlefield as the Giaour leans over him:

> I gazed upon him where he lay,
> And watched his spirit ebb away:
> Though pierced like pard by hunters' steel,
> He felt not half that now I feel.
> I search'd, but vainly searched to find,
> The workings of a wounded mind;
> Each feature of that sullen corse
> Betrayed his rage, but no remorse. (lines 1085–92)

Like the Giaour's earlier discussion of why Leila in effect deserved to die, this encounter demonstrates both an extraordinary intimacy between the two men and a careful delineation of difference.[13] In the first instance, the difference was that Hassan killed Leila for tradition's sake, whereas the Giaour imagines killing her for love's sake. In this instance, as the two men stare into each other's eyes, the difference is that the Giaour's face hides a "wounded mind," while Hassan's face hides no such complicated interiority. In looking at Hassan the Giaour searches for remorse—which is to say, he searches for another version of himself, for one who acknowledges life's irony and tragedy but is also able to take up a position vis-à-vis those things, and to understand that modern life is characterized by what Charles Taylor calls "mutual fragilization."[14] Instead he finds only rage. Thus can he conclude that Hassan "felt not half that now I feel"; absent evidence of a wounded mind, Hassan becomes simply an example of senseless fanatical anger. And that anger, however powerful and all-defining, is denied equal epistemic status with the Giaour's self-aware woundedness. For the Giaour (and thus for the reader) Hassan's face is not an interesting text; it is too easy to read.

This difference between the Giaour and Hassan, couched in the language of a "wounded mind," may thus be understood to be *reflexivity* itself. Although the two men seem remarkably similar in their aims and in their behavior, the text insists once again that in reality we are witnessing a face-off between modernity and tradition—or perhaps more accurately, we are witnessing tradition's rage *at* modernity, with its complexity and its complicated position-taking in relationship to its own beliefs.

But what the poem also documents, of course, is how the Giaour subsequently slips into his own kind of fanaticism through his single-minded devotion to the dead Leila. Earlier I described this as a paradox in Brooks's sense of the term. In other words, for this poem to work it must be simultaneously true that love and religion model mutually exclusive kinds of fidelity *and* that they model precisely the same kind of fidelity. We can now identify the moment when the Giaour reads Hassan's face as the hinge of this paradox. Even as he slides into fanaticism, the Giaour retains his wounded mind, and this makes him, as the poem obsessively demonstrates, a text worth reading precisely because it never gives up all its secrets. That, indeed, is the appeal of the Byronic hero: that he promises more than he will ever deliver, which makes him an endlessly fascinating, because ultimately elusive, object of study.

Such indeterminacy, though, pushes the poem's motivating paradox to the breaking point. For if we track the Giaour's development from the figure who searches Hassan's face to the figure whose face is searched by the curious monks, we see that his single-minded devotion to Leila is an effect of the very woundedness that he celebrates. To take reflexivity as a ground-level commitment is to make certain assumptions about which one cannot reflect critically. And this produces the unanalyzable, unspeakable, enchanted thing called "Byronism" itself.

Even though the Giaour himself is necessarily oblivious to this effect, the poem's fictive editor seems to grasp it. The editor may be unable to keep his hero from coming under the spell of his own Byronism, but he nevertheless arranges the raw materials of the story in such a way that the reader can observe how intimately Byronism is bound up with a melancholic self-enchantment that looks more and more like the religious orthodoxy against which it supposedly sets itself. This editorial apparatus is crucial: *The Giaour* offers multiple unreliable voices rather than a single authoritative one, and in so doing it places the reader in a position more reflexive than anything the Giaour himself manages. If, like the Giaour, the sympathetic reader searches Hassan's face for evidence of a shared sensibility, we also know what is behind the desire for such a common ground: "Byronism" itself, in all its powerfully attractive melancholy. Perhaps more to the point, the editorial apparatus offers a genealogy of that melancholy in the bonding that takes place between the Giaour and Hassan over the dead woman they each would kill. The source of Byronic melancholy is thus revealed to be the Giaour's deep need for the tradition (what the poem calls "the Mussulman manner") that kills Leila. Earlier I called this a paradox, and we are now in a position to see that in this poem, the paradox at the heart of Byronism, the paradox that solicits close reading, is not the exquisitely balanced tension that Brooks loved to find in poetry, but rather a deep asymmetry between killing a woman freely (that is, for love) and killing her because she is property (that is, for tradition). It is too easy to simply point out that she dies either way. What is tougher, perhaps, to swallow is that the close reading that the poem solicits valorizes one of these killings but not the other, and valorizes it moreover as the condition of possibility for its Byronism, its nameless spell, its paradox.

Like the anonymous author of the *True Account*, who does not condemn Phinehas but rather the mindset of those who read his story too literally, the Giaour's complex reading strategy needs literalism as its foil. Practitioners of paradox may dream of converting religious violence into something else. But as it turns out, paradox depends on a real violence it can "read" and then disavow: the Giaour would have killed Leila, but he did not have to, because Hassan already had, and this allows him to claim the symbolic power of the killing while keeping his distance from the actual act. That is why he is allowed to live on, in all his melancholy and fascination.

Imaginary Terrorism

In an interview with Bill Moyers that aired in the summer of 2006 as part of a PBS series called *Faith and Reason*, writer Mary Gordon offered a scenario that strikingly recalls Byron's:

> MARY GORDON: And also, I believe that if a writer can do her or his work, it is to try to imagine the other, not the comfortable other. I'm actually much more comfortable thinking of a suicide bomber as an other than I am of Donald Trump. Donald Trump—
> BILL MOYERS: The inner life of a suicide bomber—
> MARY GORDON: Yes.
> BILL MOYERS:—intrigues you more than the inner life of Donald Trump?
> MARY GORDON: I find it much more comprehensible. . . . I can very easily put myself in the imaginative place of believing that something is worth dying for and even worth killing for. And so, my imagination can understand somebody who would say, this is a life or death thing. This is about the truth. . . . And sometimes when I look, there are some things in the world that disgust me to the point of despair. So that, for example, some of the things that kids will do on the Internet now. Somebody was telling me about young girls from very good schools who will photograph each other having sex, and put it on the Internet, so that people can, you know, see them, access them having sex. Thirteen, fourteen year old girls are doing that. And I see something like that, and it makes me despair. And I think there is something so wrong with this culture that, wipe it out. Start from—start from zero. It's too corrupt. It's too far gone. . . .
> BILL MOYERS: I am sympathetic to the angst on the Christian right towards popular culture.
> MARY GORDON: Yes.
> BILL MOYERS: Towards the banality.
> MARY GORDON: Yes.

BILL MOYERS: The sheer ugliness of it.

MARY GORDON: Yes. . . . And I think if you can put yourself in that place and say, you know, and sort of ratchet it up, you can say, I understand Osama Bin Laden. That, if I have to—I mean, this is absurd—but if I have to look at all the violence, all the stupid violence that's on TV and some of the stupid violence that teenagers seem to think is fine, and kids carrying guns. And kids shooting other kids. And eleven and twelve year olds having all sorts of sex that they can't possibly really connect to pleasure. And the greed that this, to tell you the truth, to see people driving Hummers sometimes makes me feel so sick that, you know, I want to just drive them off the road and say, okay, in the name of Christ, in the name of peace and justice, I'm just going to shoot you because you have to get out of your car now. We live in a very stupid, banal, gross, greedy and rather disgusting culture.

BILL MOYERS: But it does not lead you to do what Osama Bin Laden did, to kill.

MARY GORDON: And I think that I have to go back to a religious position, which is that if reading the Gospel means anything, if Jesus means anything, it's about seeing everybody, every human being as Jesus. That's what makes sense. That—therefore, every human being is of enormous value. Every human being is sacred. So it seems to me the only thing that stops me from going out and shooting people in Hummers is a religious belief that, even though I don't like them, they are sacred and valuable in the eyes of God. And that does stop me. Because I could really, you know, go out on quite a spree.[15]

Read against the background of this chapter and the earlier discussion of Hogg, this exchange snaps into focus. Gordon's discussion moves between Benjamin's categories of divine and mythic violence. It plays with literalism before taking refuge in a figurative or symbolic violence. Symptomatically, its revulsion at the sexual availability of young women figures an accommodation to modernity that links Gordon to Phinehas, Robert Wringhim, Hassan, and the Giaour himself, who never loves Leila so well as when she is dead. Substantively, as well, Gordon's argument tries to find a connection between two disparate constituencies (fundamentalists and writers) by way of imagination. "Yet did he but what I had done" is how the Giaour puts this particular thought. Like the Giaour gazing at the face of the dying Hassan, Gordon is looking for the "inner life" of a suicide bomber. Unlike him, she claims to have found it in a shared revulsion at the soul-destroying banality of Western consumer culture. Indeed, the imaginative identification becomes so strong that she in effect loses herself in it and almost becomes the terrorist she has only imagined. This is the point at which she could "go out on quite a spree."

What keeps it potential rather than actual—what converts the terrorist into a writer, we might say—is "reading the Gospel." That reading extracts the paradox of the incarnation, with its message of "seeing . . . every human being as Jesus." Appropriately enough, the figure of a crucified Jesus, God incarnate, here comes to stand for the very kind of reflexivity that *The Giaour* had celebrated as "wounded": terrorist violence deflected into a sacrificial woundedness, modulated just enough that it retains its power to shock— hence the discomfort inspired by Gordon's remarks—without actually tip- ping over into real bloodshed.

Gordon produces this figure of Jesus through an interpretive practice ("reading") that presupposes that dramas of interpretation are at the center of a religious life. Once it begins to seem at the very least tasteless, and at the most positively bloodthirsty, to continue asserting the exclusive claims of one particular religion or sect, it becomes desirable to deflect cultural conflict into the hermeneutic domain—to turn "reading the Gospel" into a plea for tolerance rather than an excuse for bloodshed. Paradox, on this understand- ing, offers one possible answer to the inescapable fact of pluralism. Given the coexistence of a variety of mutually exclusive truth-claims on which appar- ently hang the salvation of millions and in the name of which people seem willing to die and to kill, paradox offers a method of reading that replaces violence with the indirect and ultimately inarticulable *feeling* that one is in the presence of something beyond words. To read in this way is thus to participate in a history of reading intimately bound to the transformation of Christianity itself.

I have argued in this chapter that the *doxa* beyond words is not the residue of religion but the often imperceptible presence of the secular: the air or environment that exerts variously subtle pressures on the reader, like the silence in "Frost at Midnight" suddenly revealed as "extreme." The kind of close reading solicited by *The Giaour* is less a displaced Christianity than a reading of the secular by the secular: the moment—highly stylized in the Byronic pause—when reading illuminates the conditions of its possibility, showing them to be not a neutral ground but a highly partial one: extreme, imaginatively violent, too comfortable with the asymmetries of power that make up ordinary life. If one is to step into that space, it is better to know what it means: "Not mine the act, though I the cause," as the Giaour himself puts it, indicating that to be unattached, and hence subject to various distributed agencies and unforeseen consequences, is what it means to be "free." The Giaour's melancholy shares something with Theodore's, from Walpole's *Castle of Otranto*. But it springs less from the loss of an ungrievable past than from a recognition of what it means to step into a future without attachment. Thus the hesitation, the pause. One could say that this is the time to be strong, and that the Giaour fails this test. But one might also say that he is right to demand an accounting, from others and from himself, of what that step means, of who benefits from it, and of who will not. Leila's fate may not be singular, and it is hardly redeemed by her lover's brooding melancholy. The Giaour may try to read Hassan, but we read the Giaour, and what we read there is a meditation on the literary as both the carrier of religious transformation *and* the means by which we grasp its associated costs. In an imperfect world, that kind of reading may be the best we can do. But it entails a history, and it does not come for free.

CHAPTER 8

The Constellations of Romantic Religion

You know that there is no semblance of a system in that, that still
other stars are discovered between these pictures, that even within
their limits everything is undetermined and endless.
　　　　　　—Friedrich Schleiermacher, *On Religion* (1799)

Romantic religion is all around us. I mean the term, *romantic religion*, in the
vaguest possible sense, for that is how we encounter it. Consider, for example,
the rise in the United States of those who call themselves "spiritual but not
religious," now something like 20 percent of the population.[1] And consider the
concomitant growth of a commercial sensibility meant to serve them: Krista
Tippett's popular NPR show *Speaking of Faith* (significantly renamed *On Being*
in 2010), for example, which describes itself as a "spacious conversation—and
an evolving media space—about the big questions at the center of human life."
Or a writer like Karen Armstrong, whose many books and television appearances offer intelligent and well-researched reasons to be what she calls a "free-
lance monotheist." Consider, too, Terrence Malick's 2011 film *The Tree of Life*,
which juxtaposes Job-style questions of theodicy with a pantheistic sense of the
divine presence in all things, conveyed in its luminously beautiful images and
the golden light that seems always to be filtering down onto its characters. Or
consider, in a more academic vein, Charles Taylor's *A Secular Age*, and its
lengthy meditation on our struggle for meaning under the conditions of modernity. "Somewhere," Taylor writes, "lies a fullness, a richness; . . . in that place
. . . life is fuller, richer, deeper, more worthwhile, more admirable, more what
it should be."[2] The sociological contours of this media space are not hard to
discern: Western, middle-class, educated, predominantly white. Yet whatever

the source, and whatever its limitations, the astonishing variety of spiritual practices across the contemporary landscape suggests a social world marked not only by the popular religious fervor that makes the headlines but by a dynamic cross section of movements, institutions, and individual projects of spiritual transformation.

In *The Invention of World Religions* (2005), the most institutionally focused of the books that offer genealogies of the growth of religious studies in the modern academy, Tomoko Masuzawa notes that at the beginning of the nineteenth century there were basically four categories into which Westerners divided the world's religions: Christianity, Judaism, Islam, and Idolatry. One hundred years later, there were ten to twelve religions, and the category of "world religion" was rapidly gaining acceptance in the developing field of comparative religious studies. Masuzawa's observation ought to be of interest to scholars of romanticism if for no other reason than that it was during this period that the four-part early modern division, developed largely as a way to classify peoples and what Samuel Purchas called their "customes," finally gave way to a different discourse in which religion became something that diverse peoples "have" rather than do. It was during the nineteenth century that religion itself achieved what Masuzawa calls the "overwhelming sense of objective reality . . . that now holds us in its sway."[3] For the most part, we continue to operate under this sway, perhaps especially when we imagine ourselves to have escaped from it into a putatively secular realm determined largely by its distance from "religion."

This chapter traces one of the paths by which religion's "objective reality" has come to seem a fait accompli. Some parts of this journey may be familiar: I begin with the revolutionary biblical scholarship of Robert Lowth and J. G. Herder, and track the influence of their ideas in Friedrich Schleiermacher's small book *On Religion*, arguably the most influential recasting of the term in the past two centuries.[4] As a result, perhaps, of what Taylor calls the "nova effect" of modernity, Schleiermacher's romantic religion of feeling, though a creature of the academy, has long since left it behind, taking up residence among neopagans, transcendentalists, Wiccans, meditators, druids, UFO enthusiasts, shamanic drummers, astrologers, and all those committed to beliefs and practices that seem a little crazy or maybe just a bit too optimistic—an entire landscape, in short, of citizens who are spiritual but not religious.[5]

At the end of this chapter I will be highlighting a different and more immanent romantic religion, one that does not so much abandon its institutional affiliation as learn to inhabit it differently. I take its terms from two sources: from Walter Benjamin, whose use of the figure of the "constellation" to describe a nonlinear history picks up on a largely hidden thread within the discourse of romantic religion, and from Cythna, the heroine of Percy Shelley's *Revolt of Islam*, who at a moment of revolutionary crisis creates a new language that lives differently within the boundaries of the old. Cythna calls it a "subtler language within language," characterized simultaneously by epistemological generosity and by ephemerality. Such a language, living "inside" official languages, evokes the creativity of a deterritorialized conversation across both time and space.

As the Hebrews Would Have Read It: Robert Lowth

For most of its career the Christian Bible has been understood as a repository of divine revelation and an authoritative canon belonging to the church. Not merely the source of academic theology, the Bible "also furnished [the church's] moral universe, framed its philosophic inquiries, and fitted out its liturgies."[6] It shaped the culture that surrounded it precisely because it transcended that culture. Reform whittled away at this contextualizing power, making the Bible a site of interpretive and political contest and thereby implicitly humanizing it. Seventeenth-century textual studies, whether carried out by Spinoza, Grotius, Hobbes, or Richard Simon, made the Scriptures an object of discussion, and thus a part of the process of disembedding or "explicitation" central to the phenomenology of the secular.[7] However eternal the Bible's message was still felt to be, more readers and more books meant more discussion, and perhaps more doubt, and a fractured church and multiple Bibles meant that there was no obvious place to turn in order to resolve disputes. Academic clarity and spiritual authority seemed to be locked in a zero-sum game.[8]

   In what sense, then, could Scripture still tender the eternally relevant instruction that had always been its raison d'être? Jonathan Sheehan has traced the process by which, during the eighteenth century, the Bible came to be viewed as a cultural rather than divine revelation, "recuperated," he writes, "as an essential element of that transcendent moral, literary, and historical heritage that supposedly holds together Western society."[9] And crucial to that cultural recuperation is learning to read the Bible in a literary fashion—as a fund of poetic resources, an example of what it means to be "inspired," and, eventually, in the now-familiar manner of university courses

on "the Bible as literature." In the hands first of Robert Lowth and then of
Johann Gottfried Herder, this literary or "poetic" reading of the Bible developed as a way of bridging the otherwise enormous gap between an ancient
text and its modern readership. With Lowth and Herder we can trace the
emergence of two notions that will become central pieces of intellectual culture by the early nineteenth century: a method of literary reading that celebrates language for its own sake, and a dizzying awareness of historical time.
The pastness of the past and the perplexing physicality of language came to
be seen as mutually constitutive, both inflicting and healing the wounds that
characterize the secular age.

It is to Robert Lowth (1710–87), Anglican clergyman and professor of
poetry at Oxford from 1741 to 1752, that the eighteenth century owes the
discovery of the poetic genius of the ancient Hebrews.[10] In 1741 and 1742
Lowth presented a series of lectures inspired by Warburton's *Divine Legation
of Moses*. Like many influential English divines of the late seventeenth and
early eighteenth centuries, Warburton argued that everything needful in
Scripture was clearly available to a literal reading; appeals to figurative difficulties, along with the allegorical methods developed to make sense of them,
were signs of a reactionary politics out of step with the rational, reasonable
telos of the moderate Enlightenment. (This, at least, was the official view of
the matter, though as we saw in Chapter 5 Warburton's text was rather more
complicated.) At any rate, Lowth, too, took advantage of the weakening of
allegorical interpretive practices that had fused Old and New Testaments into
a single narrative. But for him, the fading of allegory liberated the scriptural
account *into history*: freed from the weight of interpretive tradition, the Bible
could now be received as its first readers and hearers received it. This
demanded that readers celebrate the figural texture of the Bible, grasping the
metaphorical and sublime qualities of ancient Hebrew if they were to grasp
the deepest meaning of the Scriptures.[11]

Lowth had been struck by the overpowering *force* of the Hebrew
writers—a quality he described in the language of the sublime. Like Burke a
few years later, he would link the sublime to the rough, the unpolished, the
natural—it was, in short, the very opposite of the smooth and regular neoclassi-
cal diction then dominant. The Bible's "native force and beauty," he wrote,
came from the writer's simple diction, direct approach, and connection to the
land; "utmost brevity and simplicity" was the source of its power.[12] But in
order to understand this power, one must know how the poetry actually works,
"the machinery, as it were, by which this end is effected."[13]

Thus Lowth set aside the inspired character of the Old Testament in favor of an analysis of its "machinery." This is a subtle but important shift: it does not necessarily deny divine inspiration, but if that inspiration is now analytically separable from poetic genius, then the Hebrew poets are suddenly made historical in a new way: they sang as themselves, not as imperfect Christians typologically prefiguring the Christ event. Accordingly, one could not simply read "through" the language of the Old Testament in order to extract its Christological content. Rather, the content seemed to depend in some way on the form in which it was conveyed; the words themselves, in their historical and cultural rootedness, mattered. In the language of Scripture, things call to things and words call to words, and the reader must learn to attend to a process whose logic seems internal to itself. In principle, one might even remain agnostic about the question of divine inspiration and still revere the Bible for its poetry. A way of appreciating the Bible "as literature" had appeared.

This increasingly literary or autonomous quality of Scriptural language emerges in counterpoint to Lowth's acute sense of historical distance. No one, he conceded, really understood Hebrew grammar or meter, nor did eighteenth-century readers know how the words ought to sound. But that was only the beginning, for even if contemporary readers had a sense of the living language, the Hebrews themselves were radically different people: "Not only the antiquity of these writings forms a principal obstruction in many respects; but the manner of living, of speaking, of thinking, which prevailed in those times, will be found altogether different from our customs and habits."[14] In imagination, then, the reader must enter the Hebrew past: "we must even investigate their inmost sentiments, the manner and connexion of their thoughts; in one word, we must see all things with their eyes, estimate all things by their opinions: we must endeavor as much as possible to read Hebrew as the Hebrews would have read it."[15] But how does one do this?

The problem was particularly acute with figurative language, or what Lowth called "the substitution of words, or rather of ideas, for those which they resemble."[16] He refers indiscriminately to all such substitutions as metaphors, and he argues that they depend on resemblance between the two objects, and "the beauty or dignity" of the new idea. The difficulty is that objects can become detached from their appropriate ideas over time, as other associations build up: "Thus it sometimes happens, that the external form and lineaments may be sufficiently apparent, though the original and intrinsic beauty and elegance be totally erased by time."[17] The metaphors of the

sacred poets are an especial problem, separated as they are by a vast historical and cultural distance. Some metaphors "now strike the superficial reader as coarse, mean, or deformed."[18] Ideally, inspired language bridges historical distance; yet here metaphor risks becoming itself the very figure *for* historical distance, as our inability to appreciate the actual sublimity of the Hebrew writers marks our distance from them.

Long, Cold Paraphrases: J. G. Herder

"We must endeavor as much as possible to read Hebrew as the Hebrews would have read it": Lowth never really discussed how such a thing might be possible. Historical understanding and literary appreciation remained conceptually discrete endeavors for him. And in an intellectual climate still concerned more with the veracity of miracles than with their poetry, Lowth's work had little immediate influence in England in any case.[19]

But matters were different in Germany, and it was the German minister, theologian, and philosopher Johann Gottfried Herder who set himself the task of bringing literature and history together. In *The Spirit of Hebrew Poetry* (1782), Herder began by remarking that although Lowth had moved the conversation forward, he had paid too much attention to the *letter*; a proper understanding of the *spirit* of Hebrew poetry, Herder writes, would allow the reader to bridge the historical gap that had defeated Lowth. The poetry of the Hebrews, with its vivid imagery and direct style, was not a hindrance to understanding; on the contrary, poetry would help the modern reader feel his way into the lives of these quintessential *Volk*.[20]

Even before his engagement with biblical poetry, Herder had made the crucial and influential link between language and the human as such.[21] In the *Treatise on the Origin of Language* (1772), Herder set himself against both of the prominent linguistic theories of his day. Many (Lowth among them) held that language was a gift from God; others, associated with Condillac and with Enlightenment theories of language more generally, held that language derived from conventional usage and therefore had a human origin. With a characteristic flash of insight, Herder saw that these seemingly opposed theories actually shared the basic presupposition that human beings preexisted language. In the *Treatise* Herder turned this supposition upside down: there was no human being "before" language, he argued; using language simply was what it meant to *be* human: "If others found it unintelligible how a human soul was *able* to invent language, then it is unintelligible to me how a human soul was able to be what it is without precisely thereby . . . *inevitably* inventing language for itself."[22]

When Herder directed his attention to Lowth, then, he was already prepared to push beyond the Englishman's more cautious empirical approach. He followed the Orientalist scholarship of his day in holding that Eastern languages opened up to view "the childhood and youth of the human race."[23] These languages had less grammar and abstraction; they were closer to the senses, more concrete, sensuous, and image laden. Their poetic resources were therefore greater. *The Spirit of Hebrew Poetry* accordingly celebrated the immediate and intimate connection that a close reading of the Hebrew writings made possible.

Herder was particularly entranced by the lack of written vowels in Hebrew. Heard but not seen, they became a window into the childhood of the human race. In the *Treatise* he refers to this as "writing the inessential and omitting the essential"—the essential song and poetry of the language held in the "breath" and "spirit" of the unseen vowels (*TO* 71). Closer to nature, Hebrew was thus also closer to divinity: carried by breath and spirit, vowels become a channel to the mysterious, ineffable manifestation of God— the divine spirit that broods over the still unformed world. Caught in a time before abstraction and scholarly systematization, Hebrew connected the modern reader to effects that could not be precisely pointed to but only felt and experienced. In trying to describe this effect, Herder turned continually to the language of "breath," "spirit," and "soul." This was the spirit of Hebrew poetry, "the very breath of the soul" (*SHP* 35) in which the true spirit of a people allows itself to be heard.

Famously, Herder's line of argument raised the problem of cultural relativism in its modern form. For if the true spirit of a people could be heard only in their language, then it followed that there was no external or "objective" model against which either individual or group could be evaluated. Each was to be judged on its own terms: "*Moreover*, their relationships are so national, so much according to the peculiar manner of thinking and seeing of that people, of that inventor, in that land, in that time, in those circumstances, that they are infinitely difficult for a Northerner and Westerner to get right, and must suffer infinitely in long, cold paraphrases" (*TO* 114).[24] What drops out of a paraphrase, of course, is the poetry—the particular experience of language that can only be undergone and never summarized. To what kind of historical method might the modern Northerner and Westerner appeal to avoid such cold paraphrases? How does one put the poetry back into history?

No third-person method will be able to accomplish this. As Herder put it in *This Too a Philosophy of History for the Formation of Humanity* (1774), "to survey the world-sea of whole peoples, ages, and lands" was a fool's game (*TT* 291). In contrast to the wide survey of Enlightenment historiography, Herder formulated the influential notion of *Einfühlung*, or "feeling one's way in." "[G]o into the age, into the clime, the whole history, feel yourself into everything," he instructed his readers (*TT* 292). Go into the age, then—but if such empathy was not to cancel difference and thus return to Enlightenment universalism by the back door, the historical gap between now and then must be worked formally into the interpretive process itself, so that the act of interpretive understanding was always also marked by the fact of cultural and historical difference.

And it is just here that the "spirit of poetry" plays its most decisive role. We are not, after all, "Hebrews ourselves," and yet by a kind of literary magic we can become them for a time without losing our identities as modern Europeans. Because we have to deal here with differences that "can be but little grasped in rules" we are in the terrain of "obscure feelings, . . . fleeting side ideas, . . . coinciding sensations, which rise up from the bottom of the soul" (*TO* 114). The only way to get into such a world is to feel the force of its language, which is to say the literary or poetic spirit that animates it from within. So poetry emerged as the primary conduit of the empathetic historical understanding that was Herder's lifelong aim. Poetry *felt* is spirit, and spirit is the "way in" to history.

Thus does *poiesis* create for itself a new status in the closing years of the eighteenth century. The human capacity for artful creation turns out to be a way *back* to the divine, while remaining a thoroughly immanent faculty. Of course, it is hard to say just what this means in a practical sense. Frustratingly but magically, poetry seems to include everything that matters, and yet it is at the same time incorporeal, spiritual, carried on the breath and the wind, just out of reach of final explanation. We are here at the origin of a rendering of German Protestantism as a universal religion, the true inheritor and developer of a heritage stretching back to the Hebrews. Yet because Protestantism is thereby transformed into a universal religion, it loses most of the trappings of "religion." It is simply, as Herder writes, a "*subtle* spirit, 'a *deism* of *human friendship*,' . . . [a] *philosophy of heaven* that, precisely because of its loftiness and its unearthly purity, could embrace the whole earth" (*TT* 304). The metaphors are telling: Christianity is the yeast that mixes with the dough of a particular nation or culture; it is the "subtle vapor" mixed with earthly materials.

From the Interior of Every Better Soul: Friedrich Schleiermacher

When Immanuel Kant turned his attention to the organization of the academy in *The Conflict of the Faculties* (1798), he imagined a straightforward separation between the "lower" faculty of philosophy and the "higher" faculties of law, medicine, and theology. The higher faculties, Kant wrote, were higher because the government had an interest in what they taught, while the lower faculty of philosophy, because its function was "only to look after . . . science," was not of interest to the state. In service of this division Kant hit on a memorable phrase: "It [is] not a bad idea to handle the entire content of learning . . . *like a factory*, so to speak—by a division of labor."[25] This division between the higher and lower faculties recalls an analogous distinction Kant had made some years earlier, in his 1784 essay "What Is Enlightenment?" where he rather idiosyncratically distinguished between the public and private use of one's reason. Public reason is universal reason; private reason is reason in service of the state. Kant then contrasted the role of a clergyman in his "private" capacity as an employee of the state required to affirm the official positions of the church, with the role of a clergyman as a public intellectual, a citizen of the world, whose only loyalty was to universal reason and who was therefore free to criticize church doctrine.[26] So for Kant in 1798, in *The Conflict of the Faculties*, the philosophy faculty has a responsibility to reason's universal dictates, and should thus be free of state censorship; while the theology faculty, whose proper domain is religion, has a responsibility to the state, and is therefore subject to censorship.[27]

When Wilhelm von Humboldt organized the new University of Berlin in 1809, he took Kant's distinction one step further by dividing the theology faculty from the humanities faculties, including philosophy. Humboldt's distinctions aimed to liberate the humanities from theological control—a crucial step in the development of literary studies, philology, and indeed of the modern university itself.[28] Institutionally divided from both philosophy and the arts, theology came to occupy its own distinctive terrain. The undoubted preeminence of German theology, philology, and philosophy in the nineteenth century suggests that Kant and Humboldt knew what they were about; in terms of their institutional success, these disciplines were better off disentangled from one another. Yet such divisions have yielded long-term confusions about the relations among theology, literature, and philosophy—interpretive fields that remain closely allied in spite of faculty "conflict," as the recent and controversial "turn to religion" across the humanities suggests. As Stephen Prickett nicely remarks, this imperfect separation of the disciplines has left humanists with the uneasy sense that "they are somehow still in the salvation business."[29]

Humboldt's institutional limitation of "religion" follows a distinction central to Kant's "What Is Enlightenment?" essay between public, universal reason and private, state-sponsored religious belief. When the two come into conflict, it is the latter that must give way, since it would be a "crime against human nature" for a "society of clergymen" to assert that any doctrine is beyond dispute.[30] That Kant does not consider the possibility that curtailing church authority might *also* be a crime against human nature suggests a dramatic change in how religion was understood: it had come to name the local, the particular, and the time bound, while reason assumed the mantle of universality that Christianity had claimed for more than a millennium. Rather than marking a common humanity, religion became something that potentially drove people apart.[31] The influence of this line of thinking continues to be felt in manifold ways. Kant's assumption that religious truth is essentially dogmatic and unchanging, for example, is an oversimplification that puts religion on a collision course with a notion of modern reason understood as both universal and flexible. A further consequence is to make cosmopolitanism an inherently secular affair; conflicts between universal human rights and local religious traditions inevitably follow.

Taken together, then, these innovations in the university world tended to contain and delimit "religion," thereby setting up tensions within the liberal state that show no signs of abating. But they thereby also created an opening for a new kind of religion, one that would eschew dogma, that would not threaten state power, that would tie people back together again. This was a market opportunity eagerly grasped by the young Friedrich Schleiermacher, whose 1799 book *On Religion* placed Kantian intuition in the service of a religion based entirely on interior feeling, grounded in experience, and irreducible to other categories of analysis or description.[32] As Kant had formulated the notion in the *Critique of Pure Reason*, intuitions do not bring their relevant objects under general concepts but rather "relate immediately to the object"—an intuitive grasping of singular objects that is prior, as

Kant also says, to their grouping under concepts.[33] Kant notes that this relation is "sensible," by which he means that it affects the mind in a certain way. Herder's description in the *Treatise on the Origin of Language* of how verbs become nouns is clearly influential here: "Since the whole of nature resounds, there is nothing more natural for a sensuous human being than that *it lives, it speaks, it acts*," writes Herder. "That savage saw the high tree with its splendid crown and admired. The crown rustled! That is the work of divinity! The savage falls down and prays to it! Behold there the history of the sensuous human being, the obscure link, *how nouns arise from the verbs—and the easiest step to abstraction!*"[34] The pure sensuous relations of action and intuition gradually become grouped, as Kant would say, under concepts.

It is easy to see how Schleiermacher might glimpse in Kantian sensuous intuition a way back into a simpler world, a Herder-style religion of feeling prior to concepts, abstractions, and the accouterments of organized religion. Schleiermacher proposed that the religious impulse intuitively grasped the unity of mind and world before intellection had rent them asunder. Religion was thus an experiential, precognitive encounter with the truth of the universe. As such, it embraced the differentiated world of the conflict of the faculties. At once very narrow and very deep, religion "renounces herewith all claims to whatever belongs to . . . others and gives back everything that has been forced upon it. It does not wish to determine and explain the universe. . . . [Rather, it] wishes devoutly to overhear the universe's own manifestations and actions, longs to be grasped and filled by the universe's immediate influences in childlike passivity."[35] Still less does religion demand temporal power: "It springs necessarily and by itself from the interior of every better soul, it has its own province in the mind in which it reigns sovereign."[36] The political language here is not accidental; if Kant had insisted that religion be subordinate to the state, Schleiermacher argues for its sovereignty. But it is not an imperial sovereignty. Its universalism is gentle, a placeholder for humankind's best aspirations, for the spirit that drew people together across the boundaries of nation, creed, and culture.[37]

Schleiermacher's book bears the subtitle *Speeches to Its Cultured Despisers*. The cultured despisers of religion are his best friends: Friedrich Schlegel and his brother Augustus, G. P. F. von Hardenburg (who wrote under the pen name Novalis), and others steeped in the milieu of post-Kantian German philosophy. These writers, philosophers, and artists, gathered in Jena just before the turn of the century, are at the center of early German romanticism. And in his speeches Schleiermacher presents religion as their ally. He argues that both religion and romanticism are critical of cautious bourgeois life and open to new dimensions of perception and creativity. In the wake of Kant and the French Revolution, one has the choice of a stultifying conformity or the freedom of a subject at last delivered to itself. The sovereign province of religion will be the individual's salvation—its salvation, that is to say, from the numbing effects of modernity.

Constellations

That numbing effect, the sense of having crossed over into a different age— one that is historicist, reflexive, cognitive—shows up in meditations on the great difficulty of sympathetic understanding across time: the "original and intrinsic beauty" of a scriptural figure, as Lowth wrote, has faded over the centuries, so that it now appears "coarse, mean, or deformed" to the contemporary "superficial" reader.[38] If reading like the Hebrews required a movement of the imagination, then metaphor, the very figure of such movement, became for Lowth that which also blocked it. Rather than carrying us closer to them, metaphor reminds us how very far away we are.

Lowth left this problem unresolved, but in his discussion of metaphor he had recourse to a remarkable metaphor of his own. To read Hebrew as the Hebrews would have read it, he writes, is to "act as the Astronomers with regard to that branch of their science which is called comparative, who, in order to form a more perfect idea of the general system, and its different parts, conceive themselves as passing through, and surveying the whole universe, migrating from one planet to another, and becoming for a short time inhabitants of each. Thus they . . . distinguish what and how different an appearance of the universe is exhibited according to the different situations from which it is contemplated."[39] Rather than transporting himself to an ancient land and people, Lowth here imagined himself above the earth, moving into and then out of a variety of planetary systems in order to get a more accurate comparative account.[40] His is less a view from nowhere than it is a deeper recognition of perspective and partiality: of how differently the universe appears depending on the angle "from which it is contemplated."

Lowth's astronomical metaphor thus suggests a different and more figurative relationship to the historical past than is usually associated with the sympathetic understanding of *Einfühlung*. In Lowth's account, it seems, one never escapes metaphor; accordingly, one does not so much move oneself in an act of imaginative sympathy as remain open to *being moved*—nudged around the universe, affected by the power of language. And there is a social element to the experience. To become aware of the "different situations from which [the universe] is contemplated" is to be reminded that there are also other people there doing the contemplating.

Schleiermacher too discovered this intrinsically social and figural dimension to cosmological speculation. Trying to demonstrate to his romantic friends how very much alike they were, Schleiermacher claimed that they all shared the aspiration to intuit the universe. The problem with unmediated intuition was again the relativist one: a lack of shared evaluative criteria. "Others may stand right behind you, right alongside you," he wrote, "and everything can appear differently to them."[41] Schleiermacher then turned to an extended metaphor in an effort to resolve this problem:

> Elevate yourselves at once . . . to the wondrous and celebrated starry sky. The astronomical theories, which orient a thousand suns with their world systems around a common point and seek for each common point again a higher world system that could be its center, and so on into infinity. . . . You know that there is no semblance of a system in that, that still other stars are discovered between these pictures, that even within their limits everything is undetermined and endless, and that the pictures themselves remain something purely arbitrary and highly changeable. When you have persuaded another person to join you in drawing the image of the Big Dipper onto the blue background of the worlds, does he not nevertheless remain free to conceive the adjacent worlds in contours that are completely different from yours? This infinite chaos, where of course every point represents a world, is as such actually the most suitable and highest symbol of religion. In religion, as in this chaos, only the particular is true and necessary.[42]

Schleiermacher's figure, like Lowth's, suggests that a focus on a particular constellation alters one's perception of the surrounding stars—and that this is a good thing, for it indicates that all experience starts with the particular and the individual. But this claim can itself be made only in a social and comparative context. There is another person drawing the Big Dipper also; the drawings can be compared to each other and to the original; their different ways of rendering the particular constellation and the infinity that surrounds it are invitations not to judgments of whose is right but to further conversation and dialogue. Accidents of representation—of skill, angle, vision, and commitment—are intrinsic to the metaphorical situation imagined here.

While he was writing *On Religion* Schleiermacher was also contributing fragments to the *Athenaeum*, the short-lived journal founded in 1798 by Friedrich and A. W. Schlegel, two of the "cultured despisers" whom *On Religion* addresses. Schlegel argued in the pages of this journal that philosophy should begin not with a first or unconditioned principle but rather wherever we happen to find ourselves.[43] In this he follows Schleiermacher's extended stargazing metaphor, with its recommendation that we focus on a particular constellation and see how the world looks from there, rather than trying to depict the "infinite chaos" of the whole universe. Where we "find ourselves," in Schleiermacher's figure, is struggling to draw a constellation while knowing all along that nearby another person is doing the same thing. For Schlegel, the literary genre of the fragment perfectly encapsulated this unsystematic, personal, and implicitly social view, for it was itself the experience of truth as partial and provisional, its point of departure the rich world of perception and experience rather than a third-person modeling of the whole. What Schlegel called "romantic poesy" displays the ironic attitude demanded by this kind of truth. "Other genres are fixed and capable of being classified in their entirety," he wrote in the famous *Athenaeum Fragment* 116. "The romantic genre is, however, still in process of becoming; indeed, this is its essence: to be eternally in the process of becoming and never completed."[44] In this vision of things, incompleteness solicits critical conversation and transformation, and social space is *created*, not distorted, by the accidents of figuration.

A constellation is an arbitrary grouping of stars that from a certain angle make a coherent gathering. In the various fragments that make up *The Arcades Project*, and which like Schlegel's fragments blur the lines between literature and criticism, Walter Benjamin proposes the constellation as an image of how the past becomes present in concentrated form, a moment where "what has been comes together in a flash with the now."[45] "A historian who takes this as his point of departure stops telling the sequence of events like the beads of a rosary," he remarks in the *Theses on the Philosophy of History*. "Instead, he grasps the constellation which his own era has formed with a definite earlier one. Thus he establishes a conception of the present as the 'time of the now' which is shot through with chips of Messianic time."[46] Like a constellation, an era or season may gather itself at certain moments.

In contrast to Charles Taylor, who argues that what makes our age secular is that events follow each other in causal patterns without interruption, Benjamin thinks that the constellations are still there.[47] Like Schleiermacher's stargazer, Benjamin's critical historian can only see in the stars a definitive shape when he views them from a particular angle—but that angle is located in time as well as space. There is something about the current situation that will "concentrate" the object under investigation. History does not have to be a sequence of events that simply fills up the "homogenous, empty time" of modernity (*T* 261). Instead, Messianic time can emerge from within that very sequence. Or, in Schleiermacher's idiom, "still other stars are discovered between these pictures."

Discovering those stars and learning to see them as a constellation: that is the activity of the critical historian, an exercise in *poiesis* that encodes a politics of time and of history telling and functions as a critique of the phenomenology of empty time (*AP* 857). It is the very opposite of the pervasive air of melancholy that I located in the first section of this book: Theodore's endless "discourse," Emma's wish for impossible things, the pervasive feeling that lost possibilities were not only behind one as time's arrow moved relentlessly into the future, but also out of reach even in their own time. Benjamin's critical historian accepts this melancholy conclusion—that the past is ungrievable because its possibilities were always impossible—but turns it into an opportunity for the future: rather than waiting for events to unfold, the historian shapes them, "such that everything past . . . can acquire a higher grade of actuality than it had in the moment of its existing" (*AP* 392). Because the constellation illuminates connections otherwise hidden, it treats history not as past but as the site of an active intervention. Given this "revolutionary chance to fight for the oppressed past" the historian sets out to "blast a specific era out of the homogenous course of history" (*T* 263). Benjamin refers to this struggle against the age as an "awakening" (*AP* 458). As if progress has put us to sleep, and the point of writing is to wake us up from this secular slumber, to become alive once again to the multiple possibilities that adhere to each moment.

Footsteps like Those of a Wind over a Sea

The final star in our constellation is Cythna, the heroine of Percy Shelley's poem *The Revolt of Islam*. Well along in that drama, after the failure of the nonviolent revolution that she has led with her cousin/brother/lover Laon, Cythna finds herself alone, trapped in a cave by the sea. A sea-eagle carries food to her in her imprisonment, and she first tries to instruct the eagle to bring her ropes so that she can escape:

> and long in vain I sought
> By intercourse of mutual imagery
> Of objects, if such aid he could be taught;
> But fruit, and flowers, and boughs, but never ropes he brought.[48]

This kind of substitution cannot cross the species barrier. "We live in our own world," Cythna concludes (line 3091). Implicitly modifying Herder's optimistic rendering of the naturally figurative language of the primitive, Shelley suggests that symbolic language of this kind leads neither to freedom nor to communion. Trapped in her cave, fighting madness, her voice mediated by various authoritative male voices, and with only her own resources and memories to sustain her, Cythna in her radical reflexivity seems the prototypical modern subject, poised on the cusp of a new world and realizing that she must create not only her own meaning but the very conditions of its intelligibility. Or perhaps she is closer to Benjamin's famous image of the "Angel of History" blown backward toward a future she cannot see, "while the pile of debris . . . grows skyward" (*T* 257–58). But then Cythna turns inward, and the language that she invents is neither heroically autotelic nor wholly new but contingent, open to change, and implicitly social:

> And on the sand would I make signs to range
> These woofs, as they were woven, of my thought;
> Clear, elemental shapes, whose smallest change
> A subtler language within language wrought:
> The key of truths which once were dimly taught
> In old Crotona;—and sweet melodies
> Of love, in that lorn solitude I caught
> From mine own voice in dream, when thy dear eyes
> Shone thro' my sleep, and did that utterance harmonize. (lines
>   3109–16)

As Cythna discovers, the subtler language is not a new language, nor is it the kind of symbolic substitution that she had tried with the eagle. The new world she is striving to create does not require that she make meaning anew in a postmetaphysical age. Unlike the failed language of freedom that she had tried to forge with the eagle, the subtler language alters materials already available.[49] The wreckage of the old language holds the beginning of something else, scratched out temporarily on the sand, a subtler language that lives inside the language of revolution and progress. It is written on the sand and energized by prior voices of love and communion: it will change, disappear, reappear in new forms.

There is no question that *The Revolt of Islam* was one of Shelley's many efforts to replace Christianity with a new poetic and political syntax.[50] Harnessing aspects of the Radical Enlightenment to various apocalyptic scenarios, the poem offered the familiar radical argument that God was an anthropomorphic projection of "some moon-struck sophist" (line 3244) and that theology was invented to justify misery. Yet the poem also argues, strenuously, that replacing Christianity with something else does not work either: the eagle language does not take wing—nor, despite its pure and peaceful intent, does Laon and Cythna's revolt succeed. Shelley called their revolution the "beau ideal . . . of the French Revolution," and if even the best possible version of that Revolution ends terribly, then it seems likely that simply replacing one thing (tyranny) with another (liberal freedom) actually changes very little.[51]

Thanks to Earl Wasserman, the notion of the subtler language has long been associated with romanticism's distinctive poetic voice. Readers will recall that by "subtler language" Wasserman meant a language that had to be developed poetically in order to capture the new sensibility of an age in which the old verities were losing their grip:

> Until the end of the eighteenth century there was sufficient intellectual homogeneity for men to share certain assumptions. . . . In varying degrees . . . men accepted . . . the Christian interpretation of history, the sacramentalism of nature, the Great Chain of Being, the analogy of the various planes of creation. . . .
>
> By the nineteenth century these world-pictures had passed from consciousness. . . . Now . . . an additional formulative act was required of the poet. . . . Within itself the modern poem must both formulate its cosmic syntax and shape the autonomous poetic reality that the cosmic syntax permits.[52]

It is certainly possible to interpret the subtler language as the distinctive voice of the secular age, the development of a modern poetics that, as Taylor writes, "has enabled people to explore . . . meanings with their ontological commitments as it were in suspense."[53] In this formulation, the world is disenchanted, and it is up to the poet and the creative seeker to make meaning within the void, to formulate its cosmic syntax. Inevitably, such meanings will be personal, even idiosyncratic. But this is to forget, as Wasserman seems to, that Cythna's language is a language *within language*. Rather than forge a wholly new syntax of freedom with the eagle, she makes do with what she finds at hand: love, sand, memories. Arranging these disparate elements into a constellation, Cythna rescues something of the past from the storm called progress. In her efforts, she says, "the world has seen / A *type* of peace" (lines 3733–34, emphasis added). Like all typological prefigurations, this one persists, waiting for the moment of its reactivation. Here, in what she calls the "winter of the world" (line 3685), still "The seeds are sleeping in the soil" (line 3676), waiting for the right conditions in which to spring forth once again.

In her "Note" appended to *The Revolt of Islam* in the 1839 edition of the *Poems*, Mary Shelley remarks on Percy's "constant perusal" of the texts that Lowth had made central to his account of biblical poetry: "the Psalms, the Book of Job, the Prophet Isaiah, and others, the sublime poetry of which filled him with delight."[54] In the context of the *Revolt*'s celebration of the subtler language and its heterogeneous theory of history, we can read Percy's delight in "the sublime poetry" of the Bible as the delight of a fragile but ongoing conversation across space and time. Poetry, he wrote in the *Defense*, is "the interpenetration of a diviner nature through our own," but such inspiration is not a permanent condition: "its footsteps are like those of a wind over a sea, which the coming calm erases, and whose traces remain only as on the wrinkled sand which paves it."[55] Even the best words last only for a time, like Cythna's marks on the sand. Wildly inventive metaphors eventually sink into convention, "and then if no new poets should arise to create afresh the associations which have been thus disorganized, language will be dead to all the nobler purposes of human intercourse."[56] That continued revitalization of language is what Schleiermacher's friend Friedrich Schlegel had in mind when he described conversation as a "garland of fragments."[57] Conversation is the fragile, temporary process of creating a space in which to meet. And this is what Shelley means by *poiesis*: making; creating; the world that humans jointly compose every time they engage with it in a "vitally metaphorical" way, inventing new possibilities and opening new spaces in which strangers and friends, unapprehended combinations of thought, will have room to move and breathe. Cythna and Benjamin, the critical historians of this project, would add that the languages of these new worlds will be part of an ongoing engagement with the worlds that came before, a fleeting experiment in democratic language that finds its proper form when it exchanges melancholy for the fragile hope that previously unlived possibilities may yet, still, be lived.

CHAPTER 9

Shelley After Atheism

But liberty, when men act in bodies, is power.
—Edmund Burke, *Reflections on the Revolution in France*

Of the major romantic writers, Percy Shelley is most readily associated with atheism. In the early nineteenth century the word was still an epithet, yet Shelley seems to have courted it. *The Necessity of Atheism*, the 1811 pamphlet that got Shelley and Thomas Jefferson Hogg kicked out of Oxford, may have recapitulated familiar arguments from Locke and Hume, but the title itself had the desired effect. Five years later, when Shelley signed himself in the hotel registers in Chamonix and Montanvert as "Democrat, Philanthropist, and Atheist," it was again the final term that caused the uproar.[1] "Atheism" is an almost magical word.

This chapter is about *Mont Blanc*, the poem that Shelley largely wrote during his sojourn in Chamonix. I will have little to say about its content, for this is a poem that deliberately and provocatively resists any reading that focuses on content. The poem's obscure meditations on power, necessity, and death have sent critics scurrying for source texts, but these are of less interest to me than the "event" of *Mont Blanc* itself: the history of tourism in the area, the writing of the poem, the signature in the guest book, the reaction to that signature in England. I propose to read this event as a composite meditation on the possibilities and limitations of the history of atheism.

"History," Fredric Jameson famously writes in a Shelleyan idiom, "is not a type of content, but rather the inexorable *form* of events." Jameson refers here to the idea of history as an "absent cause," one "apprehended only through its effects."[2] It is significant that Jameson develops this thought from Spinoza, for *Mont Blanc* is in this sense a Spinozistic poem, a poem of effects without obvious antecedent causes. Thus the poem's speaker describes the long-range effects of the glaciers as they slowly make their way down from the mountain's peak:

> A city of death, distinct with many a tower
> And wall impregnable of beaming ice.
> Yet not a city, but a flood of ruin
> Is there, that from the boundaries of the sky
> Rolls its perpetual stream.[3]

The "absent cause" in this case is the mountain itself, made visible in the poem only briefly and seemingly remote from the slow-moving, inexorable destruction at its base. Connecting the mountain to the poem's "flood of ruin" requires that we read it by means of what it does *not* seem to be doing:

> Mont Blanc yet gleams on high:—the power is there,
> The still and solemn power of many sights,
> And many sounds, and much of life and death. (lines 127–29)

The mountain, as the speaker had earlier asserted, seems "far, far above" (line 60) the earthly ruin at its feet.

What I have sketched here is a treatment of the poem as an allegory for the Radical Enlightenment. A properly critical account of the mountain, Shelley seems to be saying, would begin with its godlike remoteness, its apparent transcendence of destruction, the way that it hides behind impressive locutions like "boundaries of the sky." Nevertheless the heroic "human mind" (line 143), by dint of its critical capacities, can trace destruction back to its ultimate source. That is a fine reading of the poem, but my argument will be Shelley himself actually goes it one better—that the event of the poem, if not the poem itself, is actually superior to the Radical Enlightenment, for the events that surround *Mont Blanc* mark something like an exit from this heroic model of the human mind. Pursuing this interpretation will involve, as we shall see, leaving *Mont Blanc* behind as well. For in his own first "reading" of the poem in Chamonix's hotel register and then more fully in *Prometheus Unbound*, written three years later, Shelley begins to undo atheism's long-standing association with heroic freethought. As such, we can

read the history in the *Mont Blanc* event not as an absent cause but as something closer to Coleridge's "strange quiet": as a secular history that regulates
the possibilities of embodied life.

Atheism as Unbelief

Because this is a rather counterintuitive argument, it will be best to begin on
familiar ground. In the late eighteenth and early nineteenth centuries, the
heavily touristed Vale of Chamonix was thought to facilitate religious awe,
even perhaps to cure atheists of unbelief. Such notions inspired Coleridge's
"Hymn Before Sunrise, in the Vale of Chamouni," which offered this
thought as part of its lengthy headnote when it first appeared in 1802: "Who
would be, who *could* be an Atheist in this valley of wonders!"[4] Notoriously,
Coleridge had never in fact been to Chamonix; even more notoriously, his
poem partly plagiarizes Sophie Christiane Friederike Brun's much shorter
poem on the same subject.[5] When Shelley signs the hotel register "Democrat,
Philanthropist, and Atheist," then, he is not only resisting the conventional
piety to which Coleridge had given voice; like the subtitle added for the
poem's 1817 publication, "Lines Written in the Vale of Chamouni," Shelley's
signature in the guest book marks the fact that he was *there*, and thinking for
himself. Thus *Mont Blanc*'s atheism betokens liberty: freedom from a past
marked by complacency, sentimentality, and lack of originality.

Putting it like this slots Shelley's atheism into the tradition of freethought that Jonathan Israel has taught us to call the "Radical Enlightenment."[6] Yet *Mont Blanc* is not a poem of the Radical Enlightenment in any
simple sense. Indeed, critics have generally seen in Shelley's poems of late
1815 and 1816 something of a turn away from the Radical Enlightenment,
particularly as Shelley had inherited that tradition from William Godwin, his
father-in-law and one of the major intellectual influences on his early
thought. Godwin assumed that revolution was first a cognitive event, and
thus that people could be convinced of its worth. By contrast, Shelley was by
this point in his career suggesting that people needed to experience change
imaginatively before they could learn its principles intellectually. Rousseau,
Wordsworth, and Coleridge began to appear more often in his writing.[7] This
inaugurated the political strategy that he described most famously in the
"Preface" to *Prometheus Unbound*: "The imagery which I have employed,"
Shelley writes there, "will be found, in many instances, to have been drawn

from the operations of the human mind, or from those external actions by which they are expressed" (*SPP* 207). According to the usual gloss, Shelley is here suggesting that revolutions do indeed happen mentally, but that Godwin was wrong to think that the contents of one mind could be simply transferred to another. The only way to grasp mental revolution is through the mediation of the outward scene.

In a general way this is what we mean by "romanticism," if we mean anything at all: rather than saying that his mind is like nature, the poet says that nature is like his mind, and accordingly that the best way of understanding what is going on there is to look at the outer scene. This is how M. H. Abrams laid it out in *Natural Supernaturalism*, and if Abrams saw this as a humanizing and therefore secularizing technique, it was secularization of a particularly "spiritual" sort. Earl Wasserman, in a roughly parallel fashion, influentially interpreted Shelley's "turn" of 1815/1816 as a shift from materialism to idealism.[8] For some years now, the political effects of this tendency to spiritualize or idealize the landscape have been a pressing critical question. Was the first generation's political apostasy a *necessary* result of an idealizing poetic theory, or merely a contingent one? That seems the crucial question for Shelley in Chamonix's Vale, invoking Coleridge in order to turn him upside down.

Yet to approach the matter at this level is to find oneself entangled in the question of religion in ways that limit what a text like *Mont Blanc* can do. Wasserman's readings of the poem are an excellent case in point, for after his subtle meditation on the relationship between skepticism and idealism, he concludes that however we decide the outcome, and however we interpret the poem's final rhetorical question, the thing itself remains "implicitly religious" (238). I think that Wasserman is correct here, though not quite for the reasons he thinks. The poem is not "implicitly religious" because it preserves a posture of submission (to Necessity, rather than to God), nor because it is an example of the *via negativa*, but because any interpretation of the poem that concentrates on its various epistemological conundrums will eventually find itself running up against the question of our knowledge of divinity. A reading that aims to extract the poem's cognitive content—that is, a reading that sets itself the task of figuring out what beliefs or unbeliefs the poem expresses—tangles itself up in the question of religion, *even if the reading concludes that the poem "expresses" atheism.*

To see why this is so, consider a basic tension in the history of modern atheism. Long before there were acknowledged atheists there were numerous refutations of atheism, and this curious fact can be explained in two different ways. Some intellectual historians infer atheism's presence in the early Enlightenment from the arguments of those writing *against* it.[9] From numerous seventeenth-century pamphlets declaring atheism to be impossible and incoherent, for example, Jonathan Israel and others conclude that there must have been atheists around then, even though there is no direct textual record. Why would authorities bother to critique, ridicule, and refute something that did not exist? By emphasizing the tradition of freethought, this story makes atheism external to religion. Atheists are the intellectual heroes of their age.

Alan Kors, by contrast, offers a different answer to the question of why there were so many early-modern refutations of atheism if there were no atheists. The educational method of early modern Europe, notes Kors, was scholastic *disputatio*, which rewarded speculative ingenuity. Theologians and other university-educated intellectuals "were taught, formally and informally, to generate 'objections' to all of their . . . cherished beliefs, indeed . . . to anticipate the strongest possible objections and to overcome these."[10] In this world the "atheist" serves a number of crucial rhetorical functions: his arguments had to be rehearsed, examined, and entertained, even if only to be at last triumphantly refuted. Early modern theists, Kors concludes, were the source or even the creators of the atheism they refuted. At this discursive level, he demonstrates, atheism was "ubiquitous" (96) in the early modern world. Rather than lurking in the recesses of the mind, waiting for the moment when it could finally be confessed, atheism was created by its opponents.

A background shift then turned such discursive atheism from a rhetorical possibility into a possible identity. That shift is the Cartesian geometric method, designed and implemented to combat the very habit of scholastic *disputatio* that had constructed atheism as a rhetorical position. The most well-known example is Descartes himself, complaining of quarrelsome students and their habit of contesting everything but not progressing toward firmer knowledge: "one cannot imagine anything so strange or unbelievable," Descartes wrote, "that it has not been said by some philosopher."[11] Scholastic shouting matches seemed to matter even more during the Thirty Years' War, when *disputatio* moved out of the lecture hall and onto the battlefield. Returning in the midst of the war to his army post in Germany, Descartes famously paused and turned inward: "the onset of winter held me up," he wrote in the *Discourse on Method*, "[and] finding no conversation with which to be diverted and, fortunately, having no worries or passions which troubled me, I remained for a whole day by myself in a small stove-heated room, where I had complete leisure for communing with my thoughts" (11). Those thoughts famously yielded the command to reason only according to a method, since so many of our prereflective beliefs about the world were groundless. In the new world struggling to be born, and where the conflict raging outside was dramatic demonstration that the organizing structures of Christendom could no longer provide a common ground, human consensus must be secured at a cognitive rather than institutional level. Descartes's project thus helped to insure the legitimacy of an increasingly mentalistic conception of religion in the early modern period. Salvation in the early modern period came more and more to hang on a method: on having the right beliefs, and on assenting to them in the right way. For the scholar, meanwhile, religion became an object of knowledge to be tabulated, compared, and understood along the lines being mapped out by the natural sciences.[12] It thus becomes possible to speak of "religions," in the plural, as distinct but relatable "things" that people or cultures "have."

This early modern transformation of religion *into* a set of cognitive beliefs makes atheism in our modern sense possible. Thus when David Berman argues in his authoritative *History of Atheism in Britain* that atheism was "repressed" and "covert" in early modern England, but could finally be "avowed" in the 1780s, he misses the historical change that really matters.[13] If atheism becomes an expressible belief at a certain historical moment, this is not simply because restrictions have finally lifted but because an entire background picture is slowly changing so that it becomes possible to think in terms of beliefs and their (dis)avowal.

Once "religion" has narrowed and deepened like this, and once its chief philosophical questions are epistemological (questions of knowledge) rather than ontological (questions of virtue, holiness, and right living), then atheism in the sense of unbelief becomes not only possible but intellectually appealing. For if God is needed mostly as a supernatural object of belief—rather than as a sustaining presence within the Creation, as God is for example in Aquinas—then God still has to be fitted somehow into a world that apparently works without him. The foremost answer to this challenge was to reconceive God as a benevolent designer of a mechanistic universe. But whatever the precise solution, intellectual culture had crossed a conceptual Rubicon: if it was once important to fit the things of this world into a theory of the divine, it now seemed necessary to fit divinity into the things of this world. At best God was now superfluous; at worst, pernicious.[14]

The final turn to this argument is the one we have been following throughout this book: that Christianity is in large part responsible for the secular sense of religious "options" in which modern atheism is embedded. This is the point that Kors makes in relation to atheism specifically, and that Charles Taylor makes in a more general way when he argues that in the early modern period, beliefs came to be understood as accompanied by their construal, so that even the most devout took up a third-person relation to them. People began to understand themselves as agents who *have* beliefs. Taylor calls this a shift toward the disenchanted world: a world of "buffered selves," where religious belief is an increasingly cognitive faculty. Initially undertaken with the aim of strengthening Christianity by clarifying areas of doctrinal and moral disagreement, the focus on belief eventually rendered Christianity irrelevant to large swaths of human experience. Concerned with policing thoughts and boundaries, doctrinal belief gradually disinvested in the social whole and withdrew from the network of activity, practice, community, and routine where religious thoughts had been embedded. Largely the product of a zealously reform-minded Christianity, this process of disenchantment ushers us into the modern secular age.[15]

This argument, if it is right, raises problems for any triumphant story of atheism as an example of heroic freethought. For it turns out that atheism, far from opposing Christianity, is a very Christian concept, a part of the tale of a secular age that arises in the early modern period because of a series of shifts within Western Christendom. It follows that the role of the Radical Enlightenment as a midwife to modernity has been overstated, its intellectualism leading to an inflated sense of its own importance. For if atheism is part of the fabric of Christian culture rather than its inveterate opponent, it cannot matter very much if a couple of freethinking Epicureans insist that atoms swerve in the void or that motion adheres in matter. Finally, this line of reasoning suggests that atheism may be a belief—a negative one, in this case—as thin as its epistemologized rival. As William Blake might say, a certain history has been adopted by both parties.[16]

Shelley's Radical Enlightenment

This is a controversial proposal. And though readers of this book will have realized that I am largely sympathetic to it, I am less interested here in whether it is entirely right than in the undeniable fact that Shelley finds it

more and more congenial as his thinking develops. This is due in large part
to his own reading of the historical situation. To be sure, he does not begin
there: between the *Necessity of Atheism* and the signature in the hotel registry,
Shelley's borrowings, references, and allusions offer a crash course in freethinking radicalism completely in line with the narrative of atheism as intellectual heroism. Some of his criticisms of Christian monotheism come from
Gibbon, and he adapts his arguments against proofs of God from Hume.
Godwin, Paine, and Wollstonecraft turn up consistently. Shelley's reading
during this period also taps into two long-standing traditions of radical Continental thought. The first is the tradition of religious syncretism, especially
as redacted in Volney's *Ruins*, which Shelley read in 1812. The first English
translation of Volney had appeared in 1792 (published by Joseph Johnson),
and the book had a direct influence on Tom Paine, Thomas Spence, Blake,
and the various members of what Iain McCalman has called London's "radical underworld."[17] The second tradition is that of Epicurianism, transmitted
through the several Lucretius revivals and then through d'Holbach's *Système
de la nature* (1770).[18] All of this material, and much more besides, found its
way into the clandestinely circulated *Queen Mab* (1812), whose notes
reprinted a modified version of the *Necessity of Atheism* and one of whose
triumphal lines declares, "There is no God!"[19] *Queen Mab* "must not be
published under pain of death, because it is too much against every existing
establishment," wrote Harriet Shelley to her Dublin friend Catherine
Nugent. "Do you [know] any one that would wish for so dangerous a gift?"[20]

Yet Shelley came late to the "New Philosophy" that had roiled elite
European cultural circles for over 150 years. Reading through this material,
and reading the accounts of it in such books as Michael Scrivener's *Radical
Shelley* and Martin Priestman's *Romantic Atheism*, one is struck by how *little*
has changed from the mid- and late seventeenth century, when thorough-
going materialism first began to seep into Europe's intellectual life. Jonathan
Israel brilliantly traces the secret networks, coteries, and groupings of the
Radical Enlightenment, the clandestine circulation of its ideas, its characteristic modes of diversion, denial, and prevarication in the late seventeenth and
early eighteenth centuries. But after reading Israel, perusing accounts of late
eighteenth and early nineteenth century radicals feels rather familiar; here
are the same sorts of pseudonymous and anonymous references, the same
clandestine circulation, the same confusion that had characterized the Radical
Enlightenment's first flowering. John Gibson Lockhart, in his hostile review
in 1819, is ironically enough correct when he notes wearily that Shelley's

notions recur "[i]n every age."[21] Whatever Lockhart's motivations, his judgment is historically accurate. In terms of philosophical sophistication or new
arguments, d'Holbach and Volney, Paine and Godwin, are for the most part
offering ideas already available to Continental initiates by 1680 or there-
abouts. The period after 1750, as Israel writes, was "basically just one of
consolidating, popularizing, and annotating revolutionary concepts introduced earlier" (*RE* 7).

This was also Shelley's view of the matter. In *A Philosophical View of
Reform* he praises the "new epoch" of the mid- and late seventeenth century,
"marked by the commencement of deeper enquiries into the point of human
nature than are compatible with an unreserved belief in any of those popular
mistakes upon which . . . systems of faith . . . with all their superstructure of
political and religious tyranny, are built." Locke, Hume, and Hartley are, by
contrast, "exact . . . but superficial," while the French *philosophes* developed
only "those particular portions of the new philosophy" that were "most popular." "[T]hey told the truth, but not the whole truth," Shelley concludes.[22]

If the "New Philosophy" that Shelley channels is no longer very new,
however, there has now been a revolution enacted in its name. The Radical
Enlightenment had arrived in France by means of Huguenots in the Netherlands, according to Israel; by 1719 Spinoza's *Tractatus Theologico-Politicus* had
been published clandestinely in French. This is Spinoza as the theorist of
radical republicanism, his philosophy "a veritable engine of war," targeting
the ancien régime and leading "in direct line of descent to the revolutionary
rhetoric of Robespierre and the French Jacobins" (*RE* 306, 22). While
Hobbes and Locke regarded the state of nature as brutal and viewed private
property as the foundation of liberty, Spinoza held that appropriation of the
land was a denial of natural liberty. Rousseau may have rejected Spinoza's
metaphysics, but he adopted his political theory, and the notion that equality
is basic to the state of nature makes its way into the *Discourse on Inequality*
and thence to the Jacobins. From this perspective the Revolution is really an
outworking of a radical intellectual tradition of the late seventeenth century.

Whether or not Israel overstates Spinoza's actual influence, his book
reveals the degree to which the Radical Enlightenment's robust concept of
liberty, formulated most powerfully in the *Tractatus*, would shape the French
Revolution. Freedom is the "freedom to philosophize," the "freedom to
think and to say what one thinks," writes Spinoza.[23] He argues that because
religion, like private property, curtails such freedom, it must be regulated *in*

the name of freedom. If for Locke religious freedom was the example of freedom par excellence, for Spinoza "religious freedom" is virtually an oxymo-
ron. In short, there is at work in Spinoza a specific anthropology—a picture
of the human as "naturally" unfettered by religion and by property—and a
theory of state power as something that may be legitimately employed to
promote that anthropology and to sideline alternatives to it. This is why
Spinoza can write that "we have established it as absolutely certain that theology should not be subordinate to reason, nor reason to theology, but rather
that each has its own domain" (*TTP* 190), but assert almost immediately that
since theology "determine[s] only what is necessary for obedience" (*TTP*
190) it is antithetical to the freedom that the ideal state will promote: "if no
one were obliged by law to obey the sovereign power in matters that he
thinks belongs to religion . . . on this pretext everyone would be able to claim
license to do anything. Since by this means the law of the state is wholly
violated, it follows that the supreme right of deciding about religion, belongs
to the sovereign power" (*TPP* 206–7). In this formulation religion always
potentially conflicts with state power. This is a crucial intellectual source of
the militant secularism of the French Revolution, which became official policy with the Civil Constitution of the Clergy of 1790: a generous acknowledgment of separate domains on the one hand, and on the other a patrolling of
that boundary so vigilant as to create the conditions of its violation. The
Radical Enlightenment bequeaths to the Revolution an image of an activist
secular state; it proposes to police religion in the effort to secure a space free
from it.

   In a widely cited essay, Charles Taylor describes a similar contrast
between two dominant models of secularism that emerged in early modern
Europe. The first is the Lockean "common ground" model, with a minimal-
ist state adjudicating among a variety of metaphysical orientations. Locke
begins by assuming that most Europeans are naturally religious, in accord
with the moderate Enlightenment's desire to modify the confessional state
without overturning the social order. This is a basically theological conception of secularism, forged in order to bring peace to warring Protestant sects;
famously, Locke would not extend toleration to atheists. Taylor's second
model, which he terms the "independent ethic," begins with a nonreligious
anthropology; it assumes, as Spinoza would put it, that "the state of nature
is not to be confused with the state of religion" (*TTP* 205), and therefore
holds it best to construct a society "as if" there were no God. Taylor traces

this idea to Hugo Grotius, but Spinoza is an even more plausible candidate; indeed, orthodox commentators often lumped both Dutchmen together as "atheistic" biblical scholars.[24]

According to the secularism of the moderate Enlightenment, then, citizens possess religious beliefs the way they possess property, namely by right, and the state agrees to leave religion alone as long as religion leaves politics alone. According to the secularism of the Radical Enlightenment, by contrast, property and religious belief limit freedom. If secularism *just is* the principle of neutrality among competing metaphysical notions, then the state's role is limited to abstention and even-handedness; but if secularism describes a certain formation of the citizen, then more intrusive measures may be required, and the state is justified in influencing the choices that people make.[25] Just as in Spinoza's *Tractatus*, the first of these tends in practice to slide into the second. When in 2003 the French government outlawed the wearing of "religious symbols" in French schools, the language of the Stasi report insisted that the state had no power over spiritual choices. But as in the Civil Constitution of 1790, it is the state that decides if its principles are threatened.

As we know, for Shelley the French Revolution was the "master-theme of the epoch in which we live," "involving pictures of all that is best qualified to interest and to instruct mankind," as he wrote to Byron just after returning from France and a few months after visiting Mont Blanc.[26] What "instruction" might he have in mind? In the famous dream vision of Volney's *Ruins*, the Genius requires all the religions of the world to justify themselves before a tribunal of free people recently liberated from superstition. But perhaps Volney's reasonable council takes the problem up at the wrong end. For if Jonathan Israel is right that the Revolution instantiates the political theories of the Radical Enlightenment, then the issue is not religious sectarianism but rather the *power of the state to name religious sectarianism as such*: a power that professes neutrality but also actively protects its own interests. On this reading, revolutionary paranoia produces "religion" as an enemy of the revolution, which can thus be eliminated by force. The manufactured possibility of religious violence justifies the actuality of secular violence. Thus the Revolution's degeneration into violence, recrimination, paranoia, and renewed political absolutism is an imminent development of the Radical Enlightenment itself. From this perspective, furthering the critique of religion aids the secular violence it claims to combat. This would be an appropriately Shelleyan turn of the screw.

A *truly* revolutionary argument, then, would disarticulate the critique of political tyranny from the critique of Christianity. This would demand a critical reading of the radical tradition itself. Shelley may very well have wished to see the last king strangled with the entrails of the last priest (a remark variously attributed to Voltaire, Diderot, and Meslier), but as a strategy this misses the point rather badly—and moreover the particular *way* that it misses the point helps explain why the French Revolution came undone in the way that it did: not only the Terror but Napoleon, years of war, and finally the restoration of thrones across post-Napoleonic Europe.[27] What if the "instruction" Shelley imagines in his letter to Byron is precisely the making visible of the violence, real and potential, that shadows the presumptively neutral operations of the state *whenever* it intervenes in the formation of its citizens, even when it intervenes to uphold a position—atheism, egalitarian property rights—that one supports? In this case Shelley's point would be his poem's point: that the content of beliefs is not the issue.

Here we return to the scene of *Mont Blanc* and the "atheism" that it may or may not express. And in doing so we can take Israel's Spinozism more seriously than he himself does. For Spinoza, necessity is not a type of content, and beliefs are not causes: what matters are *effects*. When it comes to both atheism and religion the temptation is always to talk about beliefs, and this is a temptation that *Mont Blanc*'s many voices, and its textual and literary history, continually stage. Is Shelley a Platonist? an idealist? a skeptic? What are his ideas? Whom was he reading? At a very basic level the poem insists that none of this matters; Power, "Remote, serene, and inaccessible" (97), is always there, distributing, withholding, and dispensing "life and death" (129). In such a world, "atheism," no matter how uncompromising, is pseudoradicalism.

Atheism as an Occupation

"Democrat, Philanthropist, and Atheist." These words are Shelley's own first "reading" of his poem. And these three words are of course the Radical Enlightenment in a nutshell, especially if we render "philanthropist" more literally as "lover of mankind" and hear in that phrase a certain libertinism. Already in *Queen Mab* Shelley had connected libertinism firmly to political and religious radicalism. Certainly by 1816 the charge of libertinism was in the air wherever he went.[28] And so we might read the signature in the hotel register less as an adolescent attempt to shock than an effort to reinvigorate a collection of philosophical positions that had become, on Shelley's own analysis, superficial. The Radical Enlightenment, I have suggested, was not by Shelley's estimation radical enough: it shared with the moderate Enlightenment, that is to say, the habit of viewing religion as a belief in a divine superagent, and it created thereby the possibility of modern atheism as the rejection of that belief.

Both modern religion and modern atheism are from this perspective secular, in the specific sense that there is a great deal of human life over which they no longer have authority. In post-Westphalian Europe it was generally the state that took over the management of embodied life: through various media, through networks of officials and spies, through medical innovations and humanitarian organizations it observed, measured, distributed, and supervised its subjects.[29] Indeed, the reformation of the mind demands the reformation of the body. Martin Luther, who sometimes pictured the body as merely a place of appetites and drives, famously compared it to a wild animal that must be chained, and humanity's natural, bodily condition to a state of continual warfare: "If there were no law and government, then seeing that all the world is evil and that scarcely one human being in a thousand is a true Christian, people would devour each other and no one would be able to support his wife and children, feed himself and serve God."[30] Luther developed this picture in the context of what he called the "two kingdoms": the realm of law and compulsion that characterized the earthly kingdom, the realm of freedom and grace that characterized the heavenly one. The result was a radical idea of Christian freedom (subsequently made available for Anabaptist theories of perfectionism and revolutionary anarchy and eventually, in modified form, for modern democracy) within a divinely sanctioned but institutionally secular state, where freedom was a cognitive rather than bodily property and the state held a monopoly on violence.[31] As Erasmus and More recognized, this tended to distance Christian commitment from civil society by mapping a body-mind distinction onto the earthly-heavenly one. With those divisions in place, it was not difficult for Hobbes to simply invert their values: his "Kingdome of Darknesse" replaced Luther's sphere of radical Christian freedom, but the picture of earthly life as a violent struggle against passions and desires remained the same.

In this sense early modern Europe witnessed what we can term a "secularization of the body." Driven largely by the Reforming impulse internal to

Western Christendom, such secularization organized corporeal life. It fur-
thered the process through which the body itself—its positioning, habitua-
tion, and sensory organization—came to reside outside the boundaries of
"religion." This is not to say, of course, that early modern Christianity
remained uninterested in the body. The point is, rather, that it is precisely
this "secularization" of the body, the sense that its appetites were worldly or
carnal and therefore that its energies were to be contained and productively
redirected, that contributed to the sense that there was little about the body
that aided a religious life now understood largely in mentalistic terms. Bodies
learn to apprehend the world they inhabit: institutions may deliberately culti-
vate certain attitudes and sense perceptions, but those perceptions are also
the unintended consequences of social and cultural change. The set of historical and cultural transformations known as secularism, then, has the potential
to alter the body's sensory capacities, its ability to feel in certain ways, to
access certain kinds of experiences.[32]

The Radical Enlightenment was officially dedicated to opening up possibilities heretofore beyond the pale. My argument is that its degeneration into
state-sponsored violence by the close of the eighteenth century is the logical
development of its conceptual commitment to the power of the state to
remake the affective lives of its subjects. Shelley's inscription in the hotel
register wonderfully encapsulates just this dialectical relation. For because
hotel registers do not usually offer a separate category for "beliefs," Shelley
placed his "atheism" under the category of "occupation." Simple good fortune, perhaps. But it allows us to ask a serious question: what would it mean
to understand "atheism" as an occupation—as something that one *does* rather
than something that one *is*? What if atheism were not about cognitively held
beliefs or nonbeliefs but about postures, arrangements, dispositions, embodied techniques, or disciplined actions?

"Occupation" can mean "the action of taking or maintaining possession
or control of a country, building, land, etc., esp. by (military) force," as the
OED puts it. It can also mean "the state of having one's time or attention
occupied; what a person is engaged in; employment, business; work, toil."
The first meaning is largely spatial, the second largely temporal. In the hotel
register, "occupation" means time—and yet the very presence of the mountain as an occupant of space, registered so consistently in Shelley's poem, as
well as in Mary Shelley's contributions to the *History of a Six Weeks' Tour*,
where *Mont Blanc* was first published, hints at the first meaning as well. How

can anyone or anything else occupy space when Mont Blanc's mass is so insistently *there*, and when the various military occupations of the region are so fresh in the memory? Even atheism, faced with such dominant spaces, would retreat to the mind. Indeed, this is exactly how the *Quarterly Review*, interrupting its 1818 review of Leigh Hunt's "Foliage" in order to pounce on Shelley, pictured what had happened. "If we were told," writes the *Quarterly*, "of a man who, thus witnessing the sublimest assemblage of natural objects, should retire to a cabin near and write aetheos after his name in the album, we hope our own feelings would be pity rather than disgust."[33] In the *Quarterly*'s imagination, there apparently *was* a place in the hotel register for "beliefs," and Shelley, incapable of responding to sublime objects properly, writes "atheist" there—as if his mind is the "blank" space of nothingness and nonbelief still so often taken to be the poem's own deepest aspiration.[34] This picture maps easily onto a secular distinction in which the mountain forcefully occupies all available space while doctrines and beliefs are located in the mind and "expressed."

But if the "occupation" of atheism is instead about how one organizes one's time, then a different set of concepts comes into focus. For occupations, understood temporally, involve the entire self in the organization of experience. And they centrally concern what one does with one's body—how it is trained, organized, and adjusted, what experiences it pursues and cultivates, what experiences it forecloses on—and what potentials it activates.

An incident in *Prometheus Unbound*, written around the time of the *Quarterly*'s attack, makes this point clearly. The passage, which significantly animates the static alpine scenery of *Mont Blanc*, depicts Asia describing a remote Power familiar from the earlier poem. But this time, the episode ends with an avalanche

> whose mass,
> Thrice sifted by the storm, had gathered there
> Flake after flake: in Heaven-defying minds
> As thought by thought is piled, till some great truth
> Is loosened, and the nations echo round,
> Shaken to their roots: as do the mountains now.[35]

This looks, at first, like a mental revolution—a particularly spectacular example of the technique of drawing imagery from the mind's operations that Shelley had defended in the drama's "Preface": thoughts pile up in minds until they yield a revolutionary truth. Yet by delaying the analogical "as" so long that snowflakes rather than thoughts seem to be accumulating in the mind, Shelley's syntax manages what William Keach calls a "disorienting effect." The physical world, in the form of snowflakes, seems to penetrate the mind itself, suggesting not a simple reversal of priority but an experiential undoing of any effort to draw lines between the mind and the things outside it. Shelley's "rejection of dualism," writes Keach, "forms part of the conceptual basis for a range of practices that are about remaking the world of human experience by releasing its full potential as a dynamic and differentiated totality."[36] The unsettling effect of a language that refuses to distinguish between mental life and bodily life might offer a foretaste of the kind of revolution that would *really* alter the organization of space. "Liberty, when men act in bodies, is *power*," wrote Burke about the French Revolution, glimpsing from the negative side the kinds of discomfiting potentials that adhere to an embodied life. For while power may be frozen and spatialized "on high," as in *Mont Blanc* (line 127), it might also be put into motion through the accretion of bodies that like snowflakes eventually become more than the sum of their parts, and that can learn to occupy space in a new and dynamic way. By "bodies," of course, Burke meant collections of individuals. But Shelley's syntactical disorientation allows us to take full advantage of the pun: to act as a body, we must act *in* a body.

The notorious difficulty of Shelley's writing has its source in the expanded sensory capacities toward which it points—matters of the body as much as the mind, of sensing and feeling as much as thinking.[37] This quality of Shelley's verse has bothered critics from the *Monthly Review*'s prescient description of Shelley's "licentiousness of rhythm" to F. R. Leavis's worry that with Shelley "one accepts the immediate feeling and doesn't slow down to think."[38] Often those hostile to Shelley can see this more clearly than can those who profess to admire him. In its 1819 review of *The Revolt of Islam*, for example, the *Quarterly Review* cogently recognized that Shelley's danger lay not in the content of his ideas but in what the reviewer termed his "manner." "We despair," wrote the *Quarterly*, "of convincing him directly that he has taken up false and pernicious notions; but if he pays any deference to the common laws of reasoning, we hope to show him that, let the goodness of his cause be what it may, his manner of advocating it is false and unsound."[39]

Shelley, still at work on *Prometheus Unbound*, had already described his technique of drawing the poem's images from the operations of the human mind. But after reading this review he added to the "Preface," defending his "manner" by focusing on its political potential. Although the "mass of capabilities remains at every period materially the same," he wrote, and the "power" of imagery general, changing circumstances bring images into new alignments, awakening nascent capabilities "to action" (*SPP* 208). Thus "the peculiar style of intense and comprehensive imagery which distinguishes the modern literature of England" (*SPP* 207).

Mass, power, body, action. We are back at the moving mass of *Prometheus Unbound*'s avalanche—a reading of *Mont Blanc* that extends Shelley's own first "reading" of the poem in the hotel register. It completes the turn toward a collective model of revolutionary activity—of people and arguments, of attitudes and habits involving the body as well as the mind. *Mont Blanc*'s own dense intertextuality sketches the beginnings of that collective activity, and though allusion hunting is one of the great games of *Mont Blanc* criticism, the point of Shelley's "occupation" is to avoid the temptation of wondering how certain books or authors influenced the poem's ideas; the point, rather, is to picture what it might be like to be a part of an embodied collective, a communal voice louder than the sum of its individual parts.

"[U]ntil the mind can love, and admire, and trust, and hope, and endure," Shelley wrote in the "Preface" to *Prometheus Unbound*, "reasoned principles of moral conduct are seeds cast upon the highway of life, which the unconscious passenger tramples into dust, although they would bear the harvest of his happiness" (*SPP* 209). He calls love, admiration, trust, hope, and endurance "beautiful idealisms of moral excellence," and it is easy to be misled by that phrase into cognitive speculations. But in the context of the power of embodied masses to which Shelley links his use of imagery, these "idealisms" look less like what the *Quarterly* called his "notions" and more like what it called his "manner": the project of educating the body and increasing its sensory capacities so that anger and hatred and revenge will be recognized as modes that characterize bodies lacking other, better experiences. To teach the mind other occupations—love, trust, hope, and endurance, for instance—would also require a certain education of the body, and make possible a reordered sensorium in which such adventures of human flourishing could have their way.

Vacancy

"Our age," Immanuel Kant famously wrote in the Preface to the *Critique of Pure Reason* (1781), "is the age of criticism, and to criticism everything must submit. Religion through its sanctity, and law-giving through its majesty, may seek to exempt themselves from it. But they then awaken just suspicion, and cannot claim the sincere respect which reason accords only to that which has been able to sustain the test of free and open examination."[40] Kant's is a familiar picture of enlightenment as the slow victory of rationality over reactionary forces, the gradual winning of freedom and dignity presided over by reason. Yet for at least some who lived during the age of enlightenment, the relationships among law, religion, and reason were less simple. For them, indeed, a more accurate picture of the era might be found in a passage from Kant's second preface, published with a new edition of the *Critique* in 1787. Responding to the charge that "critique" was an entirely negative exercise in establishing boundaries, Kant writes: "To deny that the service which the Critique renders is positive in character, would thus be like saying that the police are of no positive benefit, inasmuch as their main business is merely to prevent the violence of which citizens stand in mutual fear, in order that each may pursue his vocation in peace and security."[41] Characteristically, Kantian peace reduces to security and the prevention of violence. And instructively, too, Kant's image of the police as the enforcers of this peace suggests that the state has a rather different relationship to criticism than does religion. Indeed, far from trying to "exempt itself" from critique, the state serves as its administrator.

I have been arguing in this chapter that it is exactly this—enlightenment making common cause with secular power in the name of peace—that Shelley finds so "instructive" about the French Revolution. That the Revolution failed to establish even the negative peace of which Kant spoke might be regarded, from Shelley's perspective, as inevitable. In response to this lesson, I have proposed, *Mont Blanc* asks questions that are ontological rather than overtly political: What would an alternative sensorium look like? What kinds of experiences would differently organized bodies have?

And yet the poem ends with a rhetorical question that seems more like Kant's police:

And what were thou, and earth, and stars, and sea,
    If to the human mind's imaginings
Silence and solitude were vacancy? (lines 141–43)

Sometimes read as an expression of its author's philosophical idealism, the poem's final question might also be interpreted as negative liberty, whose aim is to clear a space in which freedom can thrive. Shelley's "On Life" (1819), a prose fragment inscribed in the back of the notebook that also contains the *Philosophical View of Reform*, seems to make exactly this point. Here Shelley defended the idealist conviction that "nothing exists but as it is perceived." That doctrine "establishes no new truth," he declared, but only "destroys error, and the roots of error. It leaves, what is too often the duty of the reformer in political and ethical questions to leave, a vacancy. It reduces the mind to that freedom in which it would have acted but for the misuse of words and signs, the instruments of its own creation."[42] Christopher Hitt, in an intelligent essay, argues that the "vacancy" this passage celebrates is the vacancy with which *Mont Blanc* concludes.[43] On this reading, error, like the many voices that encircle the mountain and the "large codes of fraud and woe" (line 81) that emanate from them, can be "repealed" (80) only by a philosophy that demolishes the old truths without establishing new ones in their stead.

However appealing such a negative liberty might be, the Revolution demonstrates that vacancy is not strictly negative.[44] Power will always defend its normative vision of things, stepping in with force or the promise of force whenever alternatives threaten. From this perspective, the "freedom in which [the mind] would have acted but for the mis-use of words and signs" is a chimera, a myth of reason that licenses destruction in the name of liberty. And the vacancy that it leaves behind is the vacancy into which power steps. The critical consensus that Shelley's poems of late 1815 and 1816 represent a romantic turn away from Godwinian rationalism has from this perspective not been taken far enough. Shelley's romantic turn, registered at the level of syntax and sensory organization as much as of mind and idea, interprets the tradition stretching from Descartes in his stove-heated room to the contemporary war on terror as a red herring, a way to distract the mass from the consolidation of power into fewer and fewer hands by inventing something called the problem of religion. In so doing it has blocked the kind of rethinking so obviously needed in the aftermath of the French Revolution and prevented the kind of historical analysis that would reveal how caught up secular power is in the creation of its religious opponent.

Could the Radical Enlightenment get over its obsession with religion and focus its critical energies on the process that has justified that obsession? That process is what I have called *secularism*: not simple neutrality but the peculiarly modern intervention in ordinary forms of life by state, civic, and cultural actors. Secularism validates a particular organization of the human sensorium, remaking religion as a primarily epistemological concern, a matter of minds rather than of bodies. This remaking has a politics, for at some point assimilation fails, or becomes too volatile and unpredictable, and then someone is sure to be prodded out of error a little more forcefully. Beneath that prodding, as Shelley recognizes all too well, is fear—the fear of the multitude that was present even in Spinoza himself.[45] There is of course plenty to be afraid of, and it is perhaps inevitable that dread of what might happen when, in Burke's words, "men act in bodies" would cause even the most fearless of thinkers to reassert the state's juridical power over the power of the multitude. That is the long history of which the French Revolution forms a particularly instructive chapter. To imagine a Shelley "after atheism," then, is to imagine a Shelley after secularism. And to imagine a Shelley after secularism is to imagine the noncoercive peace to which *Prometheus Unbound* gives voice in its final act: a collection of myriad embodied motions on the far side of fear, "Where all things flow to all, as rivers to the sea."[46]

Epilogue

This has been a long history, to be sure, but it has been a history nonetheless. Its links have been the unquiet things that bubble to the surface in the literature of the long romantic period: Theodore's brooding melancholy; Emma Woodhouse, who sighs and wishes for "impossible things"; the flashing eyes of the incomprehensible poet of "Kubla Khan"; the characters in Scott's fiction who accept the inevitability of Union and capitalism but who had hoped for so much more; Robert Wringhim's rage at a modernity that has passed him by; the Byronic hero who pauses in the midst of his highly stylized action while unbidden thoughts roll over his mind; Cythna in her cave, contemplating the appropriate language of revolution; and, finally, Percy Shelley's extraordinary insight into the structural violence of the secular age. Inspired by Coleridge's poem, I have attended in particular to how such disquietude registers the movements in the air around it, becoming thereby the frequency at which we can hear how extreme is the otherwise normal quiet of everyday life. And I have argued that though the figure of a film that is moved rather than moving itself may imply that subjection is the only kind of subjectivity available in the secular age, "unquiet" also has a more creative and hopeful valence: Purchas's addiction, Coleridge's delight, Scott's frivolous alembic, Schlegel's fragment, Cythna's subtler language, and Shelley's "occupation" variously articulate and embody abundant ways of living in the secular age. As Robert Lowth's meditations on metaphor unintentionally reveal, such writing does not so much move itself in an act of imaginative sympathy as remain open to being moved by forces coming from elsewhere.

In William Wordsworth's poem *The Ruined Cottage* (1798), the Pedlar instructs his listener not to "disturb / The calm of Nature with [his] restless thoughts" (lines 197–98). Those restless thoughts include the disheartening fate of the protagonist Margaret, but they also include anger at that fate's social and cultural causes: a far-off war, impossible food prices, rural indebtedness.[1] The Pedlar wants to naturalize those causes by ascribing them to illness and ill luck; he warns the listener not to turn them into *political* discontent: to do so, he says, would be "feeding on disquiet" (line 197). With his vaguely spiritual sensibility and his anxiety that local events like Margaret's suffering be understood as part of a larger pattern (to wit, a credit economy is good for most people, but unfortunately a few unlucky ones will starve), the Pedlar speaks for the project of modernity as a whole. For him the world is largely immanent, predictable, and productive; protesting against its general tendency and direction, even on behalf of those somehow passed over by a rising standard of living and by the "affirmation of ordinary life" that Charles Taylor identifies as modernity's central tenet, is quixotic and possibly dangerous.[2] And yet the Pedlar's complacency has the surprising capacity to inspire exactly the disquieting resentment that he senses in the nameless listener—let us call him the poet—who keeps pestering him for more details about Margaret, her husband, and their unhappy fate.

In this book I have argued for the ability of literary language to register such otherwise invisible effects. That the Pedlar is speaking of political economy and not religion is part of my point: the secular, as I have treated it here, is about many things *other than* religion. For some, secularism is like the Pedlar's indifference. Attuned to the workings of a global system rather than to its local effects, it participates in a social and intellectual formation that is instrumental with regard to people, cavalier with regard to debt, extractive with regard to nature, and piously sentimental only when its sentiments can no longer do any good. Such assessments may explain why forms of popular resistance to modern capitalism in the twentieth and twenty-first centuries appear so often in religious dress. For others, secularism may be more like the silence that settles over "Frost at Midnight"—a silence historically recent and, if one listens closely, perhaps a little strange, but also the condition of possibility for what we call ordinary life: labor, affective intimacy, anticipation of the future. These "numberless goings-on of life" are, Coleridge writes, "inaudible as dreams," meaning that they do not show up for him as objects of consciousness. The only things that do register in this manner are the owlet's cry, the flapping of the film in the grate, and, eventually, the sound of the quiet itself.

Whatever we may wish to call the time when church bells were, as Coleridge writes, the "poor man's only music" (line 29), there are now other melodies and other sources of music. The poem insists that its role is not to compete in this new landscape but to help us sound the silence that conditions it: to test, that is to say, both its callousness and its possibilities. Among those possibilities are habits of thought and forms of life that, whatever we choose to call them, might creatively help sustain other human beings and the earth on which we all must live. I think that romantic literature remains a resource for both kinds of sounding, not least because romantic-era writers were among the first to confront the secular world in its terror and its dullness, its splendor and its anxiety. "The moment of real poetry," wrote the Situationist International in 1963, "brings all the unsettled debts of history back into play."[3] So it is, I believe, with the real poetry discussed in these pages.

NOTES

INTRODUCTION. UNQUIET THINGS

Epigraph: Samuel Taylor Coleridge, *The Major Works*, ed. H. J. Jackson (Oxford: Oxford University Press, 2000), 87, lines 13–16.

1. Ronald Jager, "The Meetinghouse Becomes a Church," in *Granite and Grace: Essays Celebrating the Two Hundredth Anniversary of the New Hampshire Conference, United Church of Christ*, ed. Charles E. Clark and Elizabeth C. Nordbeck (Concord, N.H.: The Conference, 2001), esp. 52–55.

2. See Sarah Rivett, "Early American Religion in a Post-Secular Age," *PMLA* 128, 4 (2013): 989–96.

3. Voltaire, *Letters Concerning the English Nation*, qtd. in Roy Porter, *Enlightenment: Britain and the Creation of the Modern World*, new ed. (London: Penguin, 2001), 108.

4. C. John Sommerville, *The Secularization of Early Modern England: From Religious Culture to Religious Faith* (New York: Oxford University Press, 1992), 185.

5. Jose Casanova, *Public Religions in the Modern World* (Chicago: University of Chicago Press, 1994), 5; see also Peter L. Berger, ed., *The Desecularization of the World: Resurgent Religion and World Politics* (Grand Rapids, Mich.: Eerdmans, 1999).

6. Berger, *The Desecularization of the World*; Philip Jenkins, *The Next Christendom: The Coming of Global Christianity* (Oxford: Oxford University Press, 2002).

7. Philip S. Gorski and Ates Altinordu, "After Secularization?" *Annual Review of Sociology* 34 (2008): 76.

8. Grace Davie, *Europe, the Exceptional Case: Parameters of Faith in the Modern World* (London: Longman, 2002); S. N. Eisenstadt, "Multiple Modernities," *Daedelus* 129 (2000): 1–29; Dilip Parameshwar Gaonkar, *Alternative Modernities*, 2nd ed. (Durham, N.C.: Duke University Press, 2001); Colin Jager, *The Book of God: Secularization and Design in the Romantic Era* (Philadelphia: University of Pennsylvania Press, 2007), 26–40. It bears noting that even within "Europe," the secularization process happened very differently in Catholic and Protestant countries, northern and southern ones, and western, central, and eastern ones.

9. In the United States in the twentieth century modernization was closely correlated with religious vibrancy, not religious decline. For a "marketplace" model of religious change similar to Voltaire's, see Rodney Stark, *The Victory of Reason: How Christianity Led*

to Freedom, Capitalism, and Western Success (New York: Random House, 2006); for a critique, see Steve Bruce, *God Is Dead: Secularization in the West* (Malden, Mass.: Blackwell, 2002); for helpful and balanced commentary, see Jeffrey K. Hadden, "Toward Desacralizing Secularization Theory," *Social Forces* 65, 3 (1987): 587–611; and Gorski and Altinordu, "After Secularization?"; for "repositioning," see Callum G. Brown, "A Revisionist Approach to Religious Change," in *Religion and Modernization: Sociologists and Historians Debate the Secularization Thesis,* ed. Steve Bruce (Oxford: Clarendon, 1992), 30–58; for a fascinating argument about the social significance of enchantment in modernity, see Akeel Bilgrami, "Occidentalism, the Very Idea: An Essay on Enlightenment and Enchantment," *Critical Inquiry* 32 (Spring 2006): 381–411.

10. The question of the secular is a *political* question. "Frost at Midnight" was originally published in *Fears in Solitude* (1798), whose title poem meditates on the political moods that attend the present moment: "O my God, / It is indeed a melancholy thing, / And weighs upon the human heart, that he must think / What uproar and what strife may now be stirring / This way or that o'er these silent hills." In *The Major Works,* 93, lines 32–36.

11. T. E. Hulme, "Romanticism and Classicism [1936]," in *Romanticism: Points of View,* ed. Robert F. Gleckner and Gerald Enscoe, 2nd ed. (Englewood Cliffs, N.J.: Prentice-Hall, 1962), 58; Irving Babbitt, "The Present Outlook [1919]," in ibid., 31.

12. Earl Wasserman, *The Subtler Language* (Baltimore: Johns Hopkins University Press, 1968), 10; M. H. Abrams, *Natural Supernaturalism: Tradition and Revolution in Romantic Literature* (New York: Norton, 1971), 12, 13.

13. For two iconic and brilliant examples, see Paul de Man, "The Rhetoric of Temporality," in *Blindness and Insight: Essays in the Rhetoric of Contemporary Criticism,* 2nd ed. (Minneapolis: University of Minnesota Press, 1983); Jerome J. McGann, "The Meaning of the Ancient Mariner," *Critical Inquiry* 8, 1 (1981): 35–67.

14. Iain McCalman, *Radical Underworld: Prophets, Revolutionaries, and Pornographers in London, 1795–1840* (Oxford: Oxford University Press, 1988); Robert J. Ryan, *The Romantic Reformation: Religious Politics in English Literature, 1789–1824* (Cambridge: Cambridge University Press, 1997); Martin Priestman, *Romantic Atheism: Poetry and Freethought, 1780–1830* (Cambridge: Cambridge University Press, 1999); see also Nicholas Roe, *John Keats and the Culture of Dissent* (New York: Oxford University Press, 1997).

15. For examples of this second wave of scholarship in romantic studies, see Mark Canuel, *Religion, Toleration, and British Writing, 1790–1830* (Cambridge: Cambridge University Press, 2002); Jon Mee, *Romanticism, Enthusiasm, and Regulation: Poetics and the Policing of Culture in the Romantic Period* (Oxford: Oxford University Press, 2003); Daniel E. White, *Early Romanticism and Religious Dissent* (Cambridge: Cambridge University Press, 2006); Jager, *The Book of God,* 2007. That wave is being carried forward by several younger scholars; see for example John Savarese, "Psyche's 'Whisp'ring Fan' and Keats's Genealogy of the Secular," *Studies in Romanticism* 50, 3 (Fall 2011): 389–411; Dustin Stewart, "The Lettered Paul: Remnant and Mission in Hannah More, Walter Scott, and Critical Theory," *Studies in Romanticism* 50, 4 (2011): 591–618; Alex Eric Hernandez, "Tragedy and the Economics of Providence in Richardson's *Clarissa," Eighteenth-Century Fiction*

22, 4 (2010): 599–630; Sean Dempsey, "The Cenci: Tragedy in a Secular Age," *ELH* 79 (Winter 2012): 879–903; Humberto Garcia, *Islam and the English Enlightenment, 1670–1840* (Baltimore: Johns Hopkins University Press, 2012); and Jasper Cragwall, *Lake Methodism: Polite Literature and Popular Religion in England, 1780–1830* (Columbus: Ohio State University Press, 2013).

16. See, among many others, crucial studies by Wilfred Cantwell Smith, *Faith and Belief* (Princeton, N.J.: Princeton University Press, 1979); Peter Harrison, *"Religion" and the Religions in the English Enlightenment* (Cambridge: Cambridge University Press, 1990); Talal Asad, *Genealogies of Religion: Discipline and Reasons of Power in Christianity and Islam* (Baltimore: Johns Hopkins University Press, 1993); Tomoko Masuzawa, *The Invention of World Religions: Or, How European Universalism Was Preserved in the Language of Pluralism* (Chicago: University of Chicago Press, 2005).

17. Charles Taylor, *A Secular Age* (Cambridge, Mass.: Harvard University Press, 2007); Talal Asad, *Formations of the Secular: Christianity, Islam, Modernity* (Stanford, Calif.: Stanford University Press, 2003); Saba Mahmood, "Secularism, Hermeneutics, and Empire: The Politics of Islamic Reformation," *Public Culture* 18, 2 (2006): 323–47; Gil Anidjar, "Secularism," *Critical Inquiry* 33, 1 (Autumn 2006): 52–77; Rajeev Bhargava, *Secularism and Its Critics* (Delhi: Oxford University Press, 2005); for an excellent example of a study that anticipated this material by a few years, see Gauri Viswanathan, *Outside the Fold: Conversion, Modernity, and Belief* (Princeton, N.J.: Princeton University Press, 1998); as early as 1983, Ashis Nandy was linking colonial governance to secular governance; see Ashis Nandy, *The Intimate Enemy: Loss and Recovery of Self Under Colonialism* (Delhi: Oxford University Press, 1983).

18. Taylor, *A Secular Age*; Michael Warner, Jonathan VanAntwerpen, and Craig Calhoun, eds., *Varieties of Secularism in a Secular Age* (Cambridge, Mass.: Harvard University Press, 2010).

19. Percy Shelley, "A Defense of Poetry" (1821), in Percy Bysshe Shelley, *Shelley's Poetry and Prose*, ed. Neil Fraistat and Donald H. Reiman, 2nd ed. (New York: Norton, 2002), 521.

20. See Taylor, *A Secular Age*, 23–211; also Stephen Toulmin, *Cosmopolis: The Hidden Agenda of Modernity* (Chicago: University of Chicago Press, 1990); John W. O'Malley, *Trent and All That: Renaming Catholicism in the Early Modern Era* (Cambridge, Mass.: Harvard University Press, 2000); Michael Hardt and Antonio Negri, *Empire* (Cambridge, Mass.: Harvard University Press, 2000); Philip S. Gorski, *The Disciplinary Revolution: Calvinism and the Rise of the State in Early Modern Europe* (Chicago: University of Chicago Press, 2003).

21. Michel Foucault, "Governmentality," in *The Foucault Effect: Studies in Governmentality*, ed. Graham Burchell, Colin Gordon, and Peter Miller (Chicago: University of Chicago Press, 1991), 87–104.

22. Asad, *Formations of the Secular*, 67.

23. My description here bears on the large and difficult question of what literature can "know" of history. Earlier generations of critics have tended to rely on the language of disavowal, displacement, or symptom when confronted with this question, but some

more recent work, much of it inspired loosely by Raymond Williams, has turned to mediation as a figure for how history "enters" a text. This has the advantage of describing literary texts as objects that do not merely register a (disavowed) *knowledge* of history but that also sense and feel historical change in a way that makes them more affective participants in it. The image of the flickering film and the air currents, drawn from Coleridge's poem, is my version of this combination of mediation and participation (Coleridge calls it "dim sympathy"). For recent examples, with which I am in sympathy, see Kevis Goodman, *Georgic Modernity and British Romanticism: Poetry and the Mediation of History* (Cambridge: Cambridge University Press, 2004), esp. 1–16; Ian Baucom, *Specters of the Atlantic: Finance Capital, Slavery, and the Philosophy of History* (Durham, N.C.: Duke University Press, 2005), esp. 213–41; Mary Favret, *War at a Distance: Romanticism and the Making of Modern Wartime* (Princeton, N.J.: Princeton University Press, 2010), esp. 9–97.

24. Thomas Pfau, *Romantic Moods: Paranoia, Trauma, and Melancholy, 1794–1840* (Baltimore: Johns Hopkins University Press, 2005) 7. When he turns to melancholy itself, Pfau interprets writings by Keats and Heine as registers of the exhaustion of "literature in its by then well established self-presentation as visionary, transcendent, and permanent" (22). Keats and Heine become imminent or minority critics of this dominant cultural understanding. As should be clear from my account of "Frost at Midnight," my own interpretation of the melancholy of the secular is rather different, not least because in my account literature registers not its own expressive crisis but rather the larger and more comprehensive historical crisis that is the secular itself.

25. Walter Benjamin, *The Origin of German Tragic Drama*, trans. John Osborne (London: Verso, 1998), 66.

26. John Locke, *A Letter Concerning Toleration*, ed. James Tully, trans. William Popple (Indianapolis: Hackett, 1983), 26.

27. John Locke, "First Tract on Government (1660)," in *Political Writings*, ed. David Wootton (Indianapolis: Hackett, 1993), 144.

28. Ross Harrison, *Hobbes, Locke, and Confusion's Masterpiece: An Examination of Seventeenth-Century Political Philosophy* (Cambridge: Cambridge University Press, 2003), 10.

29. John Rawls, *Political Liberalism*, 2nd ed. (New York: Columbia University Press, 2005), xxiv. The assumed connection between religion and violence appears in the work of intelligent commentators like Karen Armstrong (*The Battle for God*) and Mark Lilla (*The Stillborn God*), as well as in the militant atheism of Sam Harris, Richard Dawkins, and Christopher Hitchens.

30. John Milbank, *Theology and Social Theory: Beyond Secular Reason*, 2nd ed. (Oxford: Wiley-Blackwell, 2006), 4; see also Stanley Hauerwas, *Against The Nations: War and Survival in Liberal Society* (South Bend, Ind.: University of Notre Dame Press, 1992); William T. Cavanaugh, *The Myth of Religious Violence: Secular Ideology and the Roots of Modern Conflict* (New York: Oxford University Press, 2009). Cavanaugh, Hauerwas, and Milbank sometimes seem to be arguing that there was no such thing as religious violence before the modern state. But this is clearly preposterous. What they must mean, then, is that such violence was importantly different, definitionally and phenomenologically, from

the way religious violence is understood today, in which irrational inner states are understood to manifest themselves in intentional acts.

31. For versions of this account see Anidjar, "Secularism"; Asad, *Formations of the Secular*; Wendy Brown, *Regulating Aversion: Tolerance in the Age of Identity and Empire* (Princeton, N.J.: Princeton University Press, 2006); Mahmood, "Secularism, Hermeneutics, and Empire"; Ashis Nandy, "The Politics of Secularism and the Recovery of Religious Tolerance," in *Secularism and Its Critics*, ed. Rajeev Bhargava (Delhi: Oxford University Press, 2005), 321–44.

32. This is most evident in Rob himself: equally comfortable in the Highlands and on the streets of Glasgow, Rob appears and disappears seemingly at will, as much a mood or ethos as a character, at home in modern life yet seemingly not of it. See Ian Duncan, *Scott's Shadow: The Novel in Romantic Edinburgh* (Princeton, N.J.: Princeton University Press, 2007), esp. 96–115. For various accounts of the notion of multiple modernities, see Dipesh Chakrabarty, *Provincializing Europe: Postcolonial Thought and Historical Difference* (Princeton, N.J.: Princeton University Press, 2000); Eisenstadt, "Multiple Modernities"; Gaonkar, *Alternative Modernities*; Taylor, *A Secular Age*, 506–617.

33. Walter Benjamin, "Critique of Violence," in *Walter Benjamin: Selected Writings*, vol. 1, *1913–1926* (Cambridge, Mass.: Belknap Press of Harvard University Press, 1996), 236–52; for "empty homogeneous time," see "Theses on the Philosophy of History," in Benjamin, *Illuminations: Essays and Reflections*, ed. Hannah Arendt, trans. Harry Zohn (New York: Schocken, 1968).

34. Viswanathan, *Outside the Fold*, xvi.

35. Taylor, *A Secular Age*, 30.

36. Jonathan Sheehan, "When Was Disenchantment? History and the Secular Age," in *Varieties of Secularism in a Secular Age*, ed. Warner, VanAntwerpen, and Calhoun, 217–42; though see Robert Miles, "Romanticism, Enlightenment, and Mediation: The Case of the Inner Stranger," in *This Is Enlightenment*, ed. Clifford Siskin and William Warner (Chicago: University of Chicago Press, 2010), 173–88 for a sympathetic account in the context of romantic literature. Discussions of disenchantment and modernity go back at least to Max Weber, *The Protestant Ethic and the Spirit of Capitalism* (New York: Scribner, 1958); see also Keith Thomas, *Religion and the Decline of Magic* (New York: Scribner, 1971); Marcel Gauchet, *The Disenchantment of the World: A Political History of Religion* (Princeton, N.J.: Princeton University Press, 1997).

37. O'Malley, *Trent and All That*; Toulmin, *Cosmopolis*; Gorski, *The Disciplinary Revolution*.

38. Of course, there is an important strand of writing throughout the romantic period, ranging from Wollstonecraft and Priestley to Hazlitt and Leigh Hunt, that was not "buffered" against institutions in this way. We might think of this, broadly, as a dissenting tradition, one that takes in both religious and political dissent and is largely comfortable within modern institutional structures *despite* its dissenting relationship to them. Such writers are not my concern here.

39. Romantic-era notions of culture as enclosed and inherently meaningful ways of life have been both a boon and a liability for a critical project: a boon, because "culture"

provides discontent with a political location and a meaningful tradition; a liability, because it hitches that discontent to an obsolescing way of life. This liability has received some attention in recent years, for it seems to point to an underlying limitation of multicultural politics: that it cannot mount a sustained critique of fundamentalism because of its culturalist premises; or, alternatively, that it patronizingly reduces minority peoples to the role of "representing" a culture or a way of life within the confines of a modernizing nation-state. The first is a critique from the right. See Paul Berman, *The Flight of the Intellectuals* (Brooklyn: Melville House, 2010); the second is a critique from the left. For an overview, see James Tully, *Strange Multiplicity: Constitutionalism in an Age of Diversity* (Cambridge: Cambridge University Press, 1995); and the thoughtful critique in David Scott, "Culture in Political Theory," *Political Theory* 31, 1 (February 2003): 92–115; also Seyla Benhabib, *The Claims of Culture: Equality and Diversity in the Global Era* (Princeton, N.J.: Princeton University Press, 2002); and the critique in Nikolas Kompridis, "Normativizing Hybridity/Neutralizing Culture," *Political Theory* 33, 3 (June 2005): 318–33. Both Scott and Kompridis point out the irony by which versions of cultural constructivism wind up neutralizing, as political forces, the very cultural diversity they officially celebrate.

40. This is one important limitation of Taylor's account. In the context of colonial and postcolonial history this problem becomes especially acute. Thus, drawing on the experience of diasporic and transnational peoples, Homi Bhabha and others have argued that "culture" was not an expression of identity but a hybrid product, arising between and among different peoples at their points of contact or overlap. Thinking of culture in this manner, the argument goes, makes possible a separation from the nation-state as the terminal apotheosis of a multicultural politics. In a somewhat different idiom, Gauri Viswanathan argues that conversion, by "undoing the concept of fixed, unalterable identities, . . . unsettles the boundaries by which selfhood, citizenship, nationhood, and community are defined, exposing these as permeable borders." See Homi K. Bhabha, *The Location of Culture* (London: Routledge, 1994); Bhabha, "Minority Maneuvers and Unsettled Negotiations," *Critical Inquiry* 23, 3 (Spring 1997): 431–59; on multiculturalism, see Charles Taylor, *Multiculturalism and the Politics of Recognition: An Essay*, ed. Amy Gutmann (Princeton, N.J.: Princeton University Press, 1992); for Bhabha's critique of Taylor, see "On Writing Rights," in *Globalizing Rights: The Oxford Amnesty Lectures 1999* (Oxford: Oxford University Press, 2003), 162–83; Gauri Viswanathan, *Outside the Fold*, 16.

41. On self-fashioning in the secular age, see Taylor, *A Secular Age*, 423–773; for an influential account of the carnivalesque that is cautious about its politics, see Peter Stallybrass and Allon White, *The Politics and Poetics of Transgression* (London: Methuen, 1986).

42. Gilles Deleuze and Felix Guattari, "What Is a Minor Literature?" in *Kafka: Toward a Minor Literature*, trans. Dana Polan (Minneapolis: University of Minnesota Press, 1986), 16–27.

43. The most concerted recent effort to deflect the "Enlightenment versus Romanticism" binary in a more useful direction can be found in Clifford Siskin and William Warner, eds., *This Is Enlightenment* (Chicago: University of Chicago Press, 2010); see especially the introduction, where the editors self-consciously move away from an emphasis on reflexivity that they associate with Kant and philosophical history more generally.

Although I, too, am uncomfortable with large categories like "Enlightenment" and "Romanticism," the shift to a history of media advocated by this volume risks losing track of the importance of intellectual history, and indeed subjectivity, altogether. By contrast, the self-critique that is central to romanticism—and indeed to literature as it was constructed during this period—is a crucial part of the account I give here.

44. Mark Lilla, *The Stillborn God: Religion, Politics, and the Modern West* (New York: Knopf, 2007). Paul Berman suggests that Islamism is a form of fascism derived in part from a romantic reading of the Qur'an "influenced by Coleridge." See Berman, "Who's Afraid of Tariq Ramadan?" *New Republic*, 4 June 2007. An influential source for this kind of analysis is Isaiah Berlin, whose various accounts of what he termed the "Counter-Enlightenment" came close to pinning National Socialism on Hamann and Herder. See Isaiah Berlin, "The Counter-Enlightenment," in *Against the Current: Essays in the History of Ideas*, ed. Henry Hardy (New York: Viking, 1980), 1–24; Berlin, *The Magus of the North: J. G. Hamann and the Origins of Modern Irrationalism*, ed. Henry Hardy (London: John Murray, 1993). For other liberal defenses of the Enlightenment, see Gary Wills, "The Day the Enlightenment Went Out," *New York Times*, 4 November 2004; Daniel Dennett, *Breaking the Spell: Religion as a Natural Phenomenon* (New York: Penguin, 2006); Christopher Hitchens, *God Is Not Great: How Religion Poisons Everything* (New York: Hachette, 2007).

45. See for example Hirsi Ali's description of the "enemies of Reason in the West: religion and the Romantic movement," in Ayaan Hirsi Ali, "Blind Faiths," *New York Times Book Review*, 6 January 2008, 14–15; also Ayaan Hirsi Ali, *Infidel* (New York: Free Press, 2008); Niall Ferguson, *Civilization: The West and the Rest* (New York: Penguin, 2011); Cheryl Benard, "Civil Democratic Islam: Partners, Resources, and Strategies" (Rand Corporation, 2003); the thinking behind much of this material is laid out in Samuel P. Huntington, "The Clash of Civilizations?" *Foreign Affairs* 72 (Summer 1993): 22–49.

46. Alain Badiou, *Saint Paul: The Foundation of Universalism*, trans. Ray Brassier (Stanford, Calif.: Stanford University Press, 2003); also Slavoj Žižek, *The Ticklish Subject: The Absent Centre of Political Ontology* (London: Verso, 1999), esp. 130–32; Hardt and Negri, *Empire*; Alain Badiou, *Ethics: An Essay on the Understanding of Evil*, trans. Peter Hallward (London: Verso, 2001). Žižek is clearest about this universalism as "a third domain, which belongs neither to the global market society nor to the new forms of ethnic fundamentalism: the domain of the *political*, the public space of civil society, of active responsible citizenship" (*Ticklish Subject*, 221).

47. Žižek, greatly influenced by Badiou on this score, writes that "what we need today is the gesture that would undermine capitalist globalization from the standpoint of universal Truth, just as Pauline Christianity did to the Roman global Empire." Žižek, *The Ticklish Subject*, 211; Badiou, *Saint Paul*, 1; helpful commentary can be found in Adam Kotsko, *Žižek and Theology* (London: T & T Clark, 2008), 71–128; and Leela Gandhi, "The Pauper's Gift: Postcolonial Theory and the New Democratic Dispensation," *Public Culture* 23, 1 (2011): 27–38.

48. For a good survey, see James A. Beckford, "Public Religions and the Postsecular: Critical Reflections," *Journal for the Scientific Study of Religion*, 51.1 (2012) 1–19.

49. Jürgen Habermas, "Notes on a Post-Secular Society," *Sign and Sight* (27 March 2014), http://print.signandsight.com/features/1714.html. It is worth noting that in Habermas's formulation, officially atheist states like the former Eastern Bloc and, in modified form, China, would not count as secular.

50. Casanova, *Public Religions in the Modern World*; also Berger, *The Desecularization of the World*.

51. Beckford, "Public Religions and the Postsecular," 16.

52. Mee, *Romanticism, Enthusiasm, and Regulation*, 3, 5, 4.

53. In Mee's account, enthusiasm, which began life as a specifically religious error, was over the course of the eighteenth century produced as an object of inquiry precisely so it could be tamed, regulated, and brought within the confines of acceptable discourse. The "discourse on enthusiasm" is in this sense structurally analogous to the discourse on religion, and thus, too, isomorphic with a process of secularization. Indeed, by the early years of the nineteenth century "enthusiasm" was beginning to shed its specifically religious connotations and denote simply the passion of any pursuit.

54. Lines 20, 18. I did not discover Robert Miles's essay on "Frost at Midnight" until I had finished my own introduction, but I am glad to see that he, too, reads the poem as a meditation on the secular. The difference between us is that, like Mee, Miles tends to see the poem as a way to "absorb the old form into the new as its content." See Miles, "Romanticism, Enlightenment, and Mediation," 187.

55. See John Modern's meditations on agency in a secular age: "For those living within a secular imaginary, decisions about religion were often one's own, yet the range of available choices had been patterned and shaped by circumstance. Institutions making their invisible demands. Media generating models of particular choices. Machines enabling you to interact with your decisions and those of others. A choice being made before it presents itself as such. Unseen somethings haunting the day." John Lardas Modern, *Secularism in Antebellum America* (Chicago: University of Chicago Press, 2011), 7. That last sentence is a quotation from Don DeLillo's novel *Underworld* (New York: Scribner, 1997).

56. David Hume, "Of Superstition and Enthusiasm," in *David Hume: Writings on Religion*, ed. Anthony Flew (Chicago: Open Court, 1992), 3–9.

57. Cragwall, *Lake Methodism*, 9, 6.

58. Isabelle Stengers, "The Cosmopolitical Proposal," in *Making Things Public: Atmospheres of Democracy*, ed. Bruno Latour and Peter Weibel (Cambridge, Mass.: MIT Press, 2005), 994.

59. Jerome Christensen, *Lord Byron's Strength: Romantic Writing and Commercial Society* (Baltimore: Johns Hopkins University Press, 1993), 324.

60. Walter Scott, *Waverley; Or, 'Tis Sixty Years Since*, ed. Andrew Hook (London: Penguin, 1985), 469.

61. Jochen Schulte-Sasse et al., eds., *Theory as Practice: A Critical Anthology of Early German Romantic Writings* (Minneapolis: University of Minnesota Press, 1997), 321.

62. Nandy, "The Politics of Secularism," 321. The key word here is *theological*: Nandy's argument is that principles of tolerance derive internally from religious traditions themselves; they are not accommodations to the "outside world."

63. For a critical but fair account, see Alastair Bonnett, "The Critical Traditionalism of Ashis Nandy: Occidentalism and the Dilemmas of Innocence," *Theory, Culture & Society* 29, 1 (January 2012): 138–57.

64. This is an implication that surfaces at times in Asad's work. For well-taken criticisms, see Mufti, "Why I Am Not a Postsecularist"; and Bruce Robbins, "Is the Postcolonial Also Postsecular?" *Boundary 2* 40, 1 (2013): 245–62.

65. And when he wrote, in the *Athenaeum* in 1800 and in the grip of his initial enthusiasm for India, that "we must seek the supreme romanticism in the Orient." See Raymond Schwab, *The Oriental Renaissance: Europe's Rediscovery of India and the East, 1680–1880* (New York: Columbia University Press, 1984), 13. By 1808, after Schlegel had learned some Sanskrit, he was less enthusiastic; see Dorothy M. Figueira, "The Politics of Exoticism and Friedrich Schlegel's Metaphorical Pilgrimage to India," *Monatshefte* 81, 4 (Winter 1989): 425–33; the question of romantic Orientalism, and in particular the emergence of a secular literature, is an extraordinarily complicated one; for an elegant account that hews more closely to a defense of the secular than I myself do, see Aamir R. Mufti, "Orientalism and the Institution of World Literatures," *Critical Inquiry* 36 (Spring 2010): 458–93; my own view is closer to that of Akeel Bilgrami, who interprets the Occidentalism (stereotypical depictions of "the West") of Nandy and others as picking up on a critique from within the West itself, beginning with Dissenters and pantheists in the seventeenth century and running through romanticism to Gandhi. See Bilgrami, "Occidentalism, the Very Idea."

66. This is not, or not only, the kind of "hauntology" that Derrida has so influentially described, and that John Lardas Modern has for example made central to his account in *Secularism in Antebellum America*. Like the stranger in "Frost at Midnight," the ghosts cast up by secularity are not only invitations to complex thoughts; they are signs of real injustice in the real world. See Jacques Derrida, *Specters of Marx: The State of the Debt, the Work of Mourning, and the New International* (New York: Routledge, 2006).

67. For a critique of secular models of public discourse, see William E. Connolly, *Why I Am Not a Secularist* (Minneapolis: University of Minnesota Press, 2000); for an engagement with Connolly and a defense of literature along these lines, see Colin Jager, "After the Secular: The Subject of Romanticism," *Public Culture* 18, 2 (Spring 2006): 301–22. For the figure of the idiot, see Stengers, "Cosmopolitical Proposal," Stengers, "Deleuze and Guattari's Last Enigmatic Message," *Angelaki* 10, 2 (2005): 152; and Gilles Deleuze and Felix Guattari, *What Is Philosophy?* (London: Verso, 1994).

68. Robert Miles, "Debating the Secular," *Eighteenth-Century Life* 37, 3 (2013): 118.

PART I INTRODUCTION

Epigraphs: A. G. Dickens and Dorothy Carr, eds., "Abbot Pyle's Surrender of Furness Abbey," in *The Reformation in England to the Accession of Elizabeth I: Documents of*

Modern History (London: Edward Arnold, 1967), 104–5; Richard Corbet, "A Proper New Ballad, Intituled the Faires' Farewell, or God-a-Mercy Will," in *The New Oxford Book of Seventeenth-Century Verse*, ed. Alastair Fowler (Oxford: Oxford University Press, 2008), 176.

1. Smith, *Faith and Belief.*

2. Harrison, *"Religion" and the Religions in the English Enlightenment*, 2–3.

3. Ibid., 24–25, 3; see also Smith, *Faith and Belief*; Michael McKeon, *The Secret History of Domesticity: Public, Private, and the Division of Knowledge* (Baltimore: Johns Hopkins University Press, 2005), 33–43.

4. Steven Shapin and Simon Schaffer, *Leviathan and the Air-Pump: Hobbes, Boyle, and the Experimental Life* (Princeton, N.J.: Princeton University Press, 1989).

5. William T. Cavanaugh, "'A Fire Strong Enough to Consume the House': The Wars of Religion and the Rise of the State," *Modern Theology* 11, 4 (October 1995): 397.

6. To be sure, there was plenty of theological discussion of revelation throughout the seventeenth and eighteenth centuries, just as there were plenty of content-based arguments in Aquinas. But the character of the concepts themselves—reason, revelation, belief—slowly shifted as the notion of a sustaining divine presence within Creation became less relevant. See John Montag SJ, "Revelation: The False Legacy of Suarez," in *Radical Orthodoxy: A New Theology*, ed. John Milbank, Catherine Pickstock, and Graham Ward (London: Routledge, 1999), 38–63.

7. C. John Sommerville, *The Secularization of Early Modern England: From Religious Culture to Religious Faith* (New York: Oxford University Press, 1992), 45; see also Richard Rex, *Henry VIII and the English Reformation* (Houndmills: Macmillan, 1993), 106–8; Stephen Prickett, *Origins of Narrative: The Romantic Appropriation of the Bible* (Cambridge: Cambridge University Press, 1996), 81.

8. These are versions of the questions asked in Talal Asad, "Thinking About Religion, Belief, and Politics," in *The Cambridge Companion to Religious Studies*, ed. Robert A. Orsi (New York: Cambridge University Press, 2012), esp. 51.

CHAPTER I. THE POWER OF THE PRINCE

1. According to Archbishop Thomas Cranmer's hostile account; see Thomas Cranmer, *The Works of Thomas Cranmer*, ed. J. E. Cox (Cambridge, 1846), 2:273; qtd. in Diane Watt, *Secretaries of God: Women Prophets in Late Medieval and Early Modern England* (Cambridge: Brewer, 1997), 60.

2. See the accounts in Watt, *Secretaries of God*, 59–60; George Bernard, *The King's Reformation: Henry VIII and the Remaking of the English Church* (New Haven, Conn.: Yale University Press, 2005), 87–90; Rex, *Henry VIII and the English Reformation*, 85.

3. Cranmer, *Works*, 2:273; qtd. in Watt, *Secretaries of God*, 62.

4. Watt, *Secretaries of God*, 63.

5. Rex, *Henry VIII and the English Reformation*, 86; Watt, *Secretaries of God*, 65.

6. See Amy Hollywood, *Sensible Ecstasy: Mysticism, Sexual Difference, and the Demands of History* (Chicago: University of Chicago Press, 2002).

7. Bernard, *The King's Reformation*, 90; Watt, *Secretaries of God*, 69.

8. Statutes of the Realm, iii, 446; qtd. in Bernard, *The King's Reformation*, 89.

9. *Letters and Papers, Foreign and Domestic, of the Reign of Henry VIII*, ed. J. S. Brewer, J. Gardiner, and R. H. Brodie (21 vols., 1862–1932), vol. 6, 1468; qtd. in Bernard, *The King's Reformation*, 89.

10. Rex, *Henry VIII and the English Reformation*, 18.

11. Public Records Office (hereafter PRO), SP1/82 fol. 80; qtd. in Bernard, *The King's Reformation*, 90.

12. PRO, SP1/82 fol. 75; qtd. in Bernard, *The King's Reformation*, 92.

13. Ibid., 95.

14. Cranmer, *Works*, 2:274; qtd. in Bernard, *The King's Reformation*, 94.

15. Rex, *Henry VIII and the English Reformation*, 21–22; Bernard, *The King's Reformation*, 98.

16. Rex, *Henry VIII and the English Reformation*, 13.

17. Bernard, *The King's Reformation*, 90.

18. For discussion, see Bernard, *The King's Reformation*, 99–101; Watt, *Secretaries of God*, 74–80; Ethan Shagan, *Popular Politics and the English Reformation* (Cambridge: Cambridge University Press, 2003), 61–88.

19. John Donne, *The Complete English Poems*, ed. Albert James Smith (London: Penguin, 1971), lines 213–14.

20. Stephen Orgel and Jonathan Goldberg, eds., *John Milton* (Oxford: Oxford University Press, 1991), 41; line 60.

21. Eamon Duffy, *The Stripping of the Altars: Traditional Religion in England, 1400–1580*, 2nd ed. (New Haven, Conn.: Yale University Press, 2005), 395; see also Sommerville, *The Secularization of Early Modern England*, 39.

22. Rex, *Henry VIII and the English Reformation*, 81, 88.

23. Ibid., 72; Sommerville, *The Secularization of Early Modern England*, 62–64; Duffy, *The Stripping of the Altars*, 407.

24. Duffy, *The Stripping of the Altars*, 398.

25. Taylor, *A Secular Age*, 79.

26. Ibid., 85.

27. Sommerville, *The Secularization of Early Modern England*, 45; Rex, *Henry VIII and the English Reformation*, 104, 122–26.

28. Also known as the "English Bible," the Great Bible was a composite, assembled by John Rogers from Tyndale's New Testament and the fragments of the Old Testament he had managed to translate before being discovered, strangled, and burned at the stake. See Prickett, *Origins of Narrative*, 82. The 1540 frontispiece was clearly influenced by the Coverdale Bible (1535), which carries a frontispiece by Hans Holbein and shows Henry with a sword in one hand and a Bible in the other.

29. Lucien Febvre, *The Problem of Unbelief in the Sixteenth Century: The Religion of Rabelais* (Cambridge Mass.: Harvard University Press, 1982), 336.

30. Rex, *Henry VIII and the English Reformation*; John Bossy, *Christianity in the West, 1400–1700* (Oxford: Oxford University Press, 1985); Sheehan, "When Was Disenchantment?"

31. Taylor, *A Secular Age*, 38.

32. Studies of popular religion in the fifteenth and sixteenth centuries are legion; for a sampling, see Keith Thomas, *Religion and the Decline of Magic: Studies in Popular Beliefs in Sixteenth and Seventeenth Century England* (New York: Oxford University Press, 1997); Carlo Ginzburg, *The Cheese and the Worms: The Cosmos of a Sixteenth-Century Miller*, trans. John Tedeschi and Anne C. Tedeschi (Baltimore: Johns Hopkins University Press, 1992); Febvre, *The Problem of Unbelief in the Sixteenth Century*; Duffy, *The Stripping of the Altars*; William A. Christian, *Local Religion in Sixteenth-Century Spain* (Princeton, N.J.: Princeton University Press, 1989); Bossy, *Christianity in the West*.

33. Taylor, *A Secular Age*, 63; O'Malley, *Trent and All That*, 137.

34. Petrus Spierenburg, *The Broken Spell: A Cultural and Anthropological History of Preindustrial Europe* (London: Macmillan, 1991), 8.

35. See especially McKeon, *The Secret History of Domesticity*.

36. "Introduction," Kaspar von Greyerz, ed., *Religion and Society in Early Modern Europe* (London: Allen & Unwin, 1984), 1–16, 4.

37. Taylor, *A Secular Age*, 107.

38. Alister McGrath, *Reformation Thought: An Introduction* (Oxford: Blackwell, 1988), 33.

39. James Simpson, *Burning to Read: English Fundamentalism and Its Reformation Opponents* (Cambridge, Mass.: Belknap Press of Harvard University Press, 2007), 2.

40. Ibid., 177, 33.

41. Catherine Pickstock, *After Writing: On the Liturgical Consummation of Philosophy* (Oxford: Blackwell, 1998), 50, 51.

42. McKeon, *The Secret History of Domesticity*, 40–41.

43. Thomas Cranmer, *Preface to the Great Bible*, in *A Reformation Reader: Primary Texts with Introductions*, ed. Denis Janz (Minneapolis: Fortress Press, 2008), 343–44.

44. McGrath, *Reformation Thought*, 32; Taylor, *A Secular Age*, 101.

45. In Stephen Toulmin's *Cosmopolis*, for example, literary skepticism embodied by Montaigne butts heads with a Cartesian desire for "quasi-geometrical certainty or necessity." For Toulmin, absolutism is a reaction to humanism's immanence, its focus on this world, and the potential power of its multitudes. In *Empire*, Michael Hardt and Antonio Negri offer a roughly similar story with a dialectical twist: the forces of order, they suggest, never achieved a complete victory over "the immanent, constructive, creative forces" of humanity. Modernity, in their analysis, just is this struggle between transcendent order and immanent disorder, mediated now by the state. See Toulmin, *Cosmopolis*, 20; Hardt and Negri, *Empire*, 75; also Harrison, *Confusion's Masterpiece*, 32–37.

46. Thus, while Toulmin's description of the murder of Henry IV at the hands of a religious zealot is certainly a powerful image, it gets at only a part of the story. By associating literary culture with humanism it tends to obscure the fact that late medieval scholastics had already developed "hermeneutic" readings of biblical texts, and by associating the church with absolutism it tends to obscure the fact that the absolutist state was already being theorized in the fifteenth century, as part of the literary Renaissance that Toulmin and others celebrate. On the former, see Christopher Ocker, *Biblical Poetics Before Humanism and Reformation* (Cambridge: Cambridge University Press, 2002); on the latter, see McKeon, *The Secret History of Domesticity*, 4, 18–26.

47. Christopher Haigh, ed., *The English Reformation Revised* (Cambridge: Cambridge University Press, 1987), 13.

48. All references are to the Arden edition of William Shakespeare, *King Henry VIII*, ed. Gordon McMullan, 3rd ed. (London: Arden Shakespeare, 2000). Scholars are now in wide agreement that the play is a collaboration between Shakespeare and John Fletcher.

49. *The Life and Letters of Sir Henry Wotton*, ed. Logan Pearsall Smith, 2 vols. (Oxford: Clarendon, 1907), 2:32–33, qtd. in McMullan, "Introduction," Shakespeare, *King Henry VIII*, 59.

50. 2.3.114–15. William Shakespeare, *Twelfth Night: Or, What You Will, The Arden Edition of the Works of William Shakespeare*, ed. J. M. Lothian and T. W. Craik (London: Methuen, 1975).

51. For the former, see Natalie Zemon Davis, *Society and Culture in Early Modern France* (Stanford, Calif.: Stanford University Press, 1975); for the latter, see Mikhail M. Bakhtin, *Rabelais and His World*, trans. Helene Iswolsky (Cambridge, Mass.: MIT Press, 1968).

52. Qtd. in Duffy, *The Stripping of the Altars*, 394.

53. Qtd. in Taylor, *A Secular Age*, 76.

54. Cranmer, *Preface to the Great Bible*, in Janz, *A Reformation Reader*, 350.

55. Rex, *Henry VIII and the English Reformation*, 96; see also Taylor, *A Secular Age*, 82; Gorski, *The Disciplinary Revolution*; Duffy, *The Stripping of the Altars*.

56. Haigh, *The English Reformation Revised*, 209; Haigh is reacting to such standard reference works as A. G. Dickens, *The English Reformation* (London: Schocken, 1964).

57. The Duke of Norfolk, leading the Royal troops, managed to negotiate a settlement by meeting the Pilgrims' demands: restore monasteries, suppress heresy, and dismiss Bishops Cranmer and Hugh Latimer, as well as "low-born" advisers, namely Cromwell and Richard Rich. Henry had no intention of keeping his side of the bargain, and in February 1537 sent Norfolk north again. He executed 130 people. For more, see Rex, *Henry VIII and the English Reformation*, 148–51.

58. Rex, *Henry VIII and the English Reformation*, 32–34; Haigh, *The English Reformation Revised*, 5.

59. Haigh, *The English Reformation Revised*, 3, 4; Rex, *Henry VIII and the English Reformation*, 41–43; Duffy, *The Stripping of the Altars*, 4–5.

60. Rex, *Henry VIII and the English Reformation*, 35.

61. Haigh, "Introduction," *The English Reformation Revised*, 6.

62. McMullan, "Introduction," Shakespeare, *King Henry VIII*, 2.

CHAPTER 2. THE MELANCHOLY OF THE SECULAR

1. The conditions for that contest had been set a bit earlier, once property came to be understood as a commodity that could circulate in the marketplace. In 1646, Parliament abolished feudal tenures and the Court of Wards, making possible an "unprecedented degree of long-term estate planning, experimentation, and investment" because landowners now possessed property outright rather than at the king's pleasure. Property thus became an economic rather than political category. Almost immediately, though, Parliament recognized that a landholder's ability to dispose of property as he wished carried its own risks: families could lose their land, go bankrupt, or get very rich. So Parliament strengthened the so-called "strict settlement" in the eighteenth century, ensuring that land could not be sold, divided, or sometimes even mortgaged, thereby helping to preserve the established order of things. See McKeon, *The Secret History of Domesticity*, 17; E. J. Clery, *The Rise of Supernatural Fiction, 1762–1800* (Cambridge: Cambridge University Press, 1999), 74, 76; Jerrold E. Hogle, "Introduction," *The Cambridge Companion to Gothic Fiction*, ed. Jerrold E. Hogle (Cambridge: Cambridge University Press, 2002), 1–20, 4. See also Michael McKeon, *The Origins of the English Novel, 1600–1740* (Baltimore: Johns Hopkins University Press, 1987), 154.

2. See Clery, *The Rise of Supernatural Fiction*, 7. For a critique of the claim that the gothic is a vehicle of bourgeois self-understanding, see James Watt, *Contesting the Gothic: Fiction, Genre, and Cultural Conflict, 1764–1832* (Cambridge: Cambridge University Press, 1999), 12–41.

3. Horace Walpole, *The Castle of Otranto*, ed. W. S. Lewis (Oxford: Oxford University Press, 1964), 108.

4. Diane Long Hoeveler interprets the gothic genre as ambivalently poised between Taylor's porous and buffered selves; Otranto, I am arguing by contrast, has room only for the buffered self. Diane Long Hoeveler, *Gothic Riffs: Secularizing the Uncanny in the European Imaginary, 1780–1820* (Columbus: Ohio State University Press, 2010), 18, 31.

5. Taylor, *A Secular Age*, 82.

6. Walpole, *The Castle of Otranto*, 12; on the history of Walpole's connection to London theater, see Marshall Brown, *The Gothic Text* (Stanford, Calif.: Stanford University Press, 2005).

7. Walpole, *The Castle of Otranto*, 49, 66; see also Carol M. Dole, "Three Tyrants in *The Castle of Otranto*," *English Language Notes* 26 (1988): 26.

8. For a discussion of these kinds of accounts, see Jager, *The Book of God*, 26–36; Michael Saler, "Modernity and Enchantment: A Historiographic Review," *American Historical Review* 111, 3 (2006): 695.

9. Accordingly, O'Malley, in *Trent and All That* suggests that the Counter-Reformation be renamed "Early Modern Catholicism."

10. Despite an official commitment to divine right, Trent conformed to a modern notion of agency that constructed an order rather than conforming to one already in nature. It was Hubert Jedin who first made the influential distinction between a "Catholic Reformation" and a "Counter-Reformation." See Jedin, *A History of the Council of Trent*, trans. Ernest Graf (London: Thomas Nelson, 1957); O'Malley, *Trent and All That*, 51–53; see also Karen Armstrong, *The Battle for God: A History of Fundamentalism* (New York: Ballantine, 2001), 5; Foucault, "Governmentality," 104; Taylor, *A Secular Age*, 129.

11. Qtd. in Susan Stewart, *Poetry and the Fate of the Senses* (Chicago: University of Chicago Press, 2002), 173.

12. *Monthly Review* 32 (May 1765): 394; qtd. in Clery, *The Rise of Supernatural Fiction*, 53.

13. Abby Coykendall, "Chance Enlightenments, Choice Superstitions: Walpole's *Historic Doubts* and Enlightened Historicism," *The Eighteenth Century: Theory and Interpretation* 54, 1 (2013): 63.

14. Clery, *The Rise of Supernatural Fiction*, 63–69.

15. Stewart, *Poetry and the Fate of the Senses*, 189.

16. Walter Benjamin, *The Origin of German Tragic Drama*, trans. John Osborne (London: Verso, 1998), 159–238; Pickstock, *After Writing*, 81–88; see also Asad, *Formations of the Secular*, 64.

17. The play's association with royalism remained strong in the eighteenth century: Colley Cibber's Drury Lane production in 1727 marked the coronation of George II, and both Covent Garden and Drury Lane mounted versions in 1761 to celebrate that of George III. Meanwhile, cultural historians have noted the importance of eighteenth-century social movements encouraging order, decency, and sobriety; the rising middle class "worked for the repression of wakes, fairs, and church ales; they suppressed brothels, ale-houses, cock-fighting, and bull-baiting; they founded schools; encouraged libraries; endowed musical festivals; hospitals and orphanages bore their names." Plumb, *The First Four Georges*, 21; See also Langford, *A Polite and Commercial People*.

18. "An Answer to the First Part of a Certaine Conference, Concerning Succession," qtd. in McKeon, *The Secret History of Domesticity*, 113. Patriarchal theory was analyzed most famously by Sir Robert Filmer in *Patriarcha; or the Natural Power of Kings* (1680), but it was operative much earlier; indeed Filmer's book may be taken as a sign that patriarchal theory was understood to be somewhat fragile by the second half of the seventeenth century.

19. As both McKeon and Foucault point out, the family-state analogy is tenuous even during the supposed heyday of absolutism. On the one hand, the family has too uncertain a meaning to support the abstract framework of sovereignty. On the other hand, as the conjugal family unit separates itself from these wider networks of relation and thereby achieves greater rhetorical and ideological importance, it begins to take precedence over the state of which it had supposedly served as a mere example: if the family was once

used as an illustration of the state, now the state becomes an illustration of the family. See McKeon, *The Secret History of Domesticity*, 115–20, 127; Foucault, "Governmentality," 98.

20. In a bravura rendering of English royalty in the seventeenth century, McKeon spins out the family saga: "The history of the royal house of Stuart must have appeared to many as a century-long allegory of family crisis: the desertion and murder of the husband-father, Charles I; the widowhood of the wife-mother, England; the belated return of the eldest son, Charles II; the rivalry of fatally defective heirs . . . ; the futile effort to extend the line through James II; the anomalous rule of the mother, Anne; and the conveyance of the estate to Hanoverian interlopers." Of course, this sounds like nothing so much as a gothic novel. McKeon, *The Secret History of Domesticity*, 113–14.

21. The bad father's crimes fall most heavily on the next generation. Manfred's desire to reverse the Oedipal dynamic and insert himself forcibly into the rising generation by marrying his son's fiancé bequeaths to the gothic genre its most sustained fantasy: the ability to halt the ascendance of the next generation—usually by torturing, imprisoning, or killing young people. When Manfred accidentally stabs his daughter Matilda this is less a "mistake" than a manifestation of the violence that accompanies any effort to hold back time. Like Cronos devouring his children, this is Manfred's last-ditch attempt to cling to a model of sovereignty that is passing away before his eyes.

22. On these transitions see Foucault, "Governmentality"; and Jürgen Habermas, *The Structural Transformation of the Public Sphere: An Inquiry into a Category of Bourgeois Society* (Cambridge Mass.: MIT Press, 1989), 28–31.

23. Steve Bruce, ed., *Religion and Modernization: Sociologists and Historians Debate the Secularization Thesis* (New York: Oxford University Press, 1992), 12; Sommerville, *The Secularization of Early Modern England*, 5; Alasdair MacIntyre, *Secularization and Moral Change*, Riddell Memorial Lectures (Oxford: Oxford University Press, 1967); Casanova, *Public Religions in the Modern World*; Jager, *The Book of God*, 26–36

24. Taylor, *A Secular Age*, 271.

25. Foucault, "Governmentality," 104.

26. Ibid., 93.

27. Habermas, *The Structural Transformation of the Public Sphere*, 29.

28. Porter, *Enlightenment*, 207.

29. Plumb, *The First Four Georges*, 78–79. Walpole was a man either loved or hated: "he was the most sought-after man in the kingdom," writes Plumb, "the most feared, the most detested, and against him there was a snarling outcry of impotent rage" (74).

30. C. B. Ricks, "Wolsey in 'The Vanity of Human Wishes'," *Modern Language Notes* 73, 8 (December 1958): 563–68.

31. For over a decade Wolsey essentially ran the country, and like Walpole he inspired equal degrees of admiration and loathing. Catherine of Aragon even blamed Wolsey for her fate, claiming it was revenge for her questioning of his "voluptuous life, and abominable lechery," and "presumptuous power and tyranny" (qtd. in Bernard, *The King's Reformation*, 1). In fact, Catherine's fall was more likely the result of the complicated diplomatic game Wolsey was playing. He wanted to give Henry the divorce he sought,

but he also wanted to preserve the church—and hence his role in the international Catholic power structure and the possibility of becoming pope himself. See Virginia Murphy, "The Literature and Proganda of Henry VIII's First Divorce," in *The Reign of Henry VIII: Politics, Policy, and Piety*, ed. Dairmaid MacCulloch (Basingstoke: Palgrave Macmillan, 1995), 135–58; also Bernard, *The King's Reformation*, 27–36. Wolsey's own fall, which came in autumn 1529, was as a triumph of national sovereignty over an international Christendom—an early foretaste of the policy of *cuius regio, eius religio* that would become the norm in the seventeenth century.

32. Qtd. in Ricks, "Wolsey in 'The Vanity of Human Wishes'," 564.

33. Qtd. as the epigraph to *Authentick Memoirs of the Life and Infamous Actions of Cardinal Wolsey. To a Certain Gentleman, Who Takes the Character of Cardinal Wolsey to Himself* (London, 1731).

34. Ibid., iv.

35. Miles, "Romanticism, Enlightenment, and Mediation"; Hoeveler, *Gothic Riffs: Secularizing the Uncanny in the European Imaginary, 1780–1820*, 6; also Robert Miles, *Gothic Writing, 1750–1820: A Genealogy* (Manchester: Manchester University Press, 2002); see also, some years earlier, Mark Canuel, "'Holy Hypocrisy' and the Government of Belief: Religion and Nationalism in the Gothic," *Studies in Romanticism* 34 (1995): 507–30: "Gothic novels imagined a . . . policy of secular government that loosened the requirements of belief upon the subjects it superintended" (508), an argument subsequently revisited in Canuel, *Religion, Toleration, and British Writing, 1790–1830*.

36. Clery argues that the dominant Walpolean narrative created the possibility of a backlash symbolized by the old values: tradition, land, stability, inheritable wealth—all things that, if not doctrinally Catholic, could be easily interpreted as a "Catholic" or superstitious alternative to a Whiggish Protestant nationalism. See Clery, *The Rise of Supernatural Fiction, 1762–1800*.

37. David Collings, *Monstrous Society: Reciprocity, Discipline, and the Political Uncanny, c. 1780–1848* (Lewisburg, Pa.: Bucknell University Press, 2009), 26, 34; E. P. Thompson, *Customs in Common: Studies in English Popular Culture* (London: Merlin, 1991); for background, see the influential writings of Victor Turner, *The Ritual Process: Structure and Anti-Structure* (New Brunswick, N.J.: Transaction, 1995); and Bahktin, *Rabelais and His World*.

38. McKeon, *The Secret History of Domesticity*, 13.

39. Foucault, "Governmentality," 99.

40. See Heather Love, *Feeling Backward: Loss and the Politics of Queer History* (Cambridge, Mass.: Harvard University Press, 2009), 5. In this sense Robert Walpole creates the conditions for his dilettantish son's gothic fantasy: not only *Otranto* but Horace's faux-Gothic mansion Strawberry Hill and his enthusiastic cultivation of a *lifestyle*—of aristocratic connoisseurship, collecting, interior decoration, eccentricity, and effeminacy.

41. See the discussion in Andrew Elfenbein, *Romantic Genius: The Prehistory of a Homosexual Role* (New York: Columbia University Press, 1999); for a deeper historical background, see McKeon, *The Secret History of Domesticity*, 272–77; also George E. Haggerty, *Men in Love: Masculinity and Sexuality in the Eighteenth Century* (New York:

Columbia University Press, 1999); and George E. Haggerty, *Queer Gothic* (Urbana: University of Illinois Press, 2006). For a nuanced account of the ambivalence that attends the coming of modern homosexuality, see Love, *Feeling Backward*.

42. See the discussion in *A Secular Age*, 30–41.

43. Robert Burton, *The anatomy of melancholy. What it is. With all the kindes, causes, symptomes, prognostickes, and severall cures of it*, 2nd ed. (Oxford: Printed by John Lichfield and James Short, for Henry Cripps, 1621), 119, 129.

44. See Thomas Pfau, *Romantic Moods*, 311.

45. Sigmund Freud, *The Ego and the Id*, in *The Standard Edition of the Complete Psychological Works of Sigmund Freud*, ed. and trans. James Strachey, 24 vols. (London: Hogarth, 1953–74), 19:29; qtd. in Judith Butler, "Melancholy Gender/Refused Identification," in *The Psychic Life of Power: Theories in Subjection* (Stanford, Calif.: Stanford University Press, 1997), 133.

46. Ibid., 139, 135. For Butler, homosexuality is also melancholic, but in a more straightforward—and thus politically useful—fashion. See also D. A. Miller, *Jane Austen; Or, the Secret of Style* (Princeton, N.J.: Princeton University Press, 2005), 67 for a discussion of melancholy identification as central to Austen's art. And see Benjamin, *The Origin of German Tragic Drama*, for a discussion of melancholy in the baroque. Only *Hamlet*, according to Benjamin, exemplified "melancholy redeemed, by being confronted with itself" (158).

47. Nandy, *The Intimate Enemy*, 4, 7.

48. Referring specifically to the debate about gay service members in the United States, Butler asks: "what would masculinity 'be' without this aggressive circuit of renunciation from which it is wrought?" (143).

49. Nandy, "The Politics of Secularism and the Recovery of Religious Tolerance," 324.

50. McKeon, *The Secret History of Domesticity*, 272.

51. As Thomas Lacquer and others have argued, the development of an "opposite sex" model, according to which the "two sexes" are to be distinguished according to fundamentally different genital anatomies rather than arranged hierarchically along a single continuum, had profound effects on the wider-ranging bodily experiences that made up premodern sexuality. Thomas W. Laquer, *Making Sex: Body and Gender from the Greeks to Freud* (Cambridge, Mass.: Harvard University Press, 1990); McKeon, *The Secret History of Domesticity*, 272; see also Lawrence Stone, *The Family, Sex and Marriage in England, 1500–1800* (New York: Harper and Row, 1977); and Tim Hitchcock, *English Sexualities, 1700–1800* (New York: St. Martin's, 1997).

52. Kathleen Coburn and B. Winer, eds., *The Collected Works of Samuel Taylor Coleridge: Table Talk.*, vol. 14 (Princeton, N.J.: Princeton University Press, 1990), 470; emphasis in original.

CHAPTER 3. WISHING FOR NOTHING

1. Jane Austen, *Mansfield Park*, ed. John Wiltshire (Cambridge: Cambridge University Press, 1995), 389–90.

2. Ibid., 390. Besides inviting the various forms of collaborative performance that seem to set playacting against reading in the moral code of *Mansfield Park*, *King Henry VIII* is itself a collaborative effort. Though this was not known in Austen's day, it is nonetheless striking that the play itself demonstrates how difficult it is to trace back motive and intention to a single person, even when that person is generally understood to be the greatest literary genius England has ever produced.

3. For a reading of Fanny's desires here, see Jager, *The Book of God*, 127–34. As I discuss in Chapter 5 of the present book, the literary possibilities of Jacobitism would be recognized and exploited especially by Walter Scott.

4. Edward Copeland, "Money," in *The Cambridge Companion to Jane Austen*, ed. Juliet McMaster and Edward Copeland (Cambridge: Cambridge University Press, 1997), 131–48; see also Beth Fowkes Tobin, "The Moral and Political Economy of Property in Austen's *Emma*," *Eighteenth-Century Fiction* 2, 3 (1990): 229–54; for readings of Emma in the context of a boom-and-bust economy, see Robert Miles, "'A Fall in Bread': Speculation and the Real in *Emma*," *NOVEL: A Forum on Fiction* 37, 1–2 (April 2003): 66–85; and "*Emma* and Bank Bills: Forgery and Romanticism," *Romantic Circles Praxis* (February 2012), http://romantic.arhu.umd.edu/praxis/forgery/.

5. Jane Austen, *Emma*, ed. Adela Pinch (New York: Oxford University Press, 2008), 281. Unless noted, all references are to this edition.

6. In this, Donwell contrasts with Sotherton, the home of the silly Mr. Rushworth in *Mansfield Park*. The excursion to Sotherton, undertaken with the professed aim of discussing the mansion's prospects for improvement, degenerates into inappropriate erotic dalliances that prefigure the later, more explicit unions licensed by the theater. Henry Crawford in particular is a most enthusiastic improver. "Here are walls of great promise," he notes—but he means to tear them down and rebuild something else. Henry's lack of respect for walls and other kinds of barriers is made clear soon afterward, when he encourages Maria Bertram to slip through a locked gate rather than wait for her fiancé, who has gone to fetch the key.

7. Slavoj Žižek, *The Sublime Object of Ideology* (London: Verso, 1989), 87.

8. Rex, *Henry VIII and the English Reformation*, 58; David Knowles, *Bare Ruined Choirs: The Dissolution of the English Monasteries* (Cambridge: Cambridge University Press, 1976), 159.

9. *Emma*, 27. For discussions of Knightley's legibility, especially as contrasted with Emma's love of intrigue and mystery, see Tobin, "The Moral and Political Economy of Property in Austen's *Emma*"; John P. McGowan, "Knowledge/Power and Jane Austen's Radicalism," *Mosaic* 18 (1985): 1–15.

10. Eve Kosofsky Sedgwick, *Tendencies* (Durham, N.C.: Duke University Press, 1993), 125.

11. Claudia L. Johnson, *Jane Austen: Women, Politics, and the Novel* (Chicago: University of Chicago Press, 1988), 26, 27.

12. For a different reading of this figure, see Pinch, "Introduction" to the Oxford edition of *Emma*: "the fact that this revelation takes this speedy, violent form can reveal to us how *natural* it would be, in contrast, for Emma to go on *not* knowing her feelings" (xxi).

13. Jane Austen, *Northanger Abbey*, ed. Marilyn Butler (London: Penguin, 1995), 212.

14. The Harriet-Knightley romance plot is very like one that appeared in the *Lady's Magazine* in November 1802: "Mr. Knightley, a country-gentleman of not very large fortune, but such as was amply sufficient for his mode of living . . . had married from the purest affection . . . a deserted orphan [left] at a boarding school near the residence of a relation of his whom he sometimes visited" (qtd. in the Cambridge edition, 536). Austen's narrator rejects this version of life by having Emma believe it, and then scolding her for it. "Emma's mistake," according to Cronin and McMillan, "is to foster in Harriet the illusion that she might be the heroine of a novel rather than the kind of minor character who serves only to swell out a scene." Jane Austen, *Emma*, ed. Richard Cronin and Dorothy McMillan, Cambridge Edition of the Works of Jane Austen (Cambridge: Cambridge University Press, 2005), liv.

15. "The whole of *Emma*," write Cronin and McMillan nicely, "is overshadowed by this missing novel." Cronin and McMillan, "Introduction," to *Emma*, lv.

16. Tobin, "The Moral and Political Economy of Property in Austen's *Emma*."

17. To be sure, Emma's Hartfield is an example of secularization gone awry: cut off from a landed economy, Hartfield indulges in a debased, capitalist verison of a popular piety given to magical thinking and making something out of nothing. But this makes the valence of Emma's imagination remarkably unstable: on the one hand, her susceptibility to romance aligns her with a Catholicism in desperate need of reform by a Protestant Knightley; on the other, the speculation to which she is so attracted is very much like Weber's famous Protestant ethic.

18. Taylor, *A Secular Age*, 85.

19. For an analysis of this "more with less" dynamic, see Miller, *Jane Austen*. Miller gives Austen's style a more utopian interpretation than do I.

20. John Wiltshire, "Emma," in *The Cambridge Companion to Jane Austen*, ed. Edward Copeland and Juliet McMaster (Cambridge: Cambridge University Press, 1997), 70.

21. Walter Scott, unsigned review of *Emma*, *Quarterly Review* 14 (March 1816): 188–201; reprinted in *Jane Austen: The Critical Heritage*, 2 vols., ed. B. C. Southam (London: Routledge, 1968), 1:58–69; 59, 64.

22. Ibid., 65; letter to Sneyd and Harriet Edgeworth, 1816; qtd. in Pinch, "Introduction," vii; letter to Miss Clavering, 1816; qtd. in *Critical Heritage*, 1:15; Anne Romily to Maria Edgeworth, 7 May 1816; qtd. in Pinch, "Introduction," vii.

23. This does not mean that letters are not subject to interpretation. Quite the contrary: they open up multiple interpretations as they are passed from hand to hand. Yet far from leading to anything new or surprising, such debates conform to what everybody already expects the case to be. As Casey Finch and Peter Bowen have famously argued, letters function as a form of community gossip, and therefore serve to reinforce inclusions and exclusions within Highbury: "voices that seem to be everywhere and nowhere at once" police the community's boundaries in remarkably efficient fashion. See Casey Finch and Peter Bowen, "'The Tittle-Tattle of Highbury': Gossip and Free Indirect Style in

Emma," *Representations* 31 (Summer 1990): 10. For a more optimistic discussion of re-reading see William H. Galperin, *The Historical Austen* (Philadelphia: University of Penn-sylvania Press, 2003).

24. The best readings of *Emma* have long wrestled with the conundrum that when Emma becomes likable and marriageable she also loses whatever it was that made her inter-esting. For Marilyn Butler, Emma the individualist is schooled by Mr. Knightley into tradi-tional, land-based government. For Nancy Armstrong, Emma finds her "true voice" when she begins to sound indistinguishable from the narrator. For Armstrong this means that the novel as conduct book teaches a new "middle-class aristocracy" how to take over from the old, land-based aristocracy it has dethroned. Critics writing in the wake of these powerful arguments have looked for resistance elsewhere. Claudia Johnson finds an uncontainable Jacobin voice in the period, and puts Austen in dialogue with what she calls the "novel of crisis." William Galperin locates political possibility (as opposed to realistic probability) in the tiresome, rambling descriptions of everyday banalities offered by Miss Bates. Marilyn Butler, *Jane Austen and the War of Ideas* (Oxford: Clarendon, 1975); Nancy Armstrong, *Desire and Domestic Fiction: A Political History of the Novel* (New York: Oxford University Press, 1987); Johnson, *Jane Austen*; Galperin, *The Historical Austen*.

25. Besides being "gentleman-like," Robert Martin reads agricultural journals and travels, exploiting the economic possibilities that the new and better roads have opened up. Enclosure generally refers to the enclosure of common land in the name of privacy and efficiency. Engrossment was the practice of combining many smaller farms into one larger farm. These innovations drove many off the land, and raised the status of those who remained. Most of the enclosure acts were passed in two groups between 1760 and 1780 and between 1793 and 1815. The pressure of the war with France, and the consequent need to increase productivity and improve transportation, lies behind the latter group, which overlaps with Austen's lifetime. She mentions enclosure specifically in *Sense and Sensibility*, and by implication in *Northanger Abbey* and *Persuasion*. See John Barrell, *The Idea of Landscape and the Sense of Place, 1730–1840: An Approach to the Poetry of John Clare* (Cambridge: Cambridge University Press, 1972), 71; Tobin, "The Moral and Political Economy of Property in Austen's *Emma*"; and Collings, *Monstrous Society*.

26. Collings, *Monstrous Society*, 11. Like Taylor, Collings draws on Bakhtin and Vic-tor Turner.

27. Duffy, *The Stripping of the Altars*, 7; see also Bossy, *Christianity in the West*; Taylor, *A Secular Age*.

28. Duffy, *The Stripping of the Altars*, 384; Knowles, *Bare Ruined Choirs*, 156.

29. Rex, *Henry VIII and the English Reformation*, 61; Knowles, *Bare Ruined Choirs*, 165.

30. Qtd. in Duffy, *The Stripping of the Altars*, 404.

31. Duffy, *The Stripping of the Altars*, 385.

32. In *Mansfield Park*, Sir Thomas Bertram is a less subtle reformer. He simply dismantles the theater his children have constructed in his absence. He hopes "that another day or two would suffice to wipe away every outward memento of what had been, even to the destruction of every unbound copy of 'Lover's Vows' in the house, for he was

burning all that met his eye" (vol. 2, chap. 2). The tone here is uneasy, as if the narrator is not quite sure whether we should be laughing at Sir Thomas's overreaction or vicariously participating in its apocalypticism. Whatever the case, events show him to be badly mistaken. By the end of the novel, Julia will elope with the ranting actor Mr. Yates, the banished Mary Crawford will recall the theatrical episodes as the happiest event of her stay, and the general topsy-turvyness, youthful eroticism, and illicit desires introduced by the theater will doom Maria Bertram.

33. For a discussion of "nothing" in *Emma*, see Pinch, "Introduction," xxi–xxix. On "reserve" as a melancholic renunciation of a plenitude one never had, see Miller, *Jane Austen*, 65–68; for a different reading of Austen and reproductive narratives, see Clara Tuite, *Romantic Austen: Sexual Politics and the Literary Canon* (Cambridge: Cambridge University Press, 2002), esp. 16–20.

34. Miller, *Jane Austen*, esp. 57–68.

35. This seems to be confirmed in one of the most famous set pieces of the novel, which also takes place at Ford's: "Emma went to the door for amusement.—Much could not be hoped from the traffic of even the busiest part of Highbury; . . . and when her eyes fell only on the butcher with his tray, a tidy old woman traveling homewards from shop with her full basket, two curs quarrelling over a dirty bone, and a string of dawdling children round the baker's little bow-window eyeing the gingerbread, she knew she had no reason to complain, and was amused enough; quite enough still to stand at the door. A mind lively and at ease, can do with seeing nothing, and can see nothing that does not answer" (183). The "nothing that does not answer" and that sustains Emma here is in clear contrast to the earlier scene at Ford's with Frank Churchill, which is full of somethings—of circulating commodities and Frank's false stories. Emma, this second passage seems to suggest, is now on her way to making due with much less: indeed, with nothing but what the scene offers, the dogs and dirty bone, the butcher and the old woman with her full basket. "[I]n the strange arithmetic of literature," remarks Adela Pinch of this passage, "nothing plus nothing plus nothing equals almost everything" ("Introduction," xxix).

36. Insisting on how sweet, pretty, and prosperous the view is, Austen makes the apple orchard blossom in July. On my reading, this "mistake" is symptomatic of the larger anxieties provoked by Donwell's symbolic importance in the novel.

37. Austen had read Gilpin's 1786 *Lakes Tour*. Like Sotherton in *Mansfield Park*, Donwell still has an old-fashioned garden, divided into walled areas and enclosed spaces. While the sexually charged young people at Sotherton reject those spaces in favor of something that gives them more room to roam, the Donwell party remains behind the wall. Yet there remains a restless, if understated, discontent in the Donwell scene as well, registered in the simple sentence "It was hot." On Austen and the picturesque, see Galperin, *The Historical Austen*; on the contrast between Donwell and Sotherton, see Prickett, *Origins of Narrative*, 137ff.

38. Finch and Bowen, "'The Tittle-Tattle of Highbury,'" 10. Finch and Bowen beautifully link gossip to Austen's mastery of free indirect style: gossip "operates as a model of social authority that both naturalizes and authenticates the new novelistic authority of free indirect style. . . . Just as the free indirect style *of* the novel functions as

a form of narrative surveillance over the novel's characters, so gossip *in* the novel deploys a mild surveillance over the members of the Highbury community" (7).

39. Samuel H. Monk, *The Sublime: A Study of Critical Theories in Eighteenth-Century England* (Ann Arbor: University of Michigan Press, 1960); Thomas Weiskel, *The Romantic Sublime: Studies in the Structure and Psychology of Transcendence* (Baltimore: Johns Hopkins University Press, 1976), esp. 3, 38–44; Neil Hertz, *The End of the Line* (New York: Columbia University Press, 1985), esp. 47–50; Frances Ferguson, *Solitude and the Sublime: The Romantic Aesthetics of Individuation* (New York: Routledge, 1992), esp. 4–5.

40. Weiskel, *The Romantic Sublime*, 3.

41. A. G. Dickens and Dorothy Carr, eds., "Robert Aske on the Dissolution of the Monasteries," in *The Reformation in England to the Accession of Elizabeth I: Documents of Modern History* (London: Edward Arnold, 1967), 103.

42. Thus the narrator insists, against the evidence, that Harriet only ever loved Robert Martin: "The fact was, as Emma could now acknowledge, that Harriet had always liked Robert Martin; and that his continuing to love her had been irresistible" (378). The only other alternative is the intolerable one that Harriet's libido is in fact completely uncontainable. Emma admits as much a page later, when she reflects that, married to Robert Martin, Harriet will be "retired enough for safety . . . would never be led into temptation, nor left for it to find her out" (379). Harriet's desire for Mr. Knightley is the one "truth" that Emma never quite gets around to telling him—even though she promises herself several times that she will do it soon. It is one of the "but"s in the "nothing but truth" so consistently celebrated by the novel. On the contingency of historical expression in Austen, see Galperin, *The Historical Austen*.

43. James Edward Austen-Leigh, *A Memoir of Jane Austen*, ed. R. W. Chapman (1926; Oxford: Oxford University Press, 1967), 157.

44. Deirdre Le Faye, ed., *Jane Austen's Letters*, 3rd ed. (Oxford: Oxford University Press, 1995), 208, 16 February 1813.

PART II INTRODUCTION

1. Patrick McGrath, *Papists and Puritans Under Elizabeth I* (London: Blandford, 1967), 3; see also Mary Fulbrook, "Legitimation Crises and the Early Modern State: The Politics of Religious Toleration," in *Religion and Society in Early Modern Europe*, ed. Kaspar von Greyerz (London: Allen & Unwin, 1984), 146–58; Anthony W. Marx, *Faith in Nation: Exclusionary Origins of Nationalism* (New York: Oxford University Press, 2003), 94–112.

2. Sommerville, *The Secularization of Early Modern England*, 126.

3. The relevant acts were the Corporation Act (1661), Act of Uniformity (1662), Conventicle Act (1663), Five Mile Act (1665), and Test Act (1673, extended 1678).

4. *Letters Concerning the English Nation*, qtd. in Porter, *Enlightenment*, 108.

5. See Jonathan Israel, "William III and Toleration," in *From Persecution to Toleration: The Glorious Revolution and Religion in England*, ed. Ole Peter Grell, Jonathan I. Israel, and Nicholas Tyacke (Oxford: Oxford University Press, 1991), esp. 135–40. See also

Israel, *Radical Enlightenment: Philosophy and the Making of Modernity 1650–1750* (New York: Oxford University Press, 2001): 1688 "was not in essence a national achievement of the English—nor was it then regarded as such—but essentially a consequence of Dutch *raison d'état* and a large-scale invasion from the continent" (22).

6. Gilbert Burnet, *Bishop Burnet's History of His Own Time*, vol. 2, *From the Revolution to the Conclusion of the Treaty of Peace at Utrecht, in the Reign of Queen Anne, To which is added, The Author's Life, by the Editor* (London, 1724), 12.

7. John Donne, *The Major Works* (Oxford: Oxford University Press, 2000), 212, line 213.

8. "Introduction," Grell, Israel, and Tyacke, *From Persecution to Toleration*, 1; Sylvan Tomaselli, "Intolerance: The Virtue of Princes and Radicals," in *Toleration in Enlightenment Europe*, ed. Ole Peter Grell and Roy Porter (Cambridge: Cambridge University Press, 2000), 86–101; Brown, *Regulating Aversion*; Kirstie M. McClure, "Difference, Diversity, and the Limits of Toleration," *Political Theory* 18, 3 (August 1990): 361–91. See also Thomas Paine's remarks on toleration, from Part One of *The Rights of Man*: "Toleration is not the *opposite* of intoleration, but is the *counterfeit* of it. Both are despotisms. The one assumes to itself the right of withholding liberty of conscience, and the other of granting it." Thomas Paine, *Common Sense and Other Political Writings*, ed. Nelson F. Adkins (Indianapolis: Bobbs-Merrill, 1953), 92.

9. John Dryden, *Religio Laici, or, A Layman's Faith* (1682), line 450. See John Dryden, *The Major Works*, ed. Keith Walker (Oxford: Oxford University Press, 1987), 239; for discussion of Dryden and the religious politics of 1688, see Colin Jager, "Common Quiet: Tolerance Around 1688," *ELH* 79 (2012): 569–96.

CHAPTER 4. COLERIDGE AT SEA

Epigraph: Coleridge, *The Major Works*, 258, Chapter 10.

1. Samuel Taylor Coleridge, *Coleridge's Poetry and Prose*, ed. Nicholas Halmi, Paul Magnuson, and Raimonda Modiano (New York: Norton, 2004), 181.

2. Coleridge, *The Major Works*, 246, 247.

3. Adam Sisman, *The Friendship: Wordsworth and Coleridge* (New York: Viking, 2007), 130–36.

4. Richard Holmes, *Coleridge: Early Visions, 1772–1804* (New York: Viking, 1990), 159.

5. Locke and Newton hardly saw eye to eye; Stillingfleet and Burnet were strongly influenced by the Cambridge neo-Platonism of the 1650s and 1660s, and thus disliked Locke's attack on innate ideas.

6. Porter, *Enlightenment*, 30.

7. J. G. A. Pocock, "Conservative Enlightenment and Democratic Revolutions: The American and French Cases in British Perspective," *Government and Opposition* 24, 1 (January 1989): 81–105; Margaret C. Jacob, *The Cultural Meaning of the Scientific Revolution* (New York: Random House, 1988); Jacob, *The Radical Enlightenment: Pantheists, Freemasons and Republicans* (London: Allen & Unwin, 1981); Israel, *Radical Enlightenment*.

8. See Pocock, "Conservative Enlightenment and Democratic Revolutions"; and Bilgrami, "Occidentalism, the Very Idea"; for a classic account, see Norman Sykes, *Church and State in England in the XVIIIth Century: The Birkbeck Lectures* (Cambridge: Cambridge University Press, 1934), esp. 343. We should not overestimate the influence of this group. Although a number of their protégés (Edward Fowler, Richard Kidder, and Benjamin Hoadly) would go on to become bishops, in the short term the conservative Counter-Enlightenment forces (country Whigs, Tory literati, nonjuring High Churchmen) retained the upper hand. They dominated Convocation, helped to defeat the Comprehension Act that was to have accompanied the Toleration Act, rejected William's proposal to repeal the Test Act, and generally made life difficult for Tillotson and Burnet. Burnet in fact claimed that they drove Tillotson to an early grave. But in the longer term the latitudinarians would win out: Convocation was suspended indefinitely, and, after enjoying great success during Anne's reign, the High Church party were defeated so soundly in 1714/15 that they never fully recovered.

9. Porter, *Enlightenment*, 30.

10. Holmes, *Coleridge*, 167.

11. The best account of this intellectual history is still E. S. Shaffer, *"Kubla Khan" and the Fall of Jerusalem: The Mythological School in Biblical Criticism and Secular Literature, 1770–1880* (Cambridge: Cambridge University Press, 1975).

12. Whether Coleridge ever discovered those "foundations" is another story; the thirteenth chapter of *Biographia Literaria* is typically read as a failure to deliver on this promise.

13. For detailed accounts, see Shaffer, *"Kubla Khan" and the Fall of Jerusalem*; Stephen Prickett, *Words and the Word: Language, Poetics, and Biblical Interpretation* (Cambridge: Cambridge University Press, 1986); Jonathan Sheehan, *The Enlightenment Bible: Translation, Scholarship, Culture* (Princeton, N.J.: Princeton University Press, 2005); Nicholas Halmi, *The Genealogy of the Romantic Symbol* (New York: Oxford University Press, 2008); Michael C. Legaspi, *The Death of Scripture and the Rise of Biblical Studies* (New York: Oxford University Press, 2010). It should be emphasized, too, that many of the crucial insights of the eighteenth century had first been proposed by seventeenth-century scholars, especially Hobbes, Spinoza, and Richard Simon.

14. For an account of the long history of this notion, see Maurice Olender, *The Languages of Paradise: Aryans and Semites, A Match Made in Heaven*, trans. Arthur Goldhammer (New York: Other Press, 2002). I return to some of this material in Chapter 8 of the present book.

15. Shaffer, *"Kubla Khan" and the Fall of Jerusalem*, 142, 141.

16. Shaffer herself acknowledges that such mythic remaking, designed in part to absorb the blows aimed at Christianity by the Radical Enlightenment, "might be seen as a major intellectual monument to bourgeois hypocrisy" (25).

17. Shaffer, in her description of Coleridge's spiritual generosity, writes that the poem's syncretism gave him "a range and depth and sympathy hardly to be found in any orthodoxy," either religious or secular. "In that primitive yet cosmopolitan dawn just before the beginning of the nineteenth century," she continues, "it was not so evidently necessary that 'The Gods of China are always Chinese,' as Wallace Stevens put it for

our own tribal times." Yet her account of the sympathetic range of Coleridge's syncretic imagination is open to the objection, familiar to readers steeped in romantic criticism, that such an interpretation is an example of what Jerome McGann more than thirty years ago labeled the "romantic ideology." In McGann's still-unsurpassed reading of *The Rime of the Ancient Mariner*, for example, that is exactly what is at stake. After tracing Coleridge's use of German biblical scholarship within the poem's Christian dialectic, McGann concludes with a ringing pronouncement: "From our present critical vantage point, what we must do is inaugurate our disbelief in Coleridge's 'poetic faith.' This Romantic ideology must be seen for what it is, a historical phenomenon of European culture, generated to save the 'traditional concepts, schemes, and values' of the Christian heritage." A related objection, of more recent vintage but part of the same intellectual genealogy, is that accounts like Shaffer's route their phenomenological universalism through the disavowed particularities of Christianity. The history of Christianity's liberal self-overcoming, as Tomoko Masuzawa and Gil Anidjar among others have pointed out, remains problematically linked to Eurocentrism and Orientalism, inconvenient facts that remain undertheorized even in the current pluralist discourse of world religions. See Shaffer, *"Kubla Khan" and the Fall of Jerusalem*, 144; Jerome J. McGann, "The Meaning of the Ancient Mariner," *Critical Inquiry* 8, 1 (1981): 65; Masuzawa, *The Invention of World Religions*; and Anidjar, "Secularism." Also, of course, Edward W. Said, *Orientalism* (New York: Vintage, 1978); and, for an account of the creation of world literature in this context, Mufti, "Orientalism and the Institution of World Literatures."

18. Samuel Purchas, *Purchas His Pilgrimage. Or Relations of the World and the Religions Observed in All Ages and Places Discovered, from the Creation unto This Present* (London: Printed by William Stansby for Henrie Fetherstone, 1613), "To the Reader," 1.

19. See "Epidemics of the Will," in Sedgwick, *Tendencies*, 130–42; also Mark Redfield, "Introduction," *Diacritics* 27, 3 (Fall 1997): 3–7.

20. Harrison, *"Religion" and the Religions in the English Enlightenment*, 2–3. See also Smith, *Faith and Belief*; and Sommerville, *The Secularization of Early Modern England*, 161–63.

21. Toulmin, *Cosmopolis*; Taylor, *A Secular Age*; McKeon, *The Secret History of Domesticity*.

22. See G. V. Bennett, *The Tory Crisis in Church and State 1688–1730: The Career of Francis Atterbury, Bishop of Rochester* (Oxford: Clarendon, 1976).

23. Sommerville, *The Secularization of Early Modern England*, 123; also Harrison, *"Religion" and the Religions in the English Enlightenment*. Remaking religion in this manner is an important part of what Taylor calls "disembedding" and McKeon calls "explicitation." J. C. D. Clark has done much to recover the importance of religion during the period, but his account largely ignores the degree to which reflexivity tends to undermine the very institutional stability for which he argues. See J. C. D. Clark, *English Society, 1660–1832: Religion, Ideology and Politics During the Ancien Régime*, 2nd ed. (Cambridge: Cambridge University Press, 2000).

24. Bennett, *The Tory Crisis*, 13; John Walsh and Stephen Taylor, "Introduction: The Church and Anglicanism in the 'Long' Eighteenth Century," in *The Church of England c.*

1689–c. 1833: From Toleration to Tractarianism, ed. John Walsh, Colin Haydon, and Stephen Taylor (Cambridge: Cambridge University Press, 2002), 16; William Gibson, *The Church of England 1688–1832: Unity and Accord* (London: Routledge, 2001), 2. The Licensing Act, which had enabled the censoring of theological books, lapsed in 1695.

25. Mark Goldie, "John Locke, Jonas Proast, and Religious Toleration," in Walsh, Haydon, and Taylor, *The Church of England*, 145. See for example Burnet's *Discourse of Pastoral Care*, commissioned by Tillotson in 1692 as a guide for parish ministers.

26. Walsh and Taylor, "Introduction," 25.

27. Smith, *Faith and Belief*, 118. For the development of the science of religion, see Harrison, *"Religion" and the Religions in the English Enlightenment*; also Donald S. Lopez, Jr., "Belief," in *Critical Terms for Religious Studies*, ed. Mark C. Taylor (Chicago: University of Chicago Press, 1998), 21–35; Sommerville, *The Secularization of Early Modern England*, chap. 1, and McKeon, *Secret History of Domesticity*, 33. For "outsider's term," see Jonathan Z. Smith, "Religion, Religions, Religious," in Taylor, *Critical Terms for Religious Studies*, 269–84.

28. Masuzawa, *The Invention of World Religions*, 47, 49.

29. Nigel Leask, "Kubla Khan and Orientalism: The Road to Xanadu Revisited," *Romanticism* 4, 1 (1998): 2; John Barrell, *The Infection of Thomas De Quincey: A Psychopathology of Imperialism* (New Haven, Conn.: Yale University Press, 1991); on "panoramic knowledge," see Donald Pearce, "'Kubla Khan' in Context," *SEL* 21 (1981): 570.

30. "The Pains of Sleep" (written 1803, pub. 1816), lines 37–40; *Coleridge's Poetry and Prose*, 185.

31. It is unclear which edition Coleridge was reading, if indeed he was reading one at all; Wordsworth owned the 1617 edition, and Coleridge may have borrowed his copy.

32. Purchas, *Purchas His Pilgrimage*, "Epistle Dedicatorie," 2.

33. Ibid., "To the Reader," 1.

34. Ibid., 2.

35. Ibid., "Epistle Dedicatorie," 2, 3.

36. Throughout his career Edward Said insisted that what he called "secular criticism" was equivalent to worldly criticism; his overt target was nationalism, not religion, and yet in his account nationalist modes of belonging seem isomorphic with religious affiliation. By insisting on the "worldly" nature of Purchas and "Kubla Khan," I am distinguishing between these two modes of Said's work, insisting on a kind of criticism that is secular only in the worldly sense; indeed, it is only because it is "religious" that it can be worldly. See Edward W. Said, "Secular Criticism," in *The World, The Text, and the Critic* (Cambridge, Mass.: Harvard University Press, 1983), 1–30; see also Aamir R. Mufti, "Auerbach in Istanbul: Edward Said, Secular Criticism, and the Question of Minority Culture," *Critical Inquiry* 25, 1 (Autumn 1998): 95–125; and Mufti, "Orientalism and the Institution of World Literatures."

37. In the Crew manuscript, our only MS of the poem, Coleridge first wrote "Amora."

38. Leask, "Kubla Khan and Orientalism," 4. Leask goes on to argue that Coleridge seems to be backing away from his attraction to this idealized and eroticized primitive

Christianity already by 1802, in "The Picture," when the maid appears as a "watery idol" (line 83), and even more so by 1816, when in the "Preface" to "Kubla Khan" Coleridge quotes "The Picture" as an example of how such idols disappear.

39. One of Purchas's own important sources offers a similar account: *De Emendatione Temporum* (1583) by the great French Huguenot scholar Joseph Justus Scaliger, a pioneer of comparative history. This version of events can also be found in Sir Thomas Herbert, *Some Years' Travels into Divers Parts of Africa and Asia the Great* (London, 1677); Hiob Ludolf, *Historia aethiopica* (Frankfurt, 1681; trans. 1682); and James Bruce, *Travels to Discover the Source of the Nile* (1790). The same account is the source for the Happy Valley of Johnson's *Rasselas*.

40. "I have seene a Manuscript in old French, pretended to be a Letter from Prester John, to the Emperor Frederike, wherin is discoursed of the site, greatnes, puissance, wealth, and other rarities of his estate: but finding so many monsters, and uncouth relations therin, I could not be so prodigall of faith or penurious of judgement, as to value his authoritie at any high rate." Purchas, *Purchas His Pilgrimage*, 560.

41. Harrison, *"Religion" and the Religions in the English Enlightenment*, 174.

42. Purchas, *Purchas His Pilgrimage*, 567. We can begin to see, perhaps, why Purchas disallowed a theory of Prester John that would have put Ethiopia in contact with China. The religions of the Far East, like those of the rest of Africa, remain for him in the vague category of the idolatrous or pagan religions, held apart from the intertwined histories of Judaism, Christianity, and Islam. It would be two hundred years before Western scholars of religion began carving up that fourth category.

43. Rather than a false paradise. In *Paradise Lost* Milton tells his reader that Mount Amara, home of the "Abássin kings" is "by some supposed / True Paradise" (4.280, 281–82). Milton may have drawn directly on Purchas, or on Peter Heylyn's *Cosmographie* (1652), which itself drew substantially from Purchas's remarkable chapter-long description of Amara in the *Pilgrimage*: "Heaven and Earth, Nature and Industry . . . all presenting their best presents, to make it of this so lovely presence, some taking this for the place of our Fore-fathers Paradise." Purchas, *Purchas His Pilgrimage*, 565.

44. Edward Herbert, *The antient religion of the gentiles, and causes of their errors considered, By the learned judicious Edward Ld Herbert of Cherbury* (London, 1711), 4.

45. Even if the idea of God *were* universal, Locke continues, that would not prove it innate: "I doubt not, but if a Colony of young Children should be placed in an Island, where no Fire was, they would certainly neither have any Notion of such a thing, nor Name for it. . . . And perhaps too, their Apprehensions would be as far removed from any Name, or Notion of a God, till some one amongst them had imployed his Thoughts, to inquire into the Constitution and Causes of things, which would easily lead him to the Notion of a God." It is reason, not intuition, that leads us "easily" to God. John Locke, *An Essay Concerning Human Understanding*, ed. Peter H. Nidditch (Oxford: Clarendon, 1975), I.iv.14, 11 (93, 90). For the full discussion see I.iv.7–17.

46. John Dunn, "The Claim to Freedom of Conscience," *From Persecution to Toleration: The Glorious Revolution and Religion in England* (New York: Oxford University Press, 1991), esp. 172–78.

47. Locke, *A Letter Concerning Toleration*, 48.

48. See, for example, Wills, "The Day the Enlightenment Went Out"; Lilla, *The Stillborn God*; Berman, *The Flight of the Intellectuals*; Ali, "Blind Faiths"; on neoconservative attempts to influence Islam, see Mahmood, "Secularism, Hermeneutics, and Empire"; on Dawkins and the so-called "new atheism," see Terry Eagleton, *Reason, Faith, and Revolution: Reflections on the God Debate* (New Haven, Conn.: Yale University Press, 2009).

49. Jürgen Habermas, "Religion in the Public Sphere," *European Journal of Philosophy* 14, 1 (2006): 17.

CHAPTER 5. HIPPOGRIFFS IN THE LIBRARY

Epigraphs: Hume, "Of Superstition and Enthusiasm," 5; Walter Scott, "Introduction," in *The Castle of Otranto: A Gothic Story, By the Honorable Horace Walpole. With Critical Introduction* (Edinburgh: James Ballantyne, 1811), xvii.

1. England and Scotland had shared a king from the time of James I, but Scotland had maintained a separate parliament. In England, the Act of Settlement of 1701 ensured that the Crown would pass to the Protestant House of Hanover; but Scotland's Parliament had made no such provision, and the possibility therefore arose that Scotland might choose a different monarch on the death of Queen Anne.

2. James Chandler, *England in 1819: The Politics of Literary Culture and the Case of Romantic Historicism* (Chicago: University of Chicago Press, 1999), 94–349; Duncan, *Scott's Shadow*, 1–69; see also Jerome J. McGann, "Walter Scott's Romantic Postmodernity," in *Scotland and the Borders of Romanticism*, ed. Leith Davis, Ian Duncan, and Janet Sorensen (Cambridge: Cambridge University Press, 2004), 113–29.

3. Paul Hamilton, *Metaromanticism: Aesthetics, Literature, Theory* (Chicago: University of Chicago Press, 2003), 125, 138.

4. Scott, *Waverley*, 489.

5. Ian Duncan, "Introduction," in *Rob Roy*, ed. Ian Duncan (Oxford: Oxford University Press, 1998), ix. Duncan offers an ingenious complication of this straightforward argument by suggesting that we view the visit as a kind of avant-garde performance piece.

6. Scott, *Waverley*, 410, 415; Austen, *Emma*, 7.

7. Walter Scott, unsigned review of *Emma*, *Quarterly Review* 14 (March 1816): 188–201; reprinted in Southam, *Jane Austen*, 1: 58–69, 59, 60.

8. Ibid., 1:59, 64, 64, 68, 68; for an argument that Austen's everyday is more disruptive than regulatory, see Galperin, *The Historical Austen*.

9. Richard Whately, unsigned review of *Northanger Abbey* and *Persuasion*," *Quarterly Review* 24 (January 1821): 352–76; reprinted in Southam, *Jane Austen*, 94.

10. Churchmen like Tillotson, Burnet, and Stillingfleet were willing to go a certain way with the new religious and scientific thinking emanating from Continental Europe. Locke pushed considerably further. As we have seen, a good portion of Locke's theory of tolerance involved rejecting doctrines and creeds that subverted the ideal of a church as a "voluntary Society of Men, joining themselves together at their own accord." While the

doctrine of the atonement might be subject to endless dispute, everything important in Christianity boiled down to a self-evident message. See for example Locke, *A Letter Concerning Toleration*, 67.

11. Newton, *An Historical Account of Two Notable Corruptions of Scripture: In a Letter to a Friend*; qtd. in Amos Funkenstein, *Theology and the Scientific Imagination from the Middle Ages to the Seventeenth Century* (Princeton, N.J.: Princeton University Press, 1989), 89–90; for an account of how "mystical" comes to mean that which eludes direct knowledge, see Michel de Certeau, *The Mystic Fable: The Sixteenth and Seventeenth Centuries*, trans. Michael B. Smith (Chicago: University of Chicago Press, 1992), esp. 1: 97; also Israel, *Radical Enlightenment*, esp. 245.

12. Shapin and Schaffer, *Leviathan and the Air-Pump*, 63, 61, 62; for further commentary, see Jonathan Lamb, *The Rhetoric of Suffering: Reading the Book of Job in the Eighteenth Century* (New York: Oxford University Press, 1995), 67–68; and McKeon, *The Secret History of Domesticity*, 66–67.

13. Niklas Luhmann, *Observations on Modernity*, trans. William Whobrey (Stanford, Calif.: Stanford University Press, 1998), 48, 58.

14. De Certeau, *The Mystic Fable*, 1:123.

15. Locke, *An Essay Concerning Human Understanding*, 508; John Locke, "Some Thoughts Concerning Education," in *The Works of John Locke in Nine Volumes*, 12th ed. (London: Rivington, 1824), 8: 167.

16. William Warburton, *Divine Legation of Moses Demonstrated, on the Principles of a Religious Deist, from the Omission of the Doctrine of a Future State of Reward and Punishment in the Jewish Dispensation. In Nine Books. . . . The Third Edition, Corrected and Enlarged*, vol. 2, 3rd ed. (London: Printed for the executor of the late Mr. Fletcher Gyles, 1742), 2.5.v., 452, 453.

17. For discussion of Warburton's technique, see Lamb, *The Rhetoric of Suffering*, 113; also John Milbank, *The Word Made Strange: Theology, Language, Culture* (Oxford: Wiley-Blackwell, 1997), 55–63; on Warburton's career, see B. W. Young, *Religion and Enlightenment in Eighteenth-Century England: Theological Debate from Locke to Burke* (Oxford: Clarendon, 1998).

18. Warburton, *Divine Legation*, 2:453.

19. Jonathan I. Israel, "Spinoza, Locke, and the Enlightenment Battle for Toleration," in *Toleration in Enlightenment Europe*, ed. Ole Peter Grell and Roy Porter (Cambridge: Cambridge University Press, 2006), 102–13; Charles Taylor, "Modes of Secularism," in *Secularism and Its Critics*, ed. Rajeev Bhargava (Delhi: Oxford University Press, 1998), 31–53.

20. Israel, *Radical Enlightenment*, 153, 359ff., demonstrates that a materialist analysis of pagan religious mystification was commonplace across the European moderate Enlightenment.

21. Warburton, *Divine Legation*, 2:545; see also Young, *Religion and Enlightenment* , 190ff.

22. Lamb, *The Rhetoric of Suffering*, 88.

23. Faced with the intolerable possibility that Job was a real person who underwent real, unwarranted suffering at God's hands without the secret comfort of a future blessed state to sustain him, Warburton overcomes his usual objection to allegory and declares the book "wholly Allegorical," with Job representing the nation of Israel during the Babylonian captivity. He writes with evident relief that the allegorical method "renders one of the most difficult and obscure Books in the whole Canon of Scripture the most easy and intelligible." Not, of course, easy and intelligible to Job, who is reduced on Warburton's reading to utterances whose purport he never understands. But this is better than the "difficult and obscure" alternative, according to which the book itself becomes a document of the unresolved tension between Job's complaint and his friends' consolation. See Warburton, *Divine Legation*, 2: 508, 544.

24. David Hume, *An Enquiry Concerning Human Understanding with A Letter from a Gentleman to His Friend in Edinburgh*, ed. Eric Steinberg (Indianapolis: Hackett, 1977), 115 (hereafter *E*). Though the *Enquiry* appeared in 1748, the miracles essay itself was extant probably from 1737.

25. Richard Hurd, "The Life of the Author," in *The Divine Legation of Moses Demonstrated, by the Right Reverend William Warburton, D.D., Lord Bishop of Gloucester, to Which Is Prefixed an Account of the Life, Writings, and Character of the Author, by Richard Hurd, D.D., Lord Bishop of Worcester*, vol. 1 (London: Printed for Thomas Tegg and Son, 1837), 1: 12. Hurd added this biographical sketch to his 1794 edition of Warburton's *Divine Legation*.

26. The first sermon is a more straightforwardly nationalist production, contrasting the "Yoke of *Rome,* now ready to be once more cast upon your Necks," with the "*Liberty in which Christ has set you free.*" William Warburton, *A Sermon Occasioned by the Present Unnatural Rebellion. . . . Preached in Mr. Allen's Chapel at Prior-Park near Bath, . . . By William Warburton* (London: Printed for J. and P. Knapton, 1745), 16, 18.

27. William Warburton, *The Nature of National Offences Truly Stated: . . . A Sermon Preached on the General Fast Day, Appointed to Be Observed December 18, 1745. By William Warburton* (London, 1745), 12.

28. Hurd, "The Life of the Author," 40–41.

29. David Hume, *A Treatise of Human Nature*, ed. L. A. Selby-Bigge and R. N. Nidditch, 2nd ed. (Oxford: Clarendon, 1978), 264.

30. Hume indeed felt himself "left utterly abandoned and disconsolate" when in 1745 he was denied an academic appointment at Edinburgh. Attacked by the masters and clergy at Edinburgh for "Heresy, Deism, Scepticism, Atheism & c." and abandoned by his friends, Hume discovered that his rhetorical pose in the *Treatise* had sprung to life: "everyone keeps at a distance, and dreads that storm, which beats upon me from every side." His later attempts to make light of his philosophical conclusions are hardly convincing. See J. Y. T. Greig, ed., *The Letters of David Hume* (Oxford: Oxford University Press, 2011), 1: 57.

31. William Warburton, *Letters from a Late Eminent Prelate to One of His Friends*, 2nd ed. (London: Printed for T. Cadell and W. Davies, 1809), 14.

32. William Warburton, "Letter to Francis Kilvert, 8 June 1755," in *A Selection from the Unpublished Papers of William Warburton* (London: John Bowyer Nichols and Son, 1841), 257.

33. Hume to Charles Erskine, 13 February 1748; Greig, *The Letters of David Hume*, 1: 112. For background see E. C. Mossner, *The Life of David Hume* (Edinburgh: Thomas Nelson, 1954), 180.

34. David Hume, "Of the Protestant Succession," in *Essays Moral, Political, and Literary*, ed. Eugene F. Miller (Indianapolis: Liberty Classics, 1985), 507.

35. I construe the distinction between Hume's philosophical and literary ambitions rather differently than does John Bender, who emphasizes Hume's transition from the "learned" context of philosophy to the "conversable" world of the literary essay. On my reading, by contrast, there is a dark and unpredictable element to Hume's literary endeavors. See John Bender, *Ends of Enlightenment* (Stanford, Calif.: Stanford University Press, 2012), 79–91. On freethinking as a stabilizing force in the eighteenth century, see Sarah Ellenzweig, *The Fringes of Belief: English Literature, Ancient Heresy, and the Politics of Freethinking, 1660–1760* (Stanford, Calif.: Stanford University Press, 2008).

36. Hume, *A Treatise of Human Nature*, 269.

37. Ibid., 270; see also Lamb, *The Rhetoric of Suffering*, 89.

38. The Dutchman Christiaan Huygens's 1657 treatise *De Ratiociniis in Ludo Aleae* (On Reasoning in Games of Chance) was the first book of probability theory; Abraham de Moive, an expatriot Huguenot and Royal Society member, developed the idea of the distribution curve in *The Doctrine of Chances* (first English translation 1718). Interestingly, the 1738 English translation of *Ludo Aleae* included some remarks on "hazard and backgammon," appended by the translator John Ham. See John Laird, *Hume's Philosophy of Human Nature* (London: Methuen, 1932), 127.

39. Lamb, *The Rhetoric of Suffering*, 89; also Bender, *Ends of Enlightenment*, 28–30.

40. Southam, *Jane Austen*, 1:68.

41. Scott, *Waverley*, 477.

42. Taylor, *A Secular Age*, 370.

43. Walter Scott, *Rob Roy*, ed. Ian Duncan (New York: Oxford University Press, 2008), 191. To suggest that the "Scottish problem" is really an *English* problem is of course a canny move for a Scottish man of letters busy turning an English literary heritage into a British one.

44. For some of the connections between Scottish Enlightenment historiography and Marxist historiography, see Chandler, *England in 1819*, 127–35.

45. Scott, *Waverley*, 492.

46. Scott, *Rob Roy*, 153.

47. Deirdre Lynch, "Gothic Libraries and National Subjects," *Studies in Romanticism* 40, 1 (2001): 32, 36.

48. For discussion of "binary" versus "dialectical" readings of modernity and enchantment, see Michael Saler, "Modernity and Enchantment: A Historiographic Review," *American Historical Review* 111, 3 (2006): 692–716.

49. This theme is so prominent in literary scholarship of the past quarter century that it defies bibliographic summary. See, for example, Terry Eagleton, *The Ideology of the Aesthetic* (Oxford: Wiley-Blackwell, 1990); John Guillory, *Cultural Capital: The Problem of Literary Canon Formation* (Chicago: University of Chicago Press, 1993); Clifford Siskin, *The Work of Writing: Literature and Social Change in Britain, 1700–1830* (Baltimore: Johns Hopkins University Press, 1998); Mary Poovey, *Genres of the Credit Economy: Mediating Value in Eighteenth- and Nineteenth-Century Britain* (Chicago: University of Chicago Press, 2008).

50. Lynch, "Gothic Libraries and National Subjects," 44; Eagleton, *Reason, Faith, and Revolution*, 44, 41.

51. Scott, *Rob Roy*, 200.

52. John Millar, *The Origin of the Distinction of Ranks, Or, An Inquiry into the Circumstances Which Give Rise to Influence and Authority, in the Different Members of Society.*, ed. Aaron Garrett, 4th ed. (Indianapolis: Liberty Fund, 2006), 140; for background, see Peter D. Garside, "Scott and the 'Philosophical' Historians," *Journal of the History of Ideas* 36, 3 (July 1, 1975): 497–512.

53. Scott, *Rob Roy*, 209, 213.

54. Virgil, *The Eclogues of Virgil*, trans. C. Day Lewis (London: Jonathan Cape, 1963), 37.

55. Scott, *Waverley*, 63; In *Redgauntlet* (1824), an account of a fictional Jacobite uprising, Scott again employs the figure as a mark of the ludicrous. See Walter Scott, *Redgauntlet*, ed. Kathryn Sutherland (Oxford: World's Classics, 1985), 35.

56. "[M]an is by his constitution a religious animal," writes Burke, yet it is possible that, "in the moment of riot, and in a drunken delirium from the hot spirit drawn out of the alembick of hell, which is in France now so furiously boiling," we might "uncover our nakedness by throwing off the Christian religion." Because "the mind will not endure a void," he continues, "some uncouth, pernicious, and degrading superstition," untethered from tradition and therefore wildly unpredictable, will rush in to take Christianity's place. Edmund Burke, *Reflections on the Revolution in France*, ed. L. G. Mitchell (Oxford: Oxford University Press, 1993), 91.

57. Scott, *Waverley*, 39; Burke, *Reflections*, 33.

58. Though Robert Boyle is traditionally credited with turning alchemy into proper chemistry, his own correspondence suggests that he retained a lifelong interest in transmutation. See Lawrence M. Principe, *The Aspiring Adept: Robert Boyle and His Alchemical Quest* (Princeton, N.J.: Princeton University Press, 2000). Long central to alchemy, distillation became in the early modern West virtually synonymous with esoteric knowledge. "Alembic" itself comes into English from the Arabic *Al-inbiq*—along with the process itself, which was invented in Persia in the eighth century. Distillation retained its association with the practices of astrology and curiosity collecting into the seventeenth century. See McKeon, *The Secret History of Domesticity*, 212–18.

59. Bennett, *The Tory Crisis*, 16.

60. John Toland, *Christianity Not Mysterious: Or, A Treatise Shewing, That There Is Nothing in the Gospel Contrary to Reason, Nor Above It: And That No Christian Doctrine*

Can Be Properly Call'd A Mystery. The Second Edition Enlarg'd (London: Printed for Sam. Buckley, 1696), xxii.

61. Charles Blount, *Great Is Diana of the Ephesians, Or, The Original of Idolatry Together with the Politick Institution of the Gentiles Sacrifices* (London, 1680), 3.

62. Qtd. in Amy Hungerford, "Postmodern Supernaturalism: Ginsberg and the Search for a Supernatural Language," *Yale Journal of Criticism* 18, 2 (2005): 283.

63. Thomas Carlyle, "Sir Walter Scott," in *Essays: Scottish and Other Miscellanies* (London: Dent, 1915), 66; qtd. in George Levine, *The Realistic Imagination: English Fiction from Frankenstein to Lady Chatterley* (Chicago: University of Chicago Press, 1983), 96.

64. Scott, "Introduction," *The Castle of Otranto: A Gothic Story, By the Honorable Horace Walpole. With Critical Introduction* (Edinburgh: James Ballantyne, 1811), xxiii, xxv.

65. F. R. Leavis, *The Great Tradition* (London: Chatto and Windus, 1960), 2, 8–9; Leavis's redemptive narrative is very much a nineteenth-century phenomenon; for a provocative reading of the eighteenth century novel as, by contrast, concerned overwhelmingly with tragedy and unintended harm, see Sandra Macpherson, *Harm's Way: Tragic Responsibility and the Novel Form* (Baltimore: Johns Hopkins University Press, 2010), esp. 1–24.

66. Levine, *The Realistic Imagination*, 5. For an account that traces the developing contrast between scientific fact and novelistic fiction during the eighteenth century, see Bender, *Ends of Enlightenment*, 38–56.

67. Stanley Cavell, *In Quest of the Ordinary: Lines of Skepticism and Romanticism* (Chicago: University of Chicago Press, 1994).

68. Scott, *Waverley*, 469.

CHAPTER 6. THE CREATION OF RELIGIOUS MINORITIES

1. Simpson, *Burning to Read*, 196.

2. Duffy, *The Stripping of the Altars*; Toulmin, *Cosmopolis*, 89–137; also Jacob, *The Cultural Meaning of the Scientific Revolution*; see also Amos Funkenstein: "This new, energetic ideal of knowing stood squarely against the old, contemplative ideal. Common to most ancient and medieval epistemologies was their receptive character: . . . knowledge or truth is found, not constructed." Funkenstein, *Theology and the Scientific Imagination*, 298.

3. Walter Scott, *Old Mortality*, ed. Jane Stevenson and Peter Davidson (New York: Oxford University Press, 1993), 438.

4. In 1560, inspired by the Protestant Elizabeth's accession to the English throne in 1558 and by the waves of Reformation still sweeping across the Continent, Scotland broke with the French and with Catholicism and established a national Reformed church. The Reformers were less successful at ridding themselves of the Episcopal polity that had been in place since Henry VIII, however, and both James I and Charles I attempted to use that political structure to nudge Scotland away from Presbyterianism and toward a High Anglican model.

5. *A Solemn League and Covenant for Reformation and Defence of Religion, the Honour and Happinesse of the King, and the Peace and Safety of the Three Kingdoms of England,*

Scotland, and Ireland, Early English Books Online (London: Printed for Edw. Husbands, Sept. 27, 1643), 4–5.

6. Oliver O'Donovan and Joan Lockwood O'Donovan, eds., *From Irenaeus to Grotius: A Sourcebook in Christian Political Thought 100–1625* (Grand Rapids, Mich.: Eerdmans, 1999), 551, 556.

7. As the ambiguous language of the Solemn League and Covenant indicates, the English Parliament was seeking a military alliance, while the Covenanters hoped to bring their Presbyterian reforms to England. When those failed to materialize, some of them, known as the "Engagers," made common cause with Charles I against Parliament. The "Kirk Party," who remained with Parliament, became known as the "Whigs" (*whiggamor* is the Gaelic word for "cattle driver").

8. "The Declaration and Testimony of the True Presbyterian, Anti-prelatic, Anti-erastian, persecuted party in Scotland. Published at Sanquhar, June 22, 1680," in Robert Simpson, *Traditions of the Covenanters; Or, Gleanings among the Mountains* (Edinburgh: John Johnston, 1846), 27.

9. Robert Wodrow, *The History of the Sufferings of the Church of Scotland, from the Restauration to the Revolution: Collected from the Publick Records, Original Papers, and Manuscripts of That Time, and Other Well Attested Narratives. By Mr. Robert Wodrow, Minister of the Gospel at Eastwood* (Edinburgh: Printed by James Watson, 1721), 2:500.

10. Ibid. For Wodrow's lengthy and famous account of the drownings of Margaret McLauchlan and Margaret Wilson, see ibid., 2:505–7.

11. Ibid., 2:499.

12. *A True Account of the Horrid Murther Committed Upon His Grace, the Late Lord Archbishop of St. Andrews, Primate and Metropolitan of All Scotland, and One of His Majesties Most Honourable Privy Council of That Kingdom. With a Detection of the Lyes Published in a Late Scandalous Relation of That Murther; and of the Pretended Occasion Thereof. Published by Authority*, Early English Books Online (Dublin: [s.n.], reprinted 1679, 1679), 4.

13. As a reward for this decisive action, God makes a covenant with Phinehas and his descendants: "Behold, I give unto him my covenant of peace, And he shall have it, and his seed after him, *even* the covenant of the Priest's office forever, because he was zealous for his God, and hath made an atonement for the children of Israel" (Numbers 25:12–13; Geneva Bible).

14. See Mark Juergensmeyer, *Terror in the Mind of God: The Global Rise of Religious Violence*, 3rd ed. (Berkeley: University of California Press, 2003), xi.

15. Scotland, Privy Council, *At Edinburgh, the Twelfth Day of December, One Thousand Six Hundred and Sixty Seven*, Early English Books Online (Edinburgh: Printed by Evan Tyler, Printer to the Kings most excellent Majesty, 1667), 1.

16. *A True Account of the Horrid Murther*, 7.

17. Mungo Murray, *On the Death and Horrid Murther of the Most Reverend Father in God, James Archbishop of Saint-Andrews, Lord Primate of Scotland*, 2nd ed. (Edinburgh, 1679), 1.

18. Scott, *Old Mortality*, 376; for good accounts of the novel, see Chandler, *England in 1819*, 212–16; George A. Drake, "'Fanciful Devotion': Ritualization in Scott's *Old Mortality*," *Studies in Romanticism* 49, 1 (2010): 133–51; Duncan, *Scott's Shadow*, 140–44.

19. Scott, *Old Mortality*, 376, emphasis added. See too Byron's use of the phrase "unquiet things" in the context of his discussion of Napoleon and other ambitious persons who have set the world aflame: "to whom add / Sophists, Bards, and Statesman, all unquiet things / Which stir too strongly the soul's secret springs." *Childe Harold's Pilgrimage*, Canto III, lines 381–83. Lord Byron, *Selected Poems*, ed. Susan J. Wolfson and Peter J. Manning (New York: Penguin, 1996), 428–29.

20. Scott, *Old Mortality*, 438.

21. Ibid., 377.

22. On anachronism, see Christensen, *Lord Byron's Strength*, 324; and *Romanticism at the End of History* (Baltimore: Johns Hopkins University Press, 2000).

23. Coleridge, *The Major Works*, 257; Coleridge is referring to Malcolm Laing, *The History of Scotland, From the Union of the Crowns on the Accession of James VI to the Throne of England, to the Union of the Kingdoms in the Reign of Queen Anne*, vol. 2 (London, 1800).

24. *The Letters of Sir Walter Scott*, ed. H. J. C. Grierson (London: Routledge & Kegan Paul, 1970), 8:376; qtd. in Hamilton, *Metaromanticism*, 130.

25. Coleridge, *The Major Works*, 256, 257. The phrasing is quite obscure here, but a paragraph earlier Coleridge suggests the link more clearly: "the Anabaptists' tenets," he writes, "differed only from those of Jacobinism by the substitution of theological for philosophical jargon" (256).

26. On the political use to which Scott puts the Covenanters, see Hamilton, *Metaromanticism*, 128–34; and Andrew D. Krull, "Spectacles of Disaffection: Politics, Ethics, and Sentiment in Walter Scott's Old Mortality," *ELH* 73, 3 (2006): 695–727.

27. Israel, *Radical Enlightenment*, 285.

28. Coleridge, *The Major Works*, 256; on the nascent working class, see E. P. Thompson, *The Making of the English Working Class* (New York: Pantheon, 1963). Thompson, of course, sees religious enthusiasm as entirely counter-revolutionary.

29. James Hogg, *The Private Memoirs and Confessions of a Justified Sinner*, ed. Adrian Hunter (Peterborough, Ont.: Broadview Press, 2001), 116.

30. Ibid., 50.

31. Linda Colley calls the Act of Union a process of inventing a distinctively British identity "superimposed over an array of internal differences in response to contact with the Other." Linda Colley, *Britons: Forging the Nation, 1707–1937* (New Haven, Conn.: Yale University Press, 1992), 6.

32. Hogg, *The Private Memoirs and Confessions of a Justified Sinner*, 56.

33. Georg Lukács, "The Historical Novel [excerpt]," in *Theory of the Novel: A Historical Approach*, ed. Michael McKeon (Baltimore: Johns Hopkins University Press, 2000), 249.

34. The editor remarks of Wringhim senior's version of predestination, for example, that "It would appear that this pharisaical doctrine is a very delicious one, and the most

grateful of all others to the worst characters" (90). This opinion echoes that of the servant John within the confession itself, who tells Wringhim senior, "Ye are the just Pharisee, sir, that gaed up wi' the poor publican to pray in the Temple; an' ye're acting the same pairt at this time, an' saying I' your heart, 'God, I thank thee that I am not as other men are'" (122–23). Here an interpretation of Wringhim senior's character within the text of the confession shapes the narrative that frames and introduces that confession.

35. Eve Kosofsky Sedgwick, *Between Men: English Literature and Male Homosocial Desire* (New York: Columbia University Press, 1985), 97–117.

36. Michael Warner, "Queer and Then?" *Chronicle Review—Chronicle of Higher Education*, 1 January 2012.

37. Again the joke is on the editor and his friends: as "literary" as they imagine themselves to be, they miss the pun: the hollow of Robert's soul is full of shit, which may be a comment on the truthfulness of his narrative or a graphic depiction of Calvinist depravity.

38. Wordsworth, *The Prelude* [1805], in William Wordsworth, *The Major Works*, ed. Stephen Gill (Oxford: Oxford University Press, 2000), 5:456–81.

39. Homer, *The Iliad*, trans. Richmond Lattimore (Chicago: University of Chicago Press, 1961), book 24, lines 603–17.

40. Benjamin, "Critique of Violence," 248, emphasis added.

41. Ibid. Benjamin contrasts mythic violence with divine violence, which suspends history and ordinary time. It comes out of nowhere: dispensing altogether with the realm of representation, it is immediately, suddenly, *there*.

42. Ibid., 250. Benjamin likely has Carl Schmitt in mind, especially the latter's claim that one may sacrifice oneself legitimately for the state; Carl Schmitt, *The Concept of the Political*, trans. George Schwab (Chicago: University of Chicago Press, 1996), esp. 35. Benjamin's account of sacrifice also distances his discussion from Kierkegaard's treatment of Abraham in *Fear and Trembling*, where the law is set aside for the sake of its preservation, secured by the substitutionary sacrifice of the ram.

43. Taylor, *A Secular Age*, 8; my description of Scott's empty characters follows the influential account in Lukács, *Theory of the Novel*, 232.

44. Warner, VanAntwerpen, and Calhoun, *Varieties of Secularism in a Secular Age*, 11–12; Sheehan, "When Was Disenchantment?"; Modern, *Secularism in Antebellum America*, 120–21.

45. See Partha Chatterjee, "Religious Minorities and the Secular State: Reflections on an Indian Impasse," *Public Culture* 8, 1 (1995): 12.

46. Saree Makdisi, "Said, Palestine, and the Humanism of Liberation," *Critical Inquiry* 31 (Winter 2005): 461; see also Stathis Gourgouris, "Transformation, Not Transcendence," *Boundary 2* 31, 2 (2004): 55–79; Homi K. Bhabha, "Untimely Ends: Homi K. Bhabha on Edward Said," *ArtForum* 42 (February 2004): 19; Lauren Berlant, *Cruel Optimism* (Durham, N.C.: Duke University Press, 2011).

47. For an argument that religion is itself structured by the internal rift named "blasphemy," see Colin Jager, "Crossing the Line: Blasphemy, Time, and Revelation," *Qui Parle* 22, 2 (2014).

PART III INTRODUCTION

Epigraph: Gilles Deleuze and Felix Guattari, "What Is a Minor Literature?" in *Kafka: Toward a Minor Literature*, trans. Dana Polan (Minneapolis: University of Minnesota Press, 1986), 27.

1. Victoria Kahn, *The Future of Illusion: Political Theology and Early Modern Texts* (Chicago: University of Chicago Press, 2014), 6. Kahn's picture of the early modern bears a strong though unremarked resemblance to those in Toulmin, *Cosmopolis*, and Hardt and Negri, *Empire*. As inspiring as these accounts are, their sharp contrast between literary humanism and state sovereignty tends to place religious uniformity solely on the reactive side of the ledger, a formation holding back a secular modernity understood as a teleological inevitability.

2. For a fascinating account of conversion along these lines, see Rob Wilson, *Be Always Converting, Be Always Converted: An American Poetics* (Cambridge, Mass.: Harvard University Press, 2009).

3. Deleuze and Guattari, "What Is a Minor Literature?" 16, 17.

4. Ibid., 19, 22.

5. Percy Bysshe Shelley, *The Revolt of Islam; A Poem, in Twelve Cantos* (London, 1818), lines 3111–12; canto 7, stanza 32.

6. Shelley, *Shelley's Poetry and Prose*, 512.

7. Deleuze and Guattari, "What Is a Minor Literature?" 17.

CHAPTER 7. BYRON AND THE PARADOX OF READING

Epigraph: Cleanth Brooks, "The Language of Paradox," in *The Well Wrought Urn: Studies in the Structure of Poetry* (San Diego: Harvest, 1947), 11.

1. Juergensmeyer, *Terror in the Mind of God*, 70.

2. The question of motivation and belief matters because we normally distinguish terrorist violence from other forms of violence precisely on the grounds of intention. Familiar military or political motivations (we wanted to control that outpost, command that hill, exploit those resources, and so on) take a back seat to different kinds of intention, which aim to disrupt normal life and thereby bring about a new psychological reality in which the usual assumptions no longer hold. Motivation, always a tricky affair even in the clearest of circumstances, thus becomes highly overdetermined when the issue is religiously motivated violence.

3. Byron, *Selected Poems*, 204.

4. In putting matters this way it might seem that I have fallen into the Byronic trap of taking expressions of fidelity too seriously. Maybe the joke is on the naive reader, who fails to see that for the Byronic hero all objects of desire are basically equivalent. For an explication of this point, see Jerome Christensen, "Perversion, Parody, and Cultural Hegemony: Lord Byron's Oriental Tales," *South Atlantic Quarterly* 88, 3 (1989): 569–603. To some extent, Christensen's approach represents a challenge to my approach in this

essay. Yet the Giaour's fidelity is an intensely serious parody, and so the point of such parody is that we take fidelity seriously, and do not take it seriously, simultaneously. This is not unlike Christensen's point that to write oppositionally Byron had to write against Byronism itself.

5. Asad, "Thinking About Religion, Belief and Politics"; and Smith, *Faith and Belief*.

6. Brooks, "The Language of Paradox," 11.

7. Guillory, *Cultural Capital*, 159.

8. See the analysis in Mahmood, "Secularism, Hermeneutics, and Empire," esp. 329.

9. The link between Byron and Brooks may seem odd, given the New Criticism's hostility toward romanticism. In my judgment, the evident similarity between their models of close reading is enough to make the comparison stick; however, two other justifications may be offered. First, Brooks's celebration of paradox over orthodoxy evinces a wariness of religiously inspired confidence, and a similar faith in the ability of literary language to redirect its worst effects, that would shortly be taken up by romantic humanists like Abrams; the sociohistorical context for both critical movements—postwar anomie, the developing cold war, religious ecumenicism—is the same. Second, it may be that Byron's amenability to Brooksian close reading provides us with another way into the often-remarked fact that Byron is an odd sort of romantic writer. It is no coincidence, surely, that Abrams essentially leaves him out of *Natural Supernaturalism*. Taken together, these two justifications begin to suggest how Byron both is and is not romantic in the sense constructed by postwar humanism: his faith in the literary partakes of the same spirit and yet remains, somehow, *different*.

10. Byron, *Selected Poems*, 1.482 (page 224); 1.210 (page 256).

11. Christensen makes the more complicated point that this moment in *The Giaour* both invites reading and resists it in the name of a superficial, repetitive appropriation— what Brooks, though not Christensen, might call paraphrase. Christensen, "Perversion, Parody, and Cultural Hegemony," 580.

12. Said, *Orientalism*; Marilyn Butler, "The Orientalism of Byron's Giaour," in *Byron and the Limits of Fiction*, ed. Bernard Beatty (Liverpool: Liverpool University Press, 1988), 78.

13. In *The Revolt of Islam* (1818), Shelley describes a similar scene, though the dynamics are less stylized and much more complex than Byron's; see bk. 5, stanza 25.

14. See in particular this passage from *A Secular Age*: "The multiplicity of faiths has little effect as long as it is neutralized by the sense that being like them is not really an option for me. As long as the alternative is strange and other . . . so long will their difference not undermine my embedding in my own faith. This changes when through increased contact, interchange, even perhaps intermarriage, the other becomes more and more like me, in everything else but faith: same activities, professions, opinions, tastes, etc. Then the issue posed by difference becomes more insistent: why my way, and not hers? There is no other difference left to make the shift preposterous or unimaginable." Taylor, *A Secular Age*, 304.

15. *Bill Moyers on Faith and Reason*, 30 June 2006, http://www.pbs.org/moyers/faithandreason/print/faithandreason102_print.html.

CHAPTER 8. THE CONSTELLATIONS OF ROMANTIC RELIGION

Epigraph: Friedrich Schleiermacher, *On Religion: Speeches to Its Cultured Despisers*, trans. Richard Crouter (Cambridge: Cambridge University Press, 1996), 27.

1. Karen Armstrong, "Bill Moyers Interviews Karen Armstrong" (PBS), 1 March 2002, http://www.pbs.org/now/transcript/transcript_armstrong.html; Pew Forum on Religion and Public Life, *"Nones" on the Rise* (Pew Research Center, 9 October 2012), http://www.pewforum.org/Unaffiliated/nones-on-the-rise-religion.aspx; Amy Hollywood, "Spiritual But Not Religious," *Harvard Divinity Bulletin* 38, 1/2 (Spring 2010): 19–23.

2. *On Being, with Krista Tippett*, American Public Media, accessed 11 March 2013, http://www.onbeing.org/about; Armstrong, "Bill Moyers Interviews Karen Armstrong"; Terrence Malick, *The Tree of Life* (Fox Searchlight, 2011); Taylor, *A Secular Age*, 5. The description of Tippett's show continues: "Krista envisioned a program that would draw out the intellectual and spiritual content of religion that should nourish our common life, but that is often obscured precisely when religion enters the news. Our sustained growth as a show has also been nurtured by a cultural shift that seeks conversation, shared life, and problem-solving within and across religious traditions and across categories of belief and non-belief."

3. Masuzawa, *The Invention of World Religions*, 2.

4. For rich intellectual background, see Hans Aarsleff, *The Study of Language in England 1780–1860* (Princeton, N.J.: Princeton University Press, 1967); and Robert E. Norton, *Herder's Aesthetics and the European Enlightenment* (Ithaca, N.Y.: Cornell University Press, 1991).

5. On the pop culture dimensions of this zeitgeist, see Victoria Nelson, *The Secret Life of Puppets* (Cambridge, Mass.: Harvard University Press, 2001); Christopher Partridge, *The Re-Enchantment of the West: Alternative Spiritualities, Sacralization, Popular Culture and Occulture*, vol. 1 (London: T & T Clark, 2005); Jeffrey J. Kripal, *Esalen: America and the Religion of No Religion* (Chicago: University of Chicago Press, 2008); Jeffrey J. Kripal, *Authors of the Impossible: The Paranormal and the Sacred* (Chicago: University of Chicago Press, 2010); Victoria Nelson, *Gothicka: Vampire Heroes, Human Gods, and the New Supernatural* (Cambridge, Mass.: Harvard University Press, 2012); For a more philosophical discussion, see Leigh Eric Schmidt, *Restless Souls: The Making of American Spirituality* (San Francisco: Harper San Francisco, 2005); Hollywood, "Spiritual But Not Religious"; Courtney Bender, *The New Metaphysicals: Spirituality and the American Religious Imagination* (Chicago: University of Chicago Press, 2010); Modern, *Secularism in Antebellum America*, 119–82.

6. Legaspi, *The Death of Scripture*, 3.

7. Taylor, *A Secular Age*; McKeon, *The Secret History of Domesticity*.

8. "As a text, an object of critical analysis, the Bible came into clearer focus; however, as Scripture, the Bible became increasingly opaque." Legaspi, *The Death of Scripture*, 4.

9. Sheehan, *The Enlightenment Bible*, ix.

10. Lowth was known more in his own lifetime for his work on grammar than for his biblical scholarship. He became a member of the Royal Society in 1765. From 1766 to 1777 he was bishop of Oxford, and from 1777 until his death ten years later he was bishop of London. Lowth's *Isaiah, a new Translation, with a Preliminary Dissertation, and Notes, Critical, Philological, and Explanatory* appeared in 1778.

11. Thus the interest in Hebrew poetry, developed in part in order to defend against the dangers of a simpleminded Lockean literalism that seemed dangerously materialist, itself opened the door for a different kind of spiritual humanism that came to be called, in due course, the Higher Criticism. In the Oxford audience for the second of Lowth's lectures was a young student named Johann David Michealis, who would go on to become the greatest German biblical scholar of his generation. Some ten years later, when the Latin text of Lowth's lectures finally appeared in print, as *Praelectiones Academicae de Sacra Poesi Hebraeorum* (1753), Michaelis quickly produced his own Latin edition of the lectures. This edition, published in Göttingen in 1758, was less expensive than Lowth's 1753 volume; just as important, it contained many of Michaelis's own observations and "corrections" in the form of a long preface, many notes, and four lengthy appendices. The names of Lowth and Michaelis would henceforth be linked: when Lowth's own lectures were eventually translated into English by George Gregory in 1787, as *Lectures on the Sacred Poetry of the Hebrews*, the edition included a selection of the "admirable criticisms of the learned Michaelis." Further English editions likewise included Michaelis's commentary, and the 1830 Oxford edition of Lowth's *Lectures* is in fact a translation of Michaelis's Göttingen edition. See Robert Lowth, *Lectures on the Sacred Poetry of the Hebrews; Translated from the Latin of the Right Rev. Robert Lowth, D. D. Late Praelector of Poetry in the University of Oxford, and Now Lord Bishop of London, by G. Gregory, F. A. S. Author of Essays Historical and Moral. To Which Are Added, The Principal Notes of Professor Michaelis, and Notes by the Translator and Others*, vol. 1 (London: Printed for J. Johnson, 1787), Preface, xi. Subsequent references will be to volume, lecture, and page number of this edition. When Lowth issued a second Latin edition of the lectures in 1763, he placed Michaelis's various interventions in a separate volume.

12. Lowth, *Lectures*, 1.2.44; 1.4.100.

13. Ibid., 1.2.45, 46. Lowth famously argued that repetition or "parallelism" was the central technique of the Hebrew poets: "The Hebrew poets frequently express a sentiment with the utmost brevity and simplicity, illustrated by no circumstances, adorned with no epithets. . . . They afterwards call in the aid of ornament; they repeat, they vary, they amplify the same sentiment; and adding one or more sentences which run parallel to each other, they express the same or a similar, and often a contrary sentiment in nearly the same form of words." Lowth, *Lectures* 1.4.100.

14. Lowth, *Lectures*, 1.5.113.

15. Ibid.

16. Ibid., 1.5.104.

17. Ibid., 1.5.115.

18. Ibid., 1.5.116.

19. Though their delayed effect was very powerful. By the last quarter of the century the *Lectures* had been widely disseminated in a variety of forms: through Gregory's 1787 translation; through monthly installments in the *Christian's Magazine* in 1767; through Lowth's translation of Isaiah, published in 1778, which summarized the *Lectures*. Hugh Blair also summarized Lowth's lectures in his widely read *Lectures on Rhetoric and Belles Lettres* (1783). Blair's *Lectures* also exerted a crucial influence on Kant's *Anthropology from a Pragmatic Point of View* (1798), especially Kant's account of the native eloquence of savage peoples. For scholars of English literary romanticism, the most famous example of Lowth's delayed influence is William Wordsworth's "Preface" to the 1800 edition of *Lyrical Ballads*. Coleridge had attended Eichhorn's lectures in Göttingen in 1798, and passed on what he heard to Wordsworth. In Germany, meanwhile, the case was rather different. Mid-century German intellectuals read English literature and literary theory avidly; Michaelis and others were appropriately entranced by Lowth's claims for the intrinsic poeticality of the Hebrews. Michaelis himself was quickly surpassed in Germany by his student Eichhorn and by others who were willing to take the new philological scholarship farther: within the world of German post-Kantianism, the ambition to write a philosophy that replaced religion seemed for a time axiomatic. Long after his star had waned in Germany, however, Michaelis enjoyed great influence in the more cautious theological context of the English nineteenth century. And thanks in part to Michaelis's enduring influence, Lowth's ideas were reimported back to his native England, where a more expansive notion of the relation of poetry and culture could finally take root a generation later. For more context, see Prickett, *Words and the Word*, 50, 84, 117; Sheehan, *The Enlightenment Bible*, 150.

20. See Olender, *The Languages of Paradise*, 37–39.

21. The origin of language was, as Alexander Regier notes, the "obsession of a generation." Rousseau, Herder, Hamann, A. W. Schlegel, Warburton, Lord Monboddo, Hugh Blair, and many others had a theory to offer. See Alexander Regier, "Figuring It Out: The Origin of Language and Anthropomorphism," *Forum for Modern Language Studies* 42, 4 (2006): 413.

22. Johann Gottfried Herder, *Philosophical Writings*, trans. and ed. Michael N. Forster (Cambridge: Cambridge University Press, 2002), 90, emphasis in original. Unless otherwise noted, all Herder quotations come from this edition; *TO* = *Treatise on the Origin of Language* (1772); *TT* = *This Too a Philosophy of History for the Formation of Humanity* (1774).

23. J. G. Herder, *The Spirit of Hebrew Poetry*, trans. James Marsh (Burlington, Vt.: Edward Smith, 1833), 21; hereafter SHP. A proper dictionary of these languages, Herder had declared in the *Treatise*, "would be a map of the course of the human spirit" (*TO* 101).

24. In view of some of the criticisms Herder has received on this score, it is important to distinguish his picture of cultural difference from the racist implications of

Enlightenment-era theories based on geographic determinism. Indeed, Herder saved some of his bitterest irony for this view (which he associated with Voltaire, among others).

25. Immanuel Kant, *The Conflict of the Faculties*, in *Immanuel Kant: Religion and Rational Theology*, trans. and ed. Allen W. Wood and George di Giovanni (Cambridge: Cambridge University Press, 1996), 247.

26. About this distinction Hamann remarked in a letter: "The distinction between public and private use of reason is [altogether] comic. . . . Of what use is to me the festive dress of freedom if I wear the costume of the slave at home?" Hamann to C. J. Krause, 18 December 1784; qtd. in "Translator's Introduction" to *Religion within the Boundaries of Mere Reason*, in Wood and di Giovanni, *Immanuel Kant: Religion and Rational Theology*, 47 n. f.

27. Indeed, one purpose of Kant's distinction is to help him escape censorship in a 1790s Prussia nervously watching the events in France. He was unsuccessful in this. When Kant published *The Conflict of the Faculties* in 1798, he included in his "Preface" Frederick William II's royal rescript demanding that he cease all publications on religion, and his private response promising to obey. Kant considered himself released from this promise after Frederick William died.

28. Prickett, *Words and the Word*, 1.

29. Ibid., 198.

30. Immanuel Kant, "An Answer to the Question: What Is Enlightenment?" in *Philosophical Writings*, ed. Ernst Behler, trans. Lewis White Beck (New York: Continuum, 1986), 266.

31. See Talal Asad's now well-known gloss on this these developments: "the construction of religion as a new historical object: anchored in personal experience, expressible as belief-statements, dependent on private institutions, and practiced in one's spare time." Asad, *Genealogies of Religion*, 207.

32. On Kant and Schleiermacher, see Graham Ward, *True Religion* (London: Wiley-Blackwell, 2003), 84ff.

33. Immanuel Kant, *Critique of Pure Reason*, trans. Norman Kemp Smith, unabridged ed. (New York: St. Martin's, 1965), 314 (A 320), 65 (A 19).

34. Herder, *TO* 101.

35. Schleiermacher, *On Religion*, 22.

36. Ibid., 17.

37. Particular religious traditions would be simply local manifestations of a global impulse, and in the nineteenth century this fully essentialized "religion" entered the domains of disciplinary knowledge, particularly anthropology and religious studies. See Asad, *Genealogies of Religion*, 27–54; see also Bender, *The New Metaphysicals*, 8; Wayne Proudfoot, *Religious Experience* (Berkeley: University of California Press, 1985); Russell T. McCutcheon, *Manufacturing Religion: The Discourse on Sui Generis Religion and the Politics of Nostalgia* (New York: Oxford University Press, 1997); Masuzawa, *The Invention of World Religions*.

38. Lowth, *Lectures*, 1.5.115, 116.

39. Ibid., 1.5.113–14.

40. Compare Hugh Blair's redaction of Lowth: "it is necessary that we transport ourselves as much as we can into the land of Judea; and place before our eyes that scenery, and those objects, with which the Hebrew Writers were conversant." Here the emphasis remains on moving oneself rather than being moved. The act of imaginative sympathy originates in the agent. Blair, *Lectures*, 3:198.

41. Schleiermacher, *On Religion*, 26.

42. Ibid., 26–27.

43. Manfred Frank, *The Philosophical Foundations of Early German Romanticism*, trans. Elizabeth Millan-Zaibert (Albany: State University of New York Press, 2004), 33, 40, 65.

44. Schulte-Sasse et al., *Theory as Practice*, 321.

45. Walter Benjamin, *The Arcades Project*, ed. Rolf Tiedemann, trans. Howard Eiland and Kevin McLaughlin (Cambridge, Mass.: Belknap Press of Harvard University Press, 2002), 462; hereafter *AP*. For helpful exposition of the constellation image see Christopher Rollason, "The Passageways of Paris: Walter Benjamin's Arcades Project and Contemporary Cultural Debate in the West," 23 October 2010, http://www.wbenjamin .org/passageways.html. For Benjamin's comments on Schlegel, see Walter Benjamin, "The Concept of Criticism in German Romanticism," in Benjamin, *Selected Writings*, vol. 1, *1913–1926*, ed. Marcus Bullock and Michael W. Jennings (Cambridge, Mass.: Belknap Press of Harvard University Press, 1996), 116–200.

46. Benjamin, "Theses on the Philosophy of History," *Illuminations*, ed. Hannah Arendt, trans. Harry Zohn (New York: Schocken, 1968), 263. Hereafter *T*.

47. "The time line encounters kairotic knots, moments whose nature and placing calls for reversal," writes Taylor. For Taylor those "higher times" have withdrawn. See Taylor, *A Secular Age*, 54.

48. Percy Bysshe Shelley, *The Revolt of Islam; A Poem, in Twelve Cantos* (London, 1818), lines 3087–90.

49. William Keach, *Shelley's Style* (New York: Methuen, 1984), 39. See also Keach's account of gender and the subtler language in Keach, *Arbitrary Power: Romanticism, Language, Politics* (Princeton, N.J.: Princeton University Press, 2004), 95–121.

50. The setting of the poem in Constantinople is incidental to the plot; Christianity is always for Shelley the type of organized religion.

51. See Percy Bysshe Shelley, *The Complete Poetry of Percy Bysshe Shelley*, ed. Donald H. Reiman, Neil Fraistat, and Nora Crook, vol. 3 (Baltimore: Johns Hopkins University Press, 2012), 552.

52. Wasserman, *The Subtler Language*, 10–11.

53. Taylor, *A Secular Age*, 351; Taylor quotes this same passage from Wasserman in both *A Secular Age* (353) and *Sources of the Self* (381).

54. Reiman, Fraistat, and Crook, *The Complete Poetry of Percy Bysshe Shelley*, 3:1073.

55. Shelley, *Shelley's Poetry and Prose*, 532.

56. Ibid., 512.

57. Schulte-Sasse et al., *Theory as Practice*, 320.

CHAPTER 9. SHELLEY AFTER ATHEISM

Epigraph: Edmund Burke, *Reflections on the Revolution in France*, ed. L. G. Mitchell (Oxford: Oxford University Press, 1993), 9.

1. On *The Necessity of Atheism*, see Michael Scrivener, *Radical Shelley: The Philosophical Anarchism and Utopian Thought of Percy Bysshe Shelley* (Princeton, N.J.:, Princeton University Press, 1982), 42; on the hotel register, see Priestman, *Romantic Atheism*, 232; Timothy Webb, *Shelley: A Voice Not Understood* (Manchester: Manchester University Press, 1977); and Richard Holmes, *Shelley: The Pursuit* (1974; London: HarperCollins, 1995) 340, 342. Byron apparently tried to scratch out Shelley's entry. News of the inscription reached England by way of Robert Southey. For good measure, Shelley entered "L'Enfer" (Hell) under "destination" in the register.

2. Frederic Jameson, *The Political Unconscious: Narrative as a Socially Symbolic Act* (Ithaca, N.Y.: Cornell University Press, 1981), 102.

3. Percy Shelley, "Mont Blanc; Lines Written in the Vale of Chamouni," lines 105–9. Shelley, *Shelley's Poetry and Prose*; hereafter *SPP*.

4. Samuel Taylor Coleridge, *Samuel Taylor Coleridge: The Complete Poems*, ed. William Keach (London: Penguin, 1997), 562. The poem first appeared in the *Morning Post* in September 1802. On the popularity of Chamonix for religious pilgrimage, see Robert M. Ryan, *The Romantic Reformation: Religious Politics in English Literature, 1789–1824* (Cambridge: Cambridge University Press, 1997) 196; Holmes, *Shelley*, 340; Cian Duffy, *Shelley and the Revolutionary Sublime* (Cambridge: Cambridge University Press, 2005), 87–90.

5. Ryan, *Romantic Reformation*, 197; Richard Holmes, *Coleridge: Early Visions* (London: Hodder and Stoughton, 1989), 334–35.

6. Israel, *Radical Enlightenment*; hereafter *RE*.

7. Scrivener, *Radical Shelley*, 7, 79. Also Gerald McNiece, *Shelley and the Revolutionary Idea* (Cambridge, Mass.: Harvard University Press, 1969), 7.

8. Abrams, *Natural Supernaturalism*; Earl R. Wasserman, *Shelley: A Critical Reading* (Baltimore: Johns Hopkins University Press, 1971).

9. Israel, *Radical Enlightenment*; David Berman, *A History of Atheism in Britain from Hobbes to Russell* (London: Routledge, 1988). Particularly in the early modern period, accusations of atheism tended to travel under other names: Epicurianism, Hobbesianism, Spinozism. Sometimes it was simply shorthand for heresy or heterodoxy.

10. Alan Charles Kors, *Atheism in France, 1650–1729: The Orthodox Sources of Disbelief* (Princeton, N.J.: Princeton University Press, 1990), 53.

11. René Descartes, *Discourse on Method* [1637], trans. Donald A. Cress (Indianapolis: Hackett, 1980), 16. Orig pub. 1637.

12. Harrison, *"Religion" and the Religions in the English Enlightenment*. Much of modern atheism conveniently forgets that "religion" is a cultural and historical construct; as a glance at the relevant anthropological literature suggests, it is not a natural kind. See Colin Jager, "Romanticism/Secularization/Secularism," *Blackwell Literature Compass*

5 (2008); and E. N. Anderson, "Attachment and Cooperation in Religious Groups," *Current Anthropology* 51, 3 (June 2010): 421–23.

13. Berman, *A History of Atheism*, 3, 110. Also Priestman, *Romantic Atheism*, 7.

14. See Gavin Hyman, "Atheism in Modern History," in *The Cambridge Companion to Atheism*, ed. Michael Martin (Cambridge: Cambridge University Press, 2007), 27–46, 42.

15. See Taylor, *A Secular Age*, 25–220.

16. One reason, perhaps, why the "debate" initiated by the so-called New Atheists (Christopher Hitchens, Richard Dawkins, et al.) is so boring.

17. Iain McCalman, *Radical Underworld*. On Godwin's influence, see Priestman, *Romantic Atheism*, 29–34; and Scrivener, *Radical Shelley*, chaps. 1 and 2.

18. England experienced its first "Lucretius revival" in the 1680s; the first full translation of *De rerum naturae* (by Thomas Creech) appeared in 1682. The years 1796 to 1813 witnessed a new wave of translations and editions of Lucretius, beginning with Gilbert Wakefield's edition of 1796. D'Holbach's *Système* arrived between these two revivals, and had its own influence on the English scene; a pamphlet entitled *An Answer to Dr. Priestley's Letters to a Philosophical Unbeliever* (1782), which David Berman identifies as the first work of "avowed" atheism in Britain, quotes long passages of d'Holbach's *Système*.

19. *Queen Mab*, VII, line 13. *The Poems of Shelley*, ed. Kelvin Everest and Geoffrey Matthews (Harlow: Pearson/Longman, 2000), 1:331.

20. Holmes, *Shelley*, 200–201; for the general discourse of atheism in England around the turn of the century, see Priestman's *Romantic Atheism*.

21. John Gibson Lockhart, unsigned review, *Blackwood's Edinburgh Magazine* 4 (January 1819): 475–82; *Shelley: The Critical Heritage*, ed. James E. Barcus (London: Routledge, 1975), 115–16.

22. Percy Shelley, *A Philosophical View of Reform*, ed. Thomas William Rolleston (Oxford: Oxford University Press, 1920), 7–8, 8, 9.

23. Benedict de Spinoza, *Theological-Political Treatise*, ed. Jonathan Israel, trans. Michael Silverthorne and Jonathan Israel (Cambridge: Cambridge University Press, 2007), 195; hereafter *TTP*.

24. Charles Taylor, "Modes of Secularism," in *Secularism and Its Critics*, ed. Rajeev Bhargava (Delhi: Oxford University Press, 1998), 31–53. For Israel's comments on the Lockean model, see *Radical Enlightenment* 108, 116, 117. Despite modifications over the years, the Lockean and Grotian/Spinozist models remain the models for how we think about secularism today. Their most familiar forms in contemporary Europe are, respectively, the multicultural model common in Great Britain and the Netherlands, and the assimilationist model that has characterized French secularism since the Revolution, generally refered to as *laïcité*. On Grotius and Spinoza as atheists, see Israel, *Radical Enlightenment* 447, 454.

25. Olivier Roy, *Secularism Confronts Islam* (New York: Columbia University Press, 2007), 26. See also Talal Asad, "Trying to Understand French Secularism," in *Political Theologies: Public Religions in a Post-Secular World*, ed. Hent deVries and Lawrence E Sullivan (New York: Fordham University Press, 2006), 494–526, 504.

26. Shelley to Byron, 8 and 29 September 1816. *The Complete Works of Percy Bysshe Shelley*, ed. Roger Ingpen and Walter E. Peck, vol. 9, *Letters 1812–1818* (New York: Gordian, 1965), 195, 199.

27. A restoration that is one key theme of *Prometheus Unbound*. Obviously this does not mean that Shelley is any more pleased by English "restraint" during the years of the Revolution. England had its own terror, or rather "war on terror" in the 1790s, which, if not as bloody as the one in France, had its own profound effect on what Kenneth Johnston has called the "lost generation of the 1790s." See Kenneth R. Johnston, "The Unromantic Lives of Others: The Lost Generation of the 1790s," *Wordsworth Circle* 40 (2009): 67–72.

28. "[I]f we might withdraw the veil of private life, and tell what we *now* know about him, it would be indeed a disgusting picture that we should exhibit." John Taylor Coleridge, review of *The Revolt of Islam, Quarterly Review* (April 1819): 460–71; reprinted in Barcus, *Shelley*, 135.

29. See Wolfgang Reinhard, "Reformation, Counter-Reformation, and the Early Modern State," *Catholic Historical Review* 75 (July 1989): 404, 402; and William T. Cavanaugh, "Does Religion Cause Violence?" *Harvard Divinity Bulletin* 35, 2–3 (Spring/Summer 2007): 22–35. Also Foucault, "Governmentality," 87–104.

30. Martin Luther, "On Secular Authority (1523)," in *Luther and Calvin on Secular Authority*, ed. Harro Höpfl (Cambridge: Cambridge University Press, 1991), 10; see also *An Open Letter Concerning the Hard Book Against the Peasants* (1525).

31. O'Donovan and O'Donovan, *From Irenaeus to Grotius*, 551.

32. Asad makes a stronger claim. The secularized body, he suggests, was in this sense an inexperienced body, for some avenues were simply closed to it. See Asad, "Thinking About Religious Belief and Politics." The argument that Reform drives secularization is the central claim in Taylor, *A Secular Age*.

33. *Poems of Shelley*, 2: 550; see also Timothy Webb, "'The Avalanche of Ages': Shelley's Defense of Atheism and *Prometheus Unbound*," *KSMB* 35 (1984): 1–39.

34. Most recently Geoffrey Hartman, "Gods, Ghosts, and Shelley's 'Atheos,'" *Literature & Theology* 24, 1 (March 2010): 4–18.

35. *Prometheus Unbound* 2.3.37–42; *SPP* 244.

36. William Keach, "The Political Poet," in *The Cambridge Companion to Shelley*, ed. Timothy Morton (Cambridge: Cambridge University Press, 2006) 123–42, 137, 123.

37. See Rob Mitchell, "The Transcendental: Deleuze, P. B. Shelley, and the Freedom of Immobility," *Romantic Circles Praxis* (January 2008), http://www.rc.umd.edu/praxis/deleuze/mitchell/mitchell.html.

38. Unsigned review of *The Revolt of Islam, Monthly Review*, March 1819, 323–24; reprinted in Barcus, *Shelley*, 123. F. R. Leavis, "Shelley," in *Revaluation: Tradition and Development in English Poetry* (1947; Chicago: Ivan R. Dee, 1998), 203–32, 207. Leavis grasps from the negative side the power of Shelley's antidualism when he writes of *Mont Blanc*: "The metaphorical and the actual, the real and the imagined, the inner and the outer, could hardly be more unsortably and indistinguishably confused" (212).

39. John Taylor Coleridge, *Quarterly Review* (April 1819): 460–71; reprinted in Barcus, *Shelley*, 126.

40. Kant, *Critique of Pure Reason*, 9.

41. Ibid., 27.

42. Shelley, *Shelley's Poetry and Prose*, 506, 507.

43. Christopher Hitt, "Unwriting Mount Blanc," *Texas Studies in Language and Literature* 47, 2 (2005): 139–66.

44. More congenial to my reading, then, is Frances Ferguson's argument that the question is a rueful acknowledgment of how hard it is to "let Mont Blanc be merely a blank." For Ferguson absolute materialism turns out to be impossible: "One can see the mountain as an example of materiality but cannot see it even as a mountain without seeing it as involving more than matter." To be sure, the poem might strive to return the mountain to a primal blankness beneath the various pious voices that have been attached to it, but as the speaker himself acknowledges early on, the valley is "many-voicèd" (line 13), and there is little guarantee that by the end we have stripped away those voices and uncovered the scene's material "truth." See Frances Ferguson, "Shelley's *Mont Blanc*: What the Mountain Said," in *Romanticism and Language*, ed. Arden Reid (London: Methuen, 1984), 202–14; 203, 211.

45. Warren Montag, "Who's Afraid of the Multitude? Between the Individual and the State," *South Atlantic Quarterly* 104, 4 (Fall 2005): 655–73; for a discussion of secularism and the fear of ordinary people, see Ashis Nandy, "Closing the Debate on Secularism: A Personal Statement," in *The Crisis of Secularism in India* (Durham, N.C.: Duke University Press, 2007), 107–17; for an analysis of the "counter-power" of the crowd, see Collings, *Monstrous Society*.

46. *Prometheus Unbound*, 4.402; *Shelley's Poetry and Prose*, 281.

EPILOGUE

1. Alan Liu, *Wordsworth: The Sense of History* (Stanford, Calif.: Stanford University Press, 1989), 311–58; Samantha Webb, "Feeding on Disquiet: 'The Ruined Cottage' and the Unmediated Event," *Essays in Romanticism* 18 (2011): 29–43.

2. Taylor, *A Secular Age*, 370.

3. Greil Marcus, *Lipstick Traces: A Secret History of the Twentieth Century* (Cambridge Mass.: Belknap Press of Harvard University Press, 2009), 21.

BIBLIOGRAPHY

Aarsleff, Hans. *The Study of Language in England 1780–1860*. Princeton, N.J.: Princeton University Press, 1967.

Abrams, M. H. *The Mirror and the Lamp: Romantic Theory and the Critical Tradition*. New York: Oxford University Press, 1953.

———. *Natural Supernaturalism: Tradition and Revolution in Romantic Literature*. New York: Norton, 1971.

Ali, Ayaan Hirsi. "Blind Faiths." *New York Times Book Review*, 6 January 2008.

———. *Infidel*. New York: Free Press, 2008.

Anidjar, Gil. "Secularism." *Critical Inquiry* 33, 1 (Autumn 2006): 52–77.

Armstrong, Karen. *The Battle for God: A History of Fundamentalism*. New York: Ballantine, 2001.

———. "Bill Moyers Interviews Karen Armstrong." PBS, 1 March 2002. http://www .pbs.org/now/transcript/transcript_armstrong.html.

Armstrong, Nancy. *Desire and Domestic Fiction: A Political History of the Novel*. New York: Oxford University Press, 1987.

Asad, Talal. *Formations of the Secular: Christianity, Islam, Modernity*. Stanford, Calif.: Stanford University Press, 2003.

———. *Genealogies of Religion: Discipline and Reasons of Power in Christianity and Islam*. Baltimore: Johns Hopkins University Press, 1993.

———. "Thinking About Religion, Belief, and Politics." In *The Cambridge Companion to Religious Studies*, ed. Robert A. Orsi, 36–57. New York: Cambridge University Press, 2012.

———. "Trying to Understand French Secularism." In *Political Theologies: Public Religions in a Post-Secular World*, ed. Hent deVries and Lawrence E Sullivan, 494–526. New York: Fordham University Press, 2006.

Austen, Jane. *Emma*. Ed. Richard Cronin and Dorothy McMillan. Cambridge Edition of the Works of Jane Austen. Cambridge: Cambridge University Press, 2005.

———. *Emma*. Ed. Adela Pinch. New York: Oxford University Press, 2008.

———. *Mansfield Park*. Ed. John Wiltshire. Cambridge Edition of the Works of Jane Austen. Cambridge: Cambridge University Press, 1995.

Austen-Leigh, James Edward. *A Memoir of Jane Austen*. Ed. R. W. Chapman. 1926. Oxford: Oxford University Press, 1967.

Authentick Memoirs of the Life and Infamous Actions of Cardinal Wolsey. To a Certain Gentleman, Who Takes the Character of Cardinal Wolsey to Himself. London, 1731.

Babbitt, Irving. "The Present Outlook [1919]." In *Romanticism: Points of View*, ed. Robert F. Gleckner and Gerald Enscoe, 26–40. 2nd ed. Englewood Cliffs, N.J.: Prentice-Hall, 1962.

Badiou, Alain. *Ethics: An Essay on the Understanding of Evil.* Trans. Peter Hallward. London: Verso, 2001.

———. *Saint Paul: The Foundation of Universalism.* Trans. Ray Brassier. Stanford, Calif.: Stanford University Press, 2003.

Bakhtin, Mikhail M. *Rabelais and His World.* Trans. Helene Iswolsky. Cambridge, Mass.: MIT Press, 1968.

Barcus, James E., ed. *Shelley: The Critical Heritage.* London: Routledge, 1975.

Barrell, John. *The Idea of Landscape and the Sense of Place, 1730–1840: An Approach to the Poetry of John Clare.* Cambridge: Cambridge University Press, 1972.

———. *The Infection of Thomas De Quincey: A Psychopathology of Imperialism.* New Haven, Conn.: Yale University Press, 1991.

Baucom, Ian. *Specters of the Atlantic: Finance Capital, Slavery, and the Philosophy of History.* Durham, N.C.: Duke University Press, 2005.

Beckford, James A. "Public Religions and the Postsecular: Critical Reflections." *Journal for the Scientific Study of Religion* 51, 1 (2012): 1–19.

Benard, Cheryl. "Civil Democratic Islam: Partners, Resources, and Strategies." Rand Corporation, 2003.

Bender, Courtney. *The New Metaphysicals: Spirituality and the American Religious Imagination.* Chicago: University of Chicago Press, 2010.

Bender, John. *Ends of Enlightenment.* Stanford, Calif.: Stanford University Press, 2012.

Benhabib, Seyla. *The Claims of Culture: Equality and Diversity in the Global Era.* Princeton, N.J.: Princeton University Press, 2002.

Benjamin, Walter. *The Arcades Project.* Ed. Rolf Tiedemann, trans. Howard Eiland and Kevin McLaughlin. Cambridge, Mass.: Belknap Press of Harvard University Press, 2002.

———. *Illuminations: Essays and Reflections.* Ed. Hannah Arendt, trans. Harry Zohn. New York: Schocken, 1968.

———. *The Origin of German Tragic Drama.* Trans. John Osborne. London: Verso, 1998.

———. *Walter Benjamin: Selected Writings.* Vol. 1, *1913–1926.* Ed. Marcus Bullock and Michael W. Jennings. Cambridge, Mass.: Belknap Press of Harvard University Press, 1996.

Bennett, G. V. *The Tory Crisis in Church and State 1688–1730: The Career of Francis Atterbury, Bishop of Rochester.* Oxford: Clarendon, 1976.

Berger, Peter L., ed. *The Desecularization of the World: Resurgent Religion and World Politics.* Grand Rapids, Mich.: Eerdmans, 1999.

Berlant, Lauren. *Cruel Optimism.* Durham, N.C.: Duke University Press, 2011.

Berman, David. *A History of Atheism in Britain from Hobbes to Russell.* London: Routledge, 1988.

Berman, Paul. *The Flight of the Intellectuals*. Brooklyn: Melville House, 2010.

Bernard, George. *The King's Reformation: Henry VIII and the Remaking of the English Church*. New Haven, Conn.: Yale University Press, 2005.

Bhabha, Homi K. *The Location of Culture*. London: Routledge, 1994.

———. "Minority Maneuvers and Unsettled Negotiations." *Critical Inquiry* 23, 3 (Spring 1997): 431–59.

———. "On Writing Rights." In *Globalizing Rights: The Oxford Amnesty Lectures 1999*, 162–83. Oxford: Oxford University Press, 2003.

———. "Untimely Ends: Homi K. Bhabha on Edward Said." *ArtForum* 42 (February 2004): 19.

Bhargava, Rajeev. *Secularism and Its Critics*. New York: Oxford University Press, 2005.

Bilgrami, Akeel. "Occidentalism, the Very Idea: An Essay on Enlightenment and Enchantment." *Critical Inquiry* 32 (Spring 2006): 381–411.

Blair, Hugh. *Lectures on Rhetoric and Belles Lettres. By Hugh Blair, D. D. In Three Volumes. . . .* Vol. 3. Dublin: Printed for Messrs. Whitestone, et al., 1783.

Blount, Charles. *Great Is Diana of the Ephesians, Or, The Original of Idolatry Together with the Politick Institution of the Gentiles Sacrifices*. London, 1680.

Bonnett, Alastair. "The Critical Traditionalism of Ashis Nandy: Occidentalism and the Dilemmas of Innocence." *Theory, Culture & Society* 29, 1 (January 2012): 138–157.

Bossy, John. *Christianity in the West 1400–1700*. Oxford: Oxford University Press, 1985.

Brooks, Cleanth. "The Language of Paradox." In *The Well Wrought Urn: Studies in the Structure of Poetry*, 3–21. San Diego: Harvest, 1947.

Brown, Callum G. "A Revisionist Approach to Religious Change." In *Religion and Modernization: Sociologists and Historians Debate the Secularization Thesis*, ed. Steve Bruce, 30–58. Oxford: Clarendon, 1992.

Brown, Marshall. *The Gothic Text*. Stanford, Calif.: Stanford University Press, 2005.

Brown, Wendy. *Regulating Aversion: Tolerance in the Age of Identity and Empire*. Princeton, N.J.: Princeton University Press, 2006.

Bruce, Steve. *God Is Dead: Secularization in the West*. Malden, Mass.: Blackwell, 2002.

———, ed. *Religion and Modernization: Sociologists and Historians Debate the Secularization Thesis*. New York: Oxford University Press, 1992.

Burke, Edmund. *Reflections on the Revolution in France*. Ed. L. G. Mitchell. Oxford: Oxford University Press, 1993.

Burnet, Gilbert. *Bishop Burnet's History of His Own Time*. Vol. 2, *From the Revolution to the Conclusion of the Treaty of Peace at Utrecht, in the Reign of Queen Anne, To Which Is Added, The Author's Life, by the Editor*. London: Printed for the Editor, by Joseph Downing and Henry Woodfall, 1724.

Burton, Robert. *The anatomy of melancholy. What it is. With all the kindes, causes, symptomes, prognostickes, and severall cures of it. By Democritus Junior*. 2nd ed. Oxford: Printed by John Lichfield and James Short, for Henry Cripps, 1621.

Butler, Judith. "Melancholy Gender/Refused Identification." In *The Psychic Life of Power: Theories in Subjection*, 132–66. Stanford, Calif.: Stanford University Press, 1997.

Butler, Marilyn. *Jane Austen and the War of Ideas*. Oxford: Clarendon, 1975.

———. "The Orientalism of Byron's *Giaour*." In *Byron and the Limits of Fiction*, ed. Bernard Beatty, 78–96. Liverpool: Liverpool University Press, 1988.

Byron, Lord George Gordon. *Selected Poems*. Ed. Susan Wolfson and Peter J. Manning. London: Penguin, 1996.

Canuel, Mark. "'Holy Hypocrisy' and the Government of Belief: Religion and Nationalism in the Gothic." *Studies in Romanticism* 34 (1995): 507–30.

———. *Religion, Toleration, and British Writing, 1790–1830*. Cambridge: Cambridge University Press, 2002.

Casanova, Jose. *Public Religions in the Modern World*. Chicago: University of Chicago Press, 1994.

Cavanaugh, William T. "'A Fire Strong Enough to Consume the House': The Wars of Religion and the Rise of the State." *Modern Theology* 11, 4 (October 1995): 397–420.

———. *The Myth of Religious Violence: Secular Ideology and the Roots of Modern Conflict*. New York: Oxford University Press, 2009.

Cavell, Stanley. *In Quest of the Ordinary: Lines of Skepticism and Romanticism*. Chicago: University of Chicago Press, 1994.

Chakrabarty, Dipesh. *Provincializing Europe: Postcolonial Thought and Historical Difference*. Princeton, N.J.: Princeton University Press, 2000.

Chandler, James. *England in 1819: The Politics of Literary Culture and the Case of Romantic Historicism*. Chicago: University of Chicago Press, 1999.

Chatterjee, Partha. "Religious Minorities and the Secular State: Reflections on an Indian Impasse." *Public Culture* 8, 1 (1995): 11–39.

Christensen, Jerome. *Lord Byron's Strength: Romantic Writing and Commercial Society*. Baltimore: Johns Hopkins University Press, 1993.

———. "Perversion, Parody, and Cultural Hegemony: Lord Byron's Oriental Tales." *South Atlantic Quarterly* 88, 3 (1989): 569–603.

———. *Romanticism at the End of History*. Baltimore: Johns Hopkins University Press, 2000.

Christian, William A. *Local Religion in Sixteenth-Century Spain*. Princeton, N.J.: Princeton University Press, 1989.

Clery, E. J. *The Rise of Supernatural Fiction, 1762–1800*. Cambridge: Cambridge University Press, 1999.

Coburn, Kathleen, and B. Winer, eds. *The Collected Works of Samuel Taylor Coleridge*. Vol. 14, *Table Talk*. Princeton, N.J.: Princeton University Press, 1990.

Coleridge, Samuel Taylor. *Coleridge's Poetry and Prose*. Ed. Nicholas Halmi, Paul Magnuson, and Raimonda Modiano. New York: Norton, 2004.

———. *The Major Works*. Ed. H. J. Jackson. Oxford: Oxford University Press, 2000.

Colley, Linda. *Britons: Forging the Nation, 1707–1937*. New Haven, Conn.: Yale University Press, 1992.

Collings, David. *Monstrous Society: Reciprocity, Discipline, and the Political Uncanny, c. 1780–1848*. Lewisburg, Pa.: Bucknell University Press, 2009.

Connolly, William E. *Why I Am Not a Secularist*. Minneapolis: University of Minnesota Press, 2000.

Copeland, Edward. "Money." In *The Cambridge Companion to Jane Austen*, ed. Juliet McMaster and Edward Copeland, 131–48. Cambridge: Cambridge University Press, 1997.

Coykendall, Abby. "Chance Enlightenments, Choice Superstitions: Walpole's Historic Doubts and Enlightened Historicism." *Eighteenth Century: Theory and Interpretation* 54, 1 (2013): 53–70.

Cragwall, Jasper. *Lake Methodism: Polite Literature and Popular Religion in England, 1780–1830*. Columbus: Ohio State University Press, 2013.

Davie, Grace. *Europe, the Exceptional Case: Parameters of Faith in the Modern World*. London: Darton Longman & Todd, 2002.

———. *Religion in Britain Since 1945: Believing Without Belonging*. Oxford: Blackwell, 1994.

Davis, Natalie Zemon. *Society and Culture in Early Modern France*. Stanford, Calif.: Stanford University Press, 1975.

De Certeau, Michel. *The Mystic Fable: The Sixteenth and Seventeenth Centuries*. Trans. Michael B. Smith. Vol. 1. Chicago: University of Chicago Press, 1992.

Deleuze, Gilles, and Felix Guattari. "What Is a Minor Literature?" In *Kafka: Toward a Minor Literature*, trans. Dana Polan, 16–27. Minneapolis: University of Minnesota Press, 1986.

———. *What Is Philosophy?* London: Verso, 1994.

De Man, Paul. "The Rhetoric of Temporality." In *Blindness and Insight: Essays in the Rhetoric of Contemporary Criticism*. 2nd ed. Minneapolis: University of Minnesota Press, 1983.

Dempsey, Sean. "The Cenci: Tragedy in a Secular Age." *ELH* 79 (Winter 2012): 879–903.

Dennett, Daniel. *Breaking the Spell: Religion as a Natural Phenomenon*. New York: Penguin, 2006.

Derrida, Jacques. *Specters of Marx: The State of the Debt, the Work of Mourning, and the New International*. New York: Routledge, 2006.

Descartes, René. *Discourse on Method* [1637]. Trans. Donald A. Cress. Indianapolis: Hackett, 1980.

Dickens, A. G. *The English Reformation*. London: Schocken, 1964.

Dickens, A. G., and Dorothy Carr, eds. "Abbot Pyle's Surrender of Furness Abbey." In *The Reformation in England to the Accession of Elizabeth I: Documents of Modern History*. London: Edward Arnold, 1967.

———, eds. "Robert Aske on the Dissolution of the Monasteries." In *The Reformation in England to the Accession of Elizabeth I: Documents of Modern History*. London: Edward Arnold, 1967.

Dole, Carol M. "Three Tyrants in *The Castle of Otranto*." *English Language Notes* 26 (1988): 26–35.

Donne, John. *The Complete English Poems*. Ed. Albert James Smith. London: Penguin, 1971.

———. *The Major Works*. Oxford: Oxford University Press, 2000.

Drake, George A. "'Fanciful Devotion': Ritualization in Scott's Old Mortality." *Studies in Romanticism* 49, 1 (2010): 133–51.

Dryden, John. *The Major Works.* Ed. Keith Walker. Oxford: Oxford University Press, 1987.

Duffy, Eamon. *The Stripping of the Altars: Traditional Religion in England, 1400–1580.* 2nd ed. New Haven, Conn.: Yale University Press, 2005.

Duncan, Ian. "Introduction." In *Rob Roy,* ed. Ian Duncan. Oxford: Oxford University Press, 1998.

———. *Scott's Shadow: The Novel in Romantic Edinburgh.* Princeton, N.J.: Princeton University Press, 2007.

Dunn, John. "The Claim to Freedom of Conscience." In *From Persecution to Toleration: The Glorious Revolution and Religion in England,* 171–93. New York: Oxford University Press, 1991.

Eagleton, Terry. *The Ideology of the Aesthetic.* Oxford: Wiley-Blackwell, 1990.

———. *Reason, Faith, and Revolution: Reflections on the God Debate.* New Haven, Conn.: Yale University Press, 2009.

Eisenstadt, S. N. "Multiple Modernities." *Daedalus* 129 (2000): 1–29.

Elfenbein, Andrew. *Romantic Genius: The Prehistory of a Homosexual Role.* New York: Columbia University Press, 1999.

Ellenzweig, Sarah. *The Fringes of Belief: English Literature, Ancient Heresy, and the Politics of Freethinking, 1660–1760.* Stanford, Calif.: Stanford University Press, 2008.

Favret, Mary. *War at a Distance: Romanticism and the Making of Modern Wartime.* Princeton, N.J.: Princeton University Press, 2010.

Febvre, Lucien. *The Problem of Unbelief in the Sixteenth Century: The Religion of Rabelais.* Cambridge, Mass.: Harvard University Press, 1982.

Ferguson, Frances. *Solitude and the Sublime: The Romantic Aesthetics of Individuation.* New York: Routledge, 1992.

Ferguson, Niall. *Civilization: The West and the Rest.* New York: Penguin, 2011.

Figueira, Dorothy M. "The Politics of Exoticism and Friedrich Schlegel's Metaphorical Pilgrimage to India." *Monatshefte* 81, 4 (Winter 1989): 425–33.

Finch, Casey, and Peter Bowen. "'The Tittle-Tattle of Highbury': Gossip and Free Indirect Style in *Emma.*" *Representations* 31 (Summer 1990): 1–18.

Foucault, Michel. "Governmentality." In *The Foucault Effect: Studies in Governmentality,* ed. Graham Burchell, Colin Gordon, and Peter Miller, 87–104. Chicago: University of Chicago Press, 1991.

Fowler, Alastair, ed. *The New Oxford Book of Seventeenth-Century Verse.* Oxford: Oxford University Press, 2008.

Frank, Manfred. *The Philosophical Foundations of Early German Romanticism.* Trans. Elizabeth Millan-Zaibert. Albany: State University of New York Press, 2004.

Fulbrook, Mary. "Legitimation Crises and the Early Modern State: The Politics of Religious Toleration." In *Religion and Society in Early Modern Europe,* ed. Kaspar von Greyerz, 146–58. London: Allen & Unwin, 1984.

Funkenstein, Amos. *Theology and the Scientific Imagination from the Middle Ages to the Seventeenth Century*. Princeton, N.J.: Princeton University Press, 1989.

Galperin, William H. *The Historical Austen*. Philadelphia: University of Pennsylvania Press, 2003.

Gandhi, Leela. "The Pauper's Gift: Postcolonial Theory and the New Democratic Dispensation." *Public Culture* 23, 1 (2011): 27–38.

Gaonkar, Dilip Parameshwar. *Alternative Modernities*. 2nd ed. Durham, N.C.: Duke University Press, 2001.

Garcia, Humberto. *Islam and the English Enlightenment, 1670–1840*. Baltimore: Johns Hopkins University Press, 2012.

Garside, Peter D. "Scott and the 'Philosophical' Historians." *Journal of the History of Ideas* 36, 3 (1 July 1975): 497–512.

Gauchet, Marcel. *The Disenchantment of the World: A Political History of Religion*. Princeton, N.J.: Princeton University Press, 1997.

Gibson, William. *The Church of England 1688–1832: Unity and Accord*. London: Routledge, 2001.

Ginzburg, Carlo. *The Cheese and the Worms: The Cosmos of a Sixteenth-Century Miller*. Trans. John Tedeschi and Anne C. Tedeschi. Baltimore: Johns Hopkins University Press, 1992.

Goldie, Mark. "John Locke, Jonas Proast, and Religious Toleration 1688–1692." In *The Church of England c. 1689–c. 1833: From Toleration to Tractarianism*, ed. John Walsh, Colin Haydon, and Stephen Taylor, 143–71. Cambridge: Cambridge University Press, 2002.

Gooch, Brad. *Godtalk: Travels in Spiritual America*. New York: Knopf, 2002.

Goodman, Kevis. *Georgic Modernity and British Romanticism: Poetry and the Mediation of History*. Cambridge: Cambridge University Press, 2004.

Gorski, Philip S. *The Disciplinary Revolution: Calvinism and the Rise of the State in Early Modern Europe*. Chicago: University of Chicago Press, 2003.

Gorski, Philip S., and Ates Altinordu. "After Secularization?" *Annual Review of Sociology* 34 (2008): 55–85.

Gourgouris, Stathis. "Transformation, Not Transcendence." *Boundary 2* 31, 2 (2004): 55–79.

Greig, J. Y. T., ed. *The Letters of David Hume*. 2 vols. Vol. 1. Oxford: Oxford University Press, 2011.

Grell, Ole Peter, Jonathan I. Israel, and Nicholas Tyacke, eds. *From Persecution to Toleration: The Glorious Revolution and Religion in England*. New York: Oxford University Press, 1991.

von Greyerz, Kaspar, ed. *Religion and Society in Early Modern Europe*. London: Allen & Unwin, 1984.

Guillory, John. *Cultural Capital: The Problem of Literary Canon Formation*. Chicago: University of Chicago Press, 1993.

Habermas, Jürgen. "Notes on a Post-Secular Society." *Sign and Sight* (27 March 2014). http://print.signandsight.com/features/1714.html.

———. "Religion in the Public Sphere." *European Journal of Philosophy* 14, 1 (2006): 1–25.

———. *The Structural Transformation of the Public Sphere: An Inquiry into a Category of Bourgeois Society*. Cambridge, Mass.: MIT Press, 1989.

Hadden, Jeffrey K. "Toward Desacralizing Secularization Theory." *Social Forces* 65, 3 (1987): 587–611.

Haggerty, George E. *Men in Love: Masculinity and Sexuality in the Eighteenth Century*. New York: Columbia University Press, 1999.

———. *Queer Gothic*. Urbana: University of Illinois Press, 2006.

Haigh, Christopher, ed. *The English Reformation Revised*. Cambridge: Cambridge University Press, 1987.

Halmi, Nicholas. *The Genealogy of the Romantic Symbol*. New York: Oxford University Press, 2008.

Hamilton, Paul. *Metaromanticism: Aesthetics, Literature, Theory*. Chicago: University of Chicago Press, 2003.

Hardt, Michael, and Antonio Negri. *Empire*. Cambridge, Mass.: Harvard University Press, 2000.

Harrison, Peter. *"Religion" and the Religions in the English Enlightenment*. Cambridge: Cambridge University Press, 1990.

Harrison, Ross. *Hobbes, Locke, and Confusion's Masterpiece: An Examination of Seventeenth-Century Political Philosophy*. Cambridge: Cambridge University Press, 2003.

Hartman, Geoffrey. "Gods, Ghosts, and Shelley's 'Atheos.'" *Literature & Theology* 24, 1 (March 2010): 4–18.

Hauerwas, Stanley. *Against the Nations: War and Survival in Liberal Society*. South Bend, Ind.: University of Notre Dame Press, 1992.

Herbert, Edward Herbert. *The antient religion of the gentiles, and causes of their errors considered, By the learned judicious Edward Ld Herbert of Cherbury*. London, 1711.

Herder, Johann Gottfried. *Philosophical Writings*. Trans. and ed. Michael N. Foster. Cambridge: Cambridge University Press, 2002.

Hernandez, Alex Eric. "Tragedy and the Economics of Providence in Richardson's *Clarissa*." *Eighteenth-Century Fiction* 22, 4 (2010): 599–630.

Hertz, Neil. *The End of the Line*. New York: Columbia University Press, 1985.

Hitchcock, Tim. *English Sexualities, 1700–1800*. New York: St. Martin's 1997.

Hitchens, Christopher. *God Is Not Great: How Religion Poisons Everything*. New York: Hachette, 2007.

Hitt, Christopher. "Unwriting Mount Blanc." *Texas Studies in Language and Literature* 47, 2 (2005): 139–66.

Hoeveler, Diane Long. *Gothic Riffs: Secularizing the Uncanny in the European Imaginary, 1780–1820*. Columbus: Ohio State University Press, 2010.

Hogg, James. *The Private Memoirs and Confessions of a Justified Sinner*. Ed. Adrian Hunter. Peterborough, Ont.: Broadview Press, 2001.

Hogle, Jerrold E., ed. *The Cambridge Companion to Gothic Fiction*. Cambridge: Cambridge University Press, 2002.

Hollywood, Amy. "Spiritual But Not Religious." *Harvard Divinity Bulletin* 38, 1/2 (Winter–Spring 2010): 19–23.

Holmes, Richard. *Coleridge: Early Visions, 1772–1804*. New York: Viking, 1990.

Homer. *The Iliad*. Trans. Richmond Lattimore. Chicago: University of Chicago Press, 1961.

Hulme, T. E. "Romanticism and Classicism [1936]." In *Romanticism: Points of View*, ed. Robert F. Gleckner and Gerald Enscoe, 55–65. 2nd ed. Englewood Cliffs, N.J.: Prentice-Hall, 1962.

Hume, David. *An Enquiry Concerning Human Understanding with A Letter from a Gentleman to His Friend in Edinburgh*. Ed. Eric Steinberg. Indianapolis: Hackett, 1977.

———. "Of the Protestant Succession." In *Essays Moral, Political, and Literary*, ed. Eugene F. Miller, 502–11. Indianapolis: Liberty Classics, 1985.

———. "Of Superstition and Enthusiasm." In *David Hume: Writings on Religion*, ed. Anthony Flew, 3–9. Chicago: Open Court, 1992.

———. *A Treatise of Human Nature*. Ed. L. A. Selby-Bigge and P. H. Nidditch. 2nd ed. Oxford: Clarendon, 1978.

Hungerford, Amy. "Postmodern Supernaturalism: Ginsberg and the Search for a Supernatural Language." *Yale Journal of Criticism* 18, 2 (2005): 269–98.

Huntington, Samuel P. "The Clash of Civilizations?" *Foreign Affairs* 72 (Summer 1993): 22–49.

Hurd, Richard. "The Life of the Author." In *The Divine Legation of Moses Demonstrated, by the Right Reverend William Warburton, D.D., Lord Bishop of Gloucester, to Which Is Prefixed an Account of the Life, Writings, and Character of the Author, by Richard Hurd, D.D., Lord Bishop of Worcester*. Vol. 1. London: Printed for Thomas Tegg and Son, 1837.

Hyman, Gavin. "Atheism in Modern History." In *The Cambridge Companion to Atheism*, ed. Michael Martin, 27–46. Cambridge: Cambridge University Press, 2007.

Israel, Jonathan I. *Radical Enlightenment: Philosophy and the Making of Modernity 1650–1750*. New York: Oxford University Press, 2001.

———. "Spinoza, Locke, and the Enlightenment Battle for Toleration." In *Toleration in Enlightenment Europe*, ed. Ole Peter Grell and Roy Porter, 102–13. Cambridge: Cambridge University Press, 2006.

———. "William III and Toleration." In *From Persecution to Toleration: The Glorious Revolution and Religion in England*, ed. Ole Peter Grell, Jonathan I. Israel, and Nicholas Tyacke, 129–70. Oxford: Oxford University Press, 1991.

Jacob, Margaret C. *The Cultural Meaning of the Scientific Revolution*. New York: Random House, 1988.

———. *The Radical Enlightenment: Pantheists, Freemasons and Republicans*. London: Allen & Unwin, 1981.

Jager, Colin. "After the Secular: The Subject of Romanticism." *Public Culture* 18, 2 (Spring 2006): 301–22.

———. *The Book of God: Secularization and Design in the Romantic Era*. Philadelphia: University of Pennsylvania Press, 2007.

———. "Common Quiet: Tolerance Around 1688." *ELH* 79 (2012): 569–96.

———. "Crossing the Line: Blasphemy, Time, and Revelation." *Qui Parle* 22, 2 (2014).

Jager, Ronald. "The Meetinghouse Becomes a Church." In *Granite and Grace: Essays Celebrating the Two Hundredth Anniversary of the New Hampshire Conference, United Church of Christ*, ed. Charles E. Clark and Elizabeth C. Nordbeck, 45–74. Concord, N.H.: The Conference, 2001.

Jameson, Frederic. *The Political Unconscious: Narrative as a Socially Symbolic Act*. Ithaca, N.Y.: Cornell University Press, 1981.

Janz, Denis, ed. *A Reformation Reader: Primary Texts with Introductions*. Minneapolis: Fortress, 2008.

Jedin, Hubert. *A History of the Council of Trent*. Trans. Ernest Graf. London: Thomas Nelson, 1957.

Jenkins, Philip. *The Next Christendom: The Coming of Global Christianity*. Oxford: Oxford University Press, 2002.

Johnson, Claudia L. *Jane Austen: Women, Politics, and the Novel*. Chicago: University of Chicago Press, 1988.

Juergensmeyer, Mark. *Terror in the Mind of God: The Global Rise of Religious Violence*. 3rd ed. Berkeley: University of California Press, 2003.

Kahn, Victoria. *The Future of Illusion: Political Theology and Early Modern Texts*. Chicago: University of Chicago Press, 2014.

Kant, Immanuel. "An Answer to the Question: What Is Enlightenment?" In *Philosophical Writings*, ed. Ernst Behler, trans. Lewis White Beck, 263–69. New York: Continuum, 1986.

———. *Critique of Pure Reason*. Trans. Norman Kemp Smith. Unabridged ed. New York: St. Martin's, 1965.

Keach, William. *Shelley's Style*. New York: Methuen, 1984.

———. "The Political Poet." In *The Cambridge Companion to Shelley*, ed. Timothy Morton. Cambridge: Cambridge University Press, 2006, 123–42.

Knowles, David. *Bare Ruined Choirs: The Dissolution of the English Monasteries*. Cambridge: Cambridge University Press, 1976.

Kompridis, Nikolas. "Normativizing Hybridity/Neutralizing Culture." *Political Theory* 33, 3 (June 2005): 318–33.

Kors, Alan Charles. *Atheism in France, 1650–1729: The Orthodox Sources of Disbelief*. Princeton, N.J.: Princeton University Press, 1990.

Kotsko, Adam. *Žižek and Theology*. London: T & T Clark, 2008.

Kripal, Jeffrey J. *Authors of the Impossible: The Paranormal and the Sacred*. Chicago: University of Chicago Press, 2010.

———. *Esalen: America and the Religion of No Religion*. Chicago: University of Chicago Press, 2008.

Krull, Andrew D. "Spectacles of Disaffection: Politics, Ethics, and Sentiment in Walter Scott's *Old Mortality*." *ELH* 73, 3 (2006): 695–727.

Laing, Malcolm. *The History of Scotland, From the Union of the Crowns on the Accession of James VI to the Throne of England, to the Union of the Kingdoms in the Reign of Queen Anne*. Vol. 2. London, 1800.

Laird, John. *Hume's Philosophy of Human Nature*. London: Methuen, 1932.

Lamb, Jonathan. *The Rhetoric of Suffering: Reading the Book of Job in the Eighteenth Century*. New York: Oxford University Press, 1995.

Langford, Paul. *A Polite and Commercial People: England 1727–1783*. Oxford: Oxford University Press, 1994.

Laqueur, Thomas W. *Making Sex: Body and Gender from the Greeks to Freud*. Cambridge, Mass.: Harvard University Press, 1990.

Leask, Nigel. "Kubla Khan and Orientalism: The Road to Xanadu Revisited." *Romanticism* 4, 1 (1998): 1–21.

Leavis, F. R. *The Great Tradition*. London: Chatto and Windus, 1960.

Le Faye, Deirdre, ed. *Jane Austen's Letters*, 3rd ed. Oxford: Oxford University Press, 1995.

Legaspi, Michael C. *The Death of Scripture and the Rise of Biblical Studies*. New York: Oxford University Press, 2010.

Levine, George. *The Realistic Imagination: English Fiction from Frankenstein to Lady Chatterley*. Chicago: University of Chicago Press, 1983.

Lilla, Mark. *The Stillborn God: Religion, Politics, and the Modern West*. New York: Knopf, 2007.

Liu, Alan. *Wordsworth: The Sense of History*. Stanford, Calif.: Stanford University Press, 1989.

Locke, John. *An Essay Concerning Human Understanding*. Ed. Peter H. Nidditch. Oxford: Clarendon Press, 1975.

———. "First Tract on Government (1660)." In *Political Writings*, ed. David Wootton. Indianapolis: Hackett, 1993.

———. *A Letter Concerning Toleration*. Ed. James Tully, trans. William Popple. Indianapolis: Hackett, 1983.

———. "Some Thoughts Concerning Education." In *The Works of John Locke in Nine Volumes*. Vol. 8. 12th ed. London: Rivington, 1824.

Lowth, Robert. *Lectures on the Sacred Poetry of the Hebrews; Translated from the Latin of the Right Rev. Robert Lowth, D. D. Late Praelector of Poetry in the University of Oxford, and Now Lord Bishop of London, by G. Gregory, F. A. S. Author of Essays Historical and Moral. To Which Are Added, The Principal Notes of Professor Michaelis, and Notes by the Translator and Others*. 2 vols. London: Printed for J. Johnson, 1787.

Luhmann, Niklas. *Observations on Modernity*. Trans. William Whobrey. Stanford, Calif.: Stanford University Press, 1998.

Lukács, Georg. "The Historical Novel [excerpt]." In *Theory of the Novel: A Historical Approach*, ed. Michael McKeon, 219–64. Baltimore: Johns Hopkins University Press, 2000.

Luther, Martin. "On Secular Authority (1523)." In *Luther and Calvin on Secular Authority*, ed. Harro Hopfl. Cambridge: Cambridge University Press, 1991.

Lynch, Deirdre. "Gothic Libraries and National Subjects." *Studies in Romanticism* 40, 1 (2001): 29–48.

MacIntyre, Alasdair. *Secularization and Moral Change.* Riddell Memorial Lectures. Oxford: Oxford University Press, 1967.

Macpherson, Sandra. *Harm's Way: Tragic Responsibility and the Novel Form.* Baltimore: Johns Hopkins University Press, 2010.

Mahmood, Saba. "Secularism, Hermeneutics, and Empire: The Politics of Islamic Reformation." *Public Culture* 18, 2 (2006): 323–47.

Makdisi, Saree. "Said, Palestine, and the Humanism of Liberation." *Critical Inquiry* 31 (Winter 2005): 443–61.

Malick, Terrence. *The Tree of Life.* Film. Fox Searchlight, 2011.

Marx, Anthony W. *Faith in Nation: Exclusionary Origins of Nationalism.* New York: Oxford University Press, 2003.

Masuzawa, Tomoko. *The Invention of World Religions: Or, How European Universalism Was Preserved in the Language of Pluralism.* Chicago: University of Chicago Press, 2005.

McCalman, Iain. *Radical Underworld: Prophets, Revolutionaries, and Pornographers in London, 1795–1840.* Oxford: Oxford University Press, 1988.

McClure, Kirstie M. "Difference, Diversity, and the Limits of Toleration," *Political Theory* 18, 3 (August 1990): 361–91.

McCutcheon, Russell T. *Manufacturing Religion: The Discourse on Sui Generis Religion and the Politics of Nostalgia.* New York: Oxford University Press, 1997.

McGann, Jerome J. "The Meaning of the Ancient Mariner." *Critical Inquiry* 8, 1 (1981): 35–67.

———. "Walter Scott's Romantic Postmodernity." In *Scotland and the Borders of Romanticism*, ed. Leith Davis, Ian Duncan, and Janet Sorensen, 113–29. Cambridge: Cambridge University Press, 2004.

McGowan, John P. "Knowledge/Power and Jane Austen's Radicalism." *Mosaic* 18 (1985): 1–15.

McGrath, Alister. *Reformation Thought: An Introduction.* Oxford: Blackwell, 1988.

McGrath, Patrick. *Papists and Puritans Under Elizabeth I.* London: Blandford, 1967.

McKeon, Michael. *The Origins of the English Novel, 1600–1740.* Baltimore: Johns Hopkins University Press, 1987.

———. *The Secret History of Domesticity: Public, Private, and the Division of Knowledge.* Baltimore: Johns Hopkins University Press, 2005.

Mee, Jon. *Romanticism, Enthusiasm, and Regulation: Poetics and the Policing of Culture in the Romantic Period.* Oxford: Oxford University Press, 2003.

Milbank, John. *Theology and Social Theory: Beyond Secular Reason.* 2nd ed. Oxford: Wiley-Blackwell, 2006.

———. *The Word Made Strange: Theology, Language, Culture.* Oxford: Wiley-Blackwell, 1997.

Miles, Robert. "Debating the Secular." *Eighteenth-Century Life* 37, 3 (2013): 110–21.

———. "*Emma* and Bank Bills: Forgery and Romanticism." *Romantic Circles Praxis* (February 2012). http://romantic.arhu.umd.edu/praxis/forgery/.

———. "'A Fall in Bread': Speculation and the Real in *Emma*." *NOVEL: A Forum on Fiction* 37, 1–2 (April 2003): 66–85.

———. *Gothic Writing, 1750–1820: A Genealogy.* Manchester: Manchester University Press, 2002.

———. "Romanticism, Enlightenment, and Mediation: The Case of the Inner Stranger." In *This Is Enlightenment*, ed. Clifford Siskin and William Warner, 173–88. Chicago: University of Chicago Press, 2010.

Millar, John. *The Origin of the Distinction of Ranks, Or, An Inquiry into the Circumstances Which Give Rise to Influence and Authority, in the Different Members of Society.* Ed. Aaron Garrett. 4th ed. Indianapolis: Liberty Fund, 2006.

Miller, D. A. *Jane Austen; Or, the Secret of Style.* Princeton, N.J.: Princeton University Press, 2005.

Modern, John Lardas. *Secularism in Antebellum America.* Chicago: University of Chicago Press, 2011.

Monk, Samuel H. *The Sublime: A Study of Critical Theories in Eighteenth-Century England.* Ann Arbor: University of Michigan Press, 1960.

Montag, John, SJ. "Revelation: The False Legacy of Suarez." In *Radical Orthodoxy: A New Theology*, ed. John Milbank, Catherine Pickstock, and Graham Ward, 38–63. London: Routledge, 1999.

Montag, Warren. "Who's Afraid of the Multitude? Between the Individual and the State." *South Atlantic Quarterly* 104, 4 (Fall 2005): 655–73.

Mossner, E. C. *The Life of David Hume.* Edinburgh: Thomas Nelson, 1954.

Mufti, Aamir R. "Auerbach in Istanbul: Edward Said, Secular Criticism, and the Question of Minority Culture." *Critical Inquiry* 25, 1 (Autumn 1998): 95–125.

———. "Orientalism and the Institution of World Literatures." *Critical Inquiry* 36 (Spring 2010): 458–93.

———. "Why I Am Not a Postsecularist." *Boundary 2* 40, 1 (2013): 7–19.

Murphy, Virginia. "The Literature and Propaganda of Henry VIII's First Divorce." In *The Reign of Henry VIII: Politics, Policy, and Piety*, ed. Dairmaid MacCulloch, 135–58. Basingstoke: Palgrave Macmillan, 1995.

Murray, Mungo. *On the Death and Horrid Murther of the Most Reverend Father in God, James Archbishop of Saint-Andrews, Lord Primate of Scotland.* 2nd ed. Edinburgh, 1679.

Nandy, Ashis. "Closing the Debate on Secularism: A Personal Statement." In *The Crisis of Secularism in India*, ed. Anuradha Dingwaney Needham and Rajeswari Sunder Rajan, 107–17. Durham, N.C.: Duke University Press, 2007.

———. *The Intimate Enemy: Loss and Recovery of Self Under Colonialism.* Delhi: Oxford University Press, 1983.

———. "The Politics of Secularism and the Recovery of Religious Tolerance." In *Secularism and Its Critics*, ed. Rajeev Bhargava, 321–44. New York: Oxford University Press, 2005.

Nelson, Victoria. *Gothicka: Vampire Heroes, Human Gods, and the New Supernatural.* Cambridge, Mass.: Harvard University Press, 2012.

———. *The Secret Life of Puppets.* Cambridge, Mass.: Harvard University Press, 2001.

Norton, Robert E. *Herder's Aesthetics and the European Enlightenment.* Ithaca, N.Y.: Cornell University Press, 1991.

Ocker, Christopher. *Biblical Poetics Before Humanism and Reformation.* Cambridge: Cambridge University Press, 2002.

O'Donovan, Oliver, and Joan Lockwood O'Donovan, eds. *From Irenaeus to Grotius: A Sourcebook in Christian Political Thought 100–1625.* Grand Rapids, Mich.: Eerdmans, 1999.

Olender, Maurice. *The Languages of Paradise: Aryans and Semites, a Match Made in Heaven.* Trans. Arthur Goldhammer. New York: Other Press, 2002.

O'Malley, John W. *Trent and All That: Renaming Catholicism in the Early Modern Era.* Cambridge, Mass.: Harvard University Press, 2000.

"On Being, with Krista Tippett." American Public Media. Accessed 11 March 2013. http://www.onbeing.org/about.

Orgel, Stephen, and Jonathan Goldberg, eds. *John Milton.* Oxford: Oxford University Press, 1991.

Partridge, Christopher. *The Re-Enchantment of the West: Alternative Spiritualities, Sacralization, Popular Culture and Occulture.* 2 vols. London: T & T Clark, 2005.

Pearce, Donald. "'Kubla Khan' in Context." *SEL* 21 (1981): 565–83.

Pew Forum on Religion and Public Life. *"Nones" on the Rise.* Pew Research Center, 9 October 2012. http://www.pewforum.org/Unaffiliated/nones-on-the-rise-religion.aspx.

Pfau, Thomas. *Romantic Moods: Paranoia, Trauma, and Melancholy, 1794–1840.* Baltimore: Johns Hopkins University Press, 2005.

Pickstock, Catherine. *After Writing: On the Liturgical Consummation of Philosophy.* Oxford: Blackwell, 1998.

Plumb, J. H. *The First Four Georges.* London: Batsford, 1956.

Pocock, J. G. A. "Conservative Enlightenment and Democratic Revolutions: The American and French Cases in British Perspective." *Government and Opposition* 24, 1 (January 1989): 81–105.

Poovey, Mary. *Genres of the Credit Economy: Mediating Value in Eighteenth- and Nineteenth-Century Britain.* Chicago: University of Chicago Press, 2008.

Porter, Roy. *Enlightenment: Britain and the Creation of the Modern World.* New ed. London: Penguin, 2001.

Prickett, Stephen. *Origins of Narrative: The Romantic Appropriation of the Bible.* Cambridge: Cambridge University Press, 1996.

———. *Words and the Word: Language, Poetics, and Biblical Interpretation.* Cambridge: Cambridge University Press, 1986.

Priestman, Martin. *Romantic Atheism: Poetry and Freethought, 1780–1830.* Cambridge: Cambridge University Press, 1999.

Principe, Lawrence M. *The Aspiring Adept: Robert Boyle and His Alchemical Quest.* Princeton, N.J.: Princeton University Press, 1998.

Proudfoot, Wayne. *Religious Experience.* Berkeley: University of California Press, 1985.

Purchas, Samuel. *Purchas His Pilgrimage. Or Relations of the World and the Religions Observed in All Ages and Places Discovered, from the Creation unto This Present.* London: Printed by William Stansby for Henrie Fetherstone, 1613.

Rawls, John. *Political Liberalism.* 2nd ed. New York: Columbia University Press, 2005.

Redfield, Mark. "Introduction." *Diacritics* 27, 3 (Fall 1997): 3–7.

Regier, Alexander. "Figuring It Out: The Origin of Language and Anthropomorphism." *Forum for Modern Language Studies* 42, 4 (2006): 412–30.

Rex, Richard. *Henry VIII and the English Reformation.* Houndmills: Macmillan, 1993.

Reinhard, Wolfgang. "Reformation, Counter-Reformation, and the Early Modern State." *Catholic Historical Review* 75 (July 1989): 383–404.

Ricks, C. B. "Wolsey in 'The Vanity of Human Wishes.'" *Modern Language Notes* 73, 8 (December 1958): 563–68.

Rivett, Sarah. "Early American Religion in a Post-Secular Age." *PMLA* 128, 4 (2013): 989–96.

Robbins, Bruce. "Is the Postcolonial Also Postsecular?" *Boundary 2* 40, 1 (2013): 245–62.

Roe, Nicholas. *John Keats and the Culture of Dissent.* New York: Oxford University Press, 1997.

Rollason, Christopher. "The Passageways of Paris: Walter Benjamin's Arcades Project and Contemporary Cultural Debate in the West." 23 October 2010. http://www.wbenjamin.org/passageways.html.

Roy, Olivier. *Secularism Confronts Islam.* New York: Columbia University Press, 2007.

Ryan, Robert J. *The Romantic Reformation: Religious Politics in English Literature, 1789–1824.* Cambridge: Cambridge University Press, 1997.

Said, Edward W. *Orientalism.* New York: Vintage, 1978.

———. "Secular Criticism." In *The World, the Text, and the Critic,* 1–30. Cambridge, Mass.: Harvard University Press, 1983.

Saler, Michael. "Modernity and Enchantment: A Historiographic Review." *American Historical Review* 111, 3 (2006): 692–716.

Savarese, John. "Psyche's 'Whisp'ring Fan' and Keats's Genealogy of the Secular." *Studies in Romanticism* 50, 3 (Fall 2011): 389–411.

Schleiermacher, Friedrich. *On Religion: Speeches to Its Cultured Despisers.* Trans. Richard Crouter. Cambridge: Cambridge University Press, 1996.

Schmidt, Leigh Eric. *Restless Souls: The Making of American Spirituality.* San Francisco: Harper San Francisco, 2005.

Schmitt, Carl. *The Concept of the Political.* Trans. George Schwab. Chicago: University of Chicago Press, 1996.

Schulte-Sasse, Jochen, Haynes Horne, Elizabeth Mittman, and Lisa C. Roetzel, eds. *Theory as Practice: A Critical Anthology of Early German Romantic Writings.* Minneapolis: University of Minnesota Press, 1997.

Schwab, Raymond. *The Oriental Renaissance: Europe's Rediscovery of India and the East, 1680–1880.* New York: Columbia University Press, 1984.

Scotland, Privy Council. *At Edinburgh, the Twelfth Day of December, One Thousand Six Hundred and Sixty Seven.* Early English Books Online. Edinburgh: Printed by Evan Tyler, Printer to the Kings most excellent Majesty, 1667.

Scott, David. "Culture in Political Theory." *Political Theory* 31, 1 (February 2003): 92–115.

Scott, Walter. "Introduction." In *The Castle of Otranto: A Gothic Story, By the Honorable Horace Walpole. With Critical Introduction.* Edinburgh: James Ballantyne, 1811.

———. *Old Mortality.* Ed. Jane Stevenson and Peter Davidson. New York: Oxford University Press, 1993.

———. *Redgauntlet.* Ed. Kathryn Sutherland. Oxford: World's Classics, 1985.

———. *Rob Roy.* Ed. Ian Duncan. New York: Oxford University Press, 2008.

———. *Waverley; Or, 'Tis Sixty Years Since.* Ed. Andrew Hook. London: Penguin, 1985.

Scrivener, Michael. *Radical Shelley: The Philosophical Anarchism and Utopian Thought of Percy Bysshe Shelley.* Princeton, N.J.:, Princeton University Press, 1982.

Sedgwick, Eve Kosofsky. *Between Men: English Literature and Male Homosocial Desire.* New York: Columbia University Press, 1985.

———. *Tendencies.* Durham, N.C.: Duke University Press, 1993.

Shaffer, E. S. *"Kubla Khan" and the Fall of Jerusalem: The Mythological School in Biblical Criticism and Secular Literature, 1770–1880.* Cambridge: Cambridge University Press, 1975.

Shagan, Ethan. *Popular Politics and the English Reformation.* Cambridge: Cambridge University Press, 2003.

Shakespeare, William. *King Henry VIII.* Ed. Gordon McMullan. 3rd ed. London: Arden Shakespeare, 2000.

Shapin, Steven, and Simon Schaffer. *Leviathan and the Air-Pump: Hobbes, Boyle, and the Experimental Life.* Princeton, N.J.: Princeton University Press, 1989.

Sheehan, Jonathan. *The Enlightenment Bible: Translation, Scholarship, Culture.* Princeton, N.J.: Princeton University Press, 2005.

———. "When Was Disenchantment? History and the Secular Age." In *Varieties of Secularism in a Secular Age*, ed. Michael Warner, Jonathan VanAntwerpen, and Craig Calhoun, 217–42. Cambridge, Mass.: Harvard University Press, 2010.

Shelley, Percy Bysshe. *The Complete Poetry of Percy Bysshe Shelley.* Ed. Donald H. Reiman, Neil Fraistat, and Nora Crook. Vol. 3. Baltimore: Johns Hopkins University Press, 2012.

———. *The Revolt of Islam; A Poem, in Twelve Cantos.* London, 1818.

———. *Shelley's Poetry and Prose.* Ed. Neil Fraistat and Donald H. Reiman. 2nd ed. New York: Norton, 2002.

Simpson, James. *Burning to Read: English Fundamentalism and Its Reformation Opponents.* Cambridge, Mass.: Belknap Press of Harvard University Press, 2007.

Simpson, Robert. *Traditions of the Covenanters; Or, Gleanings among the Mountains.* Edinburgh: John Johnston, 1846.

Siskin, Clifford. *The Work of Writing: Literature and Social Change in Britain, 1700–1830*. Baltimore: Johns Hopkins University Press, 1998.

Siskin, Clifford, and William Warner, eds. *This Is Enlightenment*. Chicago: University of Chicago Press, 2010.

Sisman, Adam. *The Friendship: Wordsworth and Coleridge*. New York: Viking, 2007.

Smith, Wilfred Cantwell. *Faith and Belief*. Princeton, N.J.: Princeton University Press, 1979.

Sockness, Brent W. "Schleiermacher and the Ethics of Authenticity: The Monologen of 1800." *Journal of Religious Ethics* 32, 3 (2004): 477–517.

A Solemn League and Covenant for Reformation and Defence of Religion, the Honour and Happinesse of the King, and the Peace and Safety of the Three Kingdoms of England, Scotland, and Ireland. London: Printed for Edw. Husbands, 27 September 1643. Early English Books Online.

Sommerville, C. John. *The Secularization of Early Modern England: From Religious Culture to Religious Faith*. New York: Oxford University Press, 1992.

Southam, B. C., ed. *Jane Austen: The Critical Heritage*. Vol. 1. London: Routledge, 1968.

Spierenburg, Petrus. *The Broken Spell: A Cultural and Anthropological History of Preindustrial Europe*. London: Macmillan, 1991.

Spinoza, Benedict de. *Theological-Political Treatise*. Ed. Jonathan Israel, trans. Michael Silverthorne and Jonathan Israel. Cambridge: Cambridge University Press, 2007.

Stallybrass, Peter, and Allon White. *The Politics and Poetics of Transgression*. London: Methuen, 1986.

Stark, Rodney. *The Victory of Reason: How Christianity Led to Freedom, Capitalism, and Western Success*. New York: Random House, 2006.

Stengers, Isabelle. "The Cosmopolitical Proposal." In *Making Things Public: Atmospheres of Democracy*, ed. Bruno Latour and Peter Weibel, 994–1003. Cambridge, Mass.: MIT Press, 2005.

———. "Deleuze and Guattari's Last Enigmatic Message." *Angelaki* 10, 2 (2005): 151–67.

Stewart, Dustin. "The Lettered Paul: Remnant and Mission in Hannah More, Walter Scott, and Critical Theory." *Studies in Romanticism* 50, 4 (2011): 591–618.

Stewart, Susan. *Poetry and the Fate of the Senses*. Chicago: University of Chicago Press, 2002.

Stone, Lawrence. *The Family, Sex and Marriage in England, 1500–1800*. New York: Harper & Row, 1977.

Sykes, Norman. *Church and State in England in the XVIIIth Century: The Birkbeck Lectures*. Cambridge: Cambridge University Press, 1934.

Taylor, Charles. "Modes of Secularism." In *Secularism and Its Critics*, ed. Rajeev Bhargava, 31–53. Delhi: Oxford University Press, 1998.

———. *Multiculturalism and the Politics of Recognition: An Essay*. Ed. Amy Gutmann. Princeton, N.J.: Princeton University Press, 1992.

———. *A Secular Age*. Cambridge, Mass.: Harvard University Press, 2007.

———. *Sources of the Self: The Making of the Modern Identity*. Cambridge, Mass.: Harvard University Press, 1989.

Taylor, Mark C., ed. *Critical Terms for Religious Studies*. Chicago: University of Chicago Press, 1998.

Thomas, Keith. *Religion and the Decline of Magic: Studies in Popular Beliefs in Sixteenth and Seventeenth Century England*. New York: Oxford University Press, 1997.

Thompson, E. P. *Customs in Common: Studies in English Popular Culture*. London: Merlin, 1991.

———. *The Making of the English Working Class*. New York: Pantheon, 1963.

Tobin, Beth Fowkes. "The Moral and Political Economy of Property in Austen's *Emma*." *Eighteenth-Century Fiction* 2, 3 (1990): 229–54.

Toland, John. *Christianity Not Mysterious: Or, A Treatise Shewing, That There Is Nothing in the Gospel Contrary to Reason, Nor Above It: And That No Christian Doctrine Can Be Properly Call'd A Mystery. The Second Edition Enlarg'd*. London: Printed for Sam. Buckley, 1696.

Tomaselli, Sylvan. "Intolerance: The Virtue of Princes and Radicals." In *Toleration in Enlightenment Europe*, ed. Ole Peter Grell and Roy Porter, 86–101. Cambridge: Cambridge University Press, 2000.

Toulmin, Stephen. *Cosmopolis: The Hidden Agenda of Modernity*. Chicago: University of Chicago Press, 1990.

A True Account of the Horrid Murther Committed upon His Grace, the Late Lord Archbishop of St. Andrews, Primate and Metropolitan of All Scotland, and One of His Majesties Most Honourable Privy Council of That Kingdom. With a Detection of the Lyes Published in a Late Scandalous Relation of That Murther; and of the Pretended Occasion Thereof. Published by Authority. Dublin: s.n., 1679. Early English Books Online.

Tuite, Clara. *Romantic Austen: Sexual Politics and the Literary Canon*. Cambridge: Cambridge University Press, 2002.

Tully, James. *Strange Multiplicity: Constitutionalism in an Age of Diversity*. Cambridge: Cambridge University Press, 1995.

Turner, Victor. *The Ritual Process: Structure and Anti-Structure*. New Brunswick, N.J.: Transaction, 1995.

Virgil. *The Eclogues of Virgil*. Trans. C. Day Lewis. London: Jonathan Cape, 1963.

Viswanathan, Gauri. *Outside the Fold: Conversion, Modernity, and Belief*. Princeton, N.J.: Princeton University Press, 1998.

Walpole, Horace. *The Castle of Otranto*. Ed. W. S. Lewis. Oxford: Oxford University Press, 1964.

Walsh, John, and Stephen Taylor. "Introduction: The Church and Anglicanism in the 'Long' Eighteenth Century." In *The Church of England c. 1689–c. 1833: From Toleration to Tractarianism*, ed. John Walsh, Colin Haydon, and Stephen Taylor, 1–66. Cambridge: Cambridge University Press, 2002.

Warburton, William. *The Divine Legation of Moses Demonstrated, on the Principles of a Religious Deist, from the Omission of the Doctrine of a Future State of Reward and Punishment in the Jewish Dispensation. In Nine Books. . . . The Third Edition, Corrected and Enlarged*. Vol. 2. 3rd ed. London: Printed for the executor of the late Mr. Fletcher Gyles, 1742.

———. "Letter to Francis Kilvert, 8 June 1755." In *A Selection from the Unpublished Papers of William Warburton*. London: John Bowyer Nichols and Son, 1841.

———. *Letters from a Late Eminent Prelate to One of His Friends*. 2nd ed. London: Printed for T. Cadell and W. Davies, 1809.

———. *The Nature of National Offences Truly Stated: . . . A Sermon Preached on the General Fast Day, Appointed to Be Observed December 18, 1745. By William Warburton*. London, 1745.

———. *A Sermon Occasioned by the Present Unnatural Rebellion. . . . Preached in Mr. Allen's Chapel at Prior-Park near Bath, . . . By William Warburton*. London: Printed for J. and P. Knapton, 1745.

Ward, Graham. *True Religion*. London: Wiley-Blackwell, 2003.

Warner, Michael. "Queer and Then?" *Chronicle Review—Chronicle of Higher Education*, 1 January 2012.

Warner, Michael, Jonathan VanAntwerpen, and Craig Calhoun, eds. *Varieties of Secularism in a Secular Age*. Cambridge, Mass.: Harvard University Press, 2010.

Wasserman, Earl. *The Subtler Language*. Baltimore: Johns Hopkins University Press, 1968.

———. *Shelley: A Critical Reading*. Baltimore: Johns Hopkins University Press, 1971.

Watt, Diane. *Secretaries of God: Women Prophets in Late Medieval and Early Modern England*. Cambridge: Brewer, 1997.

Watt, James. *Contesting the Gothic: Fiction, Genre, and Cultural Conflict, 1764–1832*. Cambridge: Cambridge University Press, 1999.

Webb, Samantha. "Feeding on Disquiet: 'The Ruined Cottage' and the Unmediated Event." *Essays in Romanticism* 18 (2011): 29–43.

Weber, Max. *The Protestant Ethic and the Spirit of Capitalism*. New York: Scribner, 1958.

Weiskel, Thomas. *The Romantic Sublime: Studies in the Structure and Psychology of Transcendence*. Baltimore: Johns Hopkins University Press, 1976.

White, Daniel E. *Early Romanticism and Religious Dissent*. Cambridge: Cambridge University Press, 2006.

Wills, Gary. "The Day the Enlightenment Went Out." *New York Times*, 4 November 2004.

Wilson, Rob. *Be Always Converting, Be Always Converted: An American Poetics*. Cambridge, Mass.: Harvard University Press, 2009.

Wiltshire, John. "Emma." In *The Cambridge Companion to Jane Austen*, ed. Edward Copeland and Juliet McMaster, 66–75. Cambridge: Cambridge University Press, 1997.

Wodrow, Robert. *The History of the Sufferings of the Church of Scotland, from the Restauration to the Revolution: Collected from the Publick Records, Original Papers, and Manuscripts of That Time, and Other Well Attested Narratives. By Mr. Robert Wodrow, Minister of the Gospel at Eastwood*. 2 vols. Vol. 2. Edinburgh: Printed by James Watson, 1721.

Wordsworth, William. *The Major Works*. Ed. Stephen Gill. Oxford: Oxford University Press, 2000.

Young, B. W. *Religion and Enlightenment in Eighteenth-Century England: Theological Debate from Locke to Burke*. Oxford: Clarendon, 1998.

Žižek, Slavoj. *The Sublime Object of Ideology*. London: Verso, 1989.

———. *The Ticklish Subject: The Absent Centre of Political Ontology*. London: Verso, 1999.

INDEX

ACKNOWLEDGMENTS

My thanks to audiences at Harvard, Yale, Columbia, Arizona, Berkeley, the CUNY Graduate Center, Wheaton College, the University of Michigan, the University of Wisconsin, and the National Humanities Center for listening to portions of this book and raising the relevant questions. Special thanks also to the American Council of Learned Societies, which provided me with a fellowship during 2007–2008, when I began work on this book. At Penn, Jerry Singerman has been a delight to work with, and Alison Anderson and Caroline Hayes made everything run smoothly. At Rutgers University, I have been fortunate in my colleagues in the English department, and in the leadership of Richard Miller, Jonah Siegel, and Carolyn Williams. The Rutgers Center for Cultural Analysis has been in an important sense my intellectual home. Several friends and colleagues from Rutgers and elsewhere deserve particular mention for their thoughtful responses to my ideas: Akeel Bilgrami, David Bromwich, Mark Canuel, David Collings, Lynn Festa, Amy Hollywood, Theresa Kelly, Jonathan Kramnick, John Kucich, George Levine, Marjorie Levinson, Michael McKeon, Anahid Nersessian, Adela Pinch, Bruce Robbins, John Savarese, Henry Turner, Jonathan VanAntwerpen, Orrin Wang, and Michael Warner. Sean Barry helped me see the outlines of my argument. Billy Galperin deserves special mention; I continue to benefit from his acute eye and generous spirit.

My own spirit has been sustained by John and Kristine Kemler and by Seth and Stephanie Kaper-Dale. Eliot Jager and Olivia Jager bring laughter and joy to my life. With remarkable grace, my wife Wendy fills our days together with happiness. Finally, this book is for my parents, models of love and constancy.

Several pages from the introduction to Part II appeared in "Common Quiet: Tolerance Around 1688," *ELH* 79, 3 (Fall 2012), used by permission of Johns

Hopkins University Press. A shorter version of Chapter 5 appeared as "Literary Enchantment and Literary Opposition from Hume to Scott," in *Secular Faiths*, ed. Vincent Lloyd and Elliot Ratzman (Cascade Books, 2010), used by permission of Wipf and Stock Publishers. A different version of Chapter 7 appeared as "Byron and Romantic Occidentalism," *Romantic Circles Praxis*, August 2008, used by permission of the series editor. A small portion of Chapter 8 appeared in "After the Secular: The Subject of Romanticism," *Public Culture* 18, 2 (Spring 2006), used by permission of Duke University Press. An earlier version of Chapter 9 appeared in *Studies in Romanticism* 49, 4 (Winter 2010), used by permission of the Trustees of Boston University.